CLINICAL APPLICATIONS OF
DRAMA THERAPY
IN CHILD AND ADOLESCENT TREATMENT

D0145651

CLINICAL APPLICATIONS OF
DRAMA THERAPY
IN CHILD AND ADOLESCENT TREATMENT

EDITED BY

ANNA MARIE WEBER & CRAIG HAEN

Brunner-Routledge
Taylor & Francis Group
NEW YORK AND HOVE

Published in 2005 by
Brunner-Routledge
270 Madison Avenue
New York, NY 10016
www.brunner-routledge.com

Published in Great Britain by
Brunner-Routledge
27 Church Road
Hove, East Sussex
BN3 2FA
www.brunner-routledge.co.uk

Copyright © 2005 by Taylor & Francis Books, Inc.

Brunner-Routledge is an imprint of the Taylor & Francis Group.

Printed in the United States of America on acid free paper.

All rights reserved. No part of this book may be reprinted or reproduced or utilized in any form or by any electronic, mechanical or other means, now known or hereafter invented, including photocopying and recording or in any information storage or retrieval system, without permission in writing from the publisher.

Library of Congress Cataloguing-in-Publication Data
Clinical applications of drama therapy in child and adolescent treatment / edited by
Anna Marie Weber, Craig Haen; foreword by Sandra L. Bloom ; introduction
by Robert J. Landy.
        p. ; cm.
        Includes bibliographical references and index.
        ISBN 0-415-94844-4 (hardback : alk. paper) — ISBN 0-415-94845-2 (pbk. : alk.
paper)
        1. Psychodrama. 2. Child psychotherapy. 3. Adolescent psychotherapy.
        [DNLM: 1. Psychodrama—methods—Adolescent. 2. Psychodrama—methods—
Child. WM 430.5.P8 C641 2004]   I. Weber, Anna Marie, 1952–   II. Haen,
Craig.   III. Title.

RJ505.P89C554 2004
618.92'89'1523—dc22
                                                                2004009362

We wish to dedicate this book
to the late Paul Weber and LaVerne Williams,
whose memories continue to enrich our lives.

Contents

Section I: Individual Drama Therapy

Editors

Anna Marie Weber, MA, RDT, CDVC Diplomate–Certified Domestic Violence Counselor, is the Director of Children's Services for Victims Information Bureau of Suffolk (New York). Services include Play and Drama Therapy for children who have witnessed domestic violence and/or experienced extrafamilial sexual assault. Along with supervising her staff and interns, she specializes in the treatment of children who have witnessed their mother's murder and/or father's suicide. She has a legislative appointment to the Suffolk County Advisory Committee on Child Protection. In 1995, she was awarded "Professional of the Year for the Prevention of Domestic Violence." She has provided numerous advanced trainings for professionals on children's trauma issues. She is currently an adjunct faculty member at New York University.

Craig Haen, MA, RDT, CGP, is a Registered Drama Therapist and a Certified Group Psychotherapist. He is currently Clinical Supervisor of Adolescent Services for Kids in Crisis, in Greenwich, Connecticut, and serves on the Advisory Board of Creative Alternatives of New York. For 5 years, Craig was employed in the Child and Adolescent Psychiatry Division of New York Presbyterian Hospital—Cornell Medical Center. He has worked with youth in shelters, community centers, hospitals, residential facilities, schools, and on Native American reservations. Craig was particularly active in the treatment of children, families, and service professionals in the New York area following the 9/11 terrorist attacks. He has presented trainings throughout the United States and has published papers internationally.

Contributors

Ann Cattanach, PhD, MSc, RDth, RDT, is a drama therapist, play therapist, and a lecturer in communication and drama. She has worked in schools and institutes of higher education in the United Kingdom, Singapore, Malaysia, and the Netherlands. She is the Course Director of Drama at Queen Margaret College, Edinburgh, and was the Course Director, Play Therapy, at the University of Surrey, Roehampton, for 10 years until 2001. Dr. Cattanach is now a freelance Consultant Therapist, living in the highlands of Scotland and working in the United Kingdom and in other countries, as well as Teaching Fellow, University of York. She provides individual and group play and drama therapy along with caregiver consultations. She offers clinical supervision and presents workshops in the United Kingdom and other countries.

Lee R. Chasen, PhD, RDT, works in a private practice on Long Island, New York, treating children and families for a range of emotional, behavioral, and developmental disorders. Lee also runs a nonprofit organization, Kid Esteem Inc., which he founded with his wife in 1997. Dedicated to the emotional health and empowerment of children, families, schools, and communities, Kid Esteem facilitates groups that focus on emotional intelligence, social skills, behavior management, and self-esteem.

Christopher Doyle, MFT, RDT, is a Licensed Marriage and Family Therapist and a Registered Drama Therapist. He has a private practice in Santa Rosa, California, where he specializes in working with boys, teens, families, and individual adults. Christopher holds a black belt in Aikido and teaches Aikido to children. He was President of the Redwood Empire Chapter of the California Association of Marriage and Family Therapists (2001).

Renée Emunah, PhD, RDT/BCT, is the Founder/Director of the Drama Therapy Program, California Institute of Integral Studies; Past President, National Association for Drama Therapy; author of *Acting for Real*, and of many chapters and articles on drama therapy; board certified trainer and long-time practitioner. Dr. Emunah's pioneering work in drama therapy has been presented extensively nationally and internationally. She was among the first four drama therapists to be officially registered (RDT) in the United States. She was recipient of the National Association for Drama Therapy Gertrud Schattner Award for Outstanding Contribution to the Field of Drama Therapy; Recipient of a Commendation by the San Francisco Board of Supervisors for Innovative Work with Ex-Psychiatric Patients; and recipient of many grants.

Alice M. Forrester, PhD, RDT/BCT, is the Associate Executive Director of the Clifford Beers Clinic in New Haven, Connecticut. She is Past President of the National Association for Drama Therapy and Chair of the National Coalition of Creative Arts Therapy Associations. She is a Doctor of Clinical Psychology and a faculty member of the Institutes for the Arts in Psychotherapy.

Loretta Gallo-Lopez, MA, RDT/BCT, is a licensed mental health counselor in private practice in Tampa, Florida. As a Registered Drama Therapist and Board Certified Trainer, she utilizes play and drama therapy and a variety of creative interventions in her work with children, adolescents, and families. She specializes in issues related to sexual abuse and trauma-related disorders. A national presenter, she has published several articles and co-edited the book, *Play Therapy with Adolescents.*

Steve Harvey, PhD, RDT, ADTR, RPT/S, is currently working as a Consultant Psychologist with the Child and Adolescent Mental Health Service in the Taranaki, New Zealand. Previously, he worked as a Child Clinical Psychologist with the U.S. government at military bases within Europe, as well as in private practice. Prior to becoming active in the mental health profession, Steve was active in improvisational dramatic performance and continues to practice Playback Theater and physical storytelling. Steve has helped pioneer the field of family play therapy and has published 16 chapters on this topic. His work has been published in major play therapy texts as well as in publications by the American Psychological Association and American Psychiatric Association.

Bernadette Hoey studied social work at the University of Melbourne and psychodrama at the Australian College of Psychodrama. She later adapted psychodrama to meet the needs of disturbed children. Her book, *Who Calls The Tune?* (Routledge, 1997), was a "first" in the literature. It graphically analyzed this adaptation against the classical psychodrama framework from which it sprang. She works in private practice at Mt. Martha, Australia, and is a visiting teacher at the Psychodrama Institute of Melbourne.

Eleanor C. Irwin, PhD, RDT, is a drama therapist, psychodramatist (TEP), clinical psychologist, and an adult and child psychoanalyst. Dr. Irwin was a founding member of the National Association for Drama Therapy (NADT), the first Registered Drama Therapist (RDT), and was the primary author of the NADT's initial "Standards for Registration" and "Standards and Ethics" documents. Dr. Irwin is a Clinical Assistant Professor of Psychiatry in the Department of Psychiatry at the University of Pittsburgh, a Certified Child Analyst, and a Teaching and Training Analyst at the Pittsburgh Psychoanalytic Society and Institute, where she is the President. Dr. Irwin's multiple publications and films focus on clinical theory and technique, and on the educational and mental health needs of children and their families. Dr. Irwin is a leading writer in the field of Drama Therapy, contributing over 17 chapters and numerous journal articles. She was the 1999 Golden Apple Award Winner at the Western Psychiatric Institute and Clinic (given by psychiatry residents to the best volunteer faculty member).

Miller James, PhD, RDT, is currently a licensed clinical psychologist in private practice. He served 4 years as a forensic psychologist at the Audrey Hepburn Children's House, Northern Regional Diagnostic Center for Child Abuse and Neglect, and was supervisor for the Creative Arts Therapies at the National Center for Post Traumatic Stress Disorder, Veteran's Administration Medical Center. He is currently a senior training faculty member for the Institutes for the Arts in Psychotherapy in New York City.

Kyongok C. Kim, MA, is a Senior Child Life Specialist/Drama Therapist at Audrey Hepburn Children's House, Northern Regional Diagnostic Center for Child Abuse and Neglect, Hackensack University Medical Center. She specializes in the treatment of abused and neglected children.

Rosalind Chaplin Kindler, MFA, RDT, DipTCPP, is a Registered Drama Therapist and psychotherapist in Toronto, Canada. She is a graduate and faculty member of the Toronto Child Psychoanalytic Program, where she is also a supervisor. Ros works in private practice treating children and their families, adolescents, and adults. She currently serves as President of the Canadian Association of Psychoanalytic Child Therapists. In her spare time, she likes to sing the blues.

Kristin Long, MA, RDT, CGP, currently lives and works in New York City, where she has a private psychotherapy/drama therapy practice. She is a member of the National Association of Drama Therapy, The American Group Psychotherapy Association, and she is currently completing analytic training at the Institute of Expressive Analysis.

Emily Nash has been running groups using theater as a therapeutic process for over 25 years. She cofounded and is the Director of Training and Supervision for Creative Alternatives of New York, which brings together the techniques of modern group psychotherapy and the theater. For the past 3 summers, she has brought her work to Bosnia with the Art Reach Foundation, working with teachers and children who have been traumatized by war. She has conducted trainings and presented her work internationally.

Ted I. Rubenstein, MFA, MA, RDT, received his MFA from the DePaul University Theatre School and his MA from the Chicago School of Professional Psychology, where he is now a Doctoral Candidate in Clinical Psychology. He is adjunct faculty at the Chicago School of Professional Psychology and at DePaul/Barat College. He is the Central Regional Representative to the National Association of Drama Therapy. He was the dramaturg for the Raven Theatre and a member of the Eclipse Theatre in Chicago.

Foreword

SANDRA L. BLOOM, MD

Every work of art points somewhere beyond itself; it transcends itself and its author; it creates a special force field around itself that moves the human mind and the human nervous system.
—Vaclav Havel

For as long as humans have been capable of pondering the nature of illness, disease has constituted a dis-integration, a loss of intactness, a separation into parts, a break up, a deterioration, a reduction to fragments. One word for the Devil is "Diabolos," referring to the divider, the splitter-into-fragments. Western medicine traces its roots to the ancient Greeks and the original therapists, the *therapeutes*, those chosen as the attendants of the cult of Asclepius, the god of healing who was—not coincidentally—also the patron of artists. Serving Asclepius required artistic performance, and the temple of Asclepius in Athens was immediately adjacent to the great Theatre of Dionysus.

Like their predecessors, the drama therapists who are the contributors to this volume have dedicated their professional lives to restoring the health of children's minds and bodies; children injured in a world that refuses to adequately protect its future. The children described in these pages have suffered injury to their brains, their sense of personal value, their capacity to trust other people, and their ability to make sense of the world. But there is an injury that is arguably even more destructive than all of these—injury to the ability to imagine something else, to imagine oneself healed and whole. Recovering from traumatic experience, illness, or affliction is not a simple project of the re-knitting of bones and muscles, but instead requires a re-working of the soul—of time, of space, of identity, of meaning. And, most importantly, it requires the revivification of the imaginative space between the here-and-now and the then. W.H. Auden observed, *"Human beings are by nature actors, who cannot become something until first they have pretended to be it."* It is this ability to create possibility, to envision alternative universes, that must be unfrozen if an ill child is to re-enter the stream of life.

From what we are learning about the psychobiology of exposure to violence, the victim experiences and remembers the trauma in nonverbal, visual, auditory, kinesthetic, visceral, and affective modalities, but is not able to "think" about it or process the experience in any way. Our cognitive processes are dependent on language function and, without words, we cannot "think."

Trauma produces a disconnection syndrome, a functional "split-brain" preparation in which the two hemispheres appear to function autonomously, at least in regard to the traumatic experience. The traumatized person becomes possessed, haunted by the theater in his mind. He cannot control the intrusive images, feelings, sensations. They come into consciousness unbidden, terrifyingly vivid, producing a vicious cycle of helpless self-revictimization and even the victimization of others. Any efforts he took to protect himself or others at the time of the trauma were a failure, and yet images of what he could have done—"failed enactment"—continue to obsess him. The inevitability of it all, the moments of irrevocable fear, loss, and longing are frozen in time and simultaneously freeze action in a continuous, repetitive loop of misery.

As a psychiatrist whose medical practice is grounded in the psychobiology of experience, I have always been impressed with how much our lives are affected by what happens to our bodies, particularly in that extraordinary organ, the human brain. Likewise, as a psychotherapist, I have never ceased being moved by the changes that occur in a patient's life as a result of therapy. For 20 years, I ran an inpatient unit for adolescents and adults who were trying to deal with every conceivable form of human suffering. In our program, patients regularly had access to psychodrama, art therapy, and movement therapy, and I became convinced that these forms of therapeutic interaction were vitally necessary to bring about the kinds of changes that were possible in the lives of the people we treated. We are now implementing sanctuary programs in residential settings for children and adolescents. As part of these programs, we are encouraging the adoption of drama therapy interventions and other forms of expressive therapies, not as "adjuncts" but as central pivots for moving children away from pathways of behavior that will inevitably lead to a reenactment of past wounding and onto entirely different trajectories that they can rehearse only in the real time and space that is safely created within the therapeutic boundaries of good treatment.

Clinical wisdom has always urged us to combine and integrate our approaches to mind, body, and spirit to achieve the greatest benefit. But, for the last 20 years, other forms of psychotherapeutic intervention have taken a back seat to the progress made in our knowledge of the neurochemistry of the brain and the emotional disorders that plague us. Now, new research methods that allow us to look at the brain in action indicate that several forms of psychotherapy are at least as effective as psychopharmaceutical agents in the treatment of a growing number of disorders, and appear to affect clinical recovery by modulating the functioning of specific sites in limbic and cortical regions—the very same regions that are affected by the drugs (Brody et al., 2001; Goldapple et al., 2004; Martin et al., 2001). In the future, studies of the impact of drama therapy and other forms of expressive treatment are likely to show what every practitioner in this book already knows—that these forms of psychotherapeutic intervention can bring about substantial changes in the lives of troubled children. Finding effective treatments for children is particularly important because the window of opportunity to influence critical stages in a child's life is relatively narrow; because we are still uncertain about the long-term effects of many medications that are used in children; and because many forms of psychotherapy that rely largely on cognitive and language-based skills may not be the most useful approaches for children, particularly young children. Children play naturally as a fundamental way of developing interpersonal and intrapersonal skills, and of safely learning about the world; and their play changes their brains as well as their minds.

Drama creates the opportunity for performative change, the creation of that *"special force field . . . that moves the human mind and the human nervous system."* It is as important for us in the twenty-first century as it was for those long-ago Greeks. The face of human tragedy has not changed in those intervening eras, and it is tragedy—and the transcendence of it—that makes engagement in the dramatic arts so critical a component of healing. As George Steiner (1961) pointed out, tragic drama starts from the fact of catastrophe, and catastrophe is often what brings these children into treatment. In their own way, each of these drama therapists is calling upon the children they work with to take a leap of faith and jump into a new time and a new space. In doing so, they are bringing the children back to life, gently urging them to use dramatic performance as the bridge across the black hole of trauma and illness.

References

Brody, A. L., Saxena, S., Stoessel, P., Gillies, L. A., Fairbanks L. A., Alborzian, S., Phelps, M. E., Huang, S. C., Wu, H. M., Ho, M. L., Ho, M. K., Au, S. C., Maidment, K., & Baxter, L. R. (2001). Regional brain metabolic changes in patients with major depression treated with either paroxetine or interpersonal therapy: Preliminary findings. *Archives of General Psychiatry, 58*(7), 631–640.

Goldapple, K., Segal, Z., Garson, C., Lau, M., Bieling, P., Kennedy, S., & Mayberg, H. (2004). Modulation of cortical-limbic pathways in major depression: Treatment-specific effects of cognitive behavior therapy. *Archives of General Psychiatry, 61*(1), 34–41.

Havel, V. (1990). *Disturbing the peace: A conversation with Karel Huizdala.* New York: Knopf.

Martin, S. D., Martin, E., Rai, S. S., Richardson, M. A., & Royall, R. (2001). Brain blood flow changes in depressed patients treated with interpersonal psychotherapy or venlafaxine hydrochloride. *Archives of General Psychiatry, 58*(7), 641–648.

Steiner, G. (1961). *The death of tragedy.* London: Faber & Faber.

Acknowledgments

The idea for this book first sparked during a chance meeting with an old friend at a holiday party. During the 2½ years that followed, its creation unfolded in magical, surprising, and often herculean ways. During this process, there have been many people who contributed to the growth of the book in your hands, through their advice, support, and endeavor.

We first must thank those who gave us counsel at various stages, from inception to completion, including Maria Hodermarska, Robert Landy, Seena Desmons, Pat and Joe Cubells, David Read Johnson, Bobbie Parini, Paul Linden, Siddharth Shah, Judith Wald, Martha Young, Tom Pilutik, and Veronica Baxter; and to Laura Lindquist for being that "old friend" whose appearance at the right time and knowledge of the publishing world allowed the book to move forward.

Our sincere appreciation to those who read drafts of the manuscript and offered their helpful comments, including Clarice Murphy, Sudi Khosropur, Robert Kuisis, Laura Cone, Stella Jang, and Kenneth Brannon. We thank the staff of Brunner-Routledge, particularly George Zimmar, Shannon Vargo, and Dana Bliss, for their guidance. Our undying gratitude to Don and Diane Weber for their printing support and to Marcia Miller of New York Presbyterian Hospital–Westchester Division's Medical Library for her patience, diligence, and devotion in offering wisdom and obtaining many difficult-to-find articles.

We wish to thank our colleagues, past and present, whose support and dedication inspire us weekly to continue to work in a challenging system: the staff at Nichols Cottage, Creative Alternatives of New York, New York University and VIBS; especially Timothy McGarvey, Sarah Woodward, Ayame Takahashi, Maria DePeña-Nowak, Victoria Gladwell, Matthew Ogala, Agnes Cindrich, Theresa Cornish, Darby Moore, Lucy McLellan, Jason Butler,

Pamela Johnston, Andrea and Andy Levenbaum, Laura, Ruth, Joanne, Melissa, Christy, Pam, Janet, and Michele.

Thank you also to our students over the years who have helped us to refine and look critically at our treatment processes.

To our friends, family, and loved ones, who have tolerated our absences, stress, excitement, and sleepless nights, we owe you our warmest appreciation. Craig thanks Stephanie Cohen and Jim and Bonnie Haen, whose ongoing love and acceptance continue to allow him to chase his dreams. Anna Marie thanks her nieces and nephews Josh, Rachel, Tim, Paul, Hannah, and Michael Weber, who keep her sense of play and love alive.

Finally, our heartfelt thanks to the children[1] whose pain, spirit, love, sadness, and joy inspire the pages to come. You have taught and given us more than you'll ever know.

Note

1. All names and identifying case details throughout the text have been changed to ensure confidentiality.

Introduction

ROBERT J. LANDY, PhD, RDT/BCT

When I was very young, I had many fears. My father had recently returned from Europe, fighting in the infantry against the original Axis of Evil. He was sick and wounded and needed time to readjust to a changed world and a family that had a desperate need to return to the status quo. I used to play among the towering apartment buildings in my city and worry that they might be bombed and fall down at any time and wonder where I might hide. From my early years at school, I remember most clearly the air raid drills, ducking under our desks, hands over our heads. Before I had time to get over my fear of the Nazis, I learned that the Russians might bomb our city at any moment. I knew what the explosion would look like, having seen so many images of the dreaded mushroom cloud in newsreels and magazines.

My play centered on war. I was a devoted player of war games with my friends and my collection of miniature soldiers. My favorite toys were the guns and bayonets and medals my father brought back from the war. Each spring, I would gather with my friends and toss spent artillery shells at old chestnut trees, hoping to knock down a chestnut or two. After each play session, however, I never quite felt finished. Over time, my play became repetitive, the same good guys and bad guys locked into the same stalemate. Neither role seemed to have sufficient power to ultimately overcome.

As I grew into my pre-teen years and eventually moved to the suburbs, my play shifted from war games to competitive sports. I learned to judge my self-worth against my ability to hit home runs or sink baskets or block others from doing the same. Playing sports seemed to sublimate my warlike needs, but my attachment to war, especially to Nazis and my father's stories of the extermination camps, never quite diminished. Reflecting on my early childhood, I realize that I needed some closure on the war, some way to play out and work through my fears of imminent destruction and death. I needed, as a child, what my father never received as an adult: an acknowledgment of the terror of war; a safe place in which to tell the war stories, to express the fear; empathic listeners; courageous grown-ups, themselves limited in understanding, who would nevertheless speak their truth about the arbitrariness and absurdity of war and, especially, genocide. My father did his best, but he was wounded and alone, and he needed me, a child, to listen and to hold his stories of horror. I didn't know how.

As an adolescent, I turned to the theater as another venue for discharging my old war fascination, fear, and anger. Perhaps on stage I could finally release my father's pain, and learn how to contain his stories that were, at the time, centered on the home front and his battles with business partners and intimates. Over an extended adolescence, my forays into acting worked to a certain degree, but I tended to use drama as a way to separate myself from my father, rather than to incorporate him, embody him, and let him go. Acting did not prove to be an effective path to healing for me.

Then, at age 22, I began working as an English teacher for emotionally disturbed adolescents. Recognizing the limits of teaching literature and grammar to those who experienced so much inner turmoil, I turned to theater as a way in. Over time, I learned that I had the capacity to help others through the process of drama in better ways than I could help myself. And as I guided them toward their wounds and listened to their war stories told eloquently in role, I found that I was battling less with myself.

As a full-fledged drama therapist and father, I have been a keen observer of my children's development, especially that which takes place through drama, as they learn to make sense of their moments of calm and chaos through a natural process of role play and storytelling. As I witness their struggles with their own wounds, I wonder about the war legacy passed on by my father. Has it resurfaced in a new generation? Is their struggle in part about my inability to resolve and transform my father's pain? Do they feel unconsciously obliged to resolve my pain?

I was led to these thoughts about my father and children after reading the very compelling papers collected in *Clinical Applications of Drama Therapy in Child and Adolescent Treatment*. The theme that runs through this book is that children in pain, those who are at war with themselves and others, those who have experienced attacks by abusers, can benefit significantly from a form of treatment that mirrors their natural developmental way of making meaning—that of drama.

Drama, in essence, is a natural process of development through role playing and storytelling that is based upon the assumption of the doubleness of all of human life. Through the lens of drama, human beings not only exist on one plane, enacting in the present the expected behaviors called for in everyday life. They also exist on planes of past and future that respond to the present moment and make revisions and adjustments to it. To be human means to be more than one thing, to be able to act and to reflect upon the action, to play one role and to then play its counterpart, to understand reality from multiple perspectives, and then to act upon that understanding in often contradictory ways. Because of the multitude of splits existing in the brain, the psyche, the family, the community, and the state, human beings are multiplicitous. At its simplest, drama concerns a moment when an actor in everyday life takes on a role and tells a story through the role. The role taken is a double of the role player. The story told is a double of the reality upon which it is based.

The following statements are all characteristic of the dramatic nature of human life:

> There is a continuity between everyday life and the life of the dramatic imagination, one reflecting the other.
> The metaphors of life as theater and theater as life have been used so often by philosophers, poets, and social scientists because they are clear and elegant descriptors of human life and, as such, have become widely accepted within Western discourse.
> Actors in role are both themselves and not themselves at the same time.
> It is possible and sometimes desirable for human beings to simultaneously act and observe their actions.
> People play many roles in their everyday lives, some of which are contradictory.
> People play roles and tell stories with a greater or lesser degree of emotional intensity in order to hide or reveal themselves to particular audiences.
> People take on and play out roles in order to express particular needs.
> People tell stories in order to make sense of their everyday experiences.

Drama therapy is a form of applied drama, a young academic and practical discipline with ancient roots. Drama therapists harness the doubleness of drama for the treatment of individuals in psychological, physical, and existential pain. Drama therapy is not only rooted in the natural developmental processes of play, role playing, and storytelling, but also in the more sophisticated art form of theater, the act of performing a dramatic text to an audience for aesthetic purposes. In drama therapy, clients do not necessarily perform scripts to audiences, although sometimes they do. But, like theatrical actors, they enact roles and stories, creating aesthetically pleasing images through movement, voice, and a wide range of emotional expression. The main difference between theatre and drama therapy is that in the former, the person is in service of the persona, the fictional role; whereas, in the latter, the persona is invoked and worked through as a means to reveal the person. There is certainly a continuity between theatre and drama therapy as both move back and forth between the doubleness of real life and fiction, of actor and role, of separation and closeness, of ethos and pathos—all in search of heightened moments of joy, release, balance, clarity, integration, transformation.

Although drama therapy is practiced widely with adults and elders, it is of special benefit to children and adolescents, whose means of expression is often more playful and imaginative and less verbal than that of their older counterparts. As implied above, even when children in need of treatment are not in treatment, they will engage in a natural process of play and drama as an attempt to make sense of their reality. My war play is one example, and as a drama therapist working with children in New York City following the terrorist attacks of 9/11, I witnessed an outpouring of drawings and role play around the themes of attack and destruction.

Throughout this book, we find example upon example of drama therapists who engage with children around their natural impulse to dramatize, helping to shape and contain their creations, helping to lead them out of the shadows of denial and compulsion into the light of acceptance and transformation. On occasion, the natural dramatic healing process will shut down, especially in children who have been severely traumatized. And yet, the impulse to play will not disappear but, instead, becomes confined to private places often inaccessible to the children. As we will see in the following articles, the drama therapist who has been trained to read the private, symbolic, non-verbal imagery of frightened children becomes a valuable guide.

The co-editors, Anna Marie Weber and Craig Haen, present a range of clinical approaches to treatment of young people through drama therapy, which attests to the growth and diversity of the field. All clinical examples presented in this book are well grounded in theory that speaks to the dual nature of drama therapy as an art form and a more scientific form of psychologically based treatment. In Section I: Individual Drama Therapy, we find a psychoanalytically based approach in the chapters by Eleanor Irwin and Rosalind Chaplin Kindler, a crisis intervention approach presented by Anna Marie Weber, a psychodramatic approach written by Bernadette Hoey, and a developmental transformations approach co-authored by Miller James, Alice Forrester, and Kyongok Kim. Later, we discover other approaches to group, family and community therapy, written by such pioneers in the field as Renée Emunah, Ann Cattanach, and Steve Harvey. In addition to articles by some of the founders of the profession, the co-editors have included new and compelling voices, such as those of Craig Haen, Emily Nash, Loretta Gallo-Lopez, Lee Chasen, Ted Rubenstein, Christopher Doyle, and Kristin Long.

We also discover throughout the book that the several approaches to drama therapy are regularly applied to a range of diagnostic conditions and treatment environments. Conditions include selective mutism, witnessing domestic violence and terrorism, sexual abuse, abandonment and bereavement, emotional disturbance and mental illness, sexual and aggressive acting out, obsessive-compulsive disorder, and attention deficit disorder. We find treatment approaches that occur in residential treatment centers, outpatient facilities, and private practice offices. We find examples of short-term, medium-term, and long-term treatment of children and adolescents through drama therapy.

To create a context for this book, let me briefly review the history of drama therapy as the field developed in relationship to the treatment of young people. The term drama therapy was first coined by British child drama expert Peter Slade (1959). Slade's (1954) early work concerned specifying a developmental view of the natural play and drama of children and applying that natural process to their education. Slade was a visionary in the area of applied drama as he imagined that the use of movement, role, and story could foster children's physical and emotional as well as cognitive development.

Sue Jennings' early work with disabled children in Europe, which she initially called *Remedial Drama* (1973), set the stage for her later entrée into pioneering a new profession, first in the UK and then internationally— that of drama therapy. In the United States, Eleanor Irwin (2000), initially a speech therapist and creative drama specialist, developed her ideas concerning the therapeutic applications of drama while working with children. She became one of the early founders of the profession of drama therapy in America. In her later training in and practice of psychoanalysis, she remained devoted to the treatment of children through dramatic means.

Other British and American pioneers in drama therapy also focused their work on young people. Renée Emunah trained in England with another drama therapy pioneer, Billie Lindkvist, the founder of the SESAME drama and movement program. Emunah returned to the United States to develop a hospital-based drama therapy approach suited to the needs of emotionally disturbed adolescents. Ann Cattanach, trained by Sue Jennings, developed an effective method of treating abused and abandoned children through play and drama therapy.

Despite this propitious beginning of a child-based drama therapy, there have been few publications specific to children and adolescents in the field. Yet, there have been some notable exceptions. Ann Cattanach published a number of books on play therapy with children (1993, 1994, 1997) and Renée Emunah (1994, 1995) has published several articles and a book discussing her work with adolescents. Sue Jennings edited an anthology of articles on drama therapy with children and adolescents in 1995, offering an international perspective. And, as recently as 2001, Carol Bouzoukis, who studied drama therapy at New York University, published an important book on her work with children in medical facilities.

Weber and Haen's volume brings us directly into the present and provides us with continuing insights from some of the pioneers, as well as new and significant voices of those who are doing ground-breaking work with young people. Both Weber and Haen trained at New York University and both supervised generations of drama therapy interns, providing a steady professional hand and eye, guiding even as they were guided. Both continued their training in drama therapy as they developed an expertise in the larger clinical arenas of trauma, abuse, and mental illness, focused specifically on young people. The multiple perspectives carefully collected and contained in this book represent the future of drama therapy that in the beginning was in part child-centered.

This book is a timely one, as we live in very uncertain times. Institutions that should provide safe environments for children have on too many occasions failed to do so. This is a time of crisis in the religious sector, as pedophiles are revealed, a time of crisis in inner city and suburban schools, as dispossessed students act out violently, and a time of crisis in the family as children are neglected and abused.

The world wars and the Cold War of the twentieth century are over. My children do not live with the threats of concentration camps and atomic bombs. They are not subject to air raid drills at school. Yet, they have lived through 9/11 and its media-generated circus. They have seen endless images of the planes attacking, the Towers burning, the bodies falling, the Towers falling. They are aware of suicide bombers, and homeland security, and militant fundamentalists. They have been searched at airports and have played simulated war games on the computer.

When my son was 11, needing an outlet for his war fears, he played paintball with his friends, a simulated war game not terribly far removed from the real thing. Players are given life-size guns that propel bullets filled with paint. They aim to shoot and destroy the enemies, usually their friends, who plan war strategies in the open field. When one is hit, a mark of paint is visible and the wounded person is out of the game. The last ones to stand, unscathed by bullets, are the winners. On this particular day at the paintball field, several teenagers appeared dressed in battle fatigues, carrying large paintball weapons. After dodging bullets and comforting a friend who had been painfully shot in the neck, my son became frightened and vowed never to play war again, at least not out in the trenches, too close to the reality of war and terror.

Far removed from my son's experience is that of children who are in the midst of or have lived through war and terror. These are the children of Afghanistan, Liberia, Iraq, the Palestinian Territories, Israel, Croatia, Bosnia, Guatemala, Colombia, and many other countries. Who will help them recover from their war trauma?

Having painted this bleak picture, I want to reassure you that there is hope. Although the nostalgia of knocking down chestnuts with shells is no longer relevant to my children or to any child who has been traumatized, young people will seek other safe ways to transform objects of violence. Children are highly resilient and, given the proper correctives, they endure and overcome. There is clear evidence that many children exposed to a potentially traumatizing experience will never develop symptoms of post-traumatic stress disorder. There is a balance in the affairs of state, just as there is balance in nature. Cycles of destruction are followed by cycles of creation. War is not the only game that children play, and yet when they need to play it, they should be encouraged to do so safely.

A further sign of hope is this book, where we engage with the ideas and the practices of creative arts therapists. The book in itself is a model for all those who work with children in need. Its collective wisdom is simple—children who have been wounded in some way need expression and validation through a therapeutic means that is once removed from the wound. The powerful clinicians and writers in this book offer their means, through play, role play, and story. Anna Marie Weber and Craig Haen have done well to let us in on their vision.

References

Bouzoukis, C. (2001). *Pediatric dramatherapy: They couldn't run, so they learned to fly.* London: Jessica Kingsley.

Cattanach, A. (1993). *Playtherapy with abused children.* London: Jessica Kingsley.

Cattanach, A. (1994). *Playtherapy: Where the sky meets the underworld.* London: Jessica Kingsley.

Cattanach, A. (1997). *Children's stories in playtherapy.* London: Jessica Kingsley.

Emunah, R. (1994). *Acting for real: Drama therapy process, technique, and performance.* New York: Brunner/Mazel.

Emunah, R. (1995). From adolescent trauma to adolescent drama: Group drama therapy with emotionally disturbed youth. In S. Jennings (Ed.), *Dramatherapy with children and adolescents* (pp. 150–168). London: Routledge.

Irwin, E. C. (2000). Psychoanalytic approach to drama therapy: Defining and finding a therapeutic framework. In P. Lewis & D. Johnson (Eds.), *Current approaches in drama therapy* (pp. 27–49). Springfield, IL: Charles C. Thomas.

Jennings, S. (1973). *Remedial drama.* London: Pitman.

Jennings, S. (Ed.). (1995). *Dramatherapy with children and adolescents.* London: Routledge.

Slade, P. (1954). *Child drama.* London: University Press.

Slade, P. (1959). *Dramatherapy as an aid to becoming a person.* London: Guild of Pastoral Psychology.

SECTION **I**

Individual Drama Therapy

CHAPTER 1

Facilitating Play with Non-Players
A Developmental Perspective

ELEANOR C. IRWIN

The Many Faces of Play

Since play is a natural way for children to express themselves and learn about the world, it is normal to expect that anyone and everyone can play. But play is an activity about which there are many points of view. Millar (1969) has captured the nebulous, multi-faceted quality of this activity in commenting that "the term play has long been a linguistic wastebasket for behavior which looks voluntary, but seems to have no obvious biological or social use" (p. 11). Most parents, educators, and therapists, however, think they know play when they see it. Asked to describe play, many observers would emphasize its spontaneous and free-flowing quality, would stress its imaginary elements and comment on the transparency of the child's wishes and fears as revealed in play activities.

It is this revealing quality of play, especially fantasy or dramatic play, that endeared this activity to psychoanalysts. When the field was in its infancy, Anna Freud (1927) and Melanie Klein (1964/1948), pioneering child psychoanalysts with different theoretical approaches and styles, began to use play as a way of understanding and treating children. Klein, whose focus on early, deep interpretations was the source of much controversy, likened the spontaneity of child play to the adult's efforts at free association in psychoanalysis. Anna Freud, on the other hand, stressed that it was necessary to have a preparatory period to form a "therapeutic alliance" with the child before making interpretations.

Other analysts, like Erik Erikson (1963), soon added to our understanding of play in the theory and practice of child therapy. Erikson thought of play as "the road to the understanding of the synthesis of the ego" (p. 209). Calling play the child's "work," Erikson stressed that through the "recreation and self cure" afforded by play, the child can learn about the world and his or her place in it. In detailed treatment vignettes, Erikson pointed to the role of anxiety, saying that when emotion becomes too intense, playfulness is disrupted (p. 223).

Donald W. Winnicott, a pediatrician and psychoanalyst, followed Klein in focusing attention away from the oedipal period to the crucial importance of the early mother–child relationship. Winnicott (1989), whose contributions are now in the mainstream of therapeutic practice, drew many analogies between the mother–child and therapist–patient relationships and the importance of play. Winnicott spoke of the mother's need to establish a "holding environment," or a "facilitating environment," that allows play and development to proceed.

Winnicott places play squarely in the center of psychotherapy with patients of all ages. Play, he said, takes place in the period of illusion, or in the "transitional space" between the imaginary and the real world, between the "me" and the "not-me" (1958, p. 215). Psychotherapy, Winnicott wrote, "has to do with two people playing together. . . . If the therapist cannot play, then he is not suitable for the work. If the patient cannot play, then something needs to be done to enable the patient to be able to play, after which psychotherapy may begin" (1971, p. 54). Winnicott further underscored the linkages between play, self development, and creativity in saying, "It is in playing and only in playing that the individual child or adult is able to be creative and to use the whole personality, and it is only in being creative that the individual discovers the self" (1971, p. 54).

Drama Therapy: Players and Non-Players

Just as there are many definitions of play, so are there many definitions of drama therapy (e.g., see Jennings et al., 1994; Lewis & Johnson, 2000). A working definition of the term is, in fact, part and parcel of each drama therapist's necessary search for a professional identity. My own description, written many years ago (Irwin, 1979), began with the attempt to distinguish between "therapeutic" and "therapy," both words stemming from the Greek word *therapeutikos*, meaning "to nurse, serve, cure." I went on to say that many activities can serve a therapeutic or healing function, particularly the creative arts.

While there is great overlap in the meaning of the two words, there are also clear distinctions between them that center on the issues of product versus process; goal and purpose; and the role of the leader. In the marriage of *drama* and *therapy*, the term, to me, implies the use of drama/theater techniques in an intentional, planned way as a specific form of intervention, designed to bring about intrapsychic, interpersonal, or behavioral changes. In drama therapy, the *process*, the *therapeutic relationship*, and the *transforming power of affect* (Fosha, 2000) are key aspects of treatment.

Drawn to the field because of a deeply felt wish to better understand themselves and those with whom they work, most drama therapists are empathic, introspective, and well trained in theater, drama and spontaneous play techniques. Relying on their intuition and training, most drama therapists try to find creative ways of connecting to others. The drama therapist works with individuals and/or groups, spanning the ages from preschool to senescence, in a variety of settings and with many populations.

Definitions aside, however, it seems to me that most drama therapists work toward the general goals of:

1. facilitating imaginative play at the highest possible level;
2. strengthening self control and affect regulation;
3. helping individuals put feelings and behaviors into words.

A core aspect of the drama therapist's work is the integration of spontaneous play and the dramatic structures of characters, plot, setting, climax, denouement, and so on. This is the stuff of which drama is made. The development and maturation of these abilities make drama possible, but more importantly, also promote creativity and social, cognitive, emotional and interpersonal growth.

The ability to be self reflective, expressive and playful in one's thoughts, feelings, and actions is the *sine qua non* of most forms of psychodynamic therapy. Unfortunately, many children and adults, burdened by a variety of difficulties, are unable to "play" in the way that Winnicott envisioned. These individuals, who might be called non-players, cannot be spontaneous, symbolize thoughts and feelings, and engage with others in an imaginative way. Non-players guard against the awareness of thoughts and feelings, often functioning at a preverbal level. While these children and adults present problems for all therapists (Greenspan, 1997), they present a particular dilemma for drama therapists, whose stock in trade is fantasy and imagination, facilitated through individual and/or group stories and enactments.

Often, the inability to play is the result of congenital, environmental or developmental difficulties. As Anna Freud pointed out (1965), development is complex and depends on the mutual interaction of constitutional, neurological, maturational and environmental factors. When one or more of these abilities is compromised, there may be impairment in many areas, including that of play. Non-players are difficult, even exasperating, to treat; mired as they are in pre-symbolic, magical, or concrete ways of thinking, unable to engage in sustained interaction with others. In such situations, it helps to have a developmental framework to understand what might be limiting or foreclosing the ability to play.

Knowledge of normal and arrested development can help the drama therapist make educated guesses about the child's difficulties, suggesting the kinds of approaches, activities, and interventions that might be successful in facilitating play. Awareness of developmental difficulties can also help the drama therapist to be patient, sensitive to the therapeutic process, and alert to the potential healing power of the relationship over time.

To illustrate work with non-players, case examples of three youngsters will be presented. This material will be supplemented with a discussion of factors such as *attachment, self and other representations,* and *affect regulation,* since difficulties in these areas often interfere with the ability to use play in the service of growth.

Children Who Are Non-Players

What might a non-player look like? Both Joey and Max had experienced significant developmental problems, as the following vignettes will illustrate.

Joey, A Frozen, Traumatized Child

In his first session, 5-year-old Joey entered the playroom hesitantly, standing as though transfixed. I pointed out the creative materials that were available for dramatic play, such as costumes, masks, puppets, sandbox materials, miniature toys, and the like (Irwin, 1983), but Joey made no move toward them. After standing still for some minutes, Joey turned his back to me and stiffly lowered himself into the nearest available chair. Taking a pencil from his pocket, he stared at it for some time and then began to make vertical marks on the blank, white paper in front of him. My empathic remarks seemed to be unheard. And there he sat for most of the hour, saying nothing, but motorically conveying a state of frozen rigidity and seeming numbness, while I sat beside him feeling increasingly out of touch.

Joey's first hour was similar to many that followed. For many sessions, I had no clue what was behind the enacted and embodied meanings conveyed through his ritualized, black pencil marks, now being "stabbed" with increased energy on white paper. Three months later, perhaps reassured that he was in a safe space (Winnicott, 1965), Joey began to make rough drawings of monster faces. By 5 months, feeling psychologically freer, Joey began to draw monsters violently attacking tiny, stick-like people, playing with his markers as though they were aggressor and victim. Becoming more verbal, Joey used puppets and doll figures to play out his stories, supplying words of anguish and rage for the victims like "Stop!" and "Get away!" It was not until he had been in therapy for 18 months that he could begin to elaborate on these attacks, linking them to beatings by his (now jailed) father. Following the monster play, Joey shifted to games of peek-a-boo and hide-and-seek, suggesting that he was working out long-delayed separation issues (Bergman, 1999).

Max: An Action-Oriented Child

Enraged because he was unable to get the devil mask and flowing red cape to stay in place for his drama, Max reacted immediately. Tearing off his costume, this twelve-year-old *became* the devil he was about to pretend to be. But, for Max, there was no pretend, no "as if." Picking up the plastic pitchfork, Max advanced dangerously close toward me. In a menacing voice, with narrowed eyes, he hissed, "I'm going to KILL you!" In a split second, he had moved from a position of tenuous control to one in which he had none. Max's fantasy of killing another slipped over the pretend boundary and became real. Only my firm re-statement of the rule: "PRETEND. No hurting for real!" averted an imminent attack.

Max laughed nervously at my intervention and backed away. I said what had been said before during similar episodes: "Max, you're ready to lose control. Let's take a breather and talk about the pictures and stories in your head." Still angry, Max narrowed his eyes and yelled, "I'm gonna stab you!"

As calmly as I could, I said that there would be no stabbing for real, but that he could draw a picture of what he wanted to do and throw darts at the picture if he wanted. Or, he could tell a story about the devil and I would write it down for him; that might help us to understand what he was thinking. Resentfully, Max chose both. Drawing a picture of a robot, he told a confused and confusing story of a devil robot that roamed the earth and killed people, especially at night. I wondered if this was the devil in the story that was about to kill me. When Max affirmed that it was so, I wondered what had happened to make the devil want to kill me. Max glowered and yelled, "'Cause you don't do what I want! *Yeah!* I'm the boss here. I'm the *devil!* And I can do it!"

Attachment Theory, Development of Self and Other Representations, and Affect Regulation

Joey's and Max's difficulties in play can be better understood through an examination of attachment theory, recent research about the development of object relations, and affect regulation. Understanding these developmental concepts can help the drama therapist navigate worrisome therapeutic paths more comfortably, especially those dangerous areas that often get bogged down in transference/countertransference swamps, particularly in work with troubled children like Joey and Max.

Attachment Theory

Our understanding of attachment, which has been the lynchpin of recent research, began with the pioneering research of John Bowlby (1969–1980), an English psychoanalyst. Studying attachment behaviors in animals and humans, Bowlby theorized that the function of early attachment to the mother is to protect the child from predators. On the *evolutionary* level, the attachment shields the infant from harm; on the *psychological* level, the attachment serves to reduce anxiety and to impart a sense of security. If the child has a *secure* base of attachment to the mother, Bowlby hypothesized, several important achievements can follow: (1) the still-vulnerable child can comfortably explore the environment with less fear and arousal, knowing that the mother is available in times of danger; (2) the secure child will have less need to develop psychological defenses; and (3) the child can form an internal mental representation of the caring protector and, over time, can identify with that internalized image. Bowlby believed that the need for attachment is never outgrown but endures throughout one's life, albeit in an attenuated way.

A proliferation of research in psychoanalysis, infant psychiatry, developmental psychology, and developmental psychopathology flowed from Bowlby's work. Researchers like Ainsworth et al. (1978), Main and Solomon (1990) and others (see Cassidy & Shaver, 1999) began to examine the attachment patterns of young children through the "Strange Situation Test." In time, researchers classified attachment patterns along a continuum from healthy to pathological. The attachment patterns they proposed include: (1) *secure*; (2) *insecure* (insecure-avoidant, insecure-ambivalent, or insecure-narcissistic); and (3) *disorganized/disoriented*.

Joey and Max manifest *disorganized/disoriented* behaviors. An examination of this category of attachment and the cumulative risk factors associated with it (e.g., low I.Q., family problems, and so on) help us to understand the multiple interrelationships between development and psychopathology. Unstable environments, financial problems, and self-preoccupied parents—who are unprepared for parenting and not able to adequately support the child's development—are common in the histories of disorganized/disoriented attachment. Because parents in such situations cannot promote self-regulation, increase sensitivity to others, or aid brain development, the child is at risk for future emotional, social, cognitive and psychological problems.

In disorganized attachment situations, the caregiver often has unresolved trauma that can easily be tapped by ongoing events. If this happens, the child may be faced with the mother's frightening, confusing, dissociated behavior. The child's core dilemma in such a situation is "fear without solution" (Lyons-Ruth & Jacobvitz, 1999, p. 549). The child can neither *approach* the mother, who is supposed to offer support, nor can the child *flee.* In such an "unresolvable paradox" (p. 549), the child often freezes, immobilized. In time, this kind of attachment pattern is followed by a host of psychological and interpersonal problems. The child may be controlling with caregivers, may be aggressive or avoidant with peers, may have academic difficulties, and often shows psychopathology in adolescence and adulthood.

Development of Self and Other Representations

Fonagy and Target (2000) stress that attachment is not an end in itself, but is of interest principally because it provides a model "for the integration of early childhood experience and later development, particularly the emergence of psychopathology" (p. 310). They and others (Schore, 2003; Siegel, 1999; Stern, 1985) have pointed out that crucial aspects of development are contingent upon and flow from attachment. Primary among these structures is the development of the brain, the central role of emotion, and their respective contributions to the *development of the self* and *the self in interaction with others* (often called object relations). Whether the attachment pattern is secure, insecure, or disorganized, there are ongoing patterns of emotional communication between mother and child over time, patterns that indelibly shape behaviors, emotions, and perception. From birth onward, through increasingly complex modes of relatedness with others, a core sense of self evolves (Broussard, 1984). The self-in-formation is a mixture of what is constitutionally innate and what is conveyed through the environment, for better or worse, in a continuous, dialectical way. Along with the development of "self-representations," are "object representations" (e.g., an internal image of the self and an internalized image of others, respectively). These self and other representations become linked with feelings, or affect states (Kernberg, 1976), that emotionally color our view of ourselves and our interactions with significant others, in time becoming a way of seeing ourselves in the world.

The child's experiences and interactions with caretakers (including fathers) and the environment are thus ingrained on the developing personality, long before the child has an autobiographical memory. These experiences and interactions, although preverbal, are remembered through bodily sensations, nonverbal behaviors, and interactions with others.

Affect Regulation

Early life events are crucial because secure attachment experiences facilitate the development of the brain, promote self-regulation, and aid in the shaping of subsequent relationships (Fonagy, 1991; Fonagy, Gergely, Jurist, & Target, 2002; Fosha, 2000; Schore, 1998, 2003; Siegel, 1999). The infant's developing brain is powerfully dependent on the mother's interactions, communicated by signals, signs, and symbols. The mind is thus created within the interaction of neurophysiological processes and interpersonal experiences, helping to shape who we are and how we are attached to others (Siegel, 1999). These self and other representations also shape the way the mind organizes its own functioning, which Fonagy and Target (2000) call "self-regulation."

Emotional regulation develops out of interpersonal experiences, shaping connections between child and others. Through secure attachment experiences with a caretaker, children can learn to regulate their affects, to label and control their own feelings, and to empathize with others. Through interactions with others, they can learn to think, reason, solve problems, organize thoughts, and especially to distinguish between inner and outer reality.

Emotions play a pivotal role in the development of the self and in cognitive development. The child who has been helped to develop a broad range of emotions will be able to distinguish his or her feelings from those of others. Conversely, the child with a limited repertoire of feelings will have a difficult time with psychological boundaries and may need to rely on primitive defenses like splitting, projection, and denial. Such a child may learn to view relationships and actions in terms of polarities, like good and bad, and either/or, and may thus be denied the opportunity to develop a rich inner life of feeling and thought.

The capacity to be self-reflective, termed "mentalization" by Fonagy et al. (2002), is a process that comes into being as the caretaker helps the child to integrate internal experiences with external reality. Mentalization, or the reflective function, helps individuals to be aware of, and make sense of, their own and other people's thoughts. Major deficits, developmental impairments, and other risk factors interfere with the development of mentalization, which is not only necessary for psychotherapy, but also for the ability to love, work, and play in a contented way.

As drama therapists well know, imaginary play fosters the development of language skills and cognitive abilities. When an adult and a child play "pretend," and both understand that the play is imaginary, the child is given a link with reality. Fonagy and Target (2000) underscore the importance of the play process, stating that playfulness indicates "the existence of an alternative perspective, which exists outside the child's mind. The challenge is the preservation of the 'as if' nature of the therapeutic exercise, and sometimes playfulness is the only ally" (p. 134). Thus, the pretend world of "make believe" helps to strengthen the boundaries between the inner world and the outer world of reality, while aiding the development of self-reflection.

Joey and Max: Attachment Patterns, Self and Other Representations, and Regulation of Affect

As can be seen from the earlier brief play vignettes, Joey and Max both came from backgrounds characteristic of children with disorganized/ disoriented attachment patterns. Surrounded by intrusive, violent adults who were preoccupied with their own needs, there was no one to help either child to form a trusting, growth-promoting relationship. No caretaker was available to help either boy to regulate emotional reactions, be self reflective, label feelings, understand cause-and-effect patterns, organize experiences, or differentiate between self and others.

Both boys showed marked impairment in symbolic, emotional, representational and cognitive domains. Joey's "freezing" behavior and Max's oppositional, defiant behaviors are common in disorganized attachment. Given the number of risk factors in the lives of both boys, it is not surprising that neither child could play imaginatively in a sustained way, regulate his emotions, or relate appropriately. Both showed pathological defenses and immature play patterns that reflected problems from earlier levels of development. They also had severe difficulties with self-regulation and the ability to focus attention, with Joey showing signs of ADD (Attention Deficit Disorder), and Max of ADHD (Attention Deficit/Hyperactivity Disorder).

Children (and adults) like Joey reflect their inner, unmetabolized psychological states through their somatic and behavioral patterns. Unable to express themselves symbolically in imaginative, thematic play, they communicate nonverbally, as Joey did with his rigid, immobile stance and his avoidance of interaction. Non-players may show signs of trauma, including dissociation and numbing (Joey), and/or hyperarousal states and destructiveness against others (Max). Fear-ridden, seeing aggression everywhere, Max would "hit back first," expressing his wishes in the same controlling, impulse-ridden manner as his father. Demonstrating disturbed regulation of affect, such youngsters express too much or too little and are over-controlled or under-controlled. Joey was painfully still, dead-like, much like his drugged mother; whereas Max was over-reactive, unable to control his (often frightening) affect.

The drama therapist's attempts to help the child gain control of frightening affect through imaginary play can bear fruit, as can be seen with Joey's changes in themes over time. When he began therapy, Joey could be characterized as demonstrating the "autistic contiguous position," a primitive, sensory-dominated defense mechanism that defends against thought, anxiety, and unspeakable terror (Ogden, 1979). After 18 months of drama therapy, however, this traumatized child began to play and talk in a spontaneous way. Less afraid of the monsters within and without, Joey began to play peek-a-boo and hide-and-seek, toddler separation games. In doing so, he was expressing his anxieties about being abandoned and being lost (from mother, in her depression and drug taking), while hoping to find and be found by mother. His play was less reflective of his fear of his monster father who beat him, and more appropriate in addressing separation fears.

Max, on the other hand, flooded me with words that he used as weapons to penetrate, attack, and frighten. Fixated on issues of power, control, and inappropriate aggression, Max also functioned at an earlier level of development, one that psychoanalysts might characterize as the pregenital or anal stage. This impulse-dominated child was unable to express emotions appropriately, sublimate his fantasies, or show sensitivity toward others. Because, at age 8, Max had never been able to develop the age-appropriate defense of repression (Sarnoff, 1976, 1987), sublimation of aggression was impossible. Demonstrating poor ego development and low frustration tolerance, Max was unable to put away (through repression) his frightening fantasies. Impulses were immediately acted out, conveying raw, unmetabolized aggression, with the use of primitive defenses such as splitting, projection, and denial. In many ways, Max's identification was with his violent father. As illustrated earlier, one aspect of his self-representation was that of a devil: "Hey! I'm like my dad!" he once said proudly. "I do what I want!" It was only after Max began to take medication for his ADHD that he was able to be slightly more controlled in his play, although major developmental problems remained.

Facilitating Play with a Selectively Mute Child

The following case example illustrates the impact of the developmental problems of disorganized attachment, impaired sense of self, and poorly developed emotional regulation. Play with Timmy, a non-player and non-talker, highlights the difficulty of engaging in drama therapy with a child who needs to develop play skills before further progress is possible—either in the small world of therapy or the larger world of life. This drama therapy case example, while necessarily abstract and rife with the many problems of selection characteristic of case example material, nevertheless attempts to focus on key interventions that aid progress toward play. For, as Winnicott has reminded us, it is only when the child can play freely that therapy can begin.

Referral

Five-year-old Timmy was the youngest child and only boy in a sibling line of four children. When he was 3½ years old, Timmy stopped talking to everyone except members of his immediate family. Since neither speech therapy nor play therapy was effective in helping him to talk, Timmy's kindergarten teachers, concerned that his mutism was interfering with all aspects of his development, insisted on another referral. Since I enjoyed the challenge of working with children with this disorder, I was happy to see Timmy in a community-based, low-fee clinic once a week for about 18 months. I also met with his mother once a month. Although Timmy's distressed mother had weekly sessions with a colleague, his father refused treatment, except for his quarterly medication checks with a psychiatrist.

Background   Timmy's father, who had a manic-depressive disorder, periodically demonstrated manic, psychotic behavior in episodes that lasted for months at a time over several years. When Timmy was 3½ years old, father was hospitalized and took medication for the first time. This helped to control father's mood swings. However, when he was psychotic, father was especially abusive to Timmy, his only son. Mother, a well-meaning woman, felt helpless in dealing with her husband. The best she could do, she said, was to send the children to her parents' home to temporarily shield them from father's paranoid and violent outbursts and his "bad moods."

Creating a Holding Environment for Play   In weekly therapy, Timmy avoided eye contact and was completely silent for 4 months. Avoiding me, as well as all of the tempting materials in the playroom, Timmy obsessively and wordlessly fingered toy soldiers, playing with them in a joyless way. In the third session, concerned about his excessive passivity, I tried to facilitate play by suggesting that he try using the sandbox, a formless, sensory medium that many nonverbal children seem to find relaxing (Irwin, 1983).

Silent and ramrod straight, Timmy moved to the sandbox and began to move the soldiers around, as though passively and compliantly acquiescing with my suggestion. I placed materials nearby and enumerated the choices he could include in his sandbox play (for example, people figures, transportation toys, digging materials, hospital equipment, miniature houses, village items, and the like). I also tried to gauge and respect his need for distance, since he made it clear that he was afraid of my coming too close to him.

Some minutes after he began to play, I noticed a change in the tempo of the action. Timmy began to push the soldiers down into the sand, head first, with slightly more energy. After this burial, as it were, Timmy unearthed the soldiers and repeated the process. This kind of defense, that might be called "doing and undoing," went on for two sessions. I limited my comments to brief descriptions of his actions. By the end of the third sand play session, however, Timmy, apparently feeling more comfortable, began to knock the soldiers down more forcibly, all the while delaying their resurrection.

Joining the Play, Narrating His Behaviors   Although mute, Timmy continued to show minor elaborations in his play in the next few sessions. He built defenses, forts and hideouts in the sand, but did not use these structures to enact a battle. He set the stage and made preparations for battle, but did not move into action. This seemed to be more a defense against play. Timmy's actions suggested, but simultaneously denied, any aggressive engagement. More emotionally engaged, however, Timmy's continual theme of killing and resurrecting seemed to reflect a fierce internal struggle with his aggressive wishes. His play conveyed the wish to *reveal*, countered by the opposite wish to *conceal*. I narrated his play, trying to follow his actions as closely as possible, feeling encouraged, however, that his nonverbal, stereotypic behaviors were beginning to change.

Gradually Timmy's projected and displaced aggression began to be expressed. Less defended against play, he began by elaborating a theme of good guys and bad guys. This kind of play is characteristic of the toddler period of development, seen in either/or themes of good versus bad or power versus powerless. One of Timmy's groups, the "green beret" soldiers, fought a second group of "regular army" guys. Interestingly, the "green beret" soldiers were much smaller than the big "regulars," but they always carried the day even though there were fewer of them. When I commented that it was funny, but the little guys *always* seemed to win, Timmy smiled. Becoming more invested in play, Timmy's affect brightened, his spontaneity increased, and his icy facade thawed a bit. But there was still no verbal dialogue with me.

Creating an Alliance with Mother and the School   Responding to an inquiry from his teacher, I spoke to Timmy and his family about the request for a school consultation. Explaining that we wanted to help him talk in school, I told Timmy that we would try to make a plan to help him talk when he was ready. I also said that his mom and I would give him feedback about our meeting. Meeting at the school with mother, teacher, the speech therapist, and others, I wondered if Timmy could have a friend join him for his speech session, and that he be told to whisper his words when he felt ready to do so. When he was ready, he could choose a second friend to join his small speech group. After the visit, I told Timmy about our plan, and he seemed pleased to know that we were working on his behalf.

Therapist and Child, Playing in Synchrony   In time, more changes in the play were evident. In concert with these, I also began to be more active in reflecting on his activities, often adding feeling words and an affective tone. Perhaps we were both beginning to feel more hopeful, as though we had more of a therapeutic alliance. Asking for confirmation or refutation of my guesses about his play, I added action words and playful affect: e.g., "Oh oh!

Another worry, *another* hideout discovered. Yikes! Betcha he's scared! But the green beret guy wins again!" Occasionally, Timmy smiled briefly; but, by and large, he continued to avoid my gaze and nonverbally let me know that I was to continue to keep my physical distance.

By making comments about the action and the presumed emotional tone of the dramas, I hoped to call Timmy's attention to what he was doing, creating a meaningful story. In a *practical* way, I hoped to demonstrate encouragement for an expanded language and repertoire of dramatic play, giving the message, "Play is spoken here." In a *psychological* way, I hoped to loosen Timmy's censorious attitude (in other words, his superego defenses) against play, and, at a deeper level, help lessen his (unconscious) shame and guilt about the powerful feelings hidden behind the mask of mutism. Occasionally, I commented that the good guys must be happy to win, especially because they were smaller and outnumbered. And once, when the big, bad guys were sent to jail, I said, "Oh, boy . . . what if in real life *little people* could be the boss of *big people*: wouldn't that be something!" In this way, I began to make symbolic interpretations within the play structure. Although there was no verbal response, it was clear that Timmy's silent campaign, enacted in the sandbox war, was becoming a more pleasurable, creative experience.

Breaking Through the (Unconscious) Vow of Silence   Three months after beginning therapy, Timmy began to whisper in school, and a month later he began to openly communicate in therapy. First, he nodded yes or no to my guesses about the play. Then, he began to make ever-louder sounds of gunfire and bombs. Much as one would do with a toddler, I encouraged his elaboration of speech and language development. In subsequent weeks and months, Timmy moved from single words to phrases, to sentences, and then to elaborate spontaneous language. After 5 months, Timmy became more verbal in his kindergarten class, as well.

Once Timmy began to talk, chaotic aggression gushed forth in his play, like a pipe striking oil. Seemingly unfazed by the tumultuous, confusing scenes in his sand play dramas, this heretofore inhibited child played with increasing aggression and gusto, making loud shouts and noises. Giving evidence of increasing enjoyment, he enacted ever more violent scenes in the sandbox, often commenting on what he was going to do in our next session.

Hoping to encourage dramatic play using other media, I asked Timmy if he wanted to use the puppets, make a story, and maybe even make scenery for his play. That way, I said, we could give the main characters a name; have a beginning, middle, and end; and maybe even give the play a title and a theme that would indicate the main idea of the story (Irwin, 1983, 1991).

Since puppets, like the sandbox, afford a certain amount of psychological safety (hiding behind the characters), I thought this might be a stepping stone to his taking roles in a drama.

Accepting my suggestion, Timmy selected characters and prepared to create a puppet story. He made elaborate background drawings of a forest and a bright red hospital room, with blood splattered everywhere. What I hoped to accomplish by suggesting greater structure was to help Timmy gain greater (ego) control of his play, making order out of the rapidly emerging inner chaos. I reasoned that the addition of dramatic structure would provide greater organization (internal and external) that could strengthen his (shaky) observing ego, aiding self reflection. In addition, while his wishes to kill seemed to be his dominant focus, there were also wishes to make reparation, an almost imperceptible theme in his play from the beginning (Klein, 1964/1948).

Emerging Aggression and Play Disruption   Perhaps anxious at the sight of so much blood in his drawings, perhaps nervous about leaving the safety of the sandbox, Timmy shifted his focus on drama (play disruption?) and turned to art. Avoiding the planned puppet story, Timmy drew elaborate drawings of knights in battle. Primitive, yet controlled violence emerged in his artwork, but Timmy did not seem frightened by the obsessively bloody scenes. On ever-larger pieces of paper, Timmy drew knights fighting powerful dinosaurs that spouted flames of fire. Huge creatures bloodied the scenes, as they pierced and sliced other dinosaurs with sharp claws, pointed teeth, and gigantic, spiked tails. Phallic aggression, castration, and pieces of dismembered heads, teeth and legs were in grisly evidence everywhere.

Startlingly clear was the theme of big animals fighting little ones. Whereas, in his soldier play, Timmy had made the little guys the winners, in *this* battle, the reverse was true. Here, the *big* guys were triumphant, as though might makes right! Timmy, seemingly identified with the biggest, fiercest dinosaurs, who dispensed death to the little guys. These images of gross carnage gave a hint of fears of aggression that had been walled off for years through silence. These graphic images from his inner world depicted a vivid picture of his terror and wishes for revenge, displaced onto the characters in his drawings. After three sessions, as though emboldened by his art work, Timmy finally announced, "Now. *Okay!* Let's do the show. Where's that big guy I was gonna use?"

Moving from Drawing to Puppetry   In the next few weeks, Timmy tried out new characters in his puppet shows, while also drawing scenes from his dramas. Perhaps to distance himself and gain a greater sense of safety (Landy, 1994), he said these were "cartoon characters." Saving his drawings, he proudly posted them on the corkboard. For a child who once felt such shame that he did not wish to be seen or heard, this was a welcome advance. And since Timmy showed considerable skill in art, his drawings became a new source of pride.

But in both art and drama, Timmy did something unusual that only became clear over several sessions. The opening scene, as it were, in both his drawings and puppet shows featured an attack on a small character, who was then summarily pronounced "dead." Similarly, the first action in the puppet show was an attack on a small puppet "victim," who, after being pronounced dead, was thrown away in a cavalier fashion. Timmy's pattern of killing off the little guy was easier to see in his drawings than it was in his fast-paced puppet shows. This barely perceptible image (which I took to be a baby dinosaur) in the corner was crossed out with a very large, black "X." Curious about this behavior, I pointed to the crossed-out, tiny image jammed into a corner, and asked about the "little fellow" crouched down there. Timmy's reaction was immediate. "Ha!" he answered disdainfully. "*Dummy*! Don't you know? Dummy! *He deserves to die* the worst killing of all!"

"Wow!" I said. "What kinds of crimes did *he* commit?"

"That squirt! He thinks he's *SOOO BIG*! He's just a squirt! A little squirt, always shooting off his mouth. I'll show him!" With that, Timmy wiped out the "little squirt" even more energetically.

Emerging Transference Issues: Talking to Me as Father Talks to Him   This exchange was remarkable for many reasons. First, was Timmy's intense affect. This heretofore over-controlled child was beginning to show powerful feelings of anger and contempt in his play. Second, Timmy's play was colored by spontaneous affect and elaboration. Paragraphs had replaced one-word responses. Third, equally important, Timmy's diminished anxiety allowed him to play at a higher symbolic level. And, fourth, there seemed to be evidence of transference in this material. Timmy talked to me as though I was the dumb, denigrated one. There must be something the matter with *me*, he implied in a haughty tone, that I would care about that puny "little squirt" in the corner. "Dummy!"

Timmy's denigrating way of talking, I learned from mother, echoed father's tone. Father, she said, often called Timmy a host of negative names. It was as though father was projecting onto Timmy his own denied, but deeply felt, qualities of stupidity and badness. In father's eyes, *he* was good and powerful, and *his son* was bad and powerless, without redeeming qualities. Now, addressing me, Timmy presented *himself* as the smart one, like his father, and *I* was the dumb one—a reversal of his relationship with father. In this kind of situation, sometimes called "negative projective identification," it is important to accept and contain the projection until such time as it can be talked about and understood.

Making Sense of the Play   This spontaneous play, with evidence of shared interaction and transference implications, seemed to signal the beginning of "real" play (Winnicott, 1971), evidence of a therapeutic alliance. Timmy had, I thought, entered an intermediary world where it was finally safe to project thoughts and wishes into play, talking freely. Still to be elaborated, of course, were the many meanings of the play: the theme of big versus little, the omnipresent worry that damage and death were imminent, and the self and object representations inherent in the denigrated "little squirt" and the huge, vicious, fire-breathing dinosaurs.

Although this kind of undisguised fantasy is common for both adults and children, often the patient is unaware of deeper meanings. My own experience, the comments of Winnicott and the recent research by Fonagy and Target (1996, 2000), suggest that interpretation and insight may not be useful for all children. Those with severe developmental deficits, poor reality testing, and major ego deviations (like Joey and Max) may not be able to use interpretations, which call for the ability to see the present in terms of the past. For such children, interpretation may be an inappropriate intellectual exercise. With a child like Joey, for example, the spontaneous dramatic play seemed to be curative in its own right, with progress noted by his mother and teachers. Joey was able to pick up developmentally and move on, even though he showed only a limited understanding of the poignant meanings of his play.

A bright and potentially psychologically minded child like Timmy, on the other hand, became interested in understanding and discussing his play. In time, he was able to make use of insight. What made this possible with Timmy who, like the others, was subjected to trauma, developing the defenses of depersonalization, dissociation, numbness, and freezing in fear? Timmy (unlike Joey and Max) was in touch with reality, showed no evidence of a thought disorder, and was able to form a trusting, caring relationship. Timmy could, in Fonagy and Target's words (2000), mentalize and become self-reflective about the themes of his dramas. Although not all youngsters can benefit from interpretation, all can benefit from an empathic relationship with another, in which creative play is facilitated and encouraged.

In a situation with a child like Timmy, understanding the play is a collaborative venture between therapist and patient, as both try to decipher some of the many symbolic meanings (Rubin & Irwin, 1975). The therapist may have hunches about the play's meanings, garnered from the child's behavior, symbolic play activity, past history, and symptoms, but it is the child who is the expert on what the play means.

Discerning Self and Other Representations   Watching Timmy's play, I was intrigued by the pattern of the "little squirt" crowded in the corner, who I speculated might be a self representation, an aspect of Timmy himself. I wondered if the bloodthirsty dinosaurs might also be a self-representation, *as well as* an object representation of his father. Father reportedly raged at everyone, but especially at his only son. I thought that Timmy's play, therefore, might be symbolically demonstrating (externalizing or enacting) scenes that had happened many times before: Timmy, a "little squirt," being verbally attacked by his enraged, out-of-control, fire-breathing dinosaur-father.

Observing Psychological Defenses Timmy's pleasure in killing off the soldiers and the dinosaurs seemed to reflect the use of a variety of psychological defenses, including those of *displacement, turning passive into active*, and *identification with the aggressor* (A. Freud, 1965). Derivatives of Timmy's wishes/fears of aggression were "displaced" onto the toy materials, where they could be safely expressed, since he had no conscious awareness of the meanings of the play. This "displacement of meaning" is one of the primary reasons that children can safely express frightening fantasies without resistance in their play. Whereas at home, Timmy had been *passive* in the hands of his father, in the play he could be *active*; and, potentially more worrisome, he showed identification with the aggressor (his father). Being the aggressor and *killing* the "the squirt" was fun, but in his drawings and dramas, Timmy simultaneously showed his terror of being the victim and *being killed* by a larger, vicious creature. His over-riding anxiety seemed to be the fear of annihilation, Timmy's terror that he would be killed or harmed, or that he would kill or harm another. In real life, Timmy's symptom of mutism was likely his attempt to control his oral aggressive rage, to keep himself from verbally lashing out and damaging or destroying others.

Although I began to make symbolic connections both inside and outside the play, at first Timmy seemed to pay no heed to what I said. For some months, the child gave no hint that he was ready to address his anxieties about the destructive impulses portrayed in his play. Anna Freud's (1927) admonition to address defenses before addressing content is applicable here. Timmy was still strongly defended against his awareness of his wish to hurt, actively or passively, and not psychologically prepared to see some of the ways that he was like his father (passive-aggressiveness being a powerful weapon). Timmy often said he was "nice" like his mother (who was kindhearted, but weak and passive). Timmy did, however, voice his ambivalence toward his mother. This was, perhaps in part, because she had failed to protect him from his violent father and was, therefore, also culpable. Nevertheless, the fact that Timmy had a connection with a caring other made it easier for him to establish a trusting relationship with me, despite his fear.

Timmy began to enact dramas after he became interested in his dream life. Intrigued to learn that dreams have meaning, he agreed to draw them and, after some weeks, act them out in the hope that they would "go away." The move to dream enactments happened after one session in which he confessed that he had a particularly frightening nightmare. When he awakened, he said, he was afraid it was not a dream but that it was real. I said that dreams are frequently stimulated by the previous day's events (in other words, the day residue), and this interested him.

Talking excitedly, Timmy began to sense a connection between himself and his father's behavior the previous day. He then told a repetitive dream that "I've had as long as I can remember, over and over." In his dream, "someone" is chased by a monster, and they go round and round in a building. In the dream, Timmy was afraid that "someone" would be killed, but he, as the viewer, was unable to cry out for help. Wakened by this dream, he was too terrified to go to his mother for comfort, for fear he would disturb and enrage his father. "Then things would be *really* bad!"

When I suggested acting out this dream, he agreed, as long as he could be the monster chasing me. Asked what the dream reminded him of, Timmy began to talk about how his father would walk around the house with a gun, checking and rechecking the windows, and threatening to kill the kids, especially "mouthy, noisy" Timmy. As soon as he made this association, Timmy saw quite clearly that his fearful reaction was to stop talking. Frightened and ashamed of his "big mouth," Timmy stopped making noise. After that, "things got worse and worse," he said, meaning that his depression deepened and all communication was shut off.

After playing the dream with several alterations for a month, Timmy was finally able to reverse roles and play the part of the victim. Even then, he was frightened, as though he was experiencing "fluctuating certainty" (Gould, 1972); that is, confusion about the boundaries between fantasy and reality. After two months, Timmy began to talk of other things and realized with a start that he was no longer having nightmares. His enactments by then had shifted to a "made-up story" of a boy who helps his mother and sister escape from a "bad guy" who had broken out of jail. Timmy said that he was always afraid that someone would come in the window at night to kill him. Associating to the "bad guy" who escaped from jail, Timmy remembered his disappointment when his father came out of the hospital. He thought that the hospital would keep his father forever and he was mad that his mother would take the kids to live with grandma.

Although much work remained, Timmy was now playing and talking freely in drama therapy. He had been in treatment for about 18 months and we were talking about termination. At a meeting with his parents, they talked of their surprise to learn from Timmy's teachers that he was quite a reader and the "best" artist in his class.

Conclusion

How can we account for Timmy's progress and that of others who are developmentally impaired? To answer this question, one needs only to consider the uniqueness of drama and its potential to stimulate growth in many domains. Drama therapists, who work patiently and persistently to facilitate imaginary play, are not only providing joy and creative outlets, but are also promoting emotional, cognitive and psychological growth. They do so by stimulating body and sensory-motor awareness, and by helping to make connections between actions and words. In encouraging the child to think about and share ideas and feelings, the drama therapist helps the individual to move out of a state of egocentrism to more social exchanges with others.

In addition to promoting personal growth, drama therapy also stimulates interpersonal interaction. Drama is about conflict; that is, one's relationship with oneself, with others, with the gods, and/or with the larger world. Sharing one's thoughts about these different worlds means moving from an intensely private world to a much more complicated, perhaps conflicted, one. Listening to others, while respecting similarities and differences, helps one to become more civilized, more humane. Role taking and other aspects of dramatic structure aid in this endeavor. When one plays a role, for example, one is asked to think, talk, and *be like* someone else. In this way, one can develop an appreciation, perhaps even empathy, for another's point of view.

As the vignettes in this chapter illustrate, drama therapy offers valuable help in diagnosis and treatment. In spontaneous drama, individuals tell highly personal, made-up stories. In the process of creating a story, children become playwrights, and then actors, scene designers, and directors. As the playwright–patient weaves a plot and chooses his preferred (and defensively disdained) roles, the drama therapist has a unique opportunity to see the unfolding of the child's fantasies, preoccupations, and defenses. Some emotionally damaged children with complex psychosocial problems, like Timmy, are able to benefit from an interpretive approach of their fantasies and behaviors, having developed the capacity to understand the symbolic meanings of their play. Others, however, who have poor reality testing and lack awareness of their own and other people's thoughts, cannot. Nevertheless, such youngsters, like Joey and Max, can benefit greatly from the growth-enhancing aspects of drama therapy, which can promote lagging development in many areas.

Drama therapy stimulates language and cognitive development. In the give and take of a drama, the child is asked to express and elaborate on ideas, sustain attention, focus on themes and sub-themes, attend to and negotiate with the needs and wishes of others, and so forth. When powerful emotions emerge, as they inevitably do, the child is encouraged to use language to control and understand his affective life. These crucial skills are needed to become a fully functioning individual, a group player and a citizen in our increasingly complex world.

Erikson, in his "Eight Ages of Man" essay (1963), stresses the importance of helping the child to develop trust, autonomy, and initiative in the early years. Although writing specifically about the development of autonomy versus shame and doubt, his words are applicable to all stages of the life cycle. He writes that this stage "becomes decisive for the ratio of love and hate, cooperation and willfulness, freedom of self-expression and its suppression. From a sense of self-control without loss of self-esteem comes a lasting sense of good will and pride; from a sense of loss of self-control and of foreign overcontrol comes a lasting propensity for doubt and shame" (p. 234).

If we add Erikson's comments to those of the other developmental specialists who stress the importance of the earliest experiences and relationships, it is clear that Joey, Max and Timmy's families were not able to form secure attachments with them. Nor were these mothers and fathers able to help these terrorized youngsters make sense of their emotions, regulate their affective life, or develop a sense of a core "good me." Deprived of the opportunity to interact comfortably with others, these youngsters had no models for the appropriate expression of feelings and ideas. Unfortunately, the millions of children like Joey, Max, and Timmy need long-term psychological help in order to remediate these severe impairments.

This chapter is intended to encourage drama therapists to continue to work with individuals with such difficulties. Patient and sensitive attempts to understand and help, delivered in an attuned and empathic way, can be effective in erecting a scaffold of trust out of which a healing relationship can emerge. With that as a basis, development can move from primitive levels to more age-appropriate levels, work that can be greatly enhanced by greater familiarity with current theories of child development.

References

Ainsworth, M. D. S., Blehar, M. C., Waters, E., & Wall, S. (1978). *Patterns of attachment: A psychological study of the strange situation.* Hillsdale, NJ: Erlbaum.

Bergman, A. (1999). *Ours, yours, mine: Mutuality and the emergence of the self.* Northvale, NJ: Jason Aronson.

Bowlby, J. (1969–1980). *Attachment and loss* (Vols. 1–3). New York: Basic Books.

Broussard, E. R. (1984). Maternal empathy: Its relation to emerging self-representations and empathy in infants. In J. D. Lichtenberg, M. Bornstein, & D. Silver (Eds.), *Empathy II* (pp. 81–103). New York: The Analytic Press.

Cassidy, J., & Shaver, P. R. (1999). *Handbook of attachment: Theory, research, and clinical applications.* New York: Guilford.

Erikson, E. (1963). *Child and society,* 2nd ed. New York: W. W. Norton.

Fonagy, P. (1991). Thinking about thinking: Some clinical and theoretical considerations in the treatment of a borderline patient. *International Journal of Psychoanalysis, 72*(4), 639–656.

Fonagy, P., Gergely, G., Jurist, E. L., & Target, M. (2002). *Affect regulation, mentalization, and the development of the self.* New York: Other Press.

Fonagy, P., & Target, M. (1996). Playing with reality: I. Theory of mind and the normal development of psychic reality. *International Journal of Psychoanalysis, 77*(2), 217–233.

Fonagy, P., & Target, M. (2000). Mentalisation and the changing aims of child psychoanalysis. In K. von Klitzing, P. Tyson, & D. Burgin (Eds.), *Psychoanalysis in childhood and adolescence* (pp. 129–139). Basel, Switzerland: Karger Press.

Fosha, D. (2000). *The transforming power of affect: A model for accelerated change.* New York: Basic Books.

Freud, A. (1927). Four lectures on child analysis, I: Preparation for child analysis. *The writings of Anna Freud, 1,* 3–18. New York: International Universities Press.

Freud, A. (1965). *Normality and pathology in childhood: Assessments of development* (2nd ed.). New York: International Universities Press.

Gould, R. (1972). *Child studies through fantasy.* New York: Quadrangle Books.

Greenspan, S. I. (1997). *Developmentally based psychotherapy.* Madison, WI: International Universities Press.

Irwin, E. C. (1979). Drama therapy with the handicapped. In A. Shaw & C. G. Stevens (Eds.), *Drama, theatre and the handicapped* (pp. 21–28). Washington, DC: ATA Publications.

Irwin, E. C. (1983). The diagnostic and therapeutic use of pretend play. In C. E. Schaefer & K. J. O'Connor (Eds.), *Handbook of play therapy* (pp. 149–173). New York: Wiley.

Irwin, E. C. (1991). The use of a puppet interview to understand children. In C.E. Schaefer, K. Gitlin, & A. Sandgrund (Eds.), *Play diagnosis and treatment* (2nd ed., pp. 682–703). New York: Wiley.

Jennings, S., Cattanach, A., Mitchell, S., Chesner, A., & Meldrum, B. (1994). *The handbook of dramatherapy.* London: Routledge.

Kernberg, O. (1976). *Object relations theory and clinical psychoanalysis.* New York: Jason Aronson.

Klein, M. (1964). *Contributions to psycho-analysis. 1921–1945: Developments in child and adolescent psychology.* New York: McGraw-Hill. (Original work published 1948)

Landy, R. (1994). *Drama therapy: Concepts, theories and practices* (2nd ed.). Springfield, IL: Charles C. Thomas.

Lewis, P., & Johnson, D. (2000). *Current approaches in drama therapy.* Springfield, IL: Charles C. Thomas.

Lyons-Ruth, K., & Jacobvitz, D. (1999). Attachment disorganization: Unresolved loss, relational violence, and lapses in behavioral and attentional strategies. In J. Cassidy & P. R. Shaver (Eds.), *Handbook of attachment* (pp. 520–554). New York: Guilford.

Main, M., & Solomon, J. (1990). Procedures for identifying infants as disorganized/disoriented during the Ainsworth strange situation. In M. T. Greenberg, D. Cicchetti, & E. M. Cummings (Eds.), *Attachment in the preschool years: Theory, research and intervention* (pp. 121–160). Chicago: University of Chicago Press.

Millar, S. (1969). *The psychology of play.* Baltimore: Penguin Books.

Ogden, T. H. (1979). On projective identification. *International Journal of Psychoanalysis, 60*(3), 357–373.

Rubin, J. A., & Irwin, E. C. (1975). Art and drama: Parts of a puzzle. In I. Jakab (Ed.), *Art and psychiatry,* Vol. 4 (pp. 193–200). Basel, Switzerland: Karger Press.

Sarnoff, C. A. (1976). *Latency.* New York: Jason Aronson.

Sarnoff, C. A. (1987). *Psychotherapeutic strategies in the latency years.* New York: Jason Aronson.

Schore, A. N. (1998). Early shame experiences and infant brain development. In P. Gilbert & B. Andrews (Eds.), *Shame: Interpersonal behavior, psychopathology, and culture* (pp. 57–77). New York: Oxford University Press.

Schore, A. N. (2003). *Affect regulation and the repair of the self.* New York: W. W. Norton.

Siegel, D. J. (1999). *The developing mind: How relationships and the brain interact to shape who we are.* New York: Guilford.

Stern, D. N. (1985). *The interpersonal world of the infant.* New York: Basic Books.

Winnicott, D. W. (1958). Transitional objects and transitional phenomena. In *Through paediatrics to psycho-analysis* (pp. 229–242). New York: Basic Books.

Winnicott, D. W. (1965). *The maturational processes and the facilitating environment: Studies in the theory of emotional development.* New York: International Universities Press.

Winnicott, D. W. (1971). *Playing and reality.* New York: Basic Books.

Winnicott, D. W. (1989). *Psychoanalytic explorations.* Boston: Harvard University Press.

CHAPTER 2

"Don't Hurt My Mommy"
Drama Therapy for Children Who Have Witnessed Severe Domestic Violence

ANNA MARIE WEBER

"He said he was going to kill her. I didn't think he'd do it."

Children who are exposed to severe domestic violence come face to face with horror. The one who vowed to love their mother controls and abuses her with yelling, hitting, shoving, knives, and guns. When their mothers or caregivers become injured, they are torn between wanting to protect and wanting to be taken care of. Multiple conflicting emotions are triggered for the children as they face violence at home, when one parent injures another. In the midst of crisis, they are often brought to a local domestic violence agency. Most mothers, fathers, and children survive; yet far too many, tragically, do not.

Domestic violence is the misuse of power and control over a spouse or intimate partner. The degree of violence varies; some batterers only need to give a look to send terror through their family. Within the controlling environment, the batterer often demeans his or her family with animal names and degrading language that whittles away at their self-esteem. Often, the threat of separation triggers an escalation of the ongoing violence, resulting in the brutalization or murder of a parent by another. In many homes, children hear and watch in fear. The U.S. Department of Justice (2003) reports that 1,247 women and 440 men were killed by an intimate partner in the year 2000. Given the statistics and prominence of women as victims, this chapter focuses on the treatment of children whose fathers or stepfathers battered and murdered their mothers or committed murder/suicide.

Hurting a mom wounds her children at the core of their being. Experts report an estimated 87% of children in homes with family violence witness that abuse. Even those children who do not see the fighting (including toddlers and preschoolers) know what is happening and are often "pulled in" to the violence (Straus, 1994). Children hear: "*He cursed at her.*" They see: "*He pulled out the phone cord.*" "*My daddy came into my bedroom and tried to kill my Mommy.*" They tell us: "*My daddy says my Mommy's bad.*"

When children witness violence, they learn that aggression solves conflict. They come to understand that violence will get you what you want. "*She didn't cook the right chicken so he slugged her.*" They become fearful: "*That bandage on Mommy's face is scary,*" or "*I hope he doesn't break the door again.*" Others cling to their mothers, not letting her out of their sight.

Children of all ages witness domestic violence, many from their mothers' arms. "Repeated physical abuse, which is estimated to take place between about 10% of American couples is most common in families that have small children through the age of 12" (Pelcovitz & Kaplan, 1994, p. 745). This statistic is particularly relevant in light of evidence that preschoolers are at heightened risk for suffering immediate and long-term behavioral and emotional effects in response to trauma. Young witnesses often shut down when conflict arises or intervene inappropriately. In addition, aggression and fear become the norm. Children are affected psychologically, physically, and socially. They often experience a host of emotions that they do not have the developmental skills to understand. Toddlers have piercing cries and heightened startle responses. Their cries often sound similar to their mother's screams.

Children exposed to domestic violence space out in school, missing the tasks assigned and forgetting their homework. On the playground, they find themselves in fights, misreading the social cues and body language of their peers. They tend to assume everyone with a stern or serious facial expression is angry. They use aggression to solve conflicts, or hide and withdraw. Many have a difficult time falling asleep and staying asleep. They often have stomach pains, headaches, and frequent colds and viruses due to chronic stress. Their loyalties can fluctuate between their parents, feeling that they must pick one parent's side. Often, it may feel safer to side with the aggressor.

During a drama therapy group for children exposed to domestic violence, each child created a family movie scene using dollhouse figures "*little people.*" They played out their scenes for one another and, upon completion, one child called out, "*This show's too violent for children to watch!*" Yes, what they have seen in their everyday lives many adults would stop them from watching on TV or at the movies. Children are affected at multiple levels. In addition, batterers often expose their children to violent movies that are not appropriate for their young age.

Bancroft & Silverman (2002) identified the characteristics of men who batter and described the influence that their violent behavior has on their parenting. They name three characteristics: control, entitlement, and possessiveness, along with a tendency toward "authoritarian, neglectful, and verbally abusive child-rearing" (p. 6). These characteristics influence the batterer's parenting ability and have a negative impact on the children by "creating role models that perpetuate the violence, undermining the mother's authority, retaliating against the mother for her efforts to protect the children, sowing divisions within the family, and using the children as weapons against the mother" (p. 7).

Older children often experience strong, ambivalent feelings toward their fathers who batter. Their young counterparts frequently split their feelings, one day feeling anger, the next day loneliness. Interparental violence that escalates into severe injury, murder, and/or suicide has an extremely detrimental effect on the children. Each situation is unique yet similar. Many children and their caregivers lie and say their parents died in a car accident to avoid the shame of admitting the truth. The caregivers fear that the children will be ostracized for their father's behavior.

"My Daddy Killeded My Mommy."

Children whose fathers have murdered their mothers experience confusing, overwhelming emotions. The most significant man in their lives has robbed them of a mother, a concept their little brains cannot hold. Instead, their loneliness, sadness, anger, and confusion take over.

Effects that emerge for children exposed to the murder or suicide of a parent are similar to those of child witnesses, yet magnified. Somatic symptoms, such as sleep and eating disturbances, emerge along with a strong sense of responsibility for what happened. The children often feel guilty about the death of their parent and believe that they should have stopped it. In addition, flashbacks, emotional outbursts, and difficulty concentrating in school add to their stress and confusion as they try to understand the emotions of those around them. The children frequently feel helpless and hopeless, often exhibiting an intense sadness coupled with violent images and generalized fears (i.e., fear of movies, animals, loud noises, slamming doors, being left alone, and bad weather). They can also experience an exacerbation or reactivation of prior symptoms. Acute stress and post-traumatic symptoms vary with each child and depend on the complexity of the case (American Psychiatric Association, 2000). A large number of the cases involve Type II (recurring) trauma (Terr, 1991) due to the ongoing, chronic domestic violence prior to the murder. Factors such as the weapons used to kill their mothers and whether or not their father also killed himself influence the symptom patterns. The amount of blood they saw on their mother has a major effect on a child's traumatic response, along with whether they saw her killed, walked in after the murder, or heard the incident described by family members. Addressing this, Eth and Pynoos (1985) wrote, "At the core of the child witness's trauma is the continued intrusion of the central violent action when physical harm was inflicted: the final blow with a fist, the plunge of a knife, or the blast of a shotgun. The child endures an intense perceptual experience" (p. 28). The images, sounds, smells, and sensations impact the level of trauma experienced by the child.

The remaining family members must cope with trying to meet the needs of the children left in their care, in addition to wrestling with their own pain and traumatic grief. Many are grandparents who feel exhausted by the demands of life or aunts and uncles with their own family responsibilities and financial burdens. They have the best intentions for the children, and most want them to "feel no pain." Others think the kids are not grieving because they often do not cry, at least not in front of adults. These caregivers have a relationship with the victim and the perpetrator as well as with the children. Thus, many feelings emerge: rage, sadness, confusion, and an intense sense of loss, to name only a few. The traumatic responses of the substitute caregivers influence the recovery process of the child. The crisis at hand and the need to get life back to normal take precedence, along with financial pressures. The caregivers often need the child to "get better quickly" and do not want him or her dwelling on what happened. They want the child to be happy. Many of the caregivers need a break from talking about the violence, while others want to talk about it more than the child does. All are at varying phases in the grieving process. Thus, engaging the caregivers in the healing process is vital, even if it is sporadic due to the crisis situation and the multiple responsibilities that come with tragic deaths. They, too, are traumatized and have experienced a devastating loss.

The crisis treatment process begins with the therapist reinforcing a semblance of safety so that the child may access the coping skills to work through the trauma. The therapist guides the beginning and closure of the session while following the child's lead. K. Johnson (1998) wrote, "In the case of grief compounded by trauma, the traumatic anxiety and other symptoms must be dealt with first in order to allow grief processing to commence" (p. 134). Concurring with this point are Hendriks, Black, and Kaplan (2000), who wrote:

> Traumatic reactions can interfere with grieving. The nightmares of trauma are always distressing and may prevent the child dreaming more calmly about the dead parent and gaining comfort from the feeling that mother is near. These 'grief dreams' appear to help in

coming to terms with the loss. Intrusive daytime recollections also interfere with the child's efforts to remember the dead parent. The mutilated image prevents reminiscence in tranquillity. Traumatic play can be repetitive and uncreative and interfere with the use of play to address and work through grief. (p. 48)

In light of the aforementioned issues, the following will reflect an adapted, integrated model for working with children exposed to severe domestic violence. The foundation for the work is based on elements of the protocol for crisis intervention, emergency evaluation used in treating severe cases of domestic violence (Eth & Pynoos, 1985). Several authors (Arroyo & Eth, 1995; Cattanach, 1996; Hendriks, Black, & Kaplan, 2000) utilize the protocol as a framework for their sessions and interventions. In addition, the timing for working through the trauma needs to be assessed, taking into account the unique context and symptoms of each individual client, while reinforcing their support systems. Keeping this in mind, the framework may be used in a variety of situations. Hendriks, Black, and Kaplan (2000) wrote of using the original framework for interviewing children both immediately following an "unlawful killing" and also after some time has gone by.

The "Emergency Evaluation" (Pynoos & Eth, 1986), described as a clinical approach by Arroyo & Eth (1995), provides a semi-structured, three-stage interview technique designed to facilitate a spontaneous and complete exploration of the child's subjective experience. The protocol begins with an opening phase that utilizes drawing to make direct links to the event. This leads to the trauma phase in which the therapist and child work through the trauma, exploring feelings about the event and fears about the future. In addition, Arroyo & Eth (1995) wrote, "The child witness may be strongly conflicted by his or her seemingly contradictory feelings of hate and love," complicated by "the issues of responsibility and loyalty" (p. 38). The closure takes place, with the therapist validating how understandable, realistic, and universal their responses have been. The child is encouraged to express any anger they may have, along with exploring what they wish had happened. Their bravery and courage during the interview process are complimented. This framework can be enhanced by the use of play and drama therapy. The creative process frees the child with a sense of safety to explore from a place of aesthetic distance while incorporating the use of projective techniques, metaphor, role exploration, sculpting, and scene work.

Child witnesses of domestic violence are brought in for crisis intervention at a time when the entire family is in crisis. Due to the immediacy of the events, detailed information is not always available. Thus, the task is to reduce the child's stress with limited intake information. Usually, the crisis counselors have a short description of the violence that has just taken place, whether something like this has happened before, and a limited idea of the child's support system. The advantage of working in an agency is that the caregivers often have a concurrent session with another therapist. The child witnesses in crisis often exhibit acute stress symptoms such as sleep and eating disturbances, startle responses, anxious attachment, and aggressive or withdrawn behaviors that mirror the event. Play and drama therapy assist in the engagement process while allowing the child a familiar format in which to explore the trauma and experience a sense of mastery.

The playroom at my office provides a comforting environment with a sense of safety through its design. The room is kept consistent so that returning clients can experience familiarity even if their sessions are sporadic. The soft, blue walls have a soothing effect. It has bean bag chairs in which the children can casually sit, roll or nestle and feel comforted by their cozy size. Even the older children enjoy the bean bag chairs and the large stuffed teddy bears that inhabit the corners of the room, along with medium and tiny teddy bears. The playroom contains two houses, school toys, puppets, therapeutic games, and small animals (wild and tame). Also present are: rescue heroes, musical instruments, blocks, little people (balanced for ethnicity and gender), assorted cars, a tool kit (which has objects that can symbolize weapons if needed), a medical kit, assorted telephones, an indoor baseball set, kids' indoor basketball, dishes, and a small table for drawings and feeling games. The space and toys are equipped for safe expressions of rage and anger, as well as a host of emotions. The ambulance and police car are brought out when appropriate. The water toys assist with closure and grounding. The room design, creative play materials, and choices offered throughout the sessions foster a physical, emotional, and social sense of safety (Bloom, 1997). The environment enhances the therapist's relationship with the child, supporting the drama therapist in the attunement process.

The engagement process begins with the first greeting. Groves (2002) wrote, "The first and most important principle is that we must recognize the power of a nurturing, respectful, and caring relationship with an adult to help a child recover from adversity" (p. 101). That relationship begins with the first greeting. While the child is in the waiting room, I walk in and out a few times (Perry, 2001), allowing the child to check me out, say hello, and begin the attunement process. Later in the therapy process, they begin to recognize the rhythm of my feet coming down the stairs and pride themselves on knowing when I'm going to come through the door. For the younger children, it is the jangle of my keys that lets them know it's me. The greeting is very important in reinforcing their sense of value, as they realize that someone is excited to see them and attuned to their needs. We all discuss the week, where the playroom is and where the aunt, grandparent, or caregiver will be sitting when we return. The child and I take the stairs up to the playroom while discussing his or her likes and dislikes, making a game out of finding the picture of children on one of the doors.

Treatment Process

Warm-up

Beginning with the warm-up phase of the session, children are offered a choice of seats and an opportunity to draw a house or a tree: "*You pick.*" Many traumatized child witnesses are overwhelmed by the task of drawing whatever they want; thus, specific choices are offered. If they choose to free draw, that is okay, too. The trauma themes still emerge within the house or tree drawings, in spiky leaves, blackened roofs, or blood-red windows. Older children concentrate on the task very quietly, and their silent focus is honored. We later discuss why kids come here: "*To play about their worries about fighting.*" Short relaxation games take place, along with choosing a stuffed animal to be their best friend. If the conversation focuses on the traumatic event, then a discussion at the child's developmental level and cognitive clarifications take place. For example, the child might say, "*My Mom made my Dad go to jail.*" Therapist responds: "*I think it was the police who took Dad to jail. Police and judges decide who goes to jail. What would happen if a kid hit somebody at school?*" Child responds, "*They'd go to the principal's office.*" "*How come?*" "*Cuz your not supposed to hit.*" "*How come?*" Child and therapist answer, "*Cuz it hurts.*"

The techniques are interwoven into the trauma model. The choice of interventions depends on the client's needs, developmental level, support system, capacity for resilience, and the severity of the crisis. Inviting the child to speak or, as Terr (2003) describes it, inquiring about the trauma are vital to the process due to the fact that domestic violence is a secret crime and children fear that others will be overwhelmed by what they have to say. This technique can be used throughout the process. During the session, the therapist may have a sense that the child is distracted, confused, or worried. Asking, "*Is there anything about what happened to your Mom that's still on your mind?*" might bring about a response such as, "*Yeah, her brain got really hurt—it's bad?*" Clarification can then take place. "*Her brain was protected by bone. It didn't get hurt and her head is 'all better' now. They even took out the stitches, which means the Doctor thinks she's all better.*" The invitation to speak of the violence opens the door for disclosure.

Children coming to session a few days after the traumatic event usually begin to speak very freely about what they have seen and about what worries them. Children for whom a long time has passed since the traumatic experience often say that they "*don't think about it*" or "*don't want to think about it.*" They are given permission to not talk or think about it, and are asked to "*tell me*" if they happen to "*start to think about it.*" This invitation often frees the child to speak of the trauma, be it later in the session or in a future session. During the "Not Thinking About It" phase, coping skills are reinforced through the use of projective objects (Landy, 1996), such as small animal figures, puppets, or stuffed animals. Puppets are effective models for breathing exercises and stop thought techniques. Architectural drawings work well for older children as they draw their favorite place and, later, the setting of the traumatic event. Throughout the process, the focus is on engaging and connecting with the child by building a trusting, validating relationship, a sense of safety, tolerance for painful themes, spontaneity, creativity, and fun. As Webb (2003) stated, traumatized children have a "short sadness span," and they want to be like other kids. They need permission to have fun.

Working Through

The working-through phase takes place when the child has the capacity and support to continue. Staying in tune with the child's body language and sensations, as well as the therapist's scan of his or her own internal responses, reinforces awareness of the child's emotional state and needs. The therapist enhances the sense of attunement (Perry, 2001; van der Kolk, 2000) developed with the child through out the warm-up phase. Intuitive senses and clinical skills are involved as the child's emotional distance and the projective techniques needed to facilitate the process are assessed in the moment. The child's needs are the priority. Levine (1997) wrote:

> Children may not state verbally whether they want to continue; take cues from their behavior and responses. Respect their wishes, as well as the mode in which they choose to communicate. Children should never be forced to do more than they are willing and able to do. Slow down the process if you notice signs of fear, constricted breathing, stiffening or a dazed (dissociated) demeanor. These reactions will dissipate if you simply wait quietly and patiently while reassuring the child that you are still there. Usually, the youngster's eyes and breathing will tell you when it's time to continue. (p. 262)

Staying attuned to the child, the therapist might ask, "*What's most on your mind about what happened?*" or "*What do you think about just before you go to sleep at night?*" Usually, either of these questions will invite the child to explore the trauma, and his or her processing begins to flow. I may ask the child to "*show me what happened*" by using the small animals, little people, puppets or multiple-sized teddy bears. The size of the toys chosen depends on the age of the child; for, the smaller the toys, the stronger the child's sense of control (Jennings, 1999). Assessment of the child's emotional or aesthetic distance (Landy, 1996) takes place throughout the warm-up and especially at this working-through phase of the process.

"*What was the worst part?*" Asking this question depends on a host of variables: a sense that the child is stuck, the developmental level of the child, the strength of the child's support system, and whether the child has the ability at the time to work through this portion of the trauma. If the traumatic event is interfering with the child's life, it is time to reinforce safety and explore where the child is stuck in relation to the traumatic experience.

Empowerment is vital throughout the process, particularly at this phase. Small choices and moments of success support the empowerment process, along with metaphorical interventions in which successful situations can be enacted. Cattanach (1996) wrote of "powerful endings" in which the child and therapist "invent" ways to contain monsters. A variation of this technique is power dreaming, or changing the ending of a dream, which can be easily adapted to the enactment process of the drama therapy session. Power endings also work well for "wish" segments. Following the child's lead yet having an active, non-intrusive presence frees the child to explore complex issues and new possibilities.

Closure/Grounding

"*We have five minutes to bring this story to an end or to be continued next week.*" This phrase gives the child warning that the session is coming to an end, reinforcing their sense of control. Little animals, puppets or dollhouse figures are put away, saying, "*back to being toys.*"

This technique models for the child, stopping the trauma exploration, marking that they can clearly take a break; they can walk away for a time and revisit at another time. Closure/grounding techniques are especially important here due to the fact that it is crisis intervention. Due to the nature of the events and the fact that their caregivers are also traumatized, closure is vital. If further grounding is needed for an agitated child, the scribble and figure 8 drawing exercise or self-esteem basketball takes place. The child is asked to scribble all their feelings on the page using as many colors as they would like. The colors are given "*feeling names*" by the child. After the discussion, the paper is turned over. The child makes a large figure 8 with the help of the therapist that goes left to right on the page, allowing his or her eyes to move from left to right as they slowly breathe, tracing the figure 8 over and over until they have reached a sense of calm. Changing a child's physical position (Gil, 1998) often guides them back to the here-and-now. Closing activities can incorporate this by taking place in a different part of the playroom.

In the indoor basketball game, the child and therapist shoot baskets while saying positive things about the child to reinforce his or her strengths. The therapist checks their physical and emotional responses, guiding them to a balanced, grounded sense of being. Then, the "*Goodbye Game*," water basketball, takes place as a ritual ending (Jennings, 1986). Water basketball is a game in which the ball is enclosed in water and the therapist and child push buttons to make baskets. When child and therapist get to the end of the game, it is time to leave the playroom. In this way, the child has a concrete sense of how long the rest of the session will be. The consistency and familiarity found in the ritual ending, used each week from the beginning of the treatment process, provide the child with a sense of security at a challenging moment—that of saying "*goodbye.*" As we walk down the stairs, plans for the rest of the day are discussed and the child is guided back to his or her new parent or caregiver, reinforcing their connection.

Brief Crisis Vignettes: An Invitation to Speak and Create

Shelby (1997) wrote, "traumatized children need to be heard in the presence of another who is not afraid to grieve with them. They need someone to accept their suffering in its cruel entirety" (p. 149). In addition, the therapist must communicate a willingness to stay emotionally present to the child throughout the process of playing or dramatizing the horrendous details that haunt them. At times, the thought of witnessing such pain can be daunting. Yet, once the child is greeted, his or her spirit for life inspires one to continue the process.

The following vignettes convey the clinical, creative examples of the process as the children in crisis begin to regain their sense of equilibrium, resuming their developmental tasks and connecting to their loved ones. The crisis session examples are in tune with the individual child's needs. An invitation to speak and create in a safe, comforting environment with a caring, skilled, empathic person takes place. Drama therapy provides the metaphorical, emotional distance and a creative way to explore painful, haunting events without overwhelming the child. Each child experiences his or her unique yet universal form of catharsis and release, cognitive reframing, and glimpses of hope.

Birthday Triggers

Traumatic reminders (Pynoos, Steinberg, & Goenjian, 1996), such as triggering events, often happen around the time of a child's deceased parent's birthday. A 5-year-old boy requested an appointment near the day that would have been his "*Mommy's birthday*," as he had heard everyone talking about it. He asked his grandmother if he could come to see me. The child was waking up with nightmares, and the grandmother was happy to honor his request. She admitted being surprised that the boy remembered me since it had been months since our previous sessions. They returned to the familiar waiting room, both appearing relieved to be there. We followed our initial routine with an energetic welcome, and grandma spoke openly about her grandson having nightmares. The child and I entered the playroom with grandma remaining in the waiting room.

Remembering the space, he checked it out and picked up his familiar *"best friend puppy"* and sat at the table *"to color."*

"How are your worries?"

He quickly spoke of a *"bad dream."*

"Do you want to show me?"

He nodded, and I followed him to the dollhouse where he proceeded to set up the bedroom. He placed a little boy doll in the bed and the Mommy doll next to him, also in the bed. He focused on the dolls, moving them with his tiny hands, saying, *"Mommy's heart blew up. Blood all over . . . it got on me."* (He was not present at the time when his mother was shot to death). He played out the dream again.

"I wonder who might help her heart?"

He responded by getting the doctor kit. He enroled as the Doctor, and I was cast as the Nurse. We gently doctored the Mommy doll and comforted the boy doll. Special people arrived to take care of the boy doll, then the Mommy doll went to heaven. *"She's all better in heaven; no owies in heaven."*

Turning and walking away from the dollhouse with deep sadness and loss emerging from his entire body, he curled up on the floor in the center of the room. Sitting next to him, I rubbed his back. Adding my voice for comfort, I chose a familiar modality, singing, which we had used in previous sessions to reinforce comfort, and sang "Somewhere Out There" (Horner, Mann, & Weil, 1986).

He jumped up and began singing his Angel rap song, marching around me in a circle. In our previous sessions, he would sing with a microphone: *"My Mommy's an Angel now,"* dancing around the room. At times, he asked me to join in. We sang and danced, rapping about *"Angel Mommy."* After five minutes or so, we closed the session with our *"goodbye game,"* water basketball. In the waiting room, he gave his grandmother a big hug and said, *"I'm hungry."*

Crisis Sessions for Trauma Blocking the Grieving Process

A 6-year-old girl was referred by a hospice to our children's program. During one session, after being asked if she had any worries about what happened to Mommy, she drew her mother lying on the floor. During her recent sessions, drawing had appeared to trigger an intense emotional response. I remembered the previous counselor mentioning that the girl had tried to take care of her mother (who was dead on the floor) before calling the police from a relative's house down the street. I brought up the fact that, while she was at her aunt's house, the paramedics came and took care of Mommy. Using the little people, we played out a scene in which the paramedics brought a "*soft blanket* (that I introduced) *for Mommy.*" We spent time picking out and preparing the blanket, then covering the Mommy doll. As the play ended, we put away the dolls, saying, "*back to being toys*" (a line she was very familiar with). We played self-esteem basketball, grounding her in the here-and-now, followed by our "*goodbye game,*" water basketball. The agitation that appeared in drawing activities diminished and her aunt later reported that she was sleeping through the night.

Many children fear that their new caregivers will also die, or that something bad will happen to them. We cannot make promises, only provide reassurance. Kroen (1996) wrote, ". . . two-to-five-year-olds do grieve, feel loss, and experience other strong emotions following the death of a loved one" (p. 40). He often uses the words "very, very, very, very," which I have borrowed when reassuring children that their caregivers are not going to die for a very, very, very, very, very, very, long time. This technique often assists older children who are fearful of everyone around them dying, as well. Of course, this intervention should be used with care depending on the health of the caregivers.

Dream Exploration to Work through Past Toddler Trauma

Dreams provide a metaphorical beginning point for working through a traumatic event, especially when details of the child's experience are in question. One little boy returned for services. I had seen him previously in a shelter where his piercing screams, whenever away from his mother or startled, were frightening for all around. By this time, he was 5 years old and, after several sessions, disclosed a dream about sharks. During the drawing warm-up, he chose to trace my key chain, which included three rings of various keys and a rose (pewter and flat). In the past, tracing our hands took place before long breaks. This was similar in style. He began to speak about a "*scary dream,*" and I asked, "*How about showing me the dream?*"

He proceeded to set up the "little people" and furniture for the house, saying, "*This will be the carpet,*" placing the key picture underneath the furniture. He began to draw a pool with the shark inside and a violent, bloody tale took place. "*I wonder who could be stronger than the shark . . .*" Then, through drawing and placement of objects that represented strong rescue heroes (Power Rangers), the shark was contained. The pool was made safe for children and the shark no longer had the dominant, destructive role in the story. The session ended with our ritual closure, de-roling the toys, and quiet conversation while watching two dolphins swimming back and forth as the water toy was gently rocked.

A 10-Year-Old's Metaphorical Exploration of Anger at His Father

His mother survived being beaten unconscious by his father on the boy's birthday. Days before his father was to be released from prison, the boy returned for therapy. Both he and his mother were experiencing heightened fear and exacerbated symptoms. Unable to verbalize his feelings, it appeared vital that we utilize a metaphorical approach. I asked him if he would like to draw a storm. He depicted a tornado in swirling blue colors. He added items that the twister had picked up, including a man swirling, caught in the tornado's grasp. With the older kids, instead of a story, we often create a *"movie"* using small objects, dollhouse furniture and figures on a sand tray size blue board, which provides a boundary for the enactment. The children often call the board a *"stage"* as we sit on the floor with the movie enactment, taking place between us. His *"movie"* was a detailed account of the thrashing around this man experienced while being hit by *wind-blown* objects. While enacting the movie, the boy released an intense amount of rage, later writing on his original picture: *"You tried to kill my mother and then take me away. You are saying your sorry now? It's to late for sorry! You shouldn't have done it in the first place. I'm very deprest! I am not pleased with what you have done."* He stood up and read it to me. The tornado metaphor allowed him to express his anger and discover his words that had been locked away by fear and traumatic reminders. He then took a deep breath and sat back down. He picked up another piece of paper and began to draw a rainbow, requesting that I color it with him. As we added color, he began to relax and we continued talking about his plans for the day.

A Concrete Exploration of Responsibility

Eight to 10-year-olds often feel that it was their fault—that they should have known and stopped the murder from happening. This if often best addressed later in the treatment process due to the fact that self-blame can be a necessary defense mechanism for the child. Care must be taken. Developmentally, they are beginning to explore and master issues related to rules and right versus wrong; their moral development is forming. When the timing is appropriate for the child, the issue is explored.

One girl stated, *"He said he was going to kill her but I didn't believe him."*

"I wonder if he didn't say things like that a lot?"

"Yes, he sure did!"

"Kids don't know what adults are going to do. How old were you when it happened?"

"Seven."

"Yes, you were just a kid. Look at that big stuffed bear over there and stand that small one next to it. Do you think that that short bear is old enough to understand the big one?"

"No. He's too little to know. It's not his fault."

She proceeded to make a sign for the bear, writing, *"It's NOT My Fault."* She took particular time to color in the "not." The process continued for a time, putting the blame on her stepfather. As with most of the case vignettes presented here, the batterer also killed himself; thus, contact and visitation in jail was not an issue.

Monster Masks Worn by Teddy Bears

Monster masks often provide a distanced way for young children to explore their fears and begin to master them. The masks are made for the stuffed animals to wear, not the children. Young, traumatized children lack the ego strength to wear masks on their faces (Emunah, 1994) or to see the therapist wearing the mask. Masks can be very underdistancing (Landy, 2001) and triggering, especially for young children. In order to feel enough control and safety to explore the *"scawrey monsters,"* concrete methods are employed such as only working on the masks for a short time and then putting them away in a folder, under a pile of books, or locked in a cabinet.

Following the warm-up, a 5-year-old began using markers to add color to a mask made from half of a file folder cut in an oval. He named it *"monster mask"* before he had even completed it. We discovered a safe place in the playroom to create the mask and only worked on it for short amounts of time, putting it away under heavy books where it could not get out. Coloring for a little bit and stopping when it got to be too scary was a concrete way to practice "stop thought" techniques. Then, we would use a newly learned breathing exercise. Taking a big breath, raising our arms above our heads and holding it for a quick count of 8 (it would be a slower count for an older child), then lowering our arms, we exhaled, repeating the sequence three times. This exercise was also practiced in the waiting room with the family.

The original task was to make two opposite masks, role and counter-role (Landy, 2001). Due to the stress involved, the *"monster mask"* was worked on in increments. Chaotic, dark, deeply pressed marker colors emerged for weeks. The counter-role of fearful victim was taken on through the use of small toy figures. As I modeled putting the mask away and only working on it for a short time, after building a safe space to retreat to, we began to play with the fearful feelings in short segments. Only when the *"monster mask"* was finished did the creation of the transformation mask begin. It became the guide (Landy, 2001). It also took weeks to create. Bright colors in shaky lines appeared. As each week progressed, the colors became less chaotic and almost wave-like. The masks were placed on the teddy bears and the *"rainbow mask"* told the *"monster mask," "No more scaring children!"*

Mother's Day and Father's Day Triggers

Many young children speak of wanting a new mom, and their need to be taken care of is very strong. Their Mom in heaven still exists for them. They imagine her in the clouds, yet this only becomes soothing after working through their feelings related to her murder. One first-grader requested to return to see me soon after Father's Day. She met me at the door after hearing me quickly come down the steps, as in the past. We chatted a bit and I asked her if she "remembered who her best friend bear was." She did and picked it up to hug it, setting it down to watch as she acted out a dream.

In the dream, she was a *"rescuer,"* fighting off the enemy who was against her mother. The play shifted from the actual dream play to talk of her *"old dad"* while she kicked the big stuffed bears around the room. She paused to hug her *"best friend bear"* and continued to fight the big bears. The fight concluded with her victory, and the play came to an end. She walked over to me and spoke of *"lighting candles for Mom."* She said, "I *want to draw Mommy with God,"* and we sat at the table. As we went to say goodbye, she picked up the toy phone and I asked, *"Who are you calling?"* She answered, *"God."* After speaking into the phone in a muffled tone, she asked God if she could *"speak to Mom."* After working through the trauma and releasing her anger, she could begin a child's grieving process by *"calling heaven."* She received comforting, supportive words that had been previously blocked out by terrifying images. She began to remember and internalize her Mother's Love.

Grieving and Understanding at a New Developmental Level

Children have an immature cognitive development and cannot quite understand death until age 9 or 10 (Webb, 2003). Not only is their grieving process influenced by their age, but often their ambiguous feelings toward the batterer, their father, cannot be tolerated until this age. As they grow cognitively, questions emerge and people consequently give them a more realistic picture of the dead parent. The children also try to construct their mother from what they have overheard at family gatherings. Thus, a return to treatment at this age is very important and may have multiple goals, depending on the child and his or her support system.

When he turned 9, the boy from the shark story returned to therapy after being triggered by Father's Day. He now knew more about his father's violent behavior and alcohol abuse and was grieving at a new level. At the same time, he was wishing he "*had a dad and a family like the other kids.*"

"*I know my dad drank and was sick. He did bad things.*"

"*Yes, his behavior was wrong.*"

"*I know.*"

"*I wonder if there was something fun that you and your dad did?*"

"*He played ball with me and took me to the park.*"

Birthday Messages from Heaven

Many of the children in the grieving phase choose the white stuffed animals to portray their parent in heaven. With the above child, role reversal was used. In role as the father, he gave birthday wishes to the son, represented by a teddy bear sitting across from him. This enactment allowed the child to incorporate positive, nurturing aspects of the father role. (If a child perceived the parent as a ghost and was fearful of him or her, this intervention would not be appropriate until more trauma work had taken place).

Helping the child discover something positive about their battering father can be challenging yet vital for the child, who needs something of his or her father to hold onto. Our prisons are filled with older teens that have joined their fathers in prison to fulfill their own need for connection. Identifying with their fathers in a maladaptive way, many are at risk for growing up to be batterers or victims themselves. Guiding them to discover the positive, however simple the moment may be, offers a reframed connection, freeing them to let go of the all-too-familiar aggression.

"You've Got the Whole World in Your Hands"

If the family has strong religious beliefs, conceptions of God can play a strong role in how the family talks to the child. One boy proceeded to put all the movie figures from "different kinds of families" in my two held-out hands. He meticulously piled them up, then started to sing, "*He's Got the Whole World in His Hands.*" I joined in and he leaned back on the bean bag chair, singing, "*You've got the whole world in your hands.*" We stayed there a moment, smiling in silence. Walking down the stairs after the session, he turned and looked up at me, saying, "*I want to be a good dad.*"

Therapist Responses

At times, I have felt such trepidation about the process. Yet, when I see their faces and look into their eyes, they inspire me to continue. I worry: will the sessions be adequate to contain them through the weeks or even months? The sporadic attendance, often due to financial stresses, long commutes, and other transportation issues, used to be so stressful until I had a few amazing experiences of the children asking to see me again. It is still difficult, for I see how they leave the building yet I often do not know how their nights are. I can only hope that, if they are having a difficult time, they will be brought back for at least a crisis session. Shelby's (2000) words give me support:

> I have spent a career making therapeutic moments from scraps of time, identifying the 'window' or the potential of each therapeutic instant . . . I have found that posttraumatic integration and healing are not predicated entirely on the strokes of time clocks. Short but meaningful therapeutic encounters—sometimes even a single moment of intervention—can produce powerful change and growth. (p. 71)

I believe in the working-through process, utilizing drama therapy in the appropriate environment and time, along with its healing power. If the children can go to sleep at night envisioning these horrors alone, the least I can do is be present to witness and assist them in discovering a guide and a way to moments of peace and love. I even do the scribble and figure 8 exercise that I teach the children. A music therapist colleague taught me to play music in the car as I drive home, a notch louder than usual, to release the pain from my body. Throughout the process, I use my countertransference to explore where the child is at emotionally, especially in their bodies, asking myself, "Is this feeling sensation theirs, mine, or both?" In order to do the therapeutic work, I surround myself with supervision, personal therapy, connections with loved ones, and walks along the beach.

Conclusion

The integration of the crisis intervention model and drama therapy provide a framework of security and empowerment, along with a sense of safety. This consistent container frees the child to explore and trust that an attuned adult will take care and guide them when needed, allowing them to discover their own personal power and strength.

The children loved their fathers, and they often still do. Violence enters their world disguised as love. How can these little ones cope with such atrocity and violence toward their mothers? If the perpetrator had been a stranger, it would be so much easier to be rageful, without *"mixed up"* feelings, confusion, and chaos. The best and the worst of the world become contained all in their own family. Adults can hardly understand the murder of a loved one by a loved one. It falls on the small shoulders of the young. The violence and the blood haunt their souls, minds, and hearts. The pictures and images of the events flood their brains, their dreams, and their nights. Many try to shut the images out and find that they have shut everyone out. A few take the healing journey.

As painful as their experiences are, the children exhibit an enormous amount of resilience in their spirit, energy, and love for siblings and willingness to connect to others. Battering/suicide and murder/suicide cases are predominate in this chapter. None of the children had fathers to visit in prison. The mothers of the children written of here gave such love and support to their children that they were all able to attach to their new caregivers and still stay connected to their moms "*in the clouds*" or "*in heaven*" as they looked to the stars.

Writing the stories of the children—stories forced upon them, stories they happened upon as they responded to horrifying noises—opens the doors to their secrets. With each story witnessed by an attuned therapist, new endings become possible. They change, we change, the world changes. The slightest change allows for new discoveries, new moments, of the magic of the child spirit, the magic of connection between two hearts and souls. The children on these pages and many more have inspired me to journey with them. It is my hope that the reader will also be inspired to go on such healing journeys with our wounded children—staying with them, not running away, believing in their resilience and their ability to tell their stories of blood, horror, violence, and great loss, along with the joys, loves, and happy times. They do not have to hide anymore; someone will ask them, invite them to speak, promise to listen, stay present and attuned, share the pain, and share the journey to new relationships and new possibilities.

References

American Psychiatric Association. (2000). *Diagnostic and statistical manual of mental disorders* (4th ed., text rev.). Washington, DC: Author.

Arroyo, W., & Eth, S. (1995). Assessment following violence-witnessing trauma. In E. Peled, P. G. Jaffe, & J. Edelson (Eds.), *Ending the cycle of violence: Community responses to children of battered women* (pp. 27–42). Thousand Oaks, CA: Sage.

Bancroft, L. (2002). The batterer as a parent. *Synergy, 6,* 6–8.

Bancroft, L., & Silverman, J. G. (2002). *The batterer as a parent: Addressing the impact of domestic violence on family dynamics.* Thousand Oaks, CA: Sage.

Bloom, S. L. (1997). *Creating sanctuary: Toward the evolution of sane societies.* New York: Routledge.

Cattanach, A. (1996). The use of dramatherapy and play therapy to help de-brief children after the trauma of sexual abuse. In A. Gersie (Ed.), *Dramatic approaches to brief therapy* (pp. 177–187). London: Jessica Kingsley.

Emunah, R. (1994). *Acting for real: Drama therapy process, technique, and performance.* New York: Brunner/Mazel.

Eth, S., & Pynoos, R. (1985). *Post-traumatic stress disorder in children.* Washington, DC: American Psychiatric Press.

Gil, E. (1998). *Play therapy with severe psychological trauma* [video]. New York: Guilford.

Groves, B. M. (2002). *Children who see too much: Lessons from the child witness to violence project.* Boston: Beacon Press.

Hendriks, J. H., Black, D., & Kaplan, T. (2000). *When father kills mother: Guiding children through trauma and grief* (2nd ed.). London: Routledge.

Horner, J., Mann, B., & Weil, C. (1986). Somewhere Out There. Original Soundtrack: *An American Tail*. MCA.

Jennings, S. (1986). *Creative drama in groupwork*. London: Winslow Press.

Jennings, S. (1999). *Introduction to developmental playtherapy: Playing and healing*. London: Jessica Kingsley.

Johnson, K. (1998). *Trauma in the lives of children: Crisis and stress management techniques for teachers, counselors, and student service professionals* (2nd ed.). Alameda, CA: Hunter House.

Kroen, W. (1996). *Helping children cope with the loss of a loved one*. Minneapolis, MN: Free Spirit Press.

Landy, R. (1996). *Essays in drama therapy: The double life*. London: Jessica Kingsley.

Landy, R. (2001). *New essays in drama therapy: Unfinished business*. Springfield, IL: Charles C Thomas.

Levine, P. (1997). *Waking the tiger: Healing trauma*. Berkley, CA: North Atlantic Books.

Pelcovitz, D., & Kaplan, S. J. (1994). Child witnesses of violence between parents: Psychosocial correlates and implications for treatment. *Child and Adolescent Psychiatric Clinics of North America, 3*(4), 745–758.

Perry, B. (2001, April). *Promoting the optimal development of children*. Presented at the Annual Meeting of Prevent Child Abuse New York. Albany, NY.

Pynoos, R. S., & Eth, S. (1986). Witness to violence: The child interview. *Journal of the American Academy of Child and Adolescent Psychiatry, 25*(3), 306–319.

Pynoos, R. S., Steinberg, A. M., & Goenjian, A. (1996). Traumatic stress in childhood and adolescence: Recent developments and current controversies. In B. van der Kolk, A. C. McFarlane, & L. Weisaeth (Eds.), *Traumatic stress: The effects of overwhelming experience on mind, body, and society* (pp. 331–358). New York: Guilford.

Shelby, J. S. (1997). Rubble, disruption, and tears: Helping young survivors of natural disaster. In H. G. Kaduson, D. M. Cangelosi, & C. E. Schaefer (Eds.), *The playing cure: Individualized play therapy for specific childhood problems* (pp. 143–169). Northvale, NJ: Jason Aronson.

Shelby, J. S. (2000). Brief therapy with traumatized children: A developmental perspective. In H. G. Kaduson & C. E. Schaefer (Eds.), *Short-term play therapy for children* (pp. 69–104). New York: Guilford.

Straus, M. (1994). *Beating the devil out of them: Corporal punishment in American families and its effects on children*. New York: Lexington Books.

Terr, L. (1991). Childhood traumas: An outline and overview. *American Journal of Psychiatry, 148*(1), 10–20.

Terr, L. (2003, May). *Using play therapy to mimic natural healing: What we have learned from Columbine and 9/11*. Presented at the 4th Annual Conference for the New York Association for Play Therapy. Melville, NY.

U.S. Department of Justice. (2003, February). *Bureau of Justice crime data brief, intimate partner violence, 1993–2001*. Washington, DC: Author.

van der Kolk, B. (2000, October). *Frontiers of trauma: Treatment in the year 2000*. Presented to the Long Island Committee on Sexual Abuse and Family Violence. Melville, NY.

Webb, N. (2003, May). *Using drawings in play therapy with traumatically bereaved children*. Presented at the 4th Annual Conference for the New York Association for Play Therapy. Melville, NY.

CHAPTER **3**

Children Who Whisper
A Study of Psychodramatic Methods
for Reaching Inarticulate Young People

BERNADETTE HOEY

"My object is to show what I have found, not what I am looking for."
—Pablo Picasso

For all of us, in times of overwhelming trouble and confusion, the landscape of the mind is a tangled place. Emotions, half-formed thoughts, disturbing memories collide, jostle to the surface, then take a dive before language can sift through them, label them, and file them in neat, explainable categories. So, we are left with the confusion locked inside ourselves, out of reach of our own understanding, and impossible to communicate to others. If this can be true for adults, then it is even more so for children. For, they have not yet mastered the art of analyzing and rationalizing their life experiences. And even when they can articulate their inner turmoil, what adults can be trusted with their words? For adults, they know, have undue power at times. Only a few can be allowed entry to private, secret places. And as for those confused, troubled areas of the mind, those places where words will not come . . . well, who can be trusted to walk with care there?

At such times, however, when healing is needed, children have one great advantage over adults. They are closer in time to the period marking the transition from infancy's egocentric *first universe* to the reality-based *second universe,* where the child must begin to engage with the separateness of others (Moreno & Moreno, 1944). In this early bridging period, the line between fantasy and reality is often indistinct. Imaginative play is vivid and it leads the children swiftly and readily into the area (namely, the right brain)

45

where both imagination and unconscious association patterns have their home. Reality itself takes on constantly shifting shapes.

Metaphor, too, has this shifting quality, slipping backward and forward between image and reality, stirring up hidden associations as it does so. It has a strong role in psychodrama-based child therapy, and it is not surprising to find that children respond instinctively to its multidimensional meanings, for their own natural play is laden with such symbolism.

Reviewing the literature linking metaphor, right brain functioning, and the therapeutic process, Mills and Crowley (1986) note Erickson and Rossi's (1976/1980) description of that moment in the storytelling process when the metaphors at work in the unconscious mind finally spill over into consciousness: "When this happens, the conscious mind is surprised because it is presented with a response within itself that it cannot account for" (p. 448). Psychodrama works in a similar way, and children are often surprised at what suddenly springs to the surface of their metaphor-enriched play. One traumatized 4-year-old with whom I worked demonstrated this. She arrived for her first session in a disturbed, hyperactive state. She had recently witnessed a fatal accident in which her favorite playmate was run over by a car. "I heard her head crack," she had told her mother at the time. Her first glimpse of the toys was enough to trigger associations. She made a beeline for a large, quite battered, old Humpty Dumpty. No child had ever chosen it before. Her rushing movement toward the toy was too sudden, too immediate for her choice to have been the result of conscious reasoning. I suspect it was an instinctive ability to use metaphor as a bridge between the conscious and unconscious minds, an ability so often apparent in the play of very young children. In the four therapeutic sessions that followed (Hoey, 1997), the child continued her exploration of the Humpty Dumpty metaphor. Assisted and stimulated by the psychodramatic method that enhanced her play, she was able to allow the distressing details of the accident to emerge. They were dealt with through metaphor, in safety, and she moved gently to a state of acceptance and peace.

Let us now examine this process in depth through a more comprehensive study of one-to-one based therapy sessions with disturbed children and adolescents. To do so with clarity, we shall focus on one small group whose play is characterized by frequent whispering, or whose body language at times shows the mind whispering the unspeakable. They cannot find the words? They have a need to hide some secret? They are afraid of diminishment or ridicule from the listener? They cannot bear a truth that is pressing up to the surface of their awareness? Or is there another possible reason the therapist must yet learn? (The therapist must never give his/her hypotheses the status of fact. The mind must always remain open to the insights that

RJ 504. E95 2003

✓* RJ503. R53 2000

RJ504. I567 2003

RJ504. I57 1999

* IPT for depressed adolescents
RJ506. D4 I58 2004

✓ RJ504. S76 1999

* RC488.5 .B485 2002

Treating Adolescents
✓ RJ503. T74 1996

Sarah Fried Recommendation
─────────────────────────────

RJ507. A29 G553 1996

drawer under the bills.

See the Appendix for Remittance Forms Instruct[ions], Remittance Forms, and Cash Management Polic[ies], Office.

K. _Book-sale Shelf:_

All items to be placed on the Booksale Shelf should [be] written in pencil on the title page (to facilitate remo[val after it has] been on the shelf the longest).

All newly added items to the Booksale Shelf should [be placed on the] shelves. If there is not enough room to move the ol[der items,] discard the items that have been on the shelf the lon[gest].

Price for items on the Booksale Shelf:

come through continuing attention to what the child is silently revealing in the undercurrents of the play, as well as in its overt structure.)

The first of these therapy sessions illustrates some key theoretical concepts that run as connecting threads between all the case studies considered here. These concepts must be so much a part of one's thinking that they spring to mind instantly when some important event in the child's life flashes fleetingly and metaphorically to the surface in play, surprising and therefore challenging the therapist with its speed. Throughout the case studies, all names and identifying details have been changed to protect the identities of the children and their families.

Natalie (Nat) was a strong-willed, little 4-year-old placed in temporary foster care, seeing her parents during supervised access visits only. She was carrying a very uncomfortable secret while the Department of Human Services tried to sort out which of her parents was responsible for the severe physical abuse of her two younger siblings. Each parent claimed the other was to blame. It was a complex story. Nat, almost certainly, held the key to the riddle, and she guarded it well. She had been referred to me for therapy by the Department of Human Services. Although my work was that of a healer, not an investigator, others (she probably knew) wished she would tell what she'd seen. So she was very guarded.

Like many children whose lives have been turned upside down through government intervention, Nat liked to keep the therapy sessions strictly under her own control. Her early play was characterized by mainly silent, purposeful concentration and oft-repeated rituals, with the therapist used in a way that was a cross between playmate and slave. For example, day after day she ordered me to come with her while she took Child–Child for a walk (Child–Child being the name she'd given to a fluffy, spindly-legged emu chick marionette to which she was strongly attracted). I would be instructed to walk beside her, holding a mirror-bedecked Indian umbrella over them both. Any other speaking she did at such times was whispered to herself.

Our work together took many forms, as I searched for ways to slip out of my role as compliant slave. As well as Child–Child, with whom she often identified, her favorite toy was a very tiny baby doll. It was not part of the therapy collection, for it was very fragile, as were the two parent dolls that belonged with it. However, Nat set her heart on it. Metaphorically, of course, it was perfect, and from time to time it took on an active role in her play.

Sometimes, I would begin a therapeutic story knowing full well that this little controller would not suffer me to continue in the prime role of story-teller. One such story began as a tale of a small bird (which she promptly replaced with the baby as soon as I set it up it in its nest. I moved in the direction she was going, and the story took a human form). *A wild storm blew up and the tree was tossing dangerously in the wind. Mother Goose* (a graceful, white satin marionette) *decided the baby was not safe. She took the baby carefully in her beak and flew off, looking for another home for the beautiful little child.* At this, Nat raced out into my study and returned with the two parent dolls. She began to enact a re-uniting of the family and created a new home for them. (This was the first time her play had shown such a clear link with her life-story). Then, she stopped abruptly. "The father can't come," she said. "Oh," I said. "Where will we put him?" "He can sit here," she said, plonking him unceremoniously on a horse, some distance away from the others. Then, even more abruptly, she turned away from the whole scene she'd created, picked up another toy and began some inconsequential play by herself.

On another day, she again interrupted a story that had just begun, bringing in an eagle that interacted with Child–Child in a way that had clear links with her father. He had recently asserted that she would soon be coming to live with him, for he was confident he would win a formal challenge he had mounted against the Department of Human Services. Against the wishes of the temporary foster parents, he had given her a new schoolbag, telling her the name of the school he had chosen for her, thus unrealistically raising the child's hopes. Nat was caught in the middle of a stressful, uncertain situation.

So today, changing my story, she began to enact one that had parallels with her own life. She chose a wide-winged kite in the shape of an eagle as one of her central characters. Child–Child was invited by the eagle to sit with him on a magic carpet. Just as they were about to take off, Child–Child ran back to pick up his schoolbag. From then on, it became clear that the eagle represented Nat's father and she was acting out a scenario wherein his promise to take her away to live with him would be fulfilled.

The enactment, however, went no further than a fairly low-key riding off with the eagle—and the schoolbag. Whatever triumph or satisfaction or hope or fear was contained in this exploratory play, there was no chance to savor it, or to deepen it with a psychodramatic intervention such as maximizing. For, Nat again moved swiftly away from such potentially revealing material and excluded me from her pottering around among the other toys, making it clear that she had no intention of allowing me further access to her private world. As usual, I totally accepted her need to remain in control and to feel her secret was safe. The material to be explored would not surface again if I tried to push the pace. Dayton (1994), commenting on the director's obligation to work from within the protagonist's existential world, puts it well:

The primary difference between true psychodrama and applying psychodramatic or experiential techniques on top of other therapeutic models is that psychodrama follows the lead of the protagonist. . . . In a sense the director takes a walk through the protagonist's *surplus reality*—that which we carry within our psyches as personal history, which affects the whole of who we are and how we relate. Surplus reality is important and it is real. What the protagonist says 'is' simply 'is,' and the director works from there. (p. 8)

The concept of *surplus reality* is a central one in psychodrama, so we shall interrupt the thread of Nat's story to briefly explore its meaning. It is a difficult concept to pin down on paper. J. L. Moreno, the founder of psychodrama, himself wrote little about *surplus reality*. However, it suffused all his teaching, and anyone who has studied psychodrama experientially has discovered in practice exactly what it means. It involves a state of heightened awareness, and in Nat's case, at this moment, it is growing increasingly present to the child. She is experiencing the power of action, as the metaphorical power of the toys and puppets is working on her subconscious mind, bringing to the surface memories, feelings, and reactions that were not in her mind when she first interrupted the therapist's story. There is an expansion of each experience, and new light is shed on them as associations form, connect, and re-form. The prosaic real world of her daily living is beginning to be replaced by the phenomenon for which Moreno coined the interesting term *surplus reality*.

When I reflect on this phrase and wonder how it came to be invented, I recall psychodrama's power to expand the ordinary, humdrum facts of real life, sometimes to wildly generous proportions. Reality can be extended in a superabundant, lavish way that causes an upwelling of insights into the normally more restrained conscious mind. That is so in practice in the therapy room and that, at least, is one of the meanings I idiosyncratically like to take from Moreno's intriguing phrase *surplus reality*. However, carrying the knowledge and weight of her experience since the earliest days of psychodrama's development, Zerka Moreno (his wife and close collaborator in the early days of psychodrama's development) takes the discussion of origins to a deeper level:

Moreno had this idea of surplus power, taken from Marx's idea of surplus value. He believed that something similar exists in psychodrama. Moreno realized that his protagonists moved into areas that were not real to anyone else but them, and purely subjective. Psychotics are an extreme example of this. These ideas went beyond fantasy, beyond intuition, almost like a trance experience. He recalled Marx's idea of "surplus value," that what the worker produces results in capital gains by the employer, a surplus which does not belong to the capitalist but should by rights be returned to the workers. Moreno thought surplus reality is "out there" somewhere and must be made concrete and specific and returned to the center of the protagonist where it has meaning and purpose. He knew he could not truly meet the psyche of the protagonist unless he lived in the surplus reality together with the protagonist." (Moreno, Blomkvist, & Rutzel, 2000, pp. 16–17)

As Nat plays, she is on the edges of Moreno's "world without limits" (Moreno, Blomkvist, & Rutzel, 2000, p. 1). Had she, at this point, been able to allow me to combine the action of her play with powerful psychodramatic methods such as doubling, mirroring, and maximizing, the healing work would have reached a far deeper level of her consciousness. Her play would have flown on wings, surprising her into new insights, as our most surreal and telling dreams sometimes do. After the enactment, she would have carried away the impact of these insights at a deeper level than a child usually reaches through normal healing play. But Nat's need to control her environment prevented her from allowing the power of surprise (a vital element in psychodrama) to enter the therapy room. So, there were limits to the therapeutic experience that opened for her and, therefore, limits also to the depth of catharsis she experienced.

It was necessary for me as therapist to fully respect her inner process and to allow it to unfold without interruption. She needed to move in her own way. My task was to follow where she so clearly was leading and to be with her as she went. Again, Dayton (1994) expresses this well:

> As therapists, when we enter into surplus reality, we are being allowed to go into the intrapsychic world of the protagonist—where angels fear to tread. We need to trust the process of our clients as being right for them, and understand that what is opening up for them is what their own psyche intends them to know at the time. (p. 9)

With all this theoretical discussion in mind, let's take a look at what emerged with 8-year-old Rebecca, a far less heavily defended child, though one who struggled to express herself freely, both with words and with play. For all her inhibitions, she was very comfortable with allowing me to follow her hesitant play, surprising her into new awareness with the occasional insertion of important psychodrama tools for change such as *concretizing, maximizing,* and *doubling.* She allowed me to move freely from one to another, using them in combination, which, as Clayton (2002) reminds us, leads to a more complete production of a drama and a deeper warm-up to the process for the protagonist. Unlike Nat, Rebecca was open to all that unfolded, so her *surplus reality* was rich and deep and she experienced full catharsis at the end of the session.

What do these terms mean? *Concretizing* occurs when the director notices an important word picture the protagonist has just created and moves in with instructions that lead to it being enacted in visible form. The protagonist's engagement with the ideas immediately deepens. *Maximizing* occurs when the director senses significant meaning in an action just made or a sentence just spoken. The instructions then given to the protagonist result in an over-the-top expansion of the idea. *Doubling*, in psychodrama's original form, and when used with adults, refers to a role an auxiliary actor takes on when the director wants to bring a supportive figure into the drama, to move alongside the protagonist, thinking, feeling, speaking, and reacting as he or she thinks, feels, speaks, and reacts. The *double* can often go on to express for the protagonist ideas or emotions that are implicit in the action but not openly revealed. The director asks the protagonist to choose someone to be that *double.* Then, all sorts of things happen that a young child would not be able to cope with. For a child, some adaptation of the process is needed. In the pages that follow, you will see a variety of ways that this *alter ego* is brought into the room through the puppets. It is a more oblique form of the doubling that is practiced in classical psychodrama.

Those readers who are familiar with psychodrama may be surprised at the lack of prominence given to the important concept of *role reversal* in these accounts of therapeutic sessions. Questions of age, level of disturbance, and complexity of the problems being explored are the determining factors here. I have used direct role reversal methods successfully with young adolescents in other cases, but they have often been frightened by its power. With more disturbed children, I have frequently experienced the truth of Moreno's (1955) words, "Double technique is the most important therapy for lonely people, therefore important for isolated, rejected children. A lonely child, like a schizophrenic patient, may never be able to do a role reversal but he will accept a double" (p. 124).

Doubling proved to be an instrument of powerful healing for Rebecca. She had been brought to me because of an increase in a phobic fear of vomiting that had begun some years back, in response to a badly handled incident at pre-school. During the first therapy session, she had allowed me to speak quite directly about her problem. In the two that followed, she needed help to relax with the toys and to use them in play.

Today, she is creating a tentative little story about Rex, the lion, and I have invited her to choose a friend to stay by Rex's side as we play. She gives this role to the giraffe (a wonderfully agile marionette attached to a crossbar by two long springs. Standing about 1.5 meters tall, he has very long legs,

clacking wooden hooves, an elongated rope neck, and great dramatic possibilities). Rex is full of fear, and I'm encouraging Rebecca to put the fears
into words. This is difficult for her.

At one stage, I cause the giraffe to invite Rex to come with him to the top
of a mountain, which we create together using an ironing board covered by
a colorful rug. "See how beautiful it is up here," I tell her through the giraffe,
"with the sun on the trees, and that little breeze just rustling the leaves a
tiny, tiny bit." We're standing on chairs behind the ironing board mountain,
and from this vantage point we're looking through the wide floor-to-ceil-
ing windows out to the garden and surrounding bushland. It's an expansive
view. I use it as psychodrama directors often use a space to create a sense of
the universe, when they want protagonists to get in touch with their inner-
most truth. "It helps if you talk about your worries," says the giraffe. "Let
them out into the fresh air. No good keeping them locked up . . . See that
little patch of blue right out there in the distance?" Rebecca nods. "It's the
sea," says the giraffe. "Tell your worries out loud to the faraway sea."

Sharing my love of the sea, Rebecca is able to respond with ease to this
directive. She lists some worries that I know are her own: fear of her brother's
teasing, fear of being called "fraidycat." Then, she stops. "Sometimes," she
says, "sometimes, I . . . get . . . I get . . . frightened when . . . I . . .
when . . . when . . . when . . . I . . ." I call on the sun to help her set free the
words that are stuck. "They're there," I tell her. "They're fluttering behind
your tongue." I make a fluttering movement with my fingers, near my lips.
"Let them out!" Then, in the voice of the storyteller, I continue: *The sun lets
Rex look at himself in her light.* (For this, I use a mirror in the shape of the
sun.) *The sun warms Rex's frightened little heart. "It's hard for you to find
the words," says the sun. "Don't worry about them. Just take your time.
They'll come. Just rest here for a minute or two. I'll keep you warm. They'll
come in the end."* Speaking for Rex, the child struggles, literally for several
minutes, before finally saying: "I get frightened . . . when . . . when I . . . I
get . . . " (And then with a rush): *"I get frightened when I get frightened!"*

"Ah! . . . So *that's* it! Your fear gets to be like a runaway horse." I tell her
to find a horse from among the toys, while I seize a deerskin drum, using
the drumstick in a way that suggests galloping hooves. The child makes the
horse gallop around as I beat the drum. This very clear description of a
panic attack is central to the child's problem. It needs to be highlighted.
Unlike some other children with whom I work, this child needs to be encouraged to express herself strongly. Her face is already shining with the relief of
having articulated her problem. But, psychodrama provides a way of maximizing this cathartic response. We make full use of its power as we play. I go
on with the story.

"Oh dear!" said the sun. "That must be scary. That must really get your poor little heart going thump, thump, thump." We let Rex's friend, the giraffe, run with him, and this time the child plays the drum as I cause the giraffe to leap wildly over chairs and tables in his careering flight round the room. At this point, I am actually using the giraffe as the child's double—a sort of *alter ego* who can express the overwhelming fear the child feels when she is in the grip of a phobic reaction. The puppet responds wonderfully to me. Its springy nature gives it a great ability to portray terror that's gone right out of control. The child beats joyfully and exceedingly vigorously on the drum. The room is filled with our vitality. Together, we play around with this imagery for some time before moving on to different metaphors that are calming ones, involving the sea, the sun, and a little rock pool, where the sea holds her fears so that she doesn't have to take them home with her. We take time with these metaphors and we enact them simply. The child's face is radiant as she leaves. She has experienced full catharsis.

Work with Brett followed a different path. He was a painfully shy, inarticulate 17-year-old, who nevertheless was capable of making clear and insightful statements about his own inner life when we managed to break through the emotional barriers that impeded his speech. The fragments of therapy sessions that now follow are not designed to give the reader a sense of his whole story. Rather, they are intended to convey an idea of how psychodramatic method can be adapted to the needs of adolescents who have moved far beyond the world of creative play, a world perhaps once accessible at an earlier stage of life. Above all, the passages that follow will focus strongly on how to adapt the method for a young person who is trapped in his own inner world and almost inaccessible to those outside it.

Brett was adopted at the age of 6. The adopting parents had two children of their own, but they wanted to help a child with a minor disability. (Brett's right arm was withered.) They both entered into the commitment with good will and high hopes. The father retained some ability to communicate with Brett and he certainly cared about him, but as the years went on, the mother lost all rapport with him. Her anger and dislike of him grew with the passage of time, and the methods she used for handling minor disputes were rigid and increasingly punitive. At the time of his referral, Brett had retreated into almost total silence within the family, unintentionally fueling their mutual antagonism. When this persisted for almost a year, his father decided he needed help, and Brett came to me.

It took me some months to uncover the extent of the boy's troubles, as he moved hesitantly, though trustingly, along the path that opened out in the therapy room. At the beginning of the first session, I told him that I could not be of use to him unless I realized that my first job was to try to understand his world. "I'll need you to help me. Now, there are many ways we can do that. One way is by talking. But that's not always easy. I know another way, and it often works very, very well with teenagers and with adults. Would you like to hear about it?" A nod, an interested look on his face, but no eye contact. (I later realized eye contact was almost impossible for him.) The process of warming him up to this unfamiliar form of communication had begun. I continued.

"In this room, I have a lot of toys and all sorts of visual imagery. When children are working with me, they play with them. But adults use them differently. I suggest to adults that they think of themselves as sculptors who want to tell a story with the figures they create and place in different positions so that people looking at their work can see the story that is in the sculptor's mind. Some European cities have wonderful groups of figures that do just that. Or maybe, I suggest, they could come closer to home, to Australia, and think of Myer's, Melbourne's own well-known department store that, every year, creates an elaborate story without words in its Christmas Window. I tell them to think of themselves as artists working on that window, setting up a scene that speaks so strongly to the people looking in from the street outside that no words are needed. The objects they've placed so creatively are themselves the storytellers. So, today, in this room, if we have a go at doing this, you'll soon know if it seems a good idea to you. If you're not comfortable with it, let me know and we'll do something different." He agreed, and I slid back the folding doors of the large cupboards where my equipment is stored.

"Let's start with you giving me a picture of what life's like for you in your family. Choose something to be you." He needed no assistance with this. He placed a small figure of Snoopy on the floor. "Okay. Now something to be your father, and place that figure in such a position that I get an idea of what sort of relationship is going on between you two." He chose a very upright, sturdy-looking horse, made of a plaited, straw-like material, pretty much the color of his father's hair. He placed it directly behind the Snoopy figure, which lay prone on the floor. "What did you have in mind when you chose that for your father?" Brett said, "He's kind of stiff, and he walks behind me in pride, kicking me, trying to make me go where I can't." I nodded in acceptance of the image. "Find something to be your mother," I suggested. To my surprise, he chose a doll that young children often choose for someone they love or aspire to be like. "Why that one?" "Because she's beautiful, but her eyes are evil. That's how she looks at me when she's angry," he said. The doll did have a fierce intensity in her brilliant eyes.

The action method had freed Brett up considerably, and we were able to talk a little about some of the issues behind what he had been able to reveal through his picture. And so future sessions were shaped. Most times, I asked him to show me what was happening in his life, but occasionally I used the visual aids in the room to show him what I was learning about him or about life in his family. At all times, however, I remained very conscious of his extreme shyness and his difficulty with a conversational approach. I never pushed him into speech when a nod or a single, understanding "Ah" from his listener was enough to make him know he had been understood. Working in this way, he was able to lead me deeper and deeper into the lonely, isolated world he inhabited.

One day, he told me of a girl with whom he was in love. It was very much a case of love from afar, not only because he saw himself as too "shy, awkward, and deformed" to have any hope of getting to know her, but also because the girl's brother had warned him never to tell her how he felt. He suspected she was repelled by him. But she remained in his daydreams constantly. In several of the sessions that followed, he spoke of noises in his head and a feeling that he was viewing life at a distance, as if from within a glass cage. I knew my next task was to help him move to the recognition of his need for a medical assessment. Then, suddenly, he said, "I know what's the matter with me." His whole body language expressed a wish and yet an inability to go on. It was clear that the thing he wanted to tell me mattered desperately to him. His mouth moved silently, he looked distressed, but no words would come.

"It looks to me as though there's something you really want to tell me," I said, my tone of voice acknowledging I could be wrong. "You don't have to, you know . . . and you know I'd never force you. . . . But, it looks as though the words you want to say are trapped in there, behind your tongue. It's as if they're caught, and they want to get free." (I made a fluttering movement with my fingers, similar to that I'd used with Rebecca). "If you want to leave them there, that's fine. But if you want to tell me . . . well, I'm here."

"It's about Cecile," he finally said. I nodded. More silence. No eye contact, but face raised, so that its anguish was visible. Then, "She's lost her innocence!" For a split second he looked at me, just time enough for him to see that his existential experience was recognized. It would not be mocked. It would not be buried, like so much trash, under a pile of reasonable adult argument. He had taken a huge risk in letting me in. He saw my nod. He read my eyes. He heard the tone of my voice as I said: "Ah!" His face was still sad, but there was peace in it. He had not been wrong. His own inner truth had been accepted as just that. It was safe. He was no longer totally alone.

This experience was no doubt helpful to Brett in the sessions that followed, and he moved surprisingly quickly past his fears to accept his need for medical assessment. Facilitating an appointment with a psychiatrist we could trust took time and patience and, for Brett, great courage. In our final time together, I asked him if he found anything useful in all that we had covered. "Yes," he replied immediately, "when you showed me Snoopy and the bottomless pool." This was a reference to an earlier session during which I'd shown him a picture of the unhealthy communication patterns in his whole family, and his own absolute passivity in allowing those dynamics to entrap him. Using a small, helpless-looking baby monkey to represent him in the role of unresisting victim, I had shown him as drowning in a bottomless pool until Snoopy (representing the strong side of him) jumped in and fished him out.

At the time of that session, Brett had shown little reaction to this image and had bucked at taking part in a crucial discussion he agreed I should have with his father. "I don't want to talk to him," he said. "WHY?" I asked, my voice more vehement and more forceful than usual, for by now the therapeutic relationship had strengthened and Brett could handle challenges more easily. "I don't want him to know me." "What do you mean by that?" "I don't want him to know I'm growing up. I suppose I'm hanging on to the childhood I never had." Faced with a clear, therapeutically significant moment, my mind needed to move with mercurial speed at this point. I decided to take the challenge further, but I knew strength without sensitivity would be destructive.

The words of W. B. Yeats (from his poem *He Wishes for the Cloths of Heaven*) are always somewhere at the back of my mind at such key points in my interactions with fragile clients: "*Tread softly because you tread on my dreams.*" Right now, the greatest of care would be needed, with strong negative imagery balanced by an even stronger affirmation of the hidden strengths that were within the boy. I would use my voice and body language fully for both. Swiftly removing Snoopy from the scene, I left the little monkey to sink beneath the black fabric that represented the bottomless pool. "This! A substitute for childhood! It isn't even living! It's the slowest form of suicide I've ever seen." Brett looked startled. I placed a tall, very thin, very pale, male Pierrot doll on the floor, lying, dead white, in an absolutely straight line on his back. I turned to Brett, with eyes, and voice, and body language reflecting my belief in him. There was great gentleness in my tone, yet insistence and strength. I watched his reactions with care, in case there were signs the imagery was too harsh for him to handle.

"You're killing that lovely boy I get glimpses of sometimes. He actually *is* a very interesting and very beautiful person." (Turning in the direction of the pool): "I'm not going to just leave you there in that pool! I'm going to help you to climb out of it." (To Brett): "Bring Snoopy back!" (Brett, still startled, retrieved the toy). "This is the one who'll get you out in the end." I caused Snoopy to drag the black fabric aside and haul the little monkey to land. At that moment, I had shown Snoopy moving in a way that a particularly insightful *double* in classical psychodrama sometimes does. Jumping into the action independent of the protagonist, such a *double* can reveal an under-exercised or neglected role that exists, untapped, in the protagonist's hidden repertoire of potentially life-enhancing roles (in this case, active shaper of destiny). Sometimes the *double* misjudges, making a mistake in interpretation or timing. Not so here. The concentrated stillness of Brett's body language silently shouted, "Touché!" A few minutes later, Brett suddenly said he'd take part in the session with his father. And now, after many more weeks, at the end of our work together, this was the incident he recalled as distinctly useful.

"Good!" I said. "Good! Hang on to that!" So, life moved on for us both. I had to let go, as therapists always do, knowing the future would unfold with its own pattern for him, but knowing also that our work together had opened him a little to respond to life's next challenge.

In this study of three young people of varied ages and backgrounds, I have chosen to abandon the scholarly, detached style favored in much academic writing, and from time to time to bring the person of the therapist quite strongly before your mind's eye. There were several reasons for this choice. First, I did not want to merely record and analyze a series of interventions and their outcomes. I wanted to enable those of my readers who were attracted to these ideas to incorporate some of them into their own practice. To accomplish this, it takes some understanding of the inner processes of the director as decisions were made at key points in the work. This internal decision-making goes on in every therapy room. In the literature, it is not always regarded as important enough for comment, but I believe even a limited idea of how it fits into the action is necessary. Otherwise, the reader may mistakenly see the techniques as fairly mechanical devices capable of yielding predictable results.

A second reason for the choice of writing style was connected with a strong belief that the therapist's influence in the room is only partly due to the methods followed or the theories subscribed to, uniquely and centrally important though these be. In any professional analysis of a therapeutic process, the theoretical concepts are given full attention. But, in general, the literature focuses less intently on the unspoken messages that are so eloquently conveyed through the therapist's voice and body language. Clayton (2002) moves outside such practice when he links his analysis of role reversal with a thoughtful and welcome consideration of a psychodrama director's voice patterns. Zeig (2003), with Ericksonian flair, elaborates on the evocative power unleashed by a therapist's deliberate use of body language. Authors such as Bandler and Grinder (1979) provide an alternative, highly structured slant to the discussion. Such a focus, however, is comparatively rare.

Yet, whether we are aware of it or not, our bodies are part of any work we do. When used consciously, they can be exquisitely tuned instruments that bring healing at deeply significant moments in the therapeutic process. But, if we are not conscious of their impact, and if the child reads inscrutable, unfriendly, or judgmental messages in them, they can be an equally potent negative force in the room, shutting the therapist out from the child's heavily protected, private inner space. This is so, to a marked degree, for children and adolescents who are unwilling or unable to communicate freely through spoken language.

In the above studies, this silent language of the therapist was experienced by the children simultaneously with the impact of the puppet's powerful presence, for the therapist was visible in the background as the puppet was released into action. Over time, I discovered that this connectedness of therapist and puppet, when used consciously, can work as an effective healing mechanism. For example, sometimes in a therapeutic story, I used the moon as a wisdom figure. Slipping over my head a cloak made out of two large, silken scarves (the colors of a moonlit night), and donning a mask shaped like a crescent moon, I was transformed, yet I was there. As the moon, I moved with grace and gentleness. In this disguise, I could express the therapist's love, patience, and non-intrusive fidelity as she accompanied the child on the search for healing. Tenderness that would be received with embarrassment if expressed directly could do its work unobtrusively and in depth when shown through such an elliptical metaphor.

Nat was one child to whom I spoke silently through the moon imagery. Having failed in his second attempt to gain custody of the children, her father secretly abandoned them, saying he was going away for two weeks' holiday. He disappeared—out of sight and out of their lives, without a word. As the weeks stretched to three, then four, Nat, her father's favorite, was grieving. Characteristically, her grieving process was completely private. It showed in rebellious, irritable behavior with her foster mother and, in the therapy room, in a need to fiercely contradict the most insignificant comments I might make. Rather than trying to talk to her openly about the sadness, anger, and confusion raging in her, I decided to create a story that would let her know I had some understanding of her grieving, and that I was with her. The story would need to be action-oriented and very short, and it would need to hold her attention from the opening word to the end. I would use the little emu chick puppet as I spoke the clear, sparse words of the tale. At the end, I would use the moon costume to enter the story, sifting among the scarf's fringe threads to find the gentlest, softest moonbeam with which to kiss poor angry, grieving little Child–Child goodnight. This is the story that came. I'll use sketches here to convey some of the atmosphere the puppet and the moon brought in to the original telling of Nat's story.

Child-Child heard that the Sea Eagle had flown away, far away, way past the place where the sun goes down at night. No one knew where he was or when he would be back.

Day after day, Child-Child went down to the sea,
trudging through the heavy sand, searching the sky
for signs of his friend.

There was nothing.

"He didn't even say goodbye!" said Child-Child to the listening sea.

He tucked the hurt away among the soft feathers near his heart and tried to get on with life, playing with the other emu chicks and learning the things emus learn,

and finding fun

wherever

it could
be
found.

He was a strong,

brave

little chick.

But when night-time came, and the world was very still, Child-Child thought about his friend and he was sad. The moonlight shone on a tear that had squeezed out from his eye.

"What's the matter, Child-Child?" asked the Moon. Her voice was soft and gentle and her face was kind. "The Sea Eagle's gone," said Child-Child gruffly. "That's all." And he turned away from the Moon to shut her out. Child-Child didn't like to talk about things that bothered him. "Oh," said the Moon, and she stayed gently there for quite some time before she kissed Child-Child goodnight and went on her way, leaving him curled up like a little ball of fluff, keeping his hurt to himself.

The Moon understood that he was sad. She left behind one of her softest, gentlest moonbeams, waiting till he could uncurl.

Child-Child smiled a small, secret smile as he drifted off
to sleep. He knew the Moon would come back.

From the moment the Child–Child marionette opened the story (walking to the center of the room in silence, then standing motionless while the opening lines were spoken), both the images and the words had riveted Nat's attention. She had no wish to fight her customary fight for ascendancy. Her face radiated thoughtfulness and peace as the tale drew to its close. The story was left, undisturbed by comment, to do its own silent work in the shifting, sifting sands of her unconscious mind. No doubt it did. I am certain all the metaphors had reached her, including that of the moon. When she looked at me, there was an answering gentleness in her eyes. The connection between us had grown.

It's time now to draw together the final strands of these studies of therapeutic interventions with inarticulate children and young people. Running through them all are four major recognizable threads:

1. The absolute necessity for the director to be in tune with and to respect the protagonist's *surplus reality*—the experiential world emerging in the play.
2. The importance of "body language literacy" for the therapist. Speaking and reading the language are equally required skills.
3. The need for the therapist to reflect deeply on known historical facts in the child's life. They hold the key to recognizing the swift-flashing metaphors in the play.
4. The central importance of surprise—its role in the whole psychodrama method, as doubling, concretizing, maximizing, etc. are brought into the action at significant moments.

Speaking of his own craft, the Irish poet, Paul Muldoon (2002), has this to say on the question of openness to surprise:

> One enters the writing of a poem in a state of ignorance and attempts to retain that ignorance throughout the writing of the poem. One doesn't know where it is going to end up, so there's some surprise, some shock as one exits the poem. If that doesn't happen to the writer, it's unlikely it's going to happen to anyone else.

A similar process is at work when a psychodrama director engages with a protagonist. Muldoon states that a poet who sets out to write a poem knowing where it will go cannot possibly write a good one. Similarly, a psychodrama director, embarking on some healing work with a preconceived idea of how it should move, will not produce a drama that has any relevance to the true needs of the protagonist. It will not contain the element of surprise, so essential to the flow of the spontaneity-creativity nexus at the center of psychodrama. The protagonist's creative energy will not be startled into action with new insights, new upsurges from the sub-conscious mind. Spontaneous moves, blocked from developing by some preconceived plan of the director, will end in frustration and confusion, as the upward rising insights from the psyche are left stranded, while the director pushes the action into an alien space. Such a director shows no recognition of the map that is opening out from within the protagonist's inner being. That is the only map that will lead them to the place of healing they are both trying to find.

Quite another role is required of the therapist. In my teaching and writing, I have sometimes referred to it as that of a Pied Piper playing leapfrog with a child. Initially, the therapist calls a tune through the puppets, entrancing the child to play. A moment comes when the child takes up the lead and it's the therapist's turn to follow, until a twist or turn in the play reveals a specific moment that's full of healing potential. The therapist then uses a psychodramatic intervention in the play, leaping ahead of the child into the realm of the unknown and of surprise. The child follows fearlessly, imagination spurred in a new direction, taking the therapist down an equally unexpected new path. And so the dance goes on, with the child exploring new emotional depths and the therapist learning more and more of the child's inner world. It's a form of interweaving leadership that Williams (1989), working with adults, recognizes. He wrote, "as so often in psychodrama, it becomes difficult to know exactly when the protagonist is suggesting something to the director, or when the suggestion is the other way round" (p. 109).

There are several imperatives operating in this leading/following/leading pattern. As we bring this chapter to a close, it is useful to list them. At all times, the therapist must read the metaphors in the play, entering the child's surplus reality with respect and care before judging the moment to deepen the action with a psychodramatic intervention. Having done this, the therapist must again allow the child's play to take what new direction it will, in full freedom. In a therapeutic situation, the Pied Piper must learn to follow if the child is to continue down the path that now opens—a path that is at once entrancing and demanding—a path with potential for healing.

References

Bandler, R., & Grinder, J. (1979). *Frogs into princes: Neuro linguistic programming.* Moab, UT: Real People Press.

Clayton, G. M. (2002). *The spirit and purpose of role reversal, opening up fresh possibilities.* Auckland, New Zealand: Imprint Desktop Publishing.

Dayton, T. (1994). *The drama within: Psychodrama and experiential therapy.* Deerfield Beach, FL: Health Communications.

Erickson, M., & Rossi, E. (1976/1980). Two level communication and the microdynamics of trance and suggestion. In E. Rossi (Ed.), *The collected papers of Milton H. Erickson on hypnosis, Vol. 1: The nature of hypnosis and suggestion* (pp. 430–451). New York: Irvington.

Hoey, B. (1997). *Who calls the tune? A psychodramatic approach to child therapy.* London: Routledge.

Mills, J. C., & Crowley, R. J. (1986). *Therapeutic metaphors for children and the child within.* New York: Brunner/Mazel.

Moreno, J. L. (1955). The discovery of the spontaneous man: With special emphasis upon the technique of role reversal. *Group Psychotherapy, 8*(2), 103–129.

Moreno, J. L., & Moreno, F. B. (1944). Spontaneity theory of child development. *Psychodrama Monographs, 8,* p. 48.

Moreno, Z. T., Blomkvist, L. D., & Rutzel, T. (2000). *Psychodrama, surplus reality and the art of healing.* London: Routledge.

Muldoon, P. (2002). *Book Talk: Paul Muldoon in conversation with Peter Steele,* Recorded at the Melbourne Writers' Festival for ABC Radio National (08/09/02).

Williams, A. (1989). *The passionate technique: Strategic psychodrama with individuals, families and groups.* London: Routledge.

Zeig, J. K. (2003). Lessons from Ericksonian hypnosis: The A to Z of changing therapeutic postures. *Psychotherapy in Australia, 9*(4), 4–51.

CHAPTER 4

Developmental Transformations in the Treatment of Sexually Abused Children

MILLER JAMES, ALICE M. FORRESTER, and KYONGOK C. KIM

Introduction

Jamaar is an 8-year-old African-American boy referred by child protective services for a forensic evaluation of possible sexual abuse. Child protective services initially became involved with his family when Jamaar was 6. He was placed in foster care at age 7 because of parental neglect, substance abuse, domestic violence, and the family's failure to comply with services. When Jamaar was removed from his home, his biological parents did not seek further visitation or reunification, agreeing to terminate their parental rights without litigation. Unfortunately, caseworkers placed Jamaar in a foster home directly across the street from his biological parents and his 16-year-old paternal uncle. They explained the reasoning behind this decision was because of the difficulty of finding foster parents willing to take boys. After 1 year in foster placement, Jamaar disclosed sexual abuse by his 16-year-old uncle.

In order to protect Jamaar's confidentiality, all names used in this case study, including the foster mother's name, and other significant case details have been disguised. In this chapter, we will provide background information, the theoretical considerations for using *developmental transformations* for sexual abuse treatment and the case description of a 2-year therapy process.

Background Information

Shirley is an African-American who has been a foster mother for several years. Soon after Jamaar was placed with her, she became afraid of him. He was in fights three or four times a week while on the bus and in class. Some of the boys at school complained that Jamaar tried "sex stuff" with them in the bathroom. The school psychologist classified him as having low-average intelligence and emotional disturbance, and he was diagnosed with Attention-Deficit/Hyperactivity Disorder (ADHD). He urinated in his bed most nights and refused to sleep alone in his room. When Shirley woke to find Jamaar standing next to her bed staring at her, she began locking her bedroom door. She asked him why he refused to sleep in his room. He told her that "Chucky" was going to come in through the window and "stab me up with a knife." Jamaar described how he saw "Chucky's face coming through the mirror" in the bathroom.

During the year before his disclosure of sexual abuse, caseworkers took Jamaar to a psychiatrist who diagnosed him with a psychotic disorder (Not Otherwise Specified) and prescribed Haldol. He was referred for therapy. He refused to speak to the first therapist and treatment terminated. His aggression at school, nighttime waking, hypervigilance, and enuresis continued. Shirley took him to a second psychiatrist who diagnosed Jamaar with bipolar disorder and prescribed Risperidal and Depakote. He again refused to attend therapy.

Jamaar disclosed sexual abuse to Shirley. Shirley and Jamaar were watching a television show about a girl who was kidnapped. Jamaar became angry and told his foster mother that he used to play "naked games" with his uncle. He then began to cry. He did not describe further to her what happened with his uncle. His 16-year-old uncle was living in the home of his biological parents across the street from the foster home.

Jamaar told Shirley that he was afraid of his uncle and told her not to tell anyone about the "naked games." Shirley called the caseworkers. Prosecutors were called. He received medical and forensic evaluations. His story was consistent in the main facts and in many of the peripheral details. Jamaar described ongoing sexual abuse that included forced oral and anal sex, the use of derogatory names, and threats to harm his family if he told anyone. Forensic evaluators clinically substantiated sexual, physical, and emotional abuse.

However, prosecutors decided not to take the case because there was no physical evidence. Even with this new disclosure of sexual abuse, child protective services felt there was no current risk and decided not to move Jamaar to a new foster home. Jamaar continued to live in a foster home across the street from his uncle and biological parents. He was referred a third time for treatment, this time for sexual abuse.

Theoretical Considerations

Child sexual abuse is any sexual activity with a child where consent is not or cannot be given (Cohen, Berliner, & March, 2000). Most child sexual abuse is not disclosed at the time it occurs (Finkelhor, Hotaling, Lewis, & Smith, 1990). Retrospective studies indicate that 20% to 25% of women and from 5% to 15% of men experience sexual abuse before eighteen years of age in the United States (Finkelhor, 1994).

Prospective longitudinal studies of adults with documented sexual abuse histories in childhood have found that more than 30% of respondents did not report sexual abuse experiences when questioned as adults (Widom & Morris, 1997). In addition, boys, more than girls, fail to disclose sexual abuse because of the stigma associated with sexual victimization (Finkelhor, 1993). For these reasons, and because most sexual abuse does not result in physical signs, it is probable that current figures underestimate the number of children who have been sexually abused (Smith et al., 2000).

Sexually victimized children have nearly a fourfold increased lifetime risk for developing psychiatric disorders and a threefold risk for substance abuse when compared to non-victimized children (Finkelhor & Dziuba-Leatherman, 1994; Kendall-Tackett, Williams, & Finkelhor, 1993; Pynoos, Steinberg, & Wraith, 1995). Cuffe and Frick-Helms (1995) note that 30% to 50% of sexually abused children meet full diagnostic criteria for Posttraumatic Stress Disorder (PTSD). Sexualized behavior and aggression are frequently associated outcomes from sexual abuse experiences (Berliner & Briere, 1997; Friedrich, 1992; McLeer, Deblinger, Henry, & Orvaschel, 1992). Misdiagnosis, failure to respond competently to disclosure, and lack of therapeutic intervention can result in adult psychopathology (Sroufe, 1989).

Child Traumatic Stress Studies

Child traumatic stress studies document how interactions with abusive caretakers may be associated with pathological changes in developing anatomical structures and physiology in the brain (Perry et al., 1995). Functioning of right brain limbic structures, such as the amygdala and hippocampus, that are associated with arousal, behavior, emotion, memory, and language have shown alterations in maltreated children (DeBellis et al., 1999; Garber & Dodge, 1991; LeDoux, 1996; Schore, 1994). Specifically, dysregulation of the hypothalamic-pituitary-adrenal axis has been suggested to be an important mediating pathway for the chronic, autonomic hyper-arousal and dissociation frequently observed in sexually abused children.

Psychological processes such as disembodiment (dissociation), conditioned fear (implicit memory), and cognitive distortion of schemas of self and other have been proposed as targets for intervention (Briere, 1992).

Theorists recommend that intervention strategies be designed that: (1) are embodied (behavioral); (2) access implicit memory; (3) modify distorted cognitive affective representations of self and others; and (4) include imaginal exposure for gradual desensitization (Greenberg & van der Kolk, 1989; James, 1994; Rothschild, 2000; Saigh, 1992; van der Kolk, 1994).

Experiences of child maltreatment disrupt the developmental self-experience of "embodiment" (Young, 1992). Embodiment is defined here as the felt sense of safety, control, and pleasure being in the body. Disembodiment (dissociation) is frequently associated with traumatic sexual experience (Putnam, 1990). Children "leave" their bodies during experiences of sexual abuse and when under stress. Alternating chronic hyper-arousal and dissociation can disrupt normal development within social and emotional developmental pathways.

Explicit memory systems allow for the verbal narration of events. *Implicit memory* is associated with attachment behaviors, non-verbal memory, sensory experience, and conditioned fear response (Schacter, 1996). It is suggested that memory for sexual abuse may be primarily encoded in sensory-motor and imagistic representation in implicit memory and not consciously available to children for verbal report. Fear conditioning may predispose the child to state-dependent and environmental reminders of abuse (triggers) resulting in PTSD symptoms of re-experiencing such as nightmares, flashbacks, and behavioral reenactments (March, Amaya-Jackson, & Pynoos, 1997).

The Creative Arts Therapies and Child Maltreatment

The creative arts therapies of art, music, dance, drama, and poetry have been used in the assessment and psychotherapy of all types of child maltreatment. These methods are embodied (behavioral) and can effectively access implicit memory in abused children (Cattanach, 1992; Cohen & Cox, 1995; Dayton, 1997; Golub, 1985; Kluft, 1992; Spring, 1993; Winn, 1994). The symbolic media of the creative arts therapies may provide more complete access to implicit memory than do primarily verbal approaches to treatment (Johnson, 2000). Creative arts therapies can invoke cues to kinesthetic and visual sensory memories related to child abuse experiences. These structured approaches can prevent emotional flooding (hyper-arousal) by providing the child a sense of control and emotional distance through the manipulation of symbolic art materials. Rather than dissociate to cope with traumatic memory, children can be taught to use the creative mediums to represent experiences that are beyond words.

Due to dissociation, abused children are often unable to attend to abstract verbal discussion regarding traumatic material. For instance, treatment guidelines for the International Society for the Study of Dissociation (1997) recommend the use of primarily non-verbal techniques such as the creative arts therapies to access dissociated (implicit) traumatic memory. Research studies conducted with adult Vietnam combat veterans diagnosed with PTSD and alexithymia (inability to put feelings into words) documented greater treatment effect sizes when primarily action oriented creative arts therapies were compared to verbal therapeutic approaches (Johnson et al., 1997; Morgan & Johnson, 1995). Currently, psychodynamic play therapy, creative arts therapies, and cognitive behavioral approaches are used extensively in the treatment of child maltreatment. Unfortunately, to date, no treatment outcome studies have been conducted comparing these approaches in their effectiveness (Deblinger & Heflin, 1996).

Because of the wide range of symbolic media used in the arts, creative arts therapists can engage children at different cognitive developmental levels. Observers of cognitive development have often noted that representation of internal affective states proceeds through three stages of development: sensory-motor (music, dance, drama), symbolic (art), and lexical (poetry) (Bruner, 1964; Flavell, Miller, & Miller, 1993; Piaget, 1951; Werner & Kaplan, 1963). Through repeated interactions with emotionally attuned caregivers, children gradually learn to modulate the intensity of physiologic arousal and to translate affective states into forms of kinesthetic and imagistic representation of self and others in action (Lane & Schwartz, 1987; Stern, 1985). This cognitive developmental process is the interpersonal context in which the child develops internalized representations of self and other. Maltreatment disrupts this healthy developmental pathway.

Child maltreatment can create abuse-related internalized working models of self and others (Alexander, 1992; Bowlby, 1969). Negative expectations of intimate relationships based on a history of sexual abuse can distort perceptions of non-abusive others (McCann, Pearlman, Sakheim, & Abrahamson, 1988). Sexually abused children frequently present as emotionally distant, distrustful, aggressive, and hyper-vigilant due to their expectations of being abused by others. Internalized shame, diminished capacity for empathy, and identification with an aggressor are common outcomes in sexually abused children (Lewis & Haviland-Jones, 2000).

Developmental Transformations in the Treatment of Sexual Abuse

The capacity for imaginative play and the risk factors that distort this process are important indicators of psychopathology in children (Fonagy & Target, 1996; Slade & Wolf, 1994; Terr, 1994). Harris (2000), in his review of the research on children's imaginative play, privileges interpersonal *discrepant* play (co-created role-playing) over solitary *object* play (projective techniques, toys, games) as the primary pathway for overall cognitive development, including the capacity to differentiate between fantasy and reality and the development of social perspective taking (theory of mind). Drama therapy may be particularly useful for accessing internalized representations of self and others in action. Drama therapy can access in imaginative play with sexually abused children the *vulnerable self* and the *perpetrating other* for cognitive restructuring.

Developmental Transformations is an improvisational drama therapy method that privileges the embodied interpersonal encounter between the therapist and the sexually abused child. Therapists using Developmental Transformations engage the child in a healthy cognitive developmental process that is experienced as pleasurable by the child. Projective objects such as toys, masks, or puppets are removed from the playroom in order for the therapist to function as the "embodied play object" and maximize the interpersonal focus of the therapeutic process. The therapist using Developmental Transformations provides for an "emotional prosthesis" by re-engaging the sexually abused child in an embodied process for translating affective arousal into imaginative representations during the improvisational play. This process is intended to reduce arousal and increase a sense of safety and competency in affective regulation for the child.

Experiences Beyond Words

The therapist, fully aware of the child's specific sexual abuse disclosure (exact words and bodily experiences), allows the known abuse history to inform their improvisational responses to the child. The therapist follows and embodies the child's indications of abuse-related symbolic material during the improvisation. The therapist follows the cues given by the child in the course of play and does not introduce the abuse material directly to the child without indications that the child feels safe to represent the trauma story. Our experience is that, unlike using models of therapy that introduce the abuse material in a predetermined phase of treatment, in this method, the child produces trauma material as they feel safe in the relationship with a particular therapist and, comparatively, in a relatively early phase of treatment.

In approaching sexual abuse-related material, therapists using Developmental Transformations do not privilege abstract verbal expression alone. Linking initially with the child's primary expressive language such as movement, images, or words (as privileged by the child) provides diagnostic information regarding cognitive and language deficits due to abuse experiences while allowing the child to control the choice of the symbolic language for the therapy. The unique power structure provides the sexually abused child with a significant incentive to engage with the therapist using Developmental Transformations. Observed inhibitions in the child's freedom to imaginatively play and the *controlling or repetitive* play style often observed in sexually abused children are understood as emerging abuse-related personifications and abuse contexts, and are indicative of the affects of rage, shame, and loss (James & Johnson, 1996). The emergence of traumatic material and possible confusion between fantasy and reality obviously constrains the capacity to play in the child. Our experience has been that abuse material evidenced by constrained play emerges relatively early in therapy using Developmental Transformations, thus allowing the therapist to intervene from within the ongoing improvisational play for the purpose of reassuring the child and maintaining the conditions of the playspace.

The therapist intervenes primarily from *within* the playspace (Johnson, 1992), the therapeutic container or transitional space for the embodied encounter between the therapist and child (Johnson, 2000; Winnicott, 1953). The primary intervention by the therapist using Developmental Transformations is to engage the resilient aspects of the child self and the abuse-related material from *within* the playspace. Three ethical conditions need to be present in order to establish the playspace: *mutual agreement* (between child and therapist), *discrepancy* (knowing this is pretend), and *restraint against harm* (defined boundaries between representation of aggression/sexuality and reality). The therapist models for the child how to embody the flow of images, thoughts, feelings, roles, gestures, movements, impulses, and silences emerging during an extended improvisational play. The therapist notices the child's verbal and non-verbal behavior and embodies material that appears meaningful for the child. Meaning is evident in the child's behavior by *increased energy* (spontaneity) that indicates the child feels safe with particular themes and roles being represented. The therapist tracks the energy fluctuations in the child's play as an indicator of the child's subjective feelings of safety. In this manner, the child controls the gradual imaginal exposure to abuse-related material.

It is our experience that children engaged in Developmental Transformations will symbolize the abuse story when they feel safe with the specific therapist as a non-abusive and reliable adult. Nontraumatic and low-arousal themes are developed until the child can tolerate prolonged imaginal exposure to traumatic material. Through repeated imaginal exposure, traumatic representations are gradually desensitized over time.

Touch is not discouraged when initiated by the child in the playspace. However, the therapist does not introduce touch directed toward the child's body during the course of play. In contrast, the therapist's body is available to the child for contact comfort and in the service of role-play. In effect, the therapist using developmental transformations submits the use of *his or her* body in the service of telling the child's story and does not guide the child through (therapist-controlled) predetermined exercises or therapeutic techniques. For sexually abused children with poor body boundaries who use aggression instrumentally with others, the therapist models ways in which the child's aggressive impulses can be *represented* in the playspace and not *acted out* in reality, therefore creating negative consequences in interpersonal relationships.

It is our feeling that this unique organization of the power differential proposed in the theory and practice of Developmental Transformations between the child and the non-abusive adult helps the child regain a sense of empowerment. This process provides the child with an experience of adult attention and intimacy that can be differentiated from memories of sexual victimization by the perpetrator. Playful and positively toned emotional experiences with the therapist characterized by pleasure, safety, and control can be internalized in contrast to the experiences of terror, shame, loss of control, and betrayal associated with the memory of the perpetrator.

The specific goals of using Developmental Transformations with sexually victimized children are: (1) to encourage the reembodiment of the child; (2) to reduce the utilization of arousal and dissociation as coping strategies; (3) to access traumatic material for imaginal exposure and integration; and (4) to modify distorted shame-based cognitive representations of self and other. Over time, the internalization of positive interactions with the playful therapist can ameliorate the painful effects of internalized shame.

Course of Treatment

After completing the interviews, medical examinations, and forensic evaluations, Jamaar refused to speak further about his uncle or his biological parents. He did not recant his story. However, now, when his family was mentioned, Jamaar clenched his fists and became silent. He was aware that the authorities did not believe his story. He asked the therapist, "Why didn't they do anything to him?" Jamaar could remember what happened, he told us in his own words that his uncle "put his dick in my butt"; however, Jamaar now refused to speak about his sexual abuse.

The fact was, Jamaar was still living next door to his biological parents and his uncle, nothing happened to the abusive adults, and Jamaar felt he was the one who was blamed for the sexual abuse. The therapist said to Jamaar, "I can imagine you still don't feel safe." Jamaar quietly replied, "You can't do anything." Indeed, Jamaar was correct. After repeated attempts to intervene with prosecutors and child protective caseworkers, it was clear that the authorities were not swayed to change the location of Jamaar's foster placement.

In his mind, Jamaar interpreted the sexual abuse, repeated evaluations, and foster placement as his fault. What the perpetrator had warned would happen to Jamaar if he told anyone, did come to pass. Jamaar was the one who got in trouble; he had to move out of his apartment and did not get to see his parents. Jamaar felt the shame of telling his story to so many "white" strangers and became highly suspicious of authorities. He did not experience the protective interventions as they were intended, instead feeling exiled and alone. As a result of the poor response to his disclosure, Jamaar began trying to suppress the memory of what happened.

Now, when asked how he was doing, he said, "Fine." However, his arousal symptoms and dissociative coping increased. He got into more trouble at school. His foster mother complained, "I have to tell him over and over what I want him to do, he never listens." His teachers described him as "spacey, hostile, and distracted."

Assessment Phase

Jamaar was assessed to be physically expressive and predominantly nonverbal. The therapist offered Jamaar a range of expressive art materials. He obsessively drew pictures of large, muscle-bound male figures dressed in wide shoulder pads like football players. These figures held various automatic weapons and explosive devices in their gloved hands. They were a combination of football players, video game characters, World Wrestling Federation wrestlers, rappers, and Special Forces soldiers. He did not draw anything else and lost interest in drawing altogether after two assessment sessions. The therapist rehearsed Jamaar in having a puppet tell him he was safe in his room at night. Jamaar liked the puppet and took it home, keeping it until completing therapy two years later.

During the third session, Jamaar walked over to the playroom and asked if he could play instead of drawing pictures. The playroom was empty except for a few pillows in the corner (by design). He asked the therapist, "Where are the toys?" The therapist told him, "I am the toy." Jamaar smiled and began an imaginary basketball game with the therapist.

Jamaar spent his first Developmental Transformations session making imaginary basketball shots. His body was fully involved in this activity and, at the end, both he and the therapist were sweating. The therapist was never allowed to score a point. The therapist imagined making the point, throwing up his arms in triumph and saying, "Yes!" Jamaar took the imaginary ball and said, "No, you missed it." Jamaar was never blocked either, making every point, no matter how unlikely the shot. Jamaar made the rules. The therapist decided to follow cues to his imaginative world for as long as Jamaar wanted to repeat running to the backboard and making slam-dunks.

During the basketball play, the therapist commented aloud to Jamaar that these rules were "Jamaar's rules for trust." After so many adults had betrayed and abused him, or failed him, it would be a while before Jamaar would trust anyone. At the end of this session, the therapist offered Jamaar an imaginative "key" to open the "magic box." Only Jamaar and the therapist could open this particular box, using special sounds and movements. Jamaar and the therapist named everything they had created together during the session and put it in the imaginary box. This dramatic ritual, demonstrated in an embodied way, separated reality from fantasy, the imaginative world from the real world. The "box" became a framing ritual for the therapy. Jamaar and the therapist co-created the magic box at the beginning and end of every session.

During the next few sessions, Jamaar bumped or hit the therapist "accidentally." He wanted to punch, jump on, and push the therapist *for real*. Jamaar had poor body boundaries. He had to be taught how to use the conditions of the playspace, how to use his imagination. It was easy to see why he was in so much trouble on the playground and in school. The therapist explained to Jamaar that he couldn't really hit the therapist and demonstrated how to represent his aggressive impulses in the playspace. The therapist explained to Jamaar that acting on his anger *for real* at home and school gets him in trouble. The therapist told Jamaar, "Here you can pretend and you won't get into trouble." Jamaar listened intently and accepted this convention for the play. Jamaar agreed with the therapist that he didn't want to get into trouble, but he didn't know what to do with the rage inside.

Offering this imaginative convention for play was an important hook for Jamaar to engage with the therapist. Jamaar was filled with rage for obvious reasons, and needed concrete (close to the body) dramatic structures to contain and express his intense feelings in a safe way. He enjoyed learning and practicing how to hit, shoot, machine-gun, and blow up the therapist with hand grenades. The more imaginative he was, the more fun he had. The therapist got up off the floor each time, dusted off, and asked Jamaar, "What else can you do to kill me?"

During the next few months, Jamaar imported characters from external sources such as TV, video games, and movies. He was unable to elaborate his imagination to any significant degree. He did not create characters, but used only ready-made characters and settings. The therapist became aware that, as a result of neglect, Jamaar had not been engaged interpersonally in imaginative play during the course of his early development. The therapist imagined that Jamaar was probably socialized (babysat) by the TV and the

Game Boy. Robots, MTV video characters, and high levels of aggression characterized his inner world.

Initially, Jamaar would only identify with the omnipotent, all-powerful aggressor in his play. The therapist was always cast to play the weak, denigrated, ashamed, and powerless characters. By Jamaar's design, the therapist could be shot or blown up repeatedly. In contrast, Jamaar could not be wounded in any way. During this phase of treatment, Jamaar would not allow the therapist to transform the scene or offer any deviation in the themes. Jamaar's style of play was controlling and rigid, with no reciprocity. The intense sounds of rage—the yelling and growling—that he made were sometimes heard outside the playroom.

Jamaar imported into the playspace whole movie scenes from Jackie Chan action movies. He played scenes from "Chucky" (*Child's Play*) and *Friday the 13th* movies. Jamaar used imaginary knives to stab the therapist. During one session, Jamaar chopped up the therapist and ate him piece by piece. For a series of intense sessions, Jamaar played "the general" from *The Planet of the Apes* (2001). He played this role with uncanny physical skill, imitating the movements and vocal grunts of this character with great effectiveness. He jumped, rolled, and strutted around the playroom. The therapist was always cast as the weak human, locked in a prison cell, totally dependent on the ape keepers for food and shelter.

The therapist was aware that Jamaar was *teaching* him how it felt to be out of control, afraid, abused, humiliated, and bored, feelings that he probably had felt frequently before his placement in foster care. Jamaar was teaching the therapist what it felt like to be in the body of the victim by enacting the aggressor role exclusively. During one session, the therapist (from inside his prison cell) commented, "Jamaar, I bet you felt out of control most of your life." Jamaar said nothing, but the energy in his play increased.

The therapist submitted fully to the parts he was cast to play and continued to comment to Jamaar how it felt to be weak, afraid, and alone. In the beginning of this phase of treatment, Jamaar did not want to hear it. He enjoyed "taking away" the therapist's voice. With a magic wave of his hand, he would mute the therapist, and the scenes would continue in silence.

During one session, Jamaar pummeled the therapist in the boxing ring round after round. Jamaar won the world heavyweight title each time. It was not fun to play with Jamaar. The therapist commented from inside the boxing ring, "Now I understand why you don't have any friends. If you play this way with them all the time, always telling them what to do and never letting them win, they won't want to play with you anymore."

After about six months, Jamaar turned the characters of Chucky, Jason, the general, and the boxer into "made-up monsters." Jamaar still wrote the script and took the role of aggressor, but now he allowed the therapist to join him as a "helper" in killing the monsters. Jamaar began to allow the therapist to have some power in the session. The plots became more elaborate and imaginative. The therapist was the one to get wounded and captured by the monsters, for Jamaar to rescue him. However, Jamaar never got wounded himself. During this time, Jamaar demonstrated more caring behaviors toward the therapist, going into the cave of the monster to rescue him, then bringing him food and attending to his wounds. A symbolic language was fully established in the playspace. The therapist had the feeling that Jamaar knew he was communicating his thoughts and feelings in this symbolic way. His gaze was direct and intimate. This was a change that both the therapist and Jamaar noticed, as the felt intimacy between them had deepened.

Eventually, Jamaar let the therapist play the monster, as well. Jamaar was given "a freeze gun" to immobilize the monster when he wanted (and before he became hyper-aroused and disembodied). The theme of the *monster* now appeared to be both frightening and exciting for Jamaar. He was given "safe places" in the playroom, like "the cave" and "the castle," and he could fly away using his "dragon/eagle wings." During one session, Jamaar turned into a falcon, flying high above the ground. He became other animals such as tigers and snakes. Based on the reports of his foster mother and his teachers, Jamaar was more confident and relaxed outside the playroom. He had stopped fighting at school.

Jamaar "captured" the therapist and put him in a cave, a pit, and the closet. His energy was very high during this kind of play. The therapist was aware that Jamaar was slowly approaching his sexual abuse experiences from a symbolic distance. The therapist was also aware that Jamaar would still only identify with the powerful characters. Jamaar did not allow himself to identify with the vulnerable, small, hurt, or weak aspects of self. He kept his wounds at an emotional distance while he attended to the imaginary wounds of the therapist. The therapist was aware that Jamaar was teaching him what it meant to be wounded.

The therapist provided Shirley several sessions of psycho-education regarding sexually abused children. She helped identify possible triggers in Jamaar's environment. The biggest problem was that Jamaar was seeing his uncle most mornings when he went to school. In the evenings, his biological parents sometimes sat on the stoop of their apartment and stared at Jamaar and Shirley when she brought him home. Jamaar would then urinate in his bed that night, for which he felt very ashamed.

Shirley did everything she could to reduce the contact with the perpetrators. She enrolled Jamaar in a new school with a smaller classroom. Jamaar made a few friends at his new school and went to camp that summer, where he did not identify himself as "a problem." Shirley filled out the papers for a subsidized mortgage so that she could afford to move. Jamaar stopped urinating in his bed so often, which made Shirley very happy. She learned to help him put the bed sheets in the washing machine and dryer without yelling, and then remind Jamaar that he was safe in her house. She started to attach emotionally to him. Jamaar did better and Shirley did better; this was good for both of them.

After about nine months of treatment, Jamaar began to develop more trust in Shirley and the therapist. The new caregivers in Jamaar's life attempted to differentiate their behavior from that of his biological parents, his uncle, and the authorities who did not respond to his disclosure. They tried to make their behavior toward him as consistent, supportive, and firmly kind as they could. They directly communicated their high expectations for his behavior. Eventually, "Chucky" stopped coming into Jamaar's nightmares and he slept through the night in his own bed. The incidents of enuresis continued with less frequency.

Jamaar introduced into the playspace an elaborate game he had made up. In this game, the therapist was made to stand up facing the wall with his back to Jamaar, close his eyes, walk back slowly, keep his eyes closed, and try to tap Jamaar. If Jamaar got by the therapist to the wall, he got a point. If the therapist tapped Jamaar before he reached the wall, he got the point. Needless to say, it was nearly impossible to tap Jamaar. He would crawl, make leaps, sneak, dive, and simply run by the therapist in order to touch the wall and yell, "Yes!" He then humiliated the therapist by calling him "slow and stupid."

The game required actual physical skill. It was fun to play for both Jamaar and the therapist. The therapist introduced the role of a "TV announcer," and played both the denigrated competitor and the announcer who cut to commercials for Reebok. Jamaar liked these dramatic structures. He participated in the "after-the-game interviews" for the studio and TV audience.

Both the therapist and Jamaar played the studio audience, wildly cheering for Jamaar when he made a point. During some games, Jamaar played for his favorite causes, for "world hunger" or for "justice" for African-Americans. During one session, the therapist noticed that Jamaar had focused his attention on the white skin of the therapist. The game was then played between the "whites versus the blacks," then the tall versus the short, the fat versus the skinny, boys versus girls, teachers versus students, victims versus perpetrators.

Both the therapist and Jamaar became good at playing the game, which required some very particular skills. For instance, you had to be very silent or still when trying to get past the player with eyes closed (who could only listen for sounds). Conversely, you had to listen very intently for any minimal sound when trying to tap your opponent. The therapist became aware that Jamaar was teaching him what it was like to try to avoid his uncle's sexual perpetration at night. Playing the game allowed the therapist to imagine what it may have been like for Jamaar to wait, to listen for his uncle at night, to be silent and lie still, to pretend to be asleep.

During one session, Jamaar turned off the lights and the game was played in the dark. Jamaar did not want to be seen. The therapist gave him an "invisible button" that he could press whenever he wanted. The lights were turned back on. When Jamaar pressed the button, the therapist acted as if he could not see Jamaar. Jamaar loved the invisible button. He used it often.

One session, during the game, the therapist said, "I bet it would have been great to be invisible when your uncle came for you at night." He nodded and played on. The therapist then said, "I bet peeing in the bed was a good idea to keep your uncle away, too." Jamaar stopped and looked at the therapist intently. "Yes," he said. The therapist took up the imaginary microphone and announced, "Boys and girls, Jamaar is here to play the game on behalf of all of those children whose uncles put their 'dicks in their butts'; he is your champion." These were the exact words that Jamaar had used in his verbal disclosure to forensic evaluators during the initial assessment. The therapist then enrolled as his uncle trying to "tap" Jamaar. The energy in this series of sessions was very high. When Jamaar scored a point against his uncle, the crowd went wild with cheers. Jamaar put his arms up in the air whenever he would score a point against his uncle. Jamaar would then relish his wins and put down his uncle (therapist) in front of the studio and TV audience. The game went on like this for a few months. During one "post-game interview," the announcer asked Jamaar: "The boys and girls in the audience want to know how you deal with your sexual abuse?" Jamaar said, "You tell your foster mother and your therapist; you do good in school; don't fight; you just keep going."

"The boys and the girls" became regular characters in this repeating dramatic plot. Jamaar gave them a "press conference" at the end of the session, giving advice on all kinds of subjects, like how to do better in school. He explained to the "kids" what to do if someone tried to have sex with them. Jamaar told them that what his uncle did to him was wrong, and the sexual abuse was not his own fault. He told the kids that there were some good things about his uncle, that he missed his parents, and that he could not understand why the police "didn't do anything."

Soon, Shirley expressed her desire to adopt Jamaar. However, Jamaar became anxious when the topic of adoption was brought up. He did not want to discuss the possible adoption and he did not want to return home to his biological parents. He pushed aside the subject when Shirley or the therapist mentioned the topic.

During one session, Jamaar stopped playing the game. In a spacey or dreamy way, he stared at a black scuff mark on the wall of the playroom. There was a long pause. The therapist said, "You know what is behind that door, don't you?" Jamaar answered, "Yes, that is where they live." The therapist asked Jamaar what he wanted to do. "I want to kill them," he said. The therapist said, "No, you are not ready to face your uncle and your parents." Jamaar looked overwhelmed (aroused), his fists clenched. He was shaking with rage and was not in the playspace.

The therapist held up an imaginary key to the "other house" and said, "I will hold the key until you are ready to face them." Jamaar began to laugh and said, "I am ready," lunging for the key. The therapist moved out of the way and kept the key out of Jamaar's reach. They played in this way for one session. Jamaar enjoyed this game of "keep away." By the end of the session, he was back in the playspace.

During the next session, the therapist warned him that if he opened the door, he might feel sad and cry. Jamaar said, "I don't care," doubling his efforts to get the key. The therapist finally agreed to help him open the door. Together, they opened the door with pretend difficulty. Once it was opened, a huge wind came and sucked the therapist through the door. Jamaar grabbed him and held on. Jamaar pulled hard to keep the therapist from being taken into "the house." Back and forth, both Jamaar and the therapist fought to get free of the pull. Then, after an "explosion," his uncle, mother, and father came out of their house and attacked Jamaar and the therapist.

The therapist and Jamaar fought the perpetrators bravely. This time, Jamaar got wounded. An arrow pierced him in the chest, "in my heart." Jamaar allowed the therapist as "the wizard" to administer to his wounds for the first time. The wizard lived in a "safe cave" and was powerful with magic. As the wizard, the therapist dressed Jamaar's wounds and gave him nourishment to build his strength.

During one of the "battle sessions," Jamaar was wounded and crawled into the wizard's lap. The wizard attended to his wounds and sang the "warrior song." Jamaar began to cry softly. The wizard changed the song to the "song of Jamaar," using the real circumstances from his life in the lyrics of the song. Jamaar let himself cry with full sobs—tears for his lost childhood. While he cried, he listened as the therapist sang the story of his life. Slowly, his sobs became quieter and his breathing calmer and more regular.

Jamaar received some "gifts" from the wizard. The wizard gave Jamaar the potion for healing sexual abuse, the book of his life so far, and a sword to protect him in the future. Jamaar seemed pleased with these gifts.

During the next few months, Jamaar played these battle scenes repeatedly until he felt he had overcome the "monsters." He accepted his wounds and the attention of the caring therapist. Shirley was approved to adopt Jamaar, and he became comfortable with the idea of having her as his new mother. Shirley decided to move after the adoption was made final. Jamaar and the therapist prepared to say goodbye.

Closure

Jamaar had come a long way. He did not fight at school anymore, he had stopped urinating in his bed at night, and he was no longer afraid of his monsters. He now had a life story with a hard beginning, a dark period in the middle, but an open future. The adoption was finalized. Jamaar had a new last name that he chose to use.

As part of the closure process in therapy, the therapist conducted an adoption ceremony for Jamaar and his new mother. Jamaar, his mother, and a few invited guests listened as the therapist read "the story of Jamaar" to the group. During the ceremony, his foster mother stood up in front of everyone and said, "I take you as my son." Jamaar answered, "I take you as my mother." The "witnesses" at the ceremony said in unison, "We hear your story, you have done well, we witness this new family." There were tears shed and some cake was served.

Two months after the adoption ceremony, Jamaar and the therapist opened the magic box for their last session. Together, they imagined what they might be like in 20 years. They imagined the therapist walking with a cane and Jamaar visiting with his own children. He and the therapist reviewed all of the characters, games, and battles they had created over the 2-year process. They played "the game" one final time and gave each other imaginary gifts. Swords, trophies, medals, and storybooks were exchanged. Jamaar was given the real puppet to keep. At the end of the session, they gave each other a hug and said goodbye.

The therapist knew that Jamaar was inside of him forever and hoped it was the same for Jamaar. The therapist hoped that Jamaar would take the playspace inside of him, to contain his helpers and his monsters as he grows up. The therapist hoped they had had enough time in the therapy process to allow Jamaar to identify with his wounded self, not just the perpetrator.

Conclusion

Jamaar, at 8 years old, had the courage to tell his story. Because of the initially poor responses by protective adults, Jamaar began to suppress his story and try to forget what happened. This defensive process had the effect of increasing his arousal and aggression at school and at home.

Jamaar told us in words that he was "fine." However, his behavior (his body) told us a different story. He was fighting every week in school, urinating in his bed most nights, having nightmares, dissociating, and acting out sexually with other children. Hypervigilant and mistrustful of adults, he believed that the sexual abuse perpetrated by a boy eight years older and stronger than him was somehow his fault. His aggressive behaviors were understandable and adaptive in the home of his biological parents. There, his behaviors of vigilance and mistrust made sense. Jamaar developed these behaviors in an environment where he needed to survive. In treatment, Jamaar needed to learn interpersonal coping skills appropriate for the new protective environments of school, the foster home, and therapy.

When Jamaar began treatment, he was sometimes *not in* his body or, at other times, *too much* in his body. His body had been the target of sexual attention from his uncle, the locus of painful physical intrusion and shame. For Jamaar, being in his body was not experienced as safe or pleasurable. Disturbing visual images and a felt sense of painful arousal came without his control. Engaged in Developmental Transformations, Jamaar slowly reinhabited his body and regained a felt sense of safety and control. This embodied method of drama therapy provided Jamaar with a cognitive developmental *middle path* between suppressing the story (avoiding, numbing) and being continually aroused by traumatic memory (re-experiencing, hyperarousal).

The trauma story encoded in implicit memory systems needs to be translated into explicit, representational form (including words) for desensitization to occur. Affective dysregulation in sexually abused children is the failure to develop *forms for feeling*. The method of Developmental Transformations allows the traumatic sense memory to be accessed, contained, represented, and placed in the child's narrative past. The therapist using this method can provide the sexually abused and neglected child an emotional prosthesis for further cognitive affective development within a safe interpersonal environment.

Finally, for trauma therapy to have an impact beyond symptom relief, the distorted cognitive affective representations of the self and others must be accessed and modified within a novel and non-abusive interpersonal encounter for internalization. Ultimately, we do not want sexually abused boys and girls to develop into adults who are symptom-free yet identified with an aggressor; thus, replaying the trauma story in another generation of children. The deep and often distorted cognitive structures of the victimized vulnerable self and perpetrating other have to be accessed and modified in order for the child to develop internal representations of a loveable self and safe others. This is not a short-term process. To be successful, this process requires a warm, courageous, and consistent therapist, safety, symptom relief, relational work, and enough time.

References

Alexander, P. C. (1992). Application of attachment theory to the study of sexual abuse. *Journal of Consulting and Clinical Psychology, 60*(2),185–195.

American Psychiatric Association. (1994). *Diagnostic and statistical manual of mental disorders* (4th ed.). Washington, DC: Author.

Berliner, L., & Briere, J. (1997). Trauma, memory and clinical practice. In L. M. Williams & V. L. Banyard (Eds.), *Trauma and memory* (pp. 3–18). Thousand Oaks, CA: Sage.

Bowlby, J. (1969). *Attachment and loss: Vol. I. Attachment.* London: Tavistock.

Briere, J. (1992). *Child abuse trauma: Theory and treatment of the lasting effects.* Newbury Park, CA: Sage.

Bruner, J. (1964). The course of cognitive growth. *American Psychologist, 19*(1), 1–15.

Cattanach, A. (1992). *Play therapy with abused children.* London: Jessica Kingsley.

Cohen, B., & Cox, C. (1995). *Telling without talking: Art as a window into the world of multiple personality.* New York: Norton.

Cohen, J. A., Berliner, L., & March, J. S. (2000). Treatment of children and adolescents. In E. B. Foa, T. M. Keane, & M. J. Friedman (Eds.), *Effective treatments for PTSD: Practice guidelines from the International Society for Traumatic Stress Studies* (pp. 106–138). New York: Guilford.

Cuffe, S. E., & Frick-Helms, S. B. (1995). Treatment interventions for child sexual abuse. In G. A. Rekers (Ed.), *Handbook for child and adolescent sexual problems* (pp. 232–251). New York: Lexington Books.

Dayton, T. (1997). *Heartwounds: The impact of unresolved trauma and grief on relationships.* Deerfield Beach, FL: Health Communications.

DeBellis, M. D., Keshavan, M. S., Clark, D. B., Casey, B. J., Biedd, J. N., Boring, A. M., Frustaci, K., & Ryan, N. D. (1999). Developmental traumatology: II. Brain development. *Biological Psychiatry, 45*(10), 1271–1284.

Deblinger, E., & Heflin, A. H. (1996). *Cognitive behavioral interventions for treating sexually abused children.* Thousand Oaks, CA: Sage.

Finkelhor, D. (1993). Epidemiological factors in the clinical identification of child sexual abuse. *Child Abuse & Neglect, 17*(1), 67–70.

Finkelhor, D. (1994). Current information on the scope and nature of child sexual abuse. *Future of Children, 4*(2), 31–53.

Finkelhor, D., & Dziuba-Leatherman, J. (1994). Children as victims of violence: A national survey. *Pediatrics, 94*, 413–420.

Finkelhor, D., Hotaling, G., Lewis, I. A., & Smith, C. (1990). Sexual abuse in a national survey of adult men and woman: Prevalence, characteristics, and risk factors. *Child Abuse & Neglect, 14*, 19–28.

Flavell, J. H., Miller, P. H., & Miller, S. A. (1993). *Cognitive development.* Englewood Cliffs, NJ: Prentice-Hall.

Fonagy, P., & Target, M. (1996). A contemporary psychoanalytic perspective: Psychodynamic developmental therapy. In E. Hibbs & P. Jensen (Eds.), *Psychosocial treatments for child and adolescent disorders: Empirically based approaches* (pp. 619–638). Washington, DC: American Psychological Association.

Friedrich, W. N. (1992). *Psychotherapy of sexually abused children and their families.* New York: Norton.

Garber, J., & Dodge, K. A. (Eds.). (1991). *The development of emotion regulation and dysregulation.* Cambridge, UK: Cambridge University Press.

Golub, D. (1985). Symbolic expression in posttraumatic stress disorder: Vietnam combat veterans in art therapy. *Arts in Psychotherapy, 12*(4), 285–296.

Greenberg, M., & van der Kolk, B. (1989). Retrieval and integration with the "painting cure." In B. van der Kolk (Ed.), *Psychological trauma* (pp. 191–216). Washington, DC: American Psychiatric Press.

Harris, P. L. (2000). *The work of the imagination.* Boston, MA: Blackwell.

International Society for the Study of Dissociation (1997). *Treatment guidelines.* Washington, DC: ISSD Publications.

James, B. (1994). *Handbook for treatment of attachment-trauma problems in children.* New York: Lexington Books.

James, M., & Johnson, D. (1996). Drama therapy for the treatment of affective expression in posttraumatic stress disorder. In D. Nathanson (Ed.), *Knowing feeling: Affect, script, and psychotherapy* (pp. 303–326).

Johnson, D. (1987). The role of the creative arts therapies in the diagnosis and treatment of psychological trauma. *The Arts in Psychotherapy, 14*(1), 7–13.

Johnson, D. (1992). The drama therapist in role. In S. Jennings (Ed.), *Drama therapy: Theory and practice* (vol. 2, pp. 112–135). London: Routledge.

Johnson, D. (2000). Creative therapies. In E. B. Foa & T. M. Keane (Eds.), *Effective treatments for PTSD: Practice guidelines from the International Society for Traumatic Stress Studies* (pp. 356–358). New York: Guilford.

Johnson, D., Lubin, H., Hale, K., & James, M. (1997). Single session effects of treatment components within a specialized inpatient posttraumatic stress disorder program. *Journal of Traumatic Stress, 10*(3), 377–390.

Kendall-Tackett, K. A., Williams, L. M., & Finkelhor, D. (1993). Impact of sexual abuse on children: A review and synthesis of recent empirical studies. *Psychological Bulletin, 113*(1), 164–180.

Kluft, E. (Ed.). (1992). *Expressive and functional therapies in the treatment of multiple personality disorder.* Springfield, IL: Charles C. Thomas.

Lane, R. D., & Schwartz, G. F. (1987). Levels of emotional awareness: A cognitive-developmental theory and its application to psychopathology. *American Journal of Psychiatry, 144*(2), 133–143.

LeDoux, J. E. (1996). *The emotional brain.* New York: Simon & Schuster.

Lewis, M., & Haviland-Jones, J. M. (Eds.) (2000). *Handbook of emotions.* New York: Guilford.

March, J. S., Amaya-Jackson, L., & Pynoos, R. S. (1997). Pediatric posttraumatic stress disorder. In J. M. Weiner (Ed.), *Textbook of child and adolescent psychiatry* (2nd ed.). Washington, DC: American Psychiatric Press.

McCann, L., Pearlman, L. A., Sakheim, D. K., & Abrahamson, D. J. (1988). Assessment and treatment of the adult survivor of childhood sexual abuse within a schema framework. In S. M. Sgroi (Ed.), *Vulnerable populations: Evaluation and treatment of sexually abused children and adult survivors* (pp. 77–102). New York: Lexington Books.

McLeer, S. V., Deblinger, E., Henry, D., & Orvaschel, H. (1992). Sexually abused children at high risk for post-traumatic stress disorder. *Journal of the American Academy of Child and Adolescent Psychiatry, 31*(5), 875–879.

Morgan, C., & Johnson, D. (1995). Use of a drawing task in the treatment of nightmares in combat-related post-traumatic stress disorder. *Art Therapy, 12*(4), 244–247.

Perry, B. D., Pollard, R. A., Blakley, T. L., Baker, W. L., & Vigilante, D. (1995). Childhood trauma, the neurobiology of adaptation and "use-dependent" development of the brain: How "states" become "traits." *Infant Mental Health Journal, 16*(4), 271–291.

Piaget, J. (1951). *Play, dreams, and imitation in childhood.* New York: Norton

Putnam, F. W. (1990). Disturbance of "self" in victims of child sexual abuse. In P. R. Kluft (Ed.), *Incest-related syndromes of adult psychopathology* (pp. 113–132). Washington, DC: American Psychiatric Press.

Pynoos, R. S., Steinberg, A. M., & Wraith, R. (1995). A developmental model of childhood traumatic stress. In D. Cicchette & D. J. Cohen (Eds.), *Manual of developmental psychopathology* (pp. 72–95). New York: Wiley.

Rothschild, B. (2000). *The body remembers: The psychophysiology of trauma and trauma treatment.* New York: Norton.

Saigh, P. A. (1992). The behavioral treatment of child and adolescent posttraumatic stress disorder. *Advances in Behaviour Research and Therapy, 14*(4), 247–275.

Schacter, D. (1996). *Searching for memory.* New York: Basic Books.

Schore, A. N. (1994). *Affect regulation and the origin of the self: The neurobiology of emotional development.* Hillsdale, NJ: Erlbaum.

86 • Clinical Applications of Drama Therapy

Slade, A., & Wolf, D. (Eds.). (1994). *Children at play.* New York: Oxford University Press.

Smith, D. W., Letourneau, E. J., Saunders, B. E., Kilpatrick, D. G., Resnick, H. S., & Best, C. L. (2000). Delay in disclosure of childhood rape: Results from a national survey. *Child Abuse & Neglect, 24*(2), 273–287.

Spring, D. (1993). *Shattered images: Phenomenological language of sexual trauma.* Chicago: Magnolia Street.

Sroufe, L. A. (1989). Pathways to adaptation and maladaptation: Psychopathology as developmental deviation. In D. Cicchetti (Ed.), *Rochester Symposium on developmental psychopatholgy: Vol. I. The emergence of discipline* (pp. 13–40). Hillsdale, NJ: Erlbaum.

Stern, D. (1985). *The interpersonal world of the infant.* New York: Basic Books.

Terr, L. (1994). *Unchained memories: True stories of traumatic memories, lost and found.* New York: Basic Books.

van der Kolk, B. A. (1994). The body keeps the score: Memory and the evolving psychobiology of posttraumatic stress. *Harvard Review of Psychiatry, 1,* 253–265.

Werner, H., & Kaplan, S. (1963). *Symbol formation.* New York: Wiley.

Widom, C. S., & Morris, S. (1997). Accuracy of adult recollections of childhood victimization: Part 2: Childhood sexual abuse. *Psychological Assessment, 9*(1), 34–46.

Winn, L. C. (1994). *Posttraumatic stress disorder and dramatherapy: Treatment and risk reduction.* London: Jessica Kingsley.

Winnicott, D. (1953). Transitional objects and transitional phenomena: A study of the first not-me possession. *International Journal of Psychoanalysis, 34,* 89–97.

Young, L. (1992). Sexual abuse and the problem of embodiment. *Child Abuse and Neglect, 16*(1), 89–100.

CHAPTER 5

Creative Co-Constructions
A Psychoanalytic Approach to Spontaneity and Improvisation in the Therapy of a Twice Forsaken Child*

ROSALIND CHAPLIN KINDLER

Introduction

It is 1985, and I am standing in a playroom facing the door to the waiting room. I am nervous. On the other side of the door there is silence. A 6-year-old boy waits there with his mother. They've come for his first therapy session. For me, this is the first session of my very first case in the process of training to become a psychoanalytic child therapist—new territory. Until now, I have been a drama teacher. I know that the only thing I can be sure of right now is that I don't know what's going to happen for the next hour. Then, I remember a time not so long ago when, as an actor, I was about to do an improvisational exercise with another actor. I remember feeling held by the certain knowledge that, whatever happened between us in the improvisation, we would be guided by the authenticity of simply being and staying in the moment. This memory calms me. I feel much better. This is familiar ground, after all. "Just think of this as another improvisation," I tell myself, as I open the door.

Psychoanalysis and Drama Therapy

I am among the fortunate who have been able to count Dr. Eleanor Irwin as mentor, supervisor, friend, and esteemed colleague. My introduction to Ellie

---

*A version of the material in this chapter was presented at the 2003 meeting of the International Association of Relational Psychoanalysis and Psychotherapy in Rome, Italy.

and to the world of drama therapy began with the National Association for Drama Therapy (NADT) conference in San Francisco in 1986. I had a great hunger to find some way to bring my two seemingly incompatible worlds—drama and psychoanalysis—together. I was already into my second year of psychoanalytic training and had been "doing" drama, primarily with children in a variety of settings, for many years. The dramas that emerged from this work were an endless source of joy and wonder. The children's stories and scenes seemed to reveal many unexpressed conflicts, fears, wishes, and needs. I was left with the desire to find better ways to decode the meaning behind these complex communications. With her presentation in San Francisco in 1986, Ellie Irwin built bridges between psychoanalytic theory and drama therapy practice that spoke powerfully to me. At that time, one of the settings in which I worked was an integrated preschool for children with physical and neurological disabilities. I found this setting particularly fascinating because it allowed me to work with two populations: children with a wide range of disabilities and their nondisabled siblings. Dr. Irwin generously agreed to supervise me by phone and thus began my dual-track training as a drama therapist and psychoanalytic child therapist. As I made my way through my 5-year training with the Toronto Child Psychoanalytic Program, I simultaneously followed a parallel track with Ellie Irwin and the NADT.

Irwin has been a powerful voice in providing important links between psychoanalytic theory and drama therapy. In her cogent (1985) paper, "Externalizing and Improvising Imagery through Drama Therapy: A Psychoanalytic View," Dr. Irwin describes the treatment of a 5-year-old girl and beautifully illustrates how Object Relations theory helped to illuminate the child's choice of roles and her growing capacity to externalize her difficulties through the drama. Irwin has also provided us with a valuable (1999) paper, that compares two psychoanalytic perspectives, Ego Psychology and Object Relations, from the point of view of child dramatic play. For a full and comprehensive account of psychoanalytic theory, its applications to drama therapy, excellent clinical examples, and a concise outline of the various psychoanalytic theoretical models, see Dr. Irwin's chapter in *Current Approaches in Drama Therapy* (Lewis & Johnson, 2000).

Under Dr. Irwin's tutelage, the bridging of the two worlds of drama therapy and psychoanalytic theory was seamlessly managed. However, while other drama therapists have embraced elements of psychoanalytic theory as an integral part of their work (Emunah, 1994; Landy, 1993; Johnson, 2000), the process was not mutual. Psychoanalysis had not embraced the enriching possibilities coming from the world of drama therapy. In an attempt to redress this imbalance, I have described elsewhere (Kindler, 1997b) how drama therapy was a powerful tool in the psychoanalytic treatment of a severely disturbed boy. I have also, over the years, presented an integration of drama therapy and psychoanalytic theory at psychoanalytic and drama therapy conferences, meetings and workshops, and in psychoanalytic publications (Kindler, 1997a, 1997b). The recent extraordinary interest from the psychoanalytic community in the notions of spontaneity and improvisation, generated by Stern and his colleagues (1998) is exciting. Requests from psychoanalysts for experiential, improvisational workshops have been happily granted.

Psychoanalysis has always distinguished itself from other therapies by emphasizing the importance of interpretation of unconscious motivations. Interpretation, which brings the unconscious into awareness, is seen as the central curative element in the treatment process. (For a fuller discussion on the merits of the use of interpretation with children, see Irwin, 2000; Kindler, 1997b.) However, recently, psychoanalytic and developmental theorists have been exploring ideas that are also central to the practice of drama therapy. For example, there is now recognition of the "something more than interpretation" that produces change in therapy (Process of Change Study Group, 1998). This has resulted in an emerging awareness in the psychoanalytic community of the parallel between the creative spontaneity required in the therapeutic encounter and that which occurs in a two-person dramatic improvisation. Both involve the imaginative and creative collaboration of the two participants—an authentic "being-in-the-moment" on the part of each. Drama therapists have long understood this experientially, but it represents a theoretical and conceptual shift in psychoanalytic thinking that has added a rich and original perspective to theory and practice.

This chapter presents a psychoanalytic approach to drama therapy with children. The ideas presented will be based on some of the more contemporary psychoanalytic theories, such as those just described, proposed by Stern et al. (1998). The theory base includes several theoretical approaches that followed the advent of Self Psychology (Kohut, 1971; Wolf, 1988), such as Intersubjectivity Theory (Stolorow & Atwood, 1992; Stolorow, Atwood, & Brandchaft, 1987), Non Linear Dynamic Systems Theory (Shane, Shane, & Gales, 1997), and Relational Theory (Aron, 1996; Mitchell, 2000). Another important contribution, which bridges attachment and psychoanalytic theory, has come from Fonagy and his colleagues (Fonagy et al., 1993; Fonagy, Gergely, Jurist, & Target, 2002; Fonagy & Target, 1998). They have provided us with important new access to the understanding of child development and attachment with the concepts of "Reflective Function" and "Mentalization."

Many of these approaches include in their theoretical constructs assumptions developed by Attachment studies (Bowlby, 1969–1980) and Infant Research (Beebe, 1986; Beebe & Lachmann, 1988; Lichtenberg, 1983, 1989;

Stern, 1985). The result is that Bowlby's seminal writing on Attachment has emerged anew as a central influence on psychoanalytic thinking and practice. These more recent conceptualizations in psychoanalytic thinking have allowed us to view Bowlby's work, and that of his followers (Ainsworth & Wittig, 1969; Main, Kaplan, & Cassidy, 1985), from fresh perspectives.

Psychoanalytic thinking has undergone considerable revision since Freud's (1923) original drive/structural model, in which the tripartite model of the mind—Id, Ego, and Superego—are central. Recent revisions have included alternative views of Freudian concepts such as the notion of instinctual drives (Eros and Thanatos) as a model for human psychological motivation, as well as the traditional Freudian positions on the Oedipus Complex, Transference, Countertransference, and Defenses.

Self Psychology theory (Kohut, 1971; Wolf, 1988) shifted the emphasis from "guilty man to tragic man" (Kohut, 1977), focusing on the development of the self and its need for selfobject experience as the prime motivator of psychic life. Selfobject needs may be met in normal development by empathy, responsivity, and attunement in the other. Self Psychology views the Oedipus Complex as a normal phase of child development (Kohut, 1977). If appropriately responded to, the Oedipus Complex becomes a potentially comfortable developmental stage in childhood that contributes to a vigorous and resilient sense of a conflict-free self. The concept of Transference has also undergone a radical shift under Self Psychology (Kindler, 1997a, 1997b; Lachmann & Beebe, 1992; Stolorow & Lachmann, 1984/85). Stolorow and Lachmann (1984/85) propose fluid and shifting transference configurations, triggered either by life experiences that emanate from unmet selfobject needs or by repetitive patterns of relational experience. Contributions from Intersubjectivity Theory (Stolorow, Atwood, & Brandchaft, 1994) and Relational Theory (Mitchell, 2000) have provided important insights to enhance our thinking on this issue. They emphasize the importance of acknowledging the subjective experiences of both participants in the therapeutic dyad. Furthermore, the concept of Defense is understood here as primarily a self-preservative measure that should, therefore, be approached with great respect and empathy, rather than seen as an obstruction to be dismantled.

In order to clarify my position vis-à-vis psychoanalytic psychotherapy and drama therapy, it might be useful for me to locate myself within this range of theoretical models. Primarily, following the psychoanalytic model in which I was trained, I tend to follow the lead of the child, and therefore see my role as facilitator and co-creator of the dramas, rather than initiator. There are, of course, always situations in which a child is simply unable to initiate play. In those cases, one must gently step in to help relieve the child's anxiety. My interest is based on moment-to-moment interactive experiences, their mutuality, and accompanying affects. Beebe and her colleagues (Beebe,

1986; Beebe & Lachmann, 1988; Beebe, Lachmann, & Jaffe, 1997) have provided us with valuable insights into how these moments of self and mutual regulation are negotiated between parent and infant. This research has contributed importantly to our understanding of the moment-to-moment interactions that form the fabric of the therapeutic encounter. In short, I am interested in what happens moment-to-moment between therapist and client, how each is affected by the other's response, and how this "dance" of affective self and mutual regulation gets played out. I am also interested in the transformation of "invariant organizing principles" (Stolorow, Atwood, & Brandchaft, 1994) that result from damaging relational patterns and developmental attachment difficulties. This places me squarely in the arena of both the Intersubjective and Relational models.

In my early days as a drama therapist, attempting to hang my drama work onto a framework of psychoanalytic theory, I was fortunate to find myself the happy recipient of many of these theoretical ideas. As drama therapists, we consistently co-construct dramatic creations with our clients. Therefore, I have found that using a psychoanalytic framework based on an understanding of the subjectivities of both client and therapist informs and enhances my capacity to respond appropriately to the meaning revealed in my clients' dramatic communications. Using this theoretical framework also allows a different view of transference and countertransference configurations.

The clinical material that follows will illustrate the value of these theoretical ideas in the twice-weekly treatment of one young client. The vignettes will illustrate how Ben's extraordinary capacity for dramatic play helped him to work through the many losses, past and potential, in his relational world as he struggled with the double-edged sword of hope and dread inherent in the new attachments offered to him. Ornstein (1974) has coined the phrase "the dread to repeat" to describe this fear of leaving the self vulnerable to a repetition of early psychic pain.

Ben

Ben was a "twice-forsaken" 6-year-old; "twice-forsaken" in that he was abandoned by his birth mother at 4 months, adopted at age 4, and bereaved of his adoptive mother before his 7th birthday. Ben's history revealed that at 4 months of age, he was taken to an orphanage in a small town in Guatemala and abandoned there. The records from the orphanage showed only that he was 4 months old and had been premature. Nothing is known about Ben's first months of life. The orphanage environment had a child–caregiver ratio of 20 to 1. Thus, his basic physical needs were met but his emotional needs went unfulfilled. He remained there until, at the age of 4 years, he was adopted and brought to Canada. In a cruel turn of events, Ben's adoptive mother became ill soon after his arrival and died shortly before Ben turned 7.

Ben was an extremely volatile child who had trouble with all transitions. He was apparently often sent home from day care and school because of repeated, violent temper tantrums that lasted for long periods of time, during which he had to be restrained while he kicked, spat, bit, and screamed.

Clinical Vignette #1

In my first meeting with Ben, I am presented with an engaging-looking 6-year-old with a thatch of black hair and piercing, dark eyes. The eyes make brief contact with mine and then dart away into the distance. Ben marches confidently into the playroom without looking back at his father and without waiting for me. He seems to have been standing just behind the door. He walks over to the toy shelf and picks up the magic wand, asking what it is. His speech is quite difficult to understand, but remarkably good considering he spoke no English at all until 18 months ago and before that he had functioned poorly in his native language.

I tell him it's a magic wand and ask if he knows what it is to play at "pretending." He says, " No," and proceeds to play with intense concentration and creativity, inventing scene after scene in which people fall, are hit, thrown, or kicked off a high ledge, then are rushed to the hospital in the rescue vehicles. The play is full and rich, and Ben demonstrates a wonderful capacity for imagination. Suddenly, Ben makes an alarm noise. He tells me that robbers have broken into the house through the windows, and the house is on fire. This marks a shift from the projective play he has been engaged in to the creation of a full-blown drama with assigned roles for us both. Ben is in tight control of the situation and instructs me to leave everything to him. He puts out the fire, dispatches the robbers, and fixes all the damage. My role is to be powerless and terrified, and to show astonishment and admiration at his skills as he takes care of everything and deals mercilessly with the robbers. Ben's need for control is clear. Therefore, I am not surprised that, as we approach the end of the session, he haughtily orders me to clean up. I respond that, indeed, it would be nice to be like a king and have others do exactly your bidding. He softens immediately and tells me of a big fight he recently had with his parents because he wouldn't pick up his toys at home. I suggest that maybe it would be good if I made him a crown and he could pretend to be a king in here.

With his crown perched jauntily on his head, the new king looks at himself in the mirror. "Very distinguished," he says. I am astonished and delighted at his appropriate use of this sophisticated word, and the stylish wit with which it is delivered. My spontaneous laughter evokes a smile of pleasure from Ben. This moment of mutual pleasure proves to be the first of many such moments between us.

Ben is a benign king who provides me with many things and reassures me that he will take complete charge of the entire kingdom. But, he can also be cruel and unforgiving, and shows no mercy to the robbers. As the end of the session approaches, Ben looks around the playroom and begins the first of what proves to become a ritual "end-of-session" bid to be allowed to take something home with him. His tone is mild and almost sadly resigned as he holds the magic wand saying, "I don't suppose I could take this home."

"No," I say to Ben. "The toys must stay here in the playroom. But they will be here for you to play with next time you come."

He accepts this without demur. However, there soon follows a lively round of negotiations in which Ben asks for things he spies on my desk. "Maybe this pen?" or "What about that pad?" Ignoring the ghostly voice from my early psychoanalytic training, which forbade under any circumstances allowing a child to take anything away, I decided that this hungry boy's need was more akin to Winnicott's (1965) concept of the "transitional object." He requires something to help keep us connected in his mind until the next time. So, Ben finally leaves clutching a pencil to his chest.

Discussion of Vignette #1

What to make of Ben's first session? The ease with which he separated from his father might be seen as the behavior of a securely attached child. However, given Ben's history, this apparent comfort with separation actually confirmed the "promiscuity" that had already been described to me by the referral source. In other words, Ben was ready to attach to just about anyone who would stand still long enough to engage with him; a trait that is not uncommon in late-adopted children, or children who are insecurely attached. However, there must have been something about the affective tone of our interactions in that first session that signaled "Danger" to Ben and set in motion the "robber" sequence that followed. I would suggest that Ben might have begun to experience something that felt good to him—perhaps dangerously good. And so his psychic alarm went off. The "robber" theme ran like a river through our work, and I came to understand this as one of Ben's most deeply ingrained organizing principles (Stolorow, Atwood, & Brandchaft, 1987). It could be articulated in this way: "There is nothing and nobody that I can be certain I can hold on to. Anything I have will, more than likely, be taken from me, and in the most violent and assaultive way, leaving me bereft again. I must be constantly vigilant and ready to fight."

The transference configurations as they were played out in this first session were to emerge again and again as we worked together. Ben's emotional neediness, the selfobject aspect of the transference, could be seen in his assigning me the role of amazed admirer (in self psychological terms, a mirroring selfobject). Also, his wish to take something home at the end of the session revealed his hope that he might be able to fill the empty space in his emotional life with "stuff." His quest for material things was relentlessly played out both inside and outside my playroom. Even when his wish was granted, he was, of course, left feeling unsatisfied. Thus, we could understand this behavior as the "selfobject" or "needy" aspect of the transference. However, another dimension of the transference left Ben terrified to truly invest in any new intimate relationships. This is the Repetitive or Representational dimension (Stolorow & Lachmann, 1984/85), which is based on "lived experience" and "expectancies" (Stern, 1985).

In other words, at one moment his transference enactments are saying to me, "I desperately need something from you: to be recognized and understood and accepted for who I really am. I am so hungry for something nourishing to feed my emotionally starved self." At another, he might be saying, "I expect that if I let myself get close to you, you will leave me or hurt me, or worse. I will not allow that to happen again. There is no reliable help out there. I'll do it all myself. I need no one."

Yet, Ben's resilience could be seen in his seeming impatience to enter my office. Perhaps Ben had hopes that something good could happen here; perhaps the hope for a "positive new attachment experience" (Shane, Shane, & Gales, 1997). For my part, I felt myself immediately drawn to Ben. His lively capacity for dramatic play engaged me, and I felt excited and hopeful about working with him. His self-admiring comment, "Very distinguished," was a spontaneous moment that touched something in me, leaving me laughing and feeling closely in touch with him.

Parental History

Ben's adoptive mother Grace was a lawyer in her early 50s when she decided to embark on what she called her "magnificent obsession." She and Peter, her husband of 25 years, had no children. Grace described her mounting certainty and determination to adopt a child. However, Grace's "magnificent obsession" was hers alone.

Ben's adoptive father was an extremely reserved and cerebral man who ran a small electronics business. He was widely read, enjoyed classical music, and otherwise engaged in outdoor activities or immersed himself in the world of his business. He said that he had few friends and little contact with his elderly parents, who still lived in his native Holland. Peter had emigrated to Canada when he was 20. He reported that his relationship with his parents had been "pretty normal," but he had seen them rarely since he left home. Although Peter had no particular desire to adopt a child, he did not actively oppose the idea.

However, the process, although difficult, continued. When they were finally offered a 4-year-old boy from Guatemala, Peter went with his wife to get the child. When he first met his new parents, Ben could speak no English. I was able to glean only a little about Grace's background on the few occasions I met with her before her death. However, I was struck by her open manner as she spoke about herself and her relationships within her family-of-origin. She alluded to the fact that, growing up in a town in Eastern Canada, she had not had good relationships with her family members, particularly with her mother. Grace's parents had died some years earlier. It was only after Grace's death that I learned from Peter that there had been physical and emotional abuse in his wife's childhood. Peter, however, said very little about his own childhood, painting a rather bland and colorless picture as he described with sparse detail his uneventful family relationships.

There may be something of significance to be gleaned from the different narrative styles revealed in Grace's and Peter's reporting of their childhood relationships. One can only speculate what results may have emerged had these parents participated in an Adult Attachment Interview assessment (Fonagy et al., 1993; Main, Kaplan, & Cassidy, 1985). The Adult Attachment Interview (AAI) was developed to assess attachment patterns in adults. It demonstrated that the patterns of attachment revealed could predict, or were analogous to, the attachment behaviors found in their children. In this research, the parent is asked to describe childhood memories and experiences.

The AAI does not focus on the content of the memories reported, but on the style of the telling. For example, adults who can talk about their childhood experiences in a coherent and reflective way, despite severe deprivations, are predictive of strong attachments with their children; whereas a sparse or incoherent style of reporting reflects an insecure attachment style, although the content presented may be benign. It was certainly clear that, despite Peter's tremendous effort, commitment, and dedication to the care of his son, whom he perceived as the legacy left him by Grace, he struggled enormously with the demanding task of parenting Ben alone. Although he read prodigiously and kept copious notes for reference during our meetings, Peter found it extremely difficult to manage a young boy of Ben's temperament and needs.

Following Ben's arrival in Canada, Grace's diagnosis demanded frequent hospitalizations for lengthy periods of time and she was progressively less available to him. However, although less and less able to physically care for him, she was committed to his well-being. She said with disarming simplicity that, when she met Ben, she had simply fallen in love with him. She read everything she could find on adopting an older child and on childcare in general. However, at the time of referral, 1 year after his arrival in Canada, Ben was increasingly difficult for his teachers, daycare workers, and parents to manage. His mother had just been admitted to the hospital for what would be a lengthy stay. His out-of-control tantrums were causing him to be sent home from school on a regular basis. At home, he was very difficult to manage—spitting, kicking, scratching, and biting those who tried to contain him.

The Dramas

Clinical Vignette #2

One day, in the first months of therapy, Ben tells me the story of the dog Maxie, who is "driving everyone crazy," and therefore must be taken back to where he came from in another country (which, Ben says, is Africa). Maxie, whose part is played by a teddy bear, is to be flown back despite his entreaties and promises that he will be "good." Ben pilots the helicopter to take the offender back to Africa with his mother (whom Ben names Grace) and me as chaperones. Maxie doesn't want to go and protests all the way, saying he's scared and sorry, but Ben is adamant.

When we finally get to Africa, I point out that, since we are back at the orphanage where Maxie used to live but says he can't remember, maybe we should take a look around and try to see if Maxie can remember it at all.

Can he remember what it looked like? Is there anything that looks familiar here?

"No," Ben answers for Maxie.

Well, maybe the feel of the bed, the blanket?

"No."

Or what about the taste of the milk? (Ben has taken to using a baby bottle and drinking out of it in our sessions). Does Maxie remember sucking on a baby bottle when he lived there?

"Yes," he does, says Ben.

Maxie is very scared because he doesn't remember much at all, and he has no friends here now. All his friends are in Toronto and he wants to go back to his parents, Ben tells me on Maxie's behalf. "It's so hard to be good all the time," I say. Maxie agrees, but he promises to try. Ben caves in and flies us all back to Toronto.

Discussion of Vignette #2

In this session, Ben and I took turns with the role of Maxie, co-constructing and giving voice to his experience of confusion, fear, and uncertainty. Ben flipped back and forth between the roles of Maxie, the "bad kid," and himself as disciplinarian, while I gave voice to Maxie and advocated for him as his chaperone. For Ben, who had such enormous struggles with affect regulation, the fear that he would be sent back must have hovered close every time he lost control and was "bad," and this theme was played out repeatedly.

This fear of abandonment or rejection is a common theme in the play of children who have been adopted and is often felt mutually by both parent and child (Brodzinsky & Schechter, 1993; Verrier, 1996). Parents often report the terrible anxiety they feel that their child will leave them or cease to love them. This can contribute to the insecure or anxious attachments that are sometimes seen in adoption. For the therapist who works with adopted children, it is important to be alert to parallel countertransferential issues that can arise. These issues often include feelings of anxiety that the parents will prematurely remove the child from treatment. In addition, therapists often fall prey to "rescue" fantasies, as in working with bereaved children.

As my relationship with Ben evolved, and my compassion for him and his father grew, it was crucial that I kept track of how my countertransference feelings may be contributing to our interactions in the dramas we created together. My protests against the harsh punishments meted out by Ben for the misdemeanors of his charges were important to me, and I had to fight hard to make sure the "criminals" had a fair hearing. Obviously, my wish to advocate on Ben's behalf and ease his school miseries was in the foreground.

My role in the drama just described, and in all our dramas, was to articulate the affective content wherever I could. In introducing the idea that we had come back to the place where Maxie had lived in the children's home in Africa, and by asking Maxie if he recognized or remembered anything at all, I was providing the affective cues that connect feelings with events. Ben was highly defended and disavowed all negative feelings, protecting his fragile self from overwhelming affect. In trying to introduce Ben to the world of feelings and memories, I was hoping to help him find the seeds of an affective history, what Palombo (2001) refers to as a "narrative self."

With the use of the stuffed animals and the roles and experiences assigned to them, Ben was able to negotiate what Landy (1993) has described as "aesthetic distance" from the potentially overwhelming affects that threatened him. His use of role reversal, as he took on the roles of pilot, disciplinarian, and adviser, allowed a sense of mastery of his confusing and disturbing experiences. Although Ben had a photo album of the orphanage in Guatemala, he did not speak of it for many months and avoided most allusions to his past experience there. In asking about the feel of the bed or the taste of the milk, I was trying to facilitate, through his alter ego Maxie, a chance for Ben to articulate some of his early "lived experience" (Lichtenberg, 1989) within the safety of the drama.

Clinical Vignette #3

One of Ben's most enduring dramas, really an ongoing story of soap opera proportions, was the creation of the "classroom" and the "class" of five stuffed animals. He was the teacher and I was his assistant. Co-constructed by Ben and myself, the students in his class (in particular, Flopsy the rabbit) had lived through, or were currently living through, much of Ben's actual experience: one struggled with a sick and dying mother; another, a large teddy bear named Spot, told me he "came from somewhere else," and suffered from loss of memory concerning everything that was his life before coming to his adoptive home; another was terribly fearful of just about everything and couldn't sleep alone; another suffered with enormous difficulties with authority, could not manage well in groups, had huge meltdowns at school and camps, and often had to be restrained, sent to the principal's office, or sent home. In short, the class was a composite of Ben's multifaceted, lived emotional experience. On more than one occasion, these dramas would be direct re-enactments of his own miserable experiences at school, recreated in therapy with the safety net provided by role reversal.

In these sessions, Ben would enter the playroom already very much in the role of the head teacher, expecting that the "class" would be already in place, lined up on the table waiting for his arrival. It was my job to have them always ready and waiting for him, and my role as his assistant allowed me many opportunities to report to him on specific problems that I could construct as having come up that day for one of the students. In this way, we could co-construct a drama that I knew would reflect his own very recent experience, whether it was another meltdown at school or the fact that his mother was back in the hospital.

In his role as head teacher, Ben was superb. In one session following "one of those" calls from his father, Ben arrived and very quickly began a drama in which Flopsy was peremptorily sent to the office for no reason that Flopsy or any of us could understand. Ben, moving back and forth with great dexterity between the roles of Flopsy and head teacher, enacted Flopsy having a complete meltdown—spitting, kicking, and screaming—during which he had to be restrained: a faithful rendition of Ben's own experience that very morning. In my multiple roles as Flopsy, Ben's assistant, and the school principal, I was able to ask the questions and then provide the answers that might explain Flopsy's terrible distress. With this done, Ben then treated Flopsy to an articulate lecture about how important it is to be part of the team and urged him to "use his words" when he's feeling upset.

Another member of the class was a teddy bear named Freddie whose mother was very ill and often in the hospital. This was introduced during the time Ben's mother was in and out of hospital, and continued through and following her death. Freddie's primary affect was forlorn sadness. Through the medium of this character, Ben was better able to manage the articulation of the terrifying and overwhelming feelings he could not otherwise tolerate. Freddie also often felt scared or lonely and, through him, Ben could master some of his most frightening and overwhelming feelings. Freddie's mother died just about the same time that Ben's did. When Ben was told this news, he was able to confide in Freddie that his mother had died, too. Now he was all alone, "Just dad and me."

Clinical Vignette #4

We are nine months into therapy and Ben is negotiating, as he does at the end of most sessions, for something he can take home. I have suggested to Ben that his wish to take something home with him is a way he has found to keep me (and all of us in the playroom) "in his mind" until we meet the next time. Ben has agreed that this is so, but today his true developmental colors are seen.

"Maybe I could take this pencil," he suggests. "And another of these cards" (old business cards of mine).

"Ben," I ask, "What did you do with all the other pencils, cards, and things you've taken home to help keep us in your mind?"

He scarcely misses a beat. "I ate them," he tells me, poker-faced.

I roar with laughter. The thoughts flit through my mind: "But of course, you did, Ben. You are, in fact, very much still functioning in the realm of concrete thinking. The abstraction of 'keeping us in your mind,' although useful, cannot be properly understood yet. Later, those words will begin to have more meaning. But, right now, your tummy is a place you can recognize and touch. And you can tell when it's empty or full."

Ben is about to leave for the summer break. I draw him a picture of himself with all the pens, pencils, and cards in his tummy. He tells me who and what to add to the picture. Soon, his tummy is overflowing with the characters and toys in the playroom to which he is becoming attached. I add myself to the contents of his tummy. He can leave today taking with him only the picture.

Discussion of Vignette #4

Stern and his colleagues at the Process of Change Study Group (1998) would perhaps call this—Ben's "I ate them" and my laughter—a "Now Moment." If seized, these "Now Moments" can lead to what they called "Moments of Meeting." As discussed, Stern and his colleagues have broadened our thinking about the therapeutic process with the notion that what is curative in the therapeutic encounter and brings about change is the "something more" than interpretation or insight. They further propose that much of the mutative action in the process belongs in the domain of "procedural knowl-edge" (Sander, 1998).

The knowledge that we store in memory is encoded in two ways. One form, the most familiar and the basis of all "talking cures," is Declarative Memory, or that which can be expressed verbally. The other form of knowl-edge, which is at least as important in influencing the way we behave, is encoded in the domain known as "Procedural Memory." Procedural Knowl-edge is the kind of memory that allows us to know how to walk, talk, smile, ride a bike, and behave appropriately in social circumstances. It is very diffi-cult to explain to another how to smile or how to walk. We know how to do it implicitly. This knowledge is acquired in non-verbal form, and converting it into words requires effort.

Stern and his colleagues (1998) propose that the therapeutic process is one in which therapist and client "move along" in an improvisational way from "moment to moment," and that their relationship is organized by "rules" or "expectations" based on early lived experiences. They identify cer-tain particular moments they call "Now Moments" in which these expecta-tions or assumptions about relationships, which form the "shared implicit relationship" that develops between patient and therapist, are open to change if responded to in a specific or authentically creative manner.

The "moment of meeting" between Ben and me seemed to engage some of his implicit relational rules about how we separate, allowing us to talk about them in a new way. I believe that a shift did occur on that day that affected our relationship in significant ways. Ben's creative, imaginative, and humorous response to my question, "What did you do with the things you've taken home?" led me to a new understanding of his patterns in regulating himself around the issue of separation. The shift in me allowed him to shift himself. The joke, "I ate it," became part of our language, an intimate joke only we could share. I think it contributed another building block of expe-rience, what Lichtenberg (1989) called a "lived experience," that subtly al-tered Ben's relational world.

This change, I believe, was evidenced during a session that followed his mother's death. In this session, Ben's attachment to me was manifest in the transference in a new way that allowed him to express some of his grief and fear over the loss of his mother. Since he could find nothing to take home that seemed just right that day, I suggested to Ben that perhaps what he really wanted to take home was me. We talked lightly about how I could live in his basement and he could just call me anytime he wanted to see me. Ben then became pensive and spelled out to me that what he really needed was "M-O-M." He sadly told me that he was afraid, because he could not re-member his mother very well anymore, nor remember what her voice sounded like.

Ben's expression of the transference in this way was an important step for him. Shane and Shane (1990) have proposed a self psychological view of loss that emphasizes the experience less in terms of the loss of the physical person, per se, but more the loss of the self-object experiences that were integral to that relationship. Thus, for a child who loses his mother to death, the loss of her person and presence is incalculable. However, the loss of those ineffable experiences of intimacy and pleasure—of her smell, of being touched and responded to in just the right way, of being "the gleam in her eye" (Kohut, 1971)—constitute a crucial element in helping us to better understand each bereaved person's unique loss experience.

Ben's disavowal of affect permeated his play for many months, up to and including the death of his mother. No sadness, no fear, no loneliness, no worries were permitted for his chosen roles as fixer, teacher, robber, jailer, and disciplinarian. I took to using as an aid a well-worn book named "Feelings" that had bright and simple pictures of most of the primary affects. Ben became extremely fond of the book, and would often quote it to his errant students. This was an important step for Ben. He began to develop the capacity to identify his disavowed and volatile affective states and link them to events. But, more importantly, he started to understand how his feelings were linked to the affective world of interactions, which we inhabited together.

Conclusion

With the advent of the Process of Change Study Group's (1998) work, the worlds of drama therapy and psychoanalytic psychotherapy are closer now than they have ever been. The Group has proposed that there is "something more than interpretation" which is mutative in the therapeutic encounter. These ideas bring with them the recognition, new to the world of psycho-analysis, that what is curative in therapy may be grounded in experiences that are creative, spontaneous, and improvisational in nature. This notion has aroused a considerable amount of interest, and even excitement, in the psychoanalytic community.

Ben's capacity for creative and imaginative play, in spite of his early history of deprivation, allowed us to co-create not only rich dramas populated by re-creations of his "lived experience," but also a new attachment experience. It is hoped that this "positive new attachment" (Shane, Shane, & Gales, 1997) with its transformed "expectancies" (Stern, 1985) could become a prototype for future relationships.

In Emunah's valuable book, *Acting for Real* (1994), she generously re-counts a dream she had when she was a beginning drama therapist. In the dream, a client has a "breakdown" during a group session and Emunah immediately realizes that she has to "mirror" her client's every terrified, teeth-chattering, screeching, crawling sound and movement in order to success-fully calm her down. She tells us, "I include the dream because it conveys my belief that what we do in drama therapy are not really techniques but processes" (p. 152). In line with Emunah, it is my belief that whatever tech-nique or theory we employ, the basic elements of spontaneity, creativity, and "moments of meeting" are always present. Recognition of how and why we seize these moments may be implicitly known by many of us. With the help of clients like Ben, the improvisational process can continue to flourish across the theoretical spectrum.

References

Ainsworth, M. D. S., & Wittig, B. A. (1969). Attachment and exploratory behavior of one-year-olds in a strange situation. In B. M. Foss (Ed.), *Determinants of infant behavior* (Vol. 4, pp. 113–136). London: Methuen.

Aron, L. (1996). *A meeting of minds: Mutuality in psychoanalysis.* Hillsdale, NJ: Analytic Press.

Beebe, B. (1986). Mother–infant mutual influence and precursors of self-and-object representa-tions. In J. Masling (Ed.), *Empirical studies of psychoanalytic theories* (Vol. 2, pp. 7–48). Hillsdale, NJ: Analytic Press.

Beebe, B., & Lachmann, F. (1988). Mother–infant mutual influence—Precursors of psychic struc-ture. In A. Goldberg (Ed.), *Frontiers in self psychology, progress in self psychology* (Vol. 3, pp. 3–25). Hillsdale, NJ: Analytic Press.

Beebe, B., Lachmann, F., & Jaffe, J. (1997). Mother–infant interaction structures and presymbolic self- and object-representations. *Psychoanalytic Dialogues, 7*(2), 113–182.

Bowlby, J. (1969–1980). *Attachment and loss* (Vols. 1–3). New York: Basic Books.

Brodzinsky, D. M., & Schechter, M. D. (1993). *The psychology of adoption.* New York: Oxford University Press.

Emunah, R. (1994). *Acting for real: Drama therapy process, technique, and performance.* New York: Brunner/Mazel.

Fonagy, P., & Target, M. (1998). Mentalization and the changing aims of child psychoanalysis. *Psychoanalytic Dialogues, 8*(1), 87–114.

Fonagy, P., Steele, M., Moran, G., Steele, H., & Higgit, A. (1993). Measuring the ghost in the nursery: An empirical study of the relation between parents' mental representations of childhood experiences and their infants' security of attachment. *Journal of the American Psychoanalytic Association, 41*(4), 957–986.

Fonagy, P., Gergely, G., Jurist, E., & Target, M. (2002). *Affect regulation, mentalization, and the development of the self.* New York: Other Press.

Freud, S. (1923). The ego and the id. In *The standard edition of the complete works of Sigmund Freud* (Vol. 2, pp. 27–48). London: Hogarth Press.

Irwin, E. C. (1985). Externalizing and improvising imagery through drama therapy: A psycho-analytic view. *Journal of Mental Imagery, 9*(4), 35–42.

Irwin, E. C. (1999). Child dramatic play as viewed from two perspectives: Ego psychology and object relations. *Journal of Clinical Psychoanalysis, 7*(4), 505–533.

Irwin, E. C. (2000). Psychoanalytic approach to drama therapy: Defining and finding a therapeu-tic framework. In P. Lewis & D. Johnson (Eds.), *Current approaches in drama therapy* (pp. 27–49). Springfield, IL: Charles C. Thomas.

Johnson, D. (2000). Developmental transformations: Toward the body as presence. In P. Lewis & D. Johnson (Eds.), *Current approaches in drama therapy* (pp. 87–110). Springfield, IL: Charles C. Thomas.

Kindler, R. (1997a). Turning passive into active: Treatment of physically handicapped preschoolers. *Psychoanalysis and Psychotherapy, 14*(2), 323–348.

Kindler, R. (1997b). Lonely as a cloud: Finding daffodils in the house of terror. Transference and countertransference in drama therapy with a ten-year-old boy. In A. Goldberg (Ed.), *Conversations in self psychology* (pp. 272–288). Hillsdale, NJ: Analytic Press.

Kohut, H. (1971). *The analysis of the self.* New York: International Universities Press.

Kohut, H. (1977). *The restoration of the self.* New York: International Universities Press.

Lachmann, F., & Beebe, B. (1992). Representational and selfobject transferences: A developmental perspective. In A. Goldberg (Ed.), *New therapeutic visions, progress in self psychology* (Vol. 8, pp. 3–15). Hillsdale, NJ: Analytic Press.

Landy, R. (1993). *Persona and performance: The meaning of role in drama, therapy, and everyday life.* New York: Guilford.

Lewis, P., & Johnson, D. R. (Eds.). (2000). *Current approaches in drama therapy.* Springfield, IL: Charles Thomas.

Lichtenberg, J. (1983) *Psychoanalysis and infant research.* Hillsdale, NJ: Analytic Press.

Lichtenberg, J. (1989). *Psychoanalysis and motivation.* Hillsdale, NJ: Analytic Press.

Main, M., Kaplan, K., & Cassidy, J. (1985). Security in infancy, childhood and adulthood: A move to the level of representation. In I. Bretherton & E. Waters (Eds.), *Monographs of the Society for Research in Child Development, 50* (1–2, Serial No. 209).

Mitchell, S. A. (2000). *Relationality: From attachment to intersubjectivity.* Hillsdale, NJ: Analytic Press.

Ornstein, A. (1974). The dread to repeat and the new beginning: A contribution to the psychoanalysis of the narcissistic personality disorders. *The Annual of Psychoanalysis, 2,* 231–248.

Palombo, J. (2001). *Learning disorders & disorders of the self in children and adolescents.* New York: Norton.

Process of Change Study Group. (1998). Non-interpretive mechanisms in psychoanalytic therapy. *International Journal of Psycho-analysis, 79*(5), 903–921

Sander, L. (1998). Interventions that effect change in psychotherapy: A model based on infant research. *Infant Mental Health Journal, Vol. 19*(3), 280–281.

Shane, E., & Shane, M. (1990). Object loss and selfobject loss: A consideration of self psychology's contribution to understanding mourning and the failure to mourn. *The Annual of Psychoanalysis, 18,* 115–131.

Shane, M., Shane, E., & Gales, M. (1997). *Intimate attachments.* New York: Guilford.

Stern, D. (1985). *The interpersonal world of the infant.* New York: Basic Books.

Stern, D., et al. (1998). *The birth of a mother: How the motherhood experience changes you forever.* New York: Basic Books.

Stolorow, R. (1994). The intersubjective perspective. In R. Stolorow, G. Atwood, & B. Brandchaft (Eds.), *The intersubjective perspective* (pp. 3–14). Northvale, NJ: Aronson.

Stolorow, R., & Lachmann, F. (1984/1985). Transference: The future of an illusion. *The Annual of Psychoanalysis, 12/13,* 28–46.

Stolorow, R., & Atwood, G. (1992). *Contexts of being: The intersubjective foundations of psychological life.* Hillsdale, NJ: The Analytic Press.

Stolorow, R., Atwood, G., & Brandchaft, B. (1987). *Psychoanalytic treatment, an intersubjective approach.* Hillsdale, NJ: Analytic Press.

Verrier, N. (1996). *The primal wound.* Baltimore, MD: Gateway Press.

Winnicott, D. W. (1965). *The maturational processes and the facilitating environment: Studies in the theory of emotional development.* New York: International Universities Press.

Wolf, E. (1988). *Treating the self: Elements of clinical self psychology.* New York: Guilford.

Group Drama Therapy and Integrated Models

CHAPTER 6

Drama Therapy and Adolescent Resistance*

RENÉE EMUNAH

Introduction

One of the primary difficulties in therapeutic work with emotionally disturbed adolescents is their high level of resistance to treatment. The author is referring specifically to adolescents between 13 and 17 years old who have responded to severely dysfunctional family situations by resorting to substance abuse and runaway, criminal, or suicidal behavior. Their maladaptive cries for help often result in short-term psychiatric hospitalization against their will. The adolescents' anger toward their parents (which is frequently generalized to all authority figures) and sense of helplessness about their situation are compounded by this involuntary placement, and they enter the institutional setting ready to fight all aspects of treatment. Indeed, it has been noted that the adolescent "views the hospital structure as an adversary with which he is locked in combat and which he much defeat" (Rinsley & Inge, 1961). Because of the time constraints inherent in brief hospitalization, it is imperative that staff psychotherapists find ways to understand and effectively respond to the adolescents' initial resistance so that treatment can begin as soon as possible.

Although there have been other reports on drama therapy with disturbed adolescents (including Dequine & Pearson-Davis, 1983; Shuttleworth, 1981; Emunah, 1990, 1995), this chapter focuses specifically on drama therapy as it relates to resistance, and on an approach to the process and structure of

---

*Reprinted and updated from Emunah, R. (1985), Drama therapy and adolescent resistence, *The Arts in Psychotherapy, 12*(2), 71–79. With permission from Elsevier Science.

the drama therapy session intended to engage clients in a trusting relationship with the therapist and to facilitate constructive interaction with their peers. The strategies elucidated in the chapter are largely based on the author's (past) experience practicing group drama therapy over a 12-year period at Gladman Memorial Hospital Youth Center (in Oakland, California).

First, issues underlying resistance and rebelliousness during adolescence will be addressed.

Adolescent Resistance and Rebelliousness

Adolescence is a period of profound physical, psychological, and cognitive change, creating uncertainty and instability. Physical growth and sexual maturation necessitate the development of a new concept of body image. Piaget (1952) noted that the adolescent's thinking and reasoning capacities have increased qualitatively, allowing abstract and ethical concepts to be manipulated by thoughts alone without the tangible and concrete checks necessary in previous ages. Adolescent thinking can encompass future time with the possibilities of envisioning idealistic goals and acknowledging consequences of personal decision-making. Generally, in late adolescence, existential dilemmas and paradoxes, as well as moral choices and values, must be adequately resolved. Adolescent rebelliousness is often an expression of frustration at having to deal with so many physical, cognitive and emotional changes. It is a rebellion against the responsibilities that independence and developing adulthood require. The adolescent is both overwhelmed and ambivalent; he or she wants to acquire the freedom and privileges of the adult and yet still longs to be cared for and protected as a child.

During adolescence, ties to infantile object relations are loosened and modified as the self becomes more clearly differentiated. The adolescent's perception of family members changes and family conflicts generally escalate. The adolescent, struggling with independence and self-assertion, resents being told by adults what to do or how to grow up. Feelings of distrust and anger toward authority figures are apparent. There is a turn to the peer group for support. In the gradual process of shifting allegiance from the parent as the primary love object to the peer group and to the self, the adolescent goes through a tumultuous period of inner emptiness, sadness, loss, and impoverished ego-functioning. Blos (1962) describes this "narcissistic phase" as a positive stage in the disengagement process.

The rebellious acting-out of the adolescent can be understood as a normal and necessary precursor to a more integrated and better-known self. New and often paradoxical experiences and abilities, as well as previous developmental gains, are gradually integrated into a cohesive sense of identity. In contrast, however, the disturbed adolescent rigidly dissociates aspects of his or her self. Not simply struggling with areas of "identity confusion," these adolescents experience a pervasive "identity diffusion," often perpetuated by dysfunctional family dynamics (Erikson, 1968; Haley, 1980; Kernberg, 1975). Their failure to gradually and safely separate from their families often results in severe adjustment difficulties, low self-esteem, disorganized thinking, maladaptive ways of handling emotions, and destructive acting-out behaviors. Acting-out is especially rigid and deleterious when the adolescent's sense of personal power and control is blocked. When even the rebelliousness is experienced as fruitless, hopelessness, despair, and self-destructive behavior often result.

Adolescent *resistance* to treatment often can be confused with age-appropriate and healthy *rebelliousness*. Resistance to therapeutic intervention develops as the person's organized attempt at opposing the processes of becoming aware and of the emergence of unconscious forces (LaPlanche & Pontalis, 1973). For adolescents, the treatment process threatens the dichotomy of good and bad, created as an attempt to simplify conflicts and ambivalences. Adolescent rebelliousness is a developmentally appropriate reaction to both the seeming childishness of latency and the entrenched authority of adults: it is a necessary aspect of the adolescent's dramatically changing self-identity. The way in which adolescents initially resist the treatment process is by acting rebellious. It is an attempt to conceal feelings of frustration, pain, and fear of being hurt, misunderstood, rejected, or betrayed. Disturbed adolescents in institutional treatment groups struggle to maintain a mutual conformity via their shared rebelliousness, which in itself is a resistance to the treatment program.

The therapeutic approach described in this chapter makes use of the distinction and relationship between rebelliousness and resistance. The drama therapist joins with and supports the adolescents' rebelliousness, thereby engaging their interest and nurturing the sense of group identity while minimizing or even bypassing the underlying anxiety and resistance to treatment. Normal adolescent rebelliousness, a necessary determinant of healthy self-identity development, is utilized by the therapist to overcome the adolescents' resistance to the therapeutic process.

Resistance to Drama Therapy

There are specific resistances by the disturbed adolescent to the process of drama therapy. First, drama evokes anxieties related to performance. As previously mentioned, the profound physical and psychological changes during adolescence cause uncertainty and self-consciousness. Adolescents are enormously concerned about their appearance and have a strong need for approval and affirmation from their peers. While craving attention, they dare not risk disapproval by "standing out." Disturbed adolescents, whose self-esteem is particularly low, anticipate ridicule and failure.

Second, dramatic play can be criticized as being childish. Adolescents attempt to define their position and identity by opposing adult authority and by defying any activity that might be considered childish. Hence, the instruction by an adult authority figure to engage in a potentially childish activity is a prime target for resistance.

Third, drama connotes acting like someone else. Although many adults might find this liberating, it can be extremely threatening for adolescents who are undergoing a period of instability and flux. "The struggles of adolescents for a stable self-identity represent in part and to a degree dependent on the depth of their psychopathology, struggles against the loss of boundaries, hence some authors conceptualize adolescence as a struggle against disintegration" (Rinsley & Inge, 1961). Given the tenuousness of their identity and the boundary confusion that could arise through role and dramatic play, it is not surprising that they initially resist the activity. They fear being other than who they are; rather, they long to establish and assert an identity.

The skillful drama therapist takes into account the particular challenges drama therapy represents for the adolescent. Establishing a relationship with the client and engaging him or her in a constructive way is a gradual and delicate process. Both resistance and involvement take various forms during the course of a session or series of sessions, and the drama therapist must be prepared to respond to each sensitively and efficaciously. The stages that have been identified by the author will now be described. Practical examples of techniques that relate to each stage will be included. Although the techniques and approach described provide examples and ideas, they are not intended to be viewed as recipes for successful sessions. Adolescent group facilitation and therapy are not easy, and effective therapy is obviously contingent on many factors.

Stage One

Resistance is particularly acute at the very beginning of the session. Almost invariably, adolescent clients confront the drama therapist with "We're not going to do anything." They may challenge the therapist with provocative and rebellious behavior, thereby testing his or her ability to maintain control. They are prepared to instigate and engage in a power struggle; they strive to defeat authority and structure and yet are terrified of succeeding. Traditionally, therapists respond to this confrontation by exerting their authority and setting limits. Staff in many treatment facilities use both positive and negative reinforcements such as, "If you participate, you'll receive points" or "If you don't cooperate you'll be placed on 'restriction.'" Limit-setting and reinforcements, however, are often taken as cues for further opposition. Even if cooperation does ensue, an antagonistic attitude toward the leader often remains.

The author has found a very different approach—one that allows and encourages clients to behave as they actually feel—to be effective in minimizing initial resistance. For example, if the clients are hostile or aggressive, the drama therapist might incorporate these attitudes into the first exercise. The sense of permission at the beginning of the session quickly eradicates the misconception that drama means acting "other" than oneself, that it involves childish pretend games, or that it necessarily entails performance; furthermore, it destroys the image of the leader as an authority figure who will "make the group do things." When the beginning exercises allow group members to express actual feelings, defenses are minimized. Resistance in the therapeutic situation often comes from the client's fear of being deprived of his individuality, his special identity, his current state of mind (Maslow, 1968). With this approach to drama therapy, the clients have little to resist because they are allowed to act as themselves; in fact, they may even be encouraged to exaggerate their rebellious behavior.

Dramatic activity is particularly suited to this permissive approach. Drama provides an arena in which all kinds of behaviors, attitudes, and emotions can be expressed within a controlled, structured setting. Because drama affords natural boundaries within which enacted behaviors and attitudes can be observed and contained, a great deal of permission can be safely granted. This permission creates an environment in which clients will eventually feel free to experiment with alternate behaviors (Emunah, 1983).

Upon first contact with the drama therapist at the onset of a session, adolescents frequently display obstinacy; a common example is the client who stubbornly insists: "I'm not getting out of my chair."

> One day, I spontaneously approached a 14-year-old client, Tim, who insisted he wouldn't budge from his chair. In a playful tone, I said, "Try as hard as you can to stay in the chair." Gently, I took hold of Tim's hands and attempted to pull him to a standing position as he struggled to remain seated. His aggressive and hostile stance transformed into a playful one, and through the physical contact, a relationship was established between the two of us. Another client, seemingly delighted at witnessing this match, grabbed my place, claiming that he could lift Tim. Soon all the clients were pairing off with each other, alternating roles that represented resistance and surrender. I have since used this originally impromptu gesture as a deliberate "game" in opening the session.

As the above example illustrates, the client's resistance is activated rather than suppressed. Energy, which can be channeled constructively and creatively, is released. Encouraging resistance is a paradoxical process in that the client is in fact cooperating: she is both doing what she wants and following the therapist's instructions. This is reminiscent of Milton Erickson's approach to hypnosis and psychotherapy as well as of the work of family therapists Salvador Minuchin (1974) and Jay Haley (1973, 1980).

"What happens when one 'accepts' the resistance of a subject and even encourages it? The subject is thereby caught in a situation where his attempt to resist is defined as cooperative behavior. He finds himself following the hypnotist's directives no matter what he does, because what he does is defined as cooperation. Once he is cooperative, he can be diverted into new behavior . . ." (Haley, 1973).

Another example of resistance becoming cooperation is to begin with something the clients clearly want to do. The leader's initial choice of language is critical; certain words and intonations are automatic cues for opposition. For example, members of an oppositional group will want to leave. Thus, this author has often begun sessions asking for volunteers to leave the room. As the response is overwhelmingly "cooperative," the clients must take turns. Each time, the client is directed to leave, return several minutes later, and identify the group's improvisation. There are innumerable variations to this game: an instruction might be for the group to nonverbally improvise being in a particular place (movie theater, beach, amusement park) or to enact a given attitude (suspicious, sympathetic, bored). The format of the guessing game de-emphasizes performance, thereby diminishing potential self-consciousness. The fact that the focus is on the guessing rather than on the acting tends to increase concentration and imagination. Furthermore, the process of selecting a place (or attitude) of one's choice and then imagining one is, in fact, in that place conveys a sense of permission and freedom that may carry over into the realm of behavior. For adolescents who feel stuck in an intolerable family situation, confined in an institutional setting, and imprisoned by their own limited and often destructive coping mechanisms, this outlet is significant.

When the resistance is not aimed at authority (the leader), but is an expression of anxiety related to performance, any improvisation (however elementary) may be premature. The leader might begin instead with sensory awareness exercises. For example, the clients are asked to remain passively in their seats and, with eyes closed, identity various objects through touch or smell. Or, rather than asking the clients to do anything at all, the leader might begin by performing a pantomime him or herself, while the clients (from their seats) try to identify what/where/who he or she is.

When the resistance is emanating from a sense of helplessness and hopelessness, the drama therapist might begin by giving the client power within the scene. Dramatic play can enable clients to experience a degree of control over the unhappy and insecure life situation. Specific scenes that deal directly with the issue of control over one's environment or which symbolize internal self-mastery can be enacted.

Sherrie, a hospitalized 17-year-old girl, entered the drama therapy session muttering, "I hate this place." After a brief pause, she added, "And don't make me do anything. I've had enough!" I asked her what she despised most about the hospital. She spurted out a series of criticisms. I then asked her what kind of place she would rather be in. She responded, "It wouldn't be anything like this place." I asked her to describe what it would be like. Before long, Sherrie was inventing her ideal version of an adolescent therapeutic community. I appointed her director of the new facility. She selected her staff from among clients in the group. Other clients (and an actual staff member) played the parts of newly admitted patients entering from their chaotic worlds disoriented, "stoned," hostile. The "director" and her staff along with the support of teens who had already been in the program for awhile, skillfully handled each individual's case. Sherrie's affect changed remarkably as she carried out this engaging scene. She became quite animated. At the end of the session, she was able to talk about her depression and sense of hopelessness. A degree of distance and perspective, as well as some sense of hope, was apparent.

The previous example took place in a verbal and relatively high-functioning group of disturbed adolescents. The following example involves a much lower-functioning group of adolescents who were temporarily hospitalized while between foster and group home placements.

A large variety of fabrics, props, tent apparatuses, and art supplies were placed in the center of the room. The adolescents were directed to construct individual tent-like structures. Each client became involved with designing and creating his or her new habitat. Imaginative exterior forms (some utilizing actual furniture in the room), interior decorations, colorful doorpost signs adorned the room. Upon completion, each adolescent was photographed inside or beside his or her special, private "home." The clients felt proud of their creations. Each had exercised mastery over the environment during a period of their lives filled with feelings of helplessness and abandonment as a result of a long series of relocations.

With a group of adolescents who feel and act "out of control," an activity that immediately provides order and structure is needed.

As I entered a rowdy, disruptive group, I quickly observed that one boy, John, was the dominant leader who was instigating the rebelliousness. I immediately appointed him the role of judge in a court trial scene, which he readily accepted. John now had power and control *through* his role in the activity. His "influence" was being used to instill order (literally) rather than chaos. He and I were on the "same team," rather than opposing ones.

Sometimes any verbal instructions increase participants' anxiety and become cues for opposition. In this case, the leader might begin the session by bypassing the stage of instruction altogether (Emunah, 1994). This author has at times begun sessions by having a phone ring (on audiotape). The clients are surprised and intrigued and cannot resist answering the phone (an actual prop). Quite spontaneously, they begin speaking to the imaginary person at the other end of the line, often revealing to the leader their inner concerns at that moment. There are endless directions that this initial activity can take, including role play of real-life conflictual situations. The phone is a familiar and cherished object to teenagers. It is a vehicle for communication (at a distance); the fact that it is "disconnected" enables calls to be made without repercussion.

Although the approach described in this section stresses "beginning where the client is at," it is strategic in nature in that the therapist takes an active stance in facilitating involvement and bringing about change (Haley, 1973). With adolescents who are placed involuntarily in a short-term facility and who exhibit little motivation, this approach seems to be particularly appropriate. It is also based on the belief that dramatic play holds great therapeutic potential for disturbed adolescents. Dramatic play is a stage in ego development that follows acting-out behavior. It is the child's method of controlling in fantasy impulses that are difficult to control in reality, of assimilating and mastering reality, of exploring problems and discovering solutions, and of resolving internal conflict (Courtney, 1974)—all relevant issues for the hospitalized adolescent client. Dramatic play provides the distance necessary for the self-observing ego and thus a sense of self-mastery and internal control. Aggressive impulses can be discharged safely and constructively. The aspect of camouflage or disguise inherent in drama facilitates the expression of emotions and the freedom to experiment with new roles and behaviors.

Stage One, in which the therapist is confronted with a great deal of resistance, is the most challenging phase to both therapist and client. The transition to Stage Two begins once the client has become engaged in dramatic activity.

Stage Two

Once the initial resistance is passed, adolescents often become involved in drama surprisingly quickly and eagerly. Because of their recent transition from childhood, dramatic play is still easily accessible. Adolescents are capable of becoming involved with the spontaneity, enthusiasm, and concentration of children, and of deriving great satisfaction and enjoyment. However, as a result of the permissive environment established in Stage One, their "acting" appears to be on their own terms. The behavior that they portray in skits and games duplicates the destructive behavior that they have exhibited in their lives. Although they have now joined the activity, they are actually continuing to test and challenge the leader. Resistance to the structure has been relinquished, but the rebellion persists through the content of their creations. For example, in a pantomime game in which an imaginary object is passed around, a "joint" will inevitably be produced; in an improvisational scene that takes place at a bus stop, drugs and alcohol, pimps and prostitutes preponderate the action. The clients become giggly; their expressions are mischievous. They expect the leader to censor their creations and are quite surprised and disarmed when this does not occur.

Another component of these rebellious roles and behaviors is the fact that by acting "cool" or rebelling in the scene, the teenager is able to both participate in the structured activity and simultaneously win the acceptance of his or her peers. Identity and self-image are crucial issues during adolescence, and the client makes every attempt to gain approval from the group through his or her roles.

There is a third component. As mentioned earlier, resistance can be seen, in part, as a fear of regression to childish behavior; therefore, any type of dramatic activity reminiscent of child's play will be met with defiance. Adolescents apprehend any loss of their newly acquired teenage identity. If the theme and content of the drama are typical, even stereotypical, teenage issues, the client feels less threatened. She is assured a safe distance from child's play and, in fact, remains unaware of the similarity between the current improvisational activity and the dramatic play of childhood.

It is important that the drama therapist accept the client's choice of material. Were censorship to occur, the resistance of Stage One would probably immediately resume. When the clients realize that their scene is being respected rather than condemned, the mischievous glances cease and the clients become engrossed in the dramatic interactions, playing and developing the scene in a serious manner. Acceptance of the content establishes a relationship of collaboration between clients and therapist. The clients are now actors: the therapist director. Both accept the other's input. An unspoken rule forms during this second phase: Just as the clients have the theatrical license to enact scenes of their choice, the therapist has the license to direct scenes as she sees fit. It is here that the skillful drama therapist can make significant therapeutic interventions.

Stage Three

During Stage Two, the drama therapist permits and encourages the clients' spontaneity and involvement in dramatic scenes or games. Stage Three begins when their engagement is stable enough to sustain therapeutic direction without disruption or resistance. A typical scene created by the adolescents during Stage Two takes place at a party or on a street corner, and before long the use of drugs dominates the entire action. The actors appear to be perfectly content to continue this activity, devoid of any plot or character development. Several examples of possible interventions, under the auspices of theatrical direction, follow.

With the objective of instilling an awareness of consequences to given behaviors, the drama therapist may direct "cops" to bust the party or arrest the drug dealers on the street corner. More important than the delight adolescents generally display from the resulting confrontation with authority is the fact that they are obliged to see and to deal with consequences. In accordance with the leader's direction, a shoplifting scene might culminate in arrest; a drunk-driving episode might end in a near-fatal accident; a skit replete with drugs or alcohol might be followed by a portrayal of the characters the next morning experiencing aftereffects such as nausea, apathy, or disorientation. The leader may set up a scene in which the teenager visits a best friend who was a drug abuser in jail or in the hospital, thus reversing the hero image. Through these kinds of enactment, impulsive clients actually experience effects and consequences of their actions. The impact of this experience is much greater than that of passively listening to the explanations and forewarnings of adult authority figures (as to what could happen).

With the objective of encouraging the development of self-awareness and insight, the therapist as director might question precipitating events and motivations. For example, the drama therapist responds to the street corner drug scene with: "That scene looked very realistic. Now tell me, what happened before you came out to this street corner?" The teenager is likely to reply, "Oh, I had a fight with my mom." Or "My dad beat me up." The therapist might then ask, "What made you feel like going here to do drugs?" The teen answers, "To get away from it all." As theatrical director, the therapist can easily play with time and set up the scene that took place with the parents 2 hours earlier. Then he might elicit suggestions from both the client–actors and client-audience of other possible responses to the fight with mom or dad: "going to the street corner to get drugs, as in the last scene, is one possible reaction. How else can John react?" Alternative responses are discussed and improvised. Enactment helps the clients to test out, explore, and practice new ways of coping with their emotions. Insight and potential behavioral change are brought together through the activity.

After an enactment of drug abuse, the drama therapist might instead direct the focus toward the issue of peer pressure. Through improvisation, the clients can become aware of their dependency on peer approval and the self-destructive actions this dependency often engenders. The dramatic task could be phrased in the form of a challenge: "Who thinks that you would be able to turn down drugs no matter how much other kids at the party tried to convince you to take some?" To the majority of teenagers, challenges are irresistible. In fact, it is this author's experience that each person demands a turn to refuse drugs. The sense of challenge is sustained and heightened by the group, who tempts and coaxes the protagonist; tactics commonly progress from seductive to sadistic remarks. The therapist's directions consistently remind and insist: "No matter what they say, remember your dramatic task is to refuse. You've made up your mind to quit drugs and you're going to stick to your decision." The therapist/director might also ask the protagonist to state his or her reasons for abstaining, thereby facilitating the development of a defined stance and sense of conviction. The protagonist's success in assertion is rewarded by applause at the end of the scene. The original "uncool" or "loser" role becomes the winner. Following the enactments, clients are often more able to openly discuss their feelings and anxieties related to peer pressure. The session might culminate in a verbal or dramatic exploration of ways in which group members can support each other in their commitment toward change and growth.

The distance between the self and the role (Landy, 1983) can be increased through the drama therapist's use of time. For example, the drama therapist might direct the client to be 5 years older than his present age. The five-year period provides a safe distance, allowing the role or new behavioral responses to be admissible to the self and accepted by peers.

> Using video equipment, I directed a scene that was to take place at a (make-believe) television studio. Tony, a 16-year-old boy with a history of drug abuse, was asked to play himself at 21 years old: "We're going to interview you on a local TV talk show, because we feel you have much to offer teenagers today. You did a lot of drugs when you were younger, but now you're 21 and you've quit drugs altogether. There are teenagers listening to our program who I'm sure will want to know your story since you've been through many of the problems they're going through now."

In the above example, the adolescent is playing himself in a new way rather than playing the role of an authority figure reproaching drug users.

Therefore, internalization of the resulting message is more likely to occur (for the actor and for the client-audience). More importantly, the future standpoint enables perspective on the present to be achieved.

Whether through the use of time, space, or role, the drama therapist attempts to expand the adolescent's perspectives, present options, and facilitate the examination of situations from a variety of angles. A scene can be temporarily "frozen," while the client-audience offers suggestions, thoughts, and personal reactions. Some scenes might lead to discussion of values, ethical concerns, or decision-making processes. The disturbed adolescents' experience is not yet developed enough for them to be capable of fully encompassing, assessing, and constructively coping with the many conflictual and stressful elements in their lives. Through theatrical directions, the drama therapist illuminates and encourages the exploration of specific relevant issues. She fosters a sense of interconnection, at the same time encouraging the beginning of independent thinking.

Self-awareness, insight, and behavioral change most often occur while the adolescent is playing him or herself. However, role playing parents or other adult authority figures also offers therapeutic benefit. Not only does the client begin to understand the other's point of view, but he gains a reflected view of himself. For the disturbed adolescent, this other perspective most often takes the form of an authority role. Generally, disturbed adolescents portray authority figures as very controlling and sadistic. Physical and verbal abuse are common not only while role playing parents, but also teachers, counselors, policemen. The players seem to enjoy the sense of power and control that these roles allow them to experience. Not surprisingly, a great deal of repressed anger toward the roles (or the actual parents they represent) is released. What is striking, however, is that these roles are extremely short-lived. Before long, the self and the role seem to merge. In the middle of the scene, suddenly the arresting officer decides to buy the confiscated drugs or the school principal lights up a marijuana cigarette in her office. The author offers several possible explanations for this frequent and sudden shifting:

1. The "actor" is reluctant to risk the disapproval of his or her peers by playing the unpopular "bad guy" role for too long.
2. The sudden role-shift is reflective of the "double message" and hypocritical behavior manifested by the parents of many of these clients. Some of the adolescents, for example, are prohibited from drinking or using drugs by parents who are substance abusers. Many are subject to the erratic behavior of emotionally unstable parents. In drama, they replay the disorienting inconsistencies they have witnessed in their adult role-models.

3. Identity is so tenuous during adolescence that the incorporation of a role for any length of time becomes confusing or actually threatening to the ego. The only way for the scene to continue is for the "real self" (or the self-image) to merge with or to replace the character. However, this sudden shifting often is modified over a period of time, providing the drama therapist with one of many indications of the group's progress within Stage Three.

Conclusion

An understanding of the underlying issues in adolescent rebelliousness and resistance to treatment necessarily precedes the therapist's ascertainment of effective responses to opposition and confrontation. Through drama therapy, the adolescent's age-appropriate and healthy rebelliousness can be engaged within the context of the dramatic activity, thereby bypassing or minimizing the resistance to treatment. A power struggle with the therapist is averted by the playful manner in which the drama therapist permits, mobilizes, and creatively channels the client's aggression and rebelliousness. The adolescent is given an opportunity to express and "act-out" his or her feelings, but within the safety and boundaries of the dramatic play. The "acting-out" becomes "acting," which implies and entails self-observation and self-mastery as well as the possibility of discovery and change. The client experiences success at drama rather than at defeating the structure.

The drama therapist's acceptance of the client's choice of material for enactment, however rebellious or self-destructive in nature, fosters a trusting relationship between client and therapist in which the therapist's combined theatrical directions and therapeutic interventions will be respected. Should it become necessary for the therapist to "cut" or "freeze" a scene because the adolescents are losing control, this direction, too, will be adhered to. In a group context, peer interaction and group identity, seen as important to adolescent development, are supported by the leader. Dramatic play, games, and enactments encourage the exploration of shared issues and often relate specifically to conflicts, ambivalences, and difficult developmental tasks that challenge adolescents. Growing cognitive capacities, such as conceptual thinking, reality-testing, and values clarification can be exercised through improvisation. New ways of coping with situations and expressing emotions can be examined and practiced. During a period of instability and uncertain identity, in which the adolescent is constricted by the norm and image imposed by the peer group, drama enables the safe experimentation with new identities. Various aspects of the adolescent's evolving sense of self can be played out and gradually integrated. The sense of confinement and hopelessness disturbed adolescents often feel in their home and hospital situation is alleviated during dramatic play in which the possibilities are innumerable and perspective on one's actual situation can be attained. In general, realistic or real-life situations are selected by adolescents for enactment in an attempt to understand and master their conflicting emotions.

The three stages of resistance and involvement that the author has outlined may progress within a single session or over a period of time. For example, a group may remain in Stage One or Stage Two for several weeks or even months; a higher-functioning group may begin with Stage Three. The identification of stages may be helpful to the drama therapist in determining therapeutic responses and directions.

As hospitalized treatment of adolescents is often brief and client motivation minimal, breaking through the initial resistance is one of the critical tasks facing the therapist. Drama therapy can thus be seen as catalytic and precursory, paving the way for the client to benefit from other areas of the treatment program or other forms of psychotherapy. It can also be the primary treatment of choice for the resistant adolescent.

References

Blos, P. (1962). On adolescence: A psychoanalytic interpretation. Glencoe, IL: The Free Press.

Blos, P. (1979). The adolescent passage. New York: International Universities Press.

Courtney, R. (1974). Play, drama, and thought. London: Cassell.

Dequine, E., & Pearson-Davis, S. (1983). Videotaped improvisational drama with emotionally disturbed adolescents. The Arts in Psychotherapy, 10(1), 15–21.

Emunah, R. (1983). Drama therapy with adult psychiatric patients. The Arts in Psychotherapy, 10(2), 77–84.

Emunah, R. (1990). Expression and expansion in adolescence. The Arts in Psychotherapy, 17(2), 101–107.

Emunah, R. (1994). Acting for real: Drama therapy process, technique, and performance. New York: Brunner/Mazel.

Emunah, R. (1995). From adolescent trauma to adolescent drama. In S. Jennings (Ed.), Dramatherapy with children and adolescents (pp. 150–168). London: Routledge.

Erikson, E. (1968). Identity, youth, and crisis. New York: Norton.

Haley, J. (1973). Uncommon therapy: The psychiatric techniques of Milton H. Erickson, M.D. New York: Norton.

Haley, J. (1980). Leaving home: The therapy of disturbed young people. New York: McGraw-Hill.

Kernberg, O. (1975). Borderline conditions and pathological narcissism. New York: Jason Aronson.

Landy, R. (1983). The use of distancing in drama therapy. The Arts in Psychotherapy, 10(3), 175–185.

LaPlanche, J., & Pontalis, J. (1973). The language of psychoanalysis. New York: Norton.

Maslow, A. (1968). Toward a psychology of being. New York: Van Nostrand.

Minuchin, S. (1974). Families and family therapy. Boston: Harvard University Press.

Piaget, J. (1952). The origins of intelligence in children. New York: International Universities Press.

Rinsley, D. B., & Inge, G. P. (1961). Psychiatric hospital treatment of adolescents: Verbal and nonverbal resistance to treatment. Bulletin of the Menninger Clinic, 25(5), 249–263.

Shuttleworth, R. (1981). Adolescent drama therapy. In R. Courtney & G. Schattner (Eds.), Drama in therapy: Vol. 2. Adults (pp. 157–172). New York: Drama Book Publishers.

Acknowledgment

The author gratefully acknowledges the contribution of George Kitahara Kich, Ph.D.

CHAPTER 7

Healing through Strength
A Group Approach to Therapeutic Enactment

EMILY NASH AND CRAIG HAEN

It is one o'clock in the afternoon. Alex is deep asleep under the covers. For him, there is no distinction between day and night, sunlight and darkness; the darkness prevails no matter what the time of day. Alex is a patient in a residential center for emotionally disturbed adolescents. At 15 years of age, his life is a map of failed connections, broken relationships, and traumatic attachments. The confusion, rage, and sense of hopelessness that pervade Alex's inner world are practically incomprehensible to most young people his age. The usual developmental tasks of adolescence are not something Alex can even begin to attend to as he battles the emotional upheaval of each day. His feelings of isolation are profound, even as he resides within a community of other adolescents who are grappling with the same darkness of a life not being lived. Asleep under the covers, Alex can forget for a while the painful reminders that waking may bring. The last thing that Alex can imagine is an experience that would make him want to face the day.

We enter Alex's room to invite him to a "drama group." This is a group attended by nine other adolescents in the residential center. In this group, the creative experience, specifically drama, is integrated with the group process to help the members access parts of themselves that are buried, forgotten, too painful or too frightening to directly express. It is a place where they can transcend the darkness—where they can find meaningful connections to others and awaken their capacity to play, to imagine, and to have fun. It is a place where feelings of aliveness can be reawakened and feelings of hope can slowly begin to emerge.

Like Alex, many of the children and adolescents we encounter in our group work, whether in New York City schools, residential treatment centers, inpatient psychiatric units, Native American reservations, or traumatized Bosnian communities, seem to reside in darkness. The psychosocial stressors that are a part of their young lives have darkened their sense of connection to others and to the world, rendering them partially asleep to life. This chapter will examine how the introduction of drama therapy in a group context can help to awaken sleeping souls and activate dormant inner lives. Alex's journey on this particular day will be interwoven with theory that examines how the drama therapy practitioner can utilize the group process to begin to heal through strength. Rather than treating symptoms and addressing pathology, this approach focuses instead on the adaptive and functional capacities of the clients. The concept of resilience will serve as a centerpiece as we examine how it can be fostered and brought to life within the group.

The first step to this awakening process is getting Alex out of bed and into the group. He is not the only one who is sleeping. In many beds in the surrounding rooms, his fellow residents are hiding from the day. They will all be extended the same invitation.

"Hello, Alex, we are having a group now in the day room; come and join us." Alex stirs as he hears the leader's voice. Dreams interrupted, he can only feel this voice as another intrusion, another demand, a potential struggle. Alex turns over, barely registering that there is someone even in the room. The leader persists.

"Alex, you did such a great job last week. I know you can do it again. You can just sit and watch—no one is going to ask you to do anything you don't want to do."

Alex buries his head, grunting.

"Alex," the leader says with a lightness of tone, "I don't want to leave this room without you. I can't let you miss this. You can sleep the rest of the day, but for this hour I would like you to get up and come to the group. It's too much fun for you to miss—and besides, if you weren't there, we'd miss you."

Alex's eyes open.

"Maybe next week," he says.

"Maybe next week, too," the leader responds. She notices a book on his side table. "Hey, what are you reading?" she asks.

"Harry Potter," he says, with slightly more energy.

"Which one—the first, the second, the fourth?"

"The fourth."

"Good book?"

"Yeah."

"Great. . . . Come on, let's go to the group."
Alex slowly sits up, and then stands.
"Where are we going?"
"Just to the day room. I'm so glad you got up, Alex. I know it was hard.
Maybe you can help me get some of the others out of bed."

This dance of encouragement and withdrawal is one familiar to group leaders who work with young people, particularly those whose lives are filled with an absence of power and choice. Though it may appear on the surface to be merely an act of protest and defiance, Alex's refusal to get out of bed represents an important struggle for autonomy that the leader must respect. It is her task to engage Alex, to encourage him while also supporting his ability to make his own choice. Alex's initial refusal communicates his avoidance of connection and perhaps a learned suspiciousness of adults. His ability to say "no" is not just a force of resistance, but also a form of empowerment. Saying "no" represents a constructive expression of aggression, as well as an assertion of "appropriate separation needs" (Buccholz & Mishne, 1994, p. 35). Indeed, the ability to say "no" is an essential survival skill that needs to be fostered in children and adolescents (Fox, 1994).

By staying with Alex through these moments, without coercion, the leader communicated acceptance and a sense of trustworthiness. By not manipulating him into attending or resorting to the immediate enforcement of consequences, she avoided recapitulating other past experiences in which his boundaries were overcome or violated. Instead, she chose to join his resistance, meet him on common ground, and remind him of his past success in the group. She communicated the importance of the group and his place in it. In doing so, she provided him with the beginnings of a hope-giving relationship (Rachman, 1975). Her connection with him outside of the session would plant the seed for his further work within the group.

Having picked up a few other residents along the way, they enter the group. Alex seems self-conscious, shows no affect and slouches in his chair. There are strains of conversation as the other members enter.

"Yo, did you have that lunch today? It was disgusting," yells Luis to another member as he enters the space. "It tasted like they took it out of the garbage somewhere."

Delighted that the group has begun with any conversation at all, the leaders recognize this as the group's starting point. Rather than ignoring this initial communication about lunch and rushing to their "plan" for the day, they use it as an opportunity to begin building on commonalities and differences, spontaneously picking up on where the life of the group is, at that very moment.

"Tell me," one leader says, "what was the most disgusting part about it?"
"Oh my God," says Maria, "the fish. I know it was rotten even before they even cooked it."
"What did you think of the fish, Michael?" the other leader inquires.
"It was bad, real bad. But I thought the watery rice was the worst."
"What about you, Alex? Any opinions on the quality of the lunch served today?"
"I didn't eat."
"Anyone else in the group lucky enough to miss this delicious feast?" the leader asks.
Two other members say that they, too, had missed lunch.
"The three of you must be very hungry. How can we feed you in here?" wonders the leader, bringing the group to the here-and-now.
"What we are doing today, anyway?" Paul asks.
"Yeah," agrees Carlos, "You got us out of bed, now you need to wake us up."

Once the members have gathered in the space, it is then the leaders' job to begin "uniting . . . a scattered community, namely a collection of people with similar problems, but who are not yet communicating in a meaningful fashion" (Ormont, 1990, p. 4). Often, when confronting the sleepy eyes of group members who affect poses of boredom, apathy, or disconnection, this can feel like a daunting prospect. However, if the leaders can trust the group—and themselves—a flow will inevitably occur, a current that carries the group toward its own unfolding. The leader channels that current by picking up the conversational/thematic thread and weaving it among the members by building connections between them.

Bridging, as formulated by Ormont (1990), is "any technique designed to strengthen emotional connections between members, or to develop connections where they did not exist before" (p. 4). In this instance, the leader bridged by engaging other group members in offering opinions about the lunch. Alex's response to the question represented his first communication to the group, a sign that a connection was being made.

"Now you need to wake us up" was a perfect signal to the leaders that the group was ready to warm up and to begin its creative journey. As such, a group often informs its leaders where it needs to go and when it is ready to move to another stage of development.

"What do you think, Alex, should we wake up some more?" one leader asks.
Alex smiles. He identifies with his fellow sleepers and is beginning to join in the flow.

"Why doesn't everybody just stretch from your chairs, reach your arms up, keep your feet firm on the ground, and rise from your seats. Breathe while you stretch some more. Good. Now, reach over to someone in the group and warm up your voices by saying hello."

Spontaneously, a few people create their own movements, which the leader encourages the rest of the group to mirror. Bridging now begins to happen non-verbally through an exchange of movement and a sharing of energy.

The leaders put on some Latin music and ask each person to create a movement to the music that the group will mirror. In turn, the group members will pass their movement to a peer who is invited to share it and then change it into his or her own. There is an almost instant transformation as bodies discover new ways of moving in space, as the rhythms in the music invite new rhythms in people who have put to sleep the abundant life that waits inside them. There is clapping. There is connection. There is much laughter. Group members are remembering, through their bodies, what it feels like to be alive.

When it is Alex's turn, he courageously moves his arms and hips in response to his partner, and is then encouraged to find his own movement. He spontaneously begins to snap his fingers and stamp his feet, bringing the whole group into the likes of a percussive ensemble.

"This is cool, Alex," a member remarks.

"You sure do have a lot of life in you," one leader says, affirming Alex's participation. Alex seems visibly pleased.

"Didn't know you had it in you, did you?" she continues.

"I forgot," he responds.

A warm-up reconnects us to our physical selves. Energies that have been frozen, rigidified, and turned inward begin to come to life again. In this moment, sleep seems to be forgotten, illness abandoned, and darkness lifted. The group is engaged in what Ormont (1996) refers to as immediacy, which "manifests itself as charged engagement between the members" (p. 212). A group is immediate "when members experience a rush of feelings and find themselves free enough to express them" (Ormont, 1996, p. 211). The therapeutic value of this immediacy lies in the members' ongoing engagement with one another in the here-and-now.

In this session, the warm-up utilized mirroring as a form of validation and attunement. For clients who have not experienced adequate and timely provision of needs early in life, this initial emphasis on the group's ability to hold its members can be a crucial building block in the session's developmental course. Likewise, verbal recognition from the leader of "new" steps taken, emerging strengths, and expression of novel ideas is very important.

The validation of hidden capacities coming to life is ego-strengthening and provides encouragement for further exploration and risk taking.

The leaders' ability to maintain immediacy, validation, and attunement throughout the session helps to insure the success of the group, creating what Winnicott (1965) referred to as potential space. This space harbors the safety that the group members need in order to continue their process. Grotowski (as cited in Wangh, 2000) wrote about the importance of potential space in actor training, but his words could easily apply to a therapy session:

> The essential problem is to give the actor the possibility of working 'in safety.' The work of the actor is in danger, continuously supervised and observed. One must create an atmosphere, a working system, in which the actor feels that he can do anything, and that nothing he does will be mocked, that all will be understood. . . . Often, the moment that the actor understands this, he reveals himself. (p. 8)

"That felt like a party," remarks George when the group is sitting back in the circle.

"Anyone else have that experience?" asks the leader. A few others concur.

"What comes to mind when you think of parties?" the leader asks, thinking this might be an interesting theme to explore with the group.

"I think about how I never got a birthday party," George responds. A few "me toos" can be heard around the room.

"That's terrible," responds the leader, "to not have your birthday celebrated."

"I imagine other people in here understand what that's like," says the second leader, engaging the group. "I wonder what other things in your lives should have been celebrated but weren't."

Here, the leaders sensed an opportunity to give attention to what had been experienced as an omission in the development of the members and in the connections they needed at an early age in order to grow. The leaders would become very interested in their stories and look for ways to create dramatic scenes that would allow the group to provide the necessary "supportive response" (Herman, 1997), or corrective experience. This facilitation of symbolic experience is often considered a prime treatment goal with developmentally arrested clients (Newirth, 1996).

In adolescent drama therapy groups, scenes often revolve around the theme of family. In fact, in one survey, adolescent group members cited family reenactment as one of the most helpful of Yalom's 12 curative factors in groups (Scheidlinger, 1985). The metaphors that adolescents employ in their work are usually thinly veiled allusions to their own lived experience (Emunah, 1995). However, a corrective scene need not be a direct reenactment of the past. It can employ varied layers of metaphor, as well. The depth of the metaphor often correlates with the amount of distance the client needs in order to work (Landy, 1994). In a group with younger boys, the children pretended to be cars coming to the mechanic for remedy of their broken engines. In another group, the members frequently accessed super-human powers and immortality through their character choices (Haen & Brannon, 2002).

In turn, group members begin to cite moments in their lives where they either missed out on a chance for celebration or had a meaningful achievement or anniversary that was never celebrated. As they talk, it becomes obvious that for each young person there was a hole that wasn't filled. Their stories represent a lifetime of unmet needs, developmental lags, and maturational deficits. The sum total speaks volumes of ruptured family relationships, chaotic lives, buried hurts, and lost opportunities. There are stories of turning points and rites of passage never recognized or only imagined: stories of birthdays that came and went, of graduations that just passed by, of weddings not held, of sobriety never applauded. Alex is one of two members who remains silent.

Maria, who is often a strong presence in the group, is chosen by her peers to enact her ideal 15th birthday party. Though Alex is not cast in her scene, he watches closely and his hunger to act is nearly palpable.

As the group members shared their common experiences of not being seen and heard at crucial moments in their lives, they were entering into a deeper awakening of memories, feelings, wishes, and empathic connections. They were recognizing and beginning to grieve the losses of the important rituals human beings need to mark their growth and accomplishments, and to fulfill their basic desire for appreciation, recognition, and understanding. By bearing witness to Maria's experience in the group, Alex begins to feel his own maturational deficit more fully and is able to benefit from seeing a peer validated by the group (Casson, 1997).

As Maria's scene ends, Alex is listening intensely. Asked by one leader what his connection is to her enactment, he responds, "I really understand."

"In what way do you understand?" the leader asks.

"Well, that can hurt, man. You feel so alone. Like you don't matter to anyone."

"What about you, Alex?" inquires the leader. "What comes to your mind around this theme—moments in our lives not celebrated?"

"Oh, man," begins Alex. "What happened to me was that at my junior high graduation, when I made my graduation speech, my parents—who

were there—didn't really hear what I was saying in my speech. They didn't get it—they didn't really hear it. They didn't get how much I hated going to that school. How hard it was, how hard it was for me to stay there and finish it. They had no idea." Alex relates this with real feeling, and one gets the sense of an almost desperate need to reach these unreachable figures in his life. His peers seem surprised at his sudden and passionate involvement.

The leaders seized upon this opportunity for Alex to have a different experience, one that would hopefully be reparative and function as a maturational response. Here, Alex could write a new story. Even if the facts of Alex's story are not exactly accurate, it is the emotional memory—his internal experience of the events—that is important. It is Alex's inner story that needs understanding.

The group connected with the feeling memory and was called upon to provide the restorative bonds he needed to heal the wounds. In this work, theater itself becomes the bridge, connecting the here-and-now to the past and traversing different aspects of the self (Nash, 1996). Inviting Alex to develop his story, the leaders recognized that it could function as a metaphor for the stories other members shared. In group, one person's work can be healing for the other members and provide them with heightened awareness of their own issues. Alex's journey is the whole group's journey.

It was time to begin to build the drama.

"What did you want to happen?" the leader asks Alex.

In response, Alex says, "For them to really hear me—to understand what I went through."

"Well, maybe we could create a scene right here in the group where that can happen. What do you think?"

"How do you mean?"

"How do I mean?" the leader asks, consulting the group. "How might we explore Alex's story?"

"We could have his graduation day and his parents are there, only this time they treat him different," suggests Luis.

"Yeah, he could give his speech and then maybe have a scene with his father and then a scene with his mother," offers Christy.

"Then a scene with both of them. To make sure they really understand him," asserts Paul.

"What do you think, Alex, are we on the right track?" asks the other leader, checking in with him.

"Yeah, I like this. It's cool."

"What else would you want to include?"

"A principal, I guess." He laughs. "A mean principal."

"Great idea, Alex," an until-now-silent Jesse tells him. "Those guys are always wanksters."

"Good, Jesse. These are wonderful ideas," the leader says. "Anything we've left out?"

"We need students, and maybe some teachers," says Luis, with enthusiasm.

"Okay with you, Alex? Some teachers?"

"Yeah. A science teacher. My science teacher was the only one who really cared."

"A science teacher it is, then."

The group was now involved in a collective process of helping Alex to develop his experience into a role play that would tell the story in the way Alex wanted it told. In doing so, they were shaping the group into a maturational agent, "a cohesive entity that ministers to the various developmental gaps of the members" (Ormont, 1997, p. 73). His peers were invited to come aboard his journey. They were actively engaged in vital creative interaction and the forming of new relationships. This aspect of the process, including every member of the group in the building of the drama, fosters a cohesion and cooperation that promotes growth and a sustained interest in staying awake. The leaders function primarily as facilitators, asking for ideas, bridging members, exploring possibilities and providing the structure in which they can tell their stories.

"Okay," one leader says. "Let's start to put this all together so we can get it on its feet. Alex, who in the group would you want to play your parents?"

Alex chooses Christy, a compassionate 18-year-old who is nearing discharge after several years at the facility, to play his mother. He asks one of the group leaders to play his father. The other roles are cast from among the remaining group members, with the role of the science teacher being given to a compassionate, mature intern who is sitting in on the session. Each role seems to reflect an aspect of the person chosen to play it.

The more the group members are engaged in making decisions about the structure of the drama, the more the actual playing of it will flow. Giving definition to the characters, their relationships to each other, and the sequence and content of the scenes, allows the players to move freely through the world of the story. It is very important to ask group members to cast their own stories. They will unconsciously choose the right people to meet their maturational needs. These unconscious connections between group members are often referred to as "tele" (Moreno, 1940/1987). In choosing the people who will give them the right feelings, group members have the opportunity to shift repetitive patterns, patterns that keep returning them to relationships of deprivation and hurt. The corrective emotional responses enable new relationships to form that can contribute to the rebuilding of a sense of self (Herman, 1997). Alex's casting choices for the parents reflected his need for mature, healthy objects with whom he could feel safe.

A key aspect of this process involves accessing the strengths of the members so that their collective functional selves will meet Alex's deficit. Alex called upon the resilience of the group, the part of their spirit that survives and flourishes in the face of adversity. While children in a residential facility might not typically be thought of as resilient, most clinicians who work with them learn to appreciate their strong capacity for perseverance. Research suggests that one can be resilient in certain functional domains despite dysfunction in other areas (Klimes-Dougan & Kendziora, 2000). Therapists who are resilience-focused seek to bolster the number of protective factors available to the child. These factors, which include relationships, initiative, insight, coherence, and meaning (Shakoor & Fister, 2000), are easily accessed in the drama therapy group process.

"So," asks the leader who is facilitating the enactment, "How should we begin? What should be our first scene?"

"Have the principal introduce the graduation," suggests Jesse.

"And the second scene?"

The group works together on structuring the order of scenes. They begin to reorganize the room. Players who are in scenes together sit near each other and determine how they want to use the space.

The play has been cast. The characters are in their places. Alex has strategically placed his "parents" on one side of the room and the principal on the other; in between are students. He is visibly enjoying his role as a star player around whom all this activity is taking place. There is almost a sense of disbelief in his voice as he says quietly, "God, I was sleeping an hour ago."

At this point, the group members were now functioning as a working ensemble—a "company of players" jointly involved in a creative effort. They were accessing what Brooks and Goldstein (2001) have so aptly termed "islands of competency" amid "oceans of inadequacy." Together, they were taking risks and experiencing sustained engagement as they prepared to step into the unknown. This collaborative planning of scene work fosters creative competence, a skill that is characteristic of resilient children. Anthony (1987) defines the concept in this way:

In creative competence, the individual is no longer limited by the situation or the methods at hand. He can extend the dimensions of the task and invent means to carry the work further into the realm of exploration. He can move from the practical to the abstract and solve the problems "inside his head.". . . . creative competence may take flight from reality and investigate, in novel ways, the less tangible but no less important facets of a problem. (p. 149)

All that was needed before the action started was to give the characters their personality traits, so as to aid the members in embodying their roles as fully and deeply as possible. Here again, the group was enlisted in the character development.

The leader asks the group members to collaborate on detailing the physical and emotional characteristics of each role being played. The leaders ask Alex to be the one to assign qualities to the mother and father so that the "actors" playing these roles know what it is he needs from them.
"Alex, what are three characteristics of the mother?"
"The father?"
"Carlos, how do you see the principal?"
"Paul, what about the science teacher?"
All of the members contribute suggestions for the characters in the scene, including names for them.

The facilitators were most focused on the connections that were being solidified through this process. They were interested in each person having a voice in the collaboration—in evoking opinions, differences, and similarities in aesthetic choices; in members making identifications with one another; in the group finding its own momentum in moving the action forward. They wanted these young people to redirect self-destructive energies into constructive form—to transform feelings of powerlessness and confusion into experiences of being effective with their peers and respected by their community. As Jenkyns (1996) wrote, "The goal of therapy is ultimately to enable an individual or a group to move on into new life, widely speaking; to be 'en-roled' into a fuller existence where more choice is possible" (p. 14). In drama therapy, the aesthetic elements can fuel the group process; the creative can enrich the therapeutic.

The play begins. The principal makes his speech. There is laughter as Jesse, who is often withdrawn in the group, transforms into a wormy, stuttering, inarticulate principal who nevertheless makes a long and meaningless speech.

"Yo, J, you are funny," a member calls out.

The intern chosen to be the science teacher speaks of Alex as a special person with great intelligence and many talents. In his speech, he sensitively acknowledges Alex's endurance through challenging times and voices admiration for his perseverance. In a poignant interaction between him and Alex, Alex thanks the teacher for his work and, most importantly, "for being there when I really needed somebody." Mr. Florio, the teacher, tells him that it was his pleasure and that he is still there for him should he need someone to talk to.

It is now time for Alex's speech. He takes a deep breath, looks directly at his parents, and begins to speak. "Getting to this point has been long and hard. Very hard. Being in this school has been very difficult for me. I don't think you know how difficult. Much of the time I was scared, and a lot of the time I spent wishing I wasn't here. And I worked hard, Mom and Dad, really hard."

His voice starts to quiver. "I worked so hard for these Ds and Cs." He begins to cry and continues to speak at the same time. "This was a very, very difficult experience for me. I almost didn't make it. I never wanted to be here. You pushed me and pushed me and forced me to be here. So I stayed. And, here I am. But I want you to hear me, and know what I went through." He is filled with emotion. The leader quietly motions to the mother and father that it is now time to have their moments with him—first his father, then his mother.

Each, in turn, acknowledges his feelings. They acknowledge their sorrow for his pain, their grave misunderstanding of his situation.

The leader stands beside Alex. "What do you want from your Dad?"

"I want him to be a Dad, to listen to me. To believe me."

She asks the father what his response to this is, and how he is feeling toward his son.

"I'm feeling a lot of love and also sadness. . . . I am also feeling very proud of him. I want to be there for him more."

"Tell him," suggests the leader.

He does so, and Alex gives him a hug.

"What is the hug saying?"

"That I feel close to him."

"Great. Tell him that."

By asking the "characters" what they feel toward each other, and by asking them what they think the other feels or needs, the group leader is giving the person playing the role the experience of connecting with others in an emotionally meaningful way. A role becomes a safe container for feelings that might be too frightening or overwhelming to express more directly.

The continued expression of affect is central to the life of the group. It is not enough to simply have emotions. Instead, the individual needs to put these feelings into words. As Ormont (1990) asserts, "... where there is talk, there is life" (p. 4).

The leader then moves to the mother, asking her what she would like to say to her son. His mother tells him that she is very upset—that she had no idea how hard things were.

"That's the problem, Mom," Alex says, more angrily. "You had no idea. Why not? I need you to know what's going on with me."

"Word!" affirms one of the group members who is watching the scene, indicating his own connection to the story.

"You are right, son. I have to pay a lot more attention. A whole lot more."

The leader asks the mother, "What do you think your son needs?"

"He needs me to spend more time talking to him and listening to him."

"Is that true?" the leader asks Alex.

"Yes."

"Talk to him about that."

"I don't think I have spent enough time with you just talking, and I know I haven't been listening enough. I want to plan ways of spending more time together."

"How do you feel about that, Alex?"

"Great," he replies. "It's what I wanted. . . . Want."

"Let her know."

The scene continues with the leader making sure that Alex has said everything to his parents he wants to tell them. He lets her know when he has.

As Jenkyns (1996) observed, it is in the drama where the therapy resides—where the magic happens. "It is that moment of perfect tension between two realities in a moment of absolute sincerity and absorption" (p. 19) in which the group members experience a shift. As Alex heard the teacher list his strengths, he was granted the opportunity to experience himself in a new way. As he opened up and became more vulnerable, he allowed his connection with the group to begin to fill in the residing emptiness. The group could serve as an actualized support system, a key factor in the development of resilience (Klimes-Dougan & Kendziora, 2000).

Likewise, many of the roles that his fellow group members played called upon their strengths. As the principal, Jesse showed the parts of himself that were comedic. Christy's role required her empathy and maternal instincts. A role played in group lays the foundation for a role played in life, expanding and solidifying the possibilities of who the group members can be, shining lights into dark corners of the psyche (Haen, in press; Nash, 1996).

The group applauds, spontaneously offering their feedback,
"Wow, that was great, Alex."
"Dope."
"So real. I totally believed it was happening."
"I wish my parents could have heard that stuff."
"What was it like for you, Alex?" the leader who played his father in-
quires.
"It was really great. Like something that was stuck for a long, long time
(he puts his hand over his heart) has gotten out. It feels so good. Really. Oh
my God, if you had let me sleep, this never would have happened."

The group at this moment was very much a community. Many, if not all, of the group members were experiencing what it feels like to be truly connected and fully awake. These 10 adolescents, whose life circumstances forced them into the darkness, found their way to a temporary healing place where, in Edward Young's (1861) words, "dormant matter waits a call to life" (p. 142). Furthermore, their experience reminded the leaders of the truism that even in the darkness, there are dreams.

The group is about to end. They leave the dramatic space and return to
the circle. The leaders praise their efforts, particularly their ability to work
together. They ask them to concretize the symbolic by identifying a feeling,
word, or phrase to capture the experience they had this day—to name it
and carry it with them.
In turn, they speak:
"Being born."
"Love."
"Opening up."
"Sharing my heart."
"Proud."
"What a surprise."
"Being alive."
"Joy."
"Connection."
"Waking from a dream."

References

Anthony, E. J. (1987). Children at high risk for psychosis growing up successfully. In E. J. Anthony & B. J. Cohler (Eds.), *The invulnerable child* (pp. 147–184). New York: Guilford.
Brooks, R., & Goldstein, S. (2001). *Raising resilient children: Fostering strength, hope, and optimism in your child.* New York: McGraw-Hill/Contemporary Books.

Buccholz, E., & Mishne, J. (1994). Principles of group practice. In E. S. Buccholz & J. M. Mishne (Eds.), *Group interventions with children, adolescents, and parents: An ego and self psychological approach* (pp. 19–48). Northvale, NJ: Jason Aronson.

Casson, J. (1997). The therapeusis of the audience. In S. Jennings (Ed.), *Dramatherapy: Theory and practice 3* (pp. 43–54). London: Routledge.

Emunah, R. (1995). From adolescent trauma to adolescent drama: Group drama therapy with emotionally disturbed youth. In S. Jennings (Ed.), *Dramatherapy with children and adolescents* (pp. 150–168). London: Routledge.

Fox, L. (1994). The catastrophe of compliance. *Journal of Child and Youth Care, 9*(1), 13–21.

Haen, C. (in press). Rebuilding security: Group therapy with children affected by September 11th. *International Journal of Group Psychotherapy.*

Haen, C., & Brannon, K. H. (2002). Superheroes, monsters and babies: Roles of strength, destruction and vulnerability for emotionally disturbed boys. *The Arts in Psychotherapy, 29*(1), 31–40.

Herman, J. (1997). *Trauma and recovery: The aftermath of violence—from domestic abuse to political terror* (2nd ed.). New York: Basic Books.

Jenkyns, M. (1996). *The play's the thing: Exploring text in drama and therapy.* London: Routledge.

Klimes-Dougan, B., & Kendziora, K. T. (2000). Resilience in children. In C. E. Bailey (Ed.), *Children in therapy: Using the family as a resource* (pp. 407–427). New York: W. W. Norton.

Landy, R. J. (1994). *Drama therapy: Concepts, theories and practices* (2nd ed.). Springfield, IL: Charles C. Thomas.

Moreno, J. L. (1987). Spontaneity and catharsis. In J. Fox (Ed.), *The essential Moreno: Writings on psychodrama, group method, and spontaneity* (pp. 39–59). New York: Springer. (Original work published 1940)

Nash, E. (1996). Therapeutic use of theater with adolescents. In P. Kymissis & D. A. Halperin (Eds.), *Group therapy with children and adolescents* (pp. 189–215). Washington, DC: American Psychiatric Press.

Newirth, J. (1996). On not interpreting: The metaphor of the baby, enactment, and transitional experience. *The American Journal of Psychoanalysis, 56*(4), 415–429.

Ormont, L. R. (1990). The craft of bridging. *International Journal of Group Psychotherapy, 40*(1), 3–17.

Ormont, L. R. (1996). Bringing life into the group experience: The power of immediacy. *Group, 20*(3), 207–221.

Ormont, L. R. (1997). Bridging in group analysis. *Modern Psychoanalysis, 22*(1), 59–77.

Rachman, A. W. (1975). *Identity group psychotherapy with adolescents.* Springfield, IL: Charles C. Thomas.

Scheidlinger, S. (1985). Group treatment of adolescents: An overview. *American Journal of Orthopsychiatry, 55*(1), 102–111.

Shakoor, M., & Fister, D. L. (2000). Finding hope in Bosnia: Fostering resilience through group process intervention. *Journal for Specialists in Group Work, 25*(3), 269–287.

Wangh, S. (2000). *An acrobat of the heart: A physical approach to acting.* New York: Vintage Books.

Winnicott, D. W. (1965). *The maturational processes and the facilitating environment: Studies in the theory of emotional development.* New York: International Universities Press.

Young, E. (1861). *Young's night thoughts.* Edinburgh, Scotland: Ballantyne & Co.

CHAPTER 8

Drama Therapy in the Treatment of Children with Sexual Behavior Problems

LORETTA GALLO-LOPEZ

The dramatic imagination is crucial for survival, as without it we would not be able to imagine how things might be or how they could be, or indeed we would not be able to hypothesize.
—Sue Jennings (1993)

Introduction

Childhood is a time of growth and almost daily transformation. Likes and dislikes continually shift. Fears develop and subside. Behaviors change and personalities develop. Resilience and the capacity for change are two of the strengths of childhood and are what make this time period one of eternal hope. Perhaps this is why children in therapy seem to progress and heal more rapidly than adults. Their sense of self is beginning to emerge, as is their awareness of the roles they play in relation to the world around them. And they can imagine "how things could be."

Just as children differ greatly from adults, children with sexual behavior problems differ greatly from adults with sexual behavior problems. Unfortunately, however, much of the treatment available to children with sexual behavior problems has been modeled after traditional adult sexual offender treatment. The accepted approach to adult treatment is typically long-term, spanning anywhere from 2 to 5 years. Adult treatment usually follows a cognitive behavioral model and focuses on issues such as offense cycles and relapse prevention. Treatment is often punitive in nature, as clinicians both treat and monitor the offending behavior. Community notification pro-grams and social stigma are seen as natural consequences of the deviant behavior choices of adult sexual offenders.

Longo (2002) describes a "trickle down effect" in sex offender treatment, asserting that adult treatment protocols have been adapted for use with children and adolescents without considering their unique developmental needs. Likewise, assigning adult labels such as sexual abuser, sexual offender, perpetrator, or sexual predator to children with sexual behavior problems hinders the healing process of these children, leaving them stuck in a dys-functional, socially disdained role. Pithers and Gray (1998) caution that "labeling these children in a manner that even remotely implies that they may have lifelong problems with sexual assaultiveness (e.g., child sexual offender) and that denies their potential to make amazing contributions to the social good is simply wrong and should never be done" (p. 214). Treat-ment providers must always be mindful of the fact that children are contin-ually developing: morally, socially, emotionally, and intellectually. Clearly, programs that endeavor to treat young children must consider the develop-mental needs of the child from each of these perspectives. Programs must be administered in a manner that offers respect and fosters healing, avoiding a judgmental or punitive stance. The focus must be on wellness rather than pathology, identifying strengths, and empowering children to achieve posi-tive change.

The program outlined in this chapter relies on drama therapy as the pri-mary treatment modality. It seeks to identify and build on each child's indi-vidual strengths, utilizing the natural processes of childhood to work toward healing and transformation. Drama therapy seems to be a logical choice for the work that needs to be done with these children. Gil and Johnson (1993), in their groundbreaking book *Sexualized Children*, suggest that role play is the most effective way for children to learn to empathize and to appreciate the perspective of another. Dramatic enactment provides children an op-portunity to safely express inner pain and conflict (Emunah, 1995). Through role play, children are given the opportunity to move beyond their histories as they expand their role repertoires (Landy, 1994, 1996, 2001), visualize options, search for answers, and experiment with solutions. Drama therapy offers children a glimpse inside, a way to give voice to their feelings and to move toward understanding and empathy (Cattanach, 1994; Gallo-Lopez, 2000; Longo & Longo, 2003) for themselves and others.

Sexual Behavior Problems in Children

Determining the scope of the problem of sexually inappropriate behaviors in children under twelve is a difficult task because many states do not have mandatory reporting laws in cases of child-on-child sexual abuse. Cases involving sibling abuse or abuse by other family members often go unreported without outside intervention. Pithers and Gray (1998) reported the results of an examination of substantiated cases of child sexual abuse in various states and concluded that 6- to 12-year-olds were responsible for 13% to 18% of all substantiated child sexual abuse. Their data also revealed that 70.6% of these children had been sexually victimized prior to the start of their sexual behavior problem. Pithers and Gray (1998) also found that sexually abused children were 4.7 times more likely to be arrested for a sex crime as an adult than were nonabused children. Interestingly, they also reported that adults physically abused as children were 4.1 times more likely to be arrested for a sex crime and 7.6 times more likely to be arrested for rape or sodomy than adults who were not abused as children. As a result, Pithers and Gray suggest that "the etiologically significant factor in the emergence of abusive sexuality is exposure to trauma, not a unique associate of sexual victimization" (p. 206). Their data overwhelmingly support the need for early intervention and for treatment services for child victims of all types of child maltreatment.

Recognizing the connection between a history of childhood trauma and the development of problematic sexual behaviors does not, however, give us the full picture regarding the origin of such behaviors. As not all victims of child maltreatment engage in sexually abusive behaviors, other factors obviously play a role in fostering these behaviors. Rasmussen, Burton, and Christopherson (1992) identify the "trauma outcome process," which distinguishes between three different responses to trauma. The "healthy coping" response is seen in children who are able to process trauma-related feelings and concerns and achieve a sense of resolution. The "self-victimizing" response can be observed in children who internalize their trauma response and may engage in self-injurious or destructive behaviors. Finally, children who present with an "assaultive" response to trauma may identify with their aggressor, externalizing their response via abusive behavior toward someone more vulnerable. Rasmussen et al. explain that children may exhibit more than one type of trauma response or different responses at different times.

Pithers and Gray (1998), in seeking to identify other elements influencing the development of sexually assaultive behaviors in children, look to familial factors. They suggest that stressors such as high rates of poverty, family violence, intrafamilial sexual abuse, and parent criminal behavior all contribute to the development of sexual behavior problems in children. They further suggest that deficits in the parent–child relationship, specifically a parent's lack of attachment to their child and lack of pleasure in parenting, create a family environment that impedes a child's ability to resolve trauma issues, thereby negatively influencing the child's trauma response. Such information supports an approach to treating childhood trauma that incorporates parent and family treatment with a specific focus on repairing and strengthening the parent–child relationship.

In providing treatment to children with sexual behavior problems, the first question to be addressed is, "When is sexual behavior a problem?" Many infants engage in genital self-stimulation, most having discovered the pleasures of such behaviors themselves. Toddlers often masturbate as a form of self-soothing prior to nap or bedtime, serving the same purpose as thumb sucking or hair twirling. Children have been engaging in mutual exploration play (in other words, "you show me yours and I'll show you mine") probably throughout time. Such behavior, though usually normal and age appropriate, has been known to horrify many parents and daycare workers who fear a possible abuse connection.

Problematic Sexual Behaviors

Sexual behavior in children is generally thought to be problematic under the following circumstances:

1. When the sexual behavior involves threats, force, coercion, bribery, or manipulation
2. When the sexual behavior involves sexual activity between children with an age difference of 3 years or more and/or an imbalance of power
3. When the sexual behavior inflicts pain on self or other(s)
4. When the child does not respond to redirection or consequences
5. When the sexual behavior is obsessive or compulsive in nature
6. When the sexual behavior involves animals
7. When the behavior is indicative of sexual knowledge/experience that is advanced for the child's age

A Drama Therapy Approach to Treating Children with Sexual Behavior Problems

For the purposes of this chapter, the term "children with sexual behavior problems" refers to children ages 5 through 12 who have engaged in sexually abusive behaviors toward another child. In terms of the trauma outcome process, the response of these children has been externalized in the form of assaultive behavior toward another. It should be noted, however, that the approach presented here has been utilized successfully with children whose sexual behaviors are self-focused, as well as with developmentally disabled adolescents and young adults.

The drama therapy treatment protocol endeavors to merge an abuse-specific approach that directly addresses inappropriate sexual behaviors with a focus on healing the child's sense of self. In dealing with inappropriate behaviors, the drama therapy model identifies and reinforces the expected and appropriate behaviors rather than solely pointing out the behaviors to be avoided. The goal is to heal the whole child, not to single out the problematic sexual behaviors to be treated. Structure, predictability, and physical and emotional safety are provided and are balanced with the level of freedom necessary to encourage exploration and experimentation. Just as each child is unique, with individual strengths, wishes, fears, and concerns, the treatment approach should be tailored to meet the individual needs of the child. Interventions should be purposeful and carefully chosen.

Assessing Treatment Needs

A thorough assessment should be conducted before a child is placed in treatment, in order to provide effective treatment planning. Friedrich's (1997) Child Sexual Behavior Inventory (CSBI) is a standard assessment tool for use with children with sexual behavior problems. The CSBI is a 38-item measure that assesses a wide range of sexual behaviors via parent report (preferably mother or primary female caregiver). The CSBI provides information that can help to evaluate a child's risk to other children. An initial assessment should also include information related to child and family history (including history of abuse and issues related to family views about sexuality), as well as information related to the child's academic functioning, use of psychotropic medications, family functioning, child and family strengths, and parent–child relationships. Though much of this information can be obtained via clinical interviews, the parent–child relationship must be assessed through direct observation. Strategies for gathering information related to family roles and relationships include shared drawing activities and family sand tray work (Gil, 1994). Family puppet stories (Irwin, 2000; Irwin & Malloy, 1975), either with assigned or improvised themes, provide the clinician with a wealth of information about how the family interacts, problem solves, and communicates.

As part of the child's individual assessment, the Cave Drawing (Tanaka, Kakuyama, & Urhausen, 2003) is a powerful technique that can provide insight about the child's inner world. The cave, which is symbolized by a large oval drawn on a sheet of paper, provides the metaphor of a safe place. The therapist draws, or asks the child to draw, a large oval and then informs the child that the oval is the entrance to a cave. The child is asked to draw the outside world viewed from inside the cave. Sara, a 9-year-old, was referred following sexually abusive behavior toward a 5-year-old in her foster home. When asked to draw her view from inside the cave, Sara drew her dream house, a huge castle surrounded by fruit trees, flowers, grass, birds, and friendly animals. She told a story about this dream environment that offered life, protection, and a place to belong. Using doll figures and props, she created the environment and enacted her story. As a child who had suffered abandonment by both of her parents and had been moved from one foster home to another, her need for safety and belonging was apparent in her fantasy world.

The Role of the Therapist

What therapists must bring to this work, in addition to training in drama therapy and in issues related to sexual abuse and child sexual behavior problems, is sensitivity, flexibility, humor, and creativity. A level of comfort with the techniques and strategies to be employed is equally important. Cattanach (1994) describes the role of the therapist as that of facilitator of children's explorations who helps them to "develop their internal model of the outside world and a clear sense of their identity in that world" (p. 56). Although the therapist is always an observer of the child's play, she may alternately, take on the role of participant, assistant, or audience in the drama.

Whenever a therapist steps into a role in a drama with young children, it is often necessary for her to continually advise the child as to her status of being in or out of role. For young children, the lines between reality and fantasy, between "me" and "not me," can be easily obscured and confused. This ambiguity is often heightened in children who have been sexually abused, as perpetrators may utilize a distorted version of pretend play to gain the trust and compliance of their young victims. The therapist's first task is to work toward establishing a strong therapeutic relationship based on trust and respect. This relationship, which is the foundation of the work to come, is more important to the outcome of therapy then any set of techniques or therapy tools. Emphasis must be placed on the importance of establishing and maintaining boundaries in order to help children to express their feelings without becoming flooded and overwhelmed by them. These boundaries are physical on one level with regard to the arrangement of the space and the physical space between therapist and child. Many children with abuse histories do not have a sense of their own personal space, as their boundaries have been violated and exploited. Likewise, children with sexual behavior problems have, by the nature of their behavior, violated the boundaries of another. Identifying the level of physical closeness that is appropriate and comfortable for each child is an important step in establishing boundaries and personal space. The child can be asked to create a safety circle around herself using cardboard blocks, stones, beads, marbles, or other objects. The circle represents the amount of physical space that is necessary and the level of closeness that is acceptable. On another level, the boundaries are emotional and are established via the dynamics of the relationship between the therapist and child. The physical and emotional boundaries established within the therapy environment are a model for the child to apply to the outside world, as well.

The Therapy Space

Cattanach (1994) describes the play space as "a physical space, and also the psychic space which develops between child and therapist" (p. 70). Although a play room is a wonderful luxury for doing drama therapy work, it is something that not everyone has access to, and is by no means a necessity. In the absence of a dedicated space, a play space can be defined within an office, group room, or other available space. A requirement is that the space be private, allowing children to explore and experiment without fear that someone might be listening at the door or without the therapist having to censor the level of voices. Furniture can be arranged to inspire, rather than hinder, the flow of the play. Pillows, a sofa, or even an area rug can be used to establish the boundaries of the play space, providing a sense of order, containment, and safety.

Props, toys, and other play materials serve to enhance fantasy play, role development, and thematic play. They promote mastery and self expression, and are ready vehicles for projection. They are a welcoming element and provide a sense of comfort and familiarity for children. Therapists should be careful to include in their collections only toys and equipment with which they are comfortable, in order to avoid censoring the play. Toys and props that give permission for aggressive play, such as toy soldiers and swords, should be included. Props such as flashlights, sunglasses, telephones, and keys, as well as fabric in various sizes, colors and textures, encourage character development and enactment. A toy microphone is useful for role plays that involve character interviews, news reporting, or TV talk shows. As noted previously, cardboard blocks can be used to establish boundaries or to delineate space. A large dry erase board provides a place to draw environmental elements such as trees and houses. Two dollhouses, along with several sets of family figures, allow for the exploration of family issues in more then one environment. This is especially relevant for children from divorced families or children in foster care. Figures and toys for use in or out of the sand tray should include environment pieces such as trees, fences, and bridges, as well as animals and vehicles. Figures that symbolize specific themes such as good versus evil, danger and protection, nurturing, power, birth and death are very important. Puppets and masks, as well as a variety of art materials, are also helpful additions to the drama therapy space.

Drama Therapy for Children with Sexual Behavior Problems

Some young children are easily over-stimulated in a group setting and, at least initially, would reap greater benefit from involvement in individual treatment. A highly effective alternative may be dyadic therapy, pairing two children of similar age and developmental level. When treatment is provided in a group format, it is crucial to keep the numbers of children in the group to a minimum. Incorporating more than three or four children with sexual behavior problems into one group will make it difficult to contain the level of stimulation, to provide for the safety of group members, and to address the needs of individual children. Time and attention focused on behavior management takes the focus away from the therapeutic agenda. Research (Pithers & Gray, 1998) has shown significant positive results following 16 weeks of specialized treatment for children with sexual behavior problems. Treatment length should be dependent on the specific treatment needs of each child and would typically last from 12 to 24 weeks. Although it is always advisable to inform families that treatment length may be longer than anticipated based on the child's progress, some sense of a time limitation helps them to feel more hopeful for the future. Sessions should be an hour in length, should be scheduled for a set day and time, and should maintain a predictable structure. Beginning and ending rituals (Cattanach, 1994; Jennings, 1993; Landy, 1994) help to provide a sense of safety, enhancing children's ability to explore difficult issues.

Goals of treatment for children with sexual behavior problems follow. All of the goals and most of the interventions can be utilized for either individual or group therapy. Aside from the goals for the initial and termination sessions, goals and themes do not necessarily adhere to a specific order.

Initial Phase of Treatment

The focus of the first few treatment sessions should be on establishing the therapeutic relationship and building trust and rapport between group members. Whether a child is seen individually or in group therapy, every effort should be made to nurture the child's feelings of connectedness and belonging. Private boxes for storing drawings, artwork, or other treasures can be kept on a shelf to be taken out at the start of each session. Beginning and ending rituals help to establish a sense that there is something in common that is being shared. Exercises that foster group cohesion and encourage comfort with role play are important at this juncture.

Ongoing Treatment Issues

It is important for children in treatment to directly address and discuss their sexually inappropriate behaviors. Where and how the behavior(s) occurred and who the victim was should be discussed. Several strategies can be used to facilitate this process. Prior to any disclosure by the child, it is helpful to discuss and agree upon names to be used for body parts. This serves several purposes. It establishes the words that are acceptable to use and provides children with the vocabulary to talk about their sexual behaviors. It also communicates the therapist's comfort in talking about and listening to sexual material. Once a common language is agreed upon, it is necessary for children to begin to talk about their "touching problem" in order to work toward managing their behaviors. For some children, it is easier to begin by talking about how people found out about the behavior. Children can be asked to draw a picture of the first person, other than their victim, to find out about their "touching problem." The child is then asked to take on the role of that person and tell about what they saw or found out. It is also important for children to identify what occurred prior to the sexually inappropriate behavior in order to help them to identify any feelings or events that may have contributed to the behavior. A time line or road map, detailing what happened before, during and, after the sexual behavior, can help children to understand the progression of their behaviors. Role play can be utilized to help them identify alternative responses and behaviors and to identify strategies for managing their sexual impulses. Exploring the issues through the enactment of a news broadcast or TV interview and call-in show gives children the opportunity to offer advice to others in similar situations, thereby resolving issues for themselves. Cognitive restructuring of distorted thinking and issues related to values clarification can be addressed through similar interventions.

Issues of self identity and self acceptance must be explored as part of the healing process. Many children who have experienced trauma and maltreatment develop a damaged and distorted sense of self. The repercussions of the inappropriate sexual behaviors, as well as the child's identification with the abuser, serve to strengthen the negative self image. Drama therapy interventions offer these children an opportunity to explore other, more positive aspects of themselves, to identify strengths, and to move beyond their past behaviors. Role play, storytelling, and mask work (Cattanach, 1994; Gallo-Lopez, 2000; Landy, 1994) can be utilized to help children to repair their damaged sense of self.

Carlie was a 7-year-old referred for treatment following several incidents of sexual abuse of other children, including her younger sister. There was no indication that either of the girls had been sexually abused. Both girls, however, had been physically abused, had been exposed to domestic violence and substance abuse by their mother and by several of her boyfriends, and had been the victims of chronic neglect and abandonment. They were placed in foster care and, as a result of Carlie's sexual behavior, were moved through seven different foster homes. In one foster home, Carlie was made to believe that evil spirits had inhabited her body and that she was doomed to burn in hell. Not surprisingly, Carlie's problematic behaviors worsened and she was found to have forced or coerced sexual contact with several other children at school and in daycare.

Carlie's sense of self had been severely damaged and her behavior reinforced the negative view that both she and others had of her. During one session, Carlie was asked to create two masks from precut poster board. One mask was to represent her outer self, how others saw her, and the second was to represent a hidden side of herself. Carlie's outer self mask appeared angry. The colors were dark and the design was chaotic. When asked to take on the role of her outer self, Carlie described herself as bad, dirty, and evil. She was unable to identify any positive characteristics. Carlie's hidden self mask was childlike and tearful. When asked to take on the role of her hidden self, Carlie expressed feeling lonely, unloved, and unwanted. During the next several sessions, Carlie used the masks to explore the feelings of pain and hurt of her hidden self. Carlie was able to identify strengths and positive attributes, and with her therapist worked toward incorporating them into her overall self view.

Throughout treatment, interventions should continually focus on identification and expression of feelings and emotion management. Role play situations could be suggested that focus on the expression of specific feelings. Story or role play starters in the form of provocative titles such as "the family crisis," "left out," or "the great escape" enable children to explore specific feelings through role play. Feelings masks can be made to represent different feelings, enabling children to more effectively deal with feelings and emotions.

Mirroring Looks is an activity that can be done in pairs or in individual therapy using a mirror. Children are instructed to make a facial expression that represents a given feeling. The goal of the exercise is to help children to understand the connection between their feelings and the physical responses of their bodies. Examples of feelings statements that can be used in this activity are: "That's disgusting!" "I'm so embarrassed," "Nobody likes me," and "I am the best."

Sculpting (Landy, 2001; Sternberg & Garcia, 2000) is another activity that allows children to explore the connection between their emotions and their bodies. Some young children, however, have difficulty understanding the concept of sculpting. Van Fleet's (2001) Dynamic Dinosaurs activity is an effective way to introduce sculpting to young children. Using bendable dinosaurs, children are instructed to pose their dinosaurs to show how they would express a range of feelings including sad, mad, happy, and teased. Following this activity, children can be introduced to sculpting, which is a powerful tool for self expression. Sculpting themes could include "Keeping secrets," "My fault again," "Mom loves you best," "I don't care!" and "I did it!"

Several other treatment objectives are woven throughout the treatment process. Opportunities for mastery are essential to the development of feelings of empowerment and a healthy sense of self esteem. Recognizing and acknowledging positive characteristics are often difficult for children with sexual behavior problems who are used to having more attention paid to their deficits than their strengths. *Super Hero* (Haen & Brannon, 2002) is an activity that allows children to create super hero characters to represent themselves. The child is first asked to identify qualities or characteristics of the super hero, including the hero's strengths and special powers. If the child is unable to identify positive qualities, the therapist can either prompt the child or make suggestions. The child then draws the super hero or instructs the therapist to do so, deciding on a specific costume, including colors and any tools, gear, or weapons. The child is asked to name the super hero and to create a story about the hero. Some children may choose to develop a comic book story or to create a mask or puppet to represent the super hero. Stories may then be enacted.

The *TV Storyboard* (Gallo-Lopez, 2001) technique can help facilitate story making and dramatic enactment with children who have difficulty getting started on their own. This technique borrows from the idea of storyboards used in animation, telling a story frame by frame. Several sheets of paper are supplied that have been divided into six sections. The papers are preprinted with storyboard frames shaped like TV sets. Children are directed to create their own TV show. The first TV introduces the show, for example, "The Sharon Show" or "The Super Rocket Man Show." The next frame introduces the characters, and subsequent frames tell the story. The stories can then lead to enactments. Some children have videotaped their shows using live actors or figures, and have even created theme songs.

An important element of treatment for children with sexual behavior problems is the exploration of personal victimization issues (Gallo-Lopez, 2000). Using puppets or role play, themes representing the dynamics of abuse such as threats, bribes, secrecy, and fear can be enacted and the connection to personal experiences can be explored. A focus on safety issues, including the establishment of physical boundaries and journey/rescue themes, can be reparative and healing.

Empathy work is an integral part of treatment for children with sexual behavior problems (Gallo-Lopez, 2000; Gil & Johnson, 1993; Longo & Longo, 2003). Role play is an effective way to empathize with another, to foster understanding of how someone else might feel. For children who have engaged in sexually abusive behavior, empathy work focuses on understanding the impact of this behavior on others. Role playing situations in which someone else is hurt or victimized allow children to gain insight into the experiences of another. The use of puppets, storytelling, or scene work can help to facilitate this goal. It is important for children who have engaged in sexually abusive behaviors to understand the far-reaching effects of their behavior. A group of 10- to 12-year-old boys with sexual behavior problems were asked to take turns playing the mother of a sexual abuse victim. The "mothers" were interviewed about how they felt when they first found out what had happened to their child, and were asked to tell about their fears and concerns for the future. This is an incredibly powerful exercise that may not be appropriate for younger children.

When children are victimized by someone stronger or more powerful, they lack the ability to exert control over what is happening. As a result, many victimized children feel powerless and respond by seeking to control anyone or anything they can. *Power Masks* (Gallo-Lopez, 2000) guide children to identify the source of their own personal power, countering feelings of powerlessness and vulnerability. The therapist should begin the session by engaging the children in a discussion or activity that could help them to view power as an internal process rather than the result of physical force or prowess. Once children identify the source of their personal power, they should be instructed to create a mask that symbolizes that power. Children who are able to tolerate the sensation of a plaster craft mask being created directly on their face will be thrilled to see the resulting replica of their visage. Mask making can be done as a group experience with groups that have established adequate levels of trust. This activity requires group members to be able to accept positive, non-sexual touch from each other and should not be attempted until trust and adequate physical boundaries are established. Following the mask making experience, children should be asked to speak as the source of their power. A prompt such as, "I am powerful because . . ." can be used to facilitate enactment. Joseph, a 10-year-old who sexually abused a 3-year-old cousin, created a mask that resembled a clown. A child with a wonderful sense of humor, Joseph was able to recognize that his power came from his ability to make people laugh.

Future Orientation

One of the main goals of termination is for children to be positively oriented toward their future. It is helpful to provide several levels to the termination process. One level should allow the child to experience the successful completion of treatment. This should take place with group members or between the therapist and child. Another level, if appropriate, should involve the child and the family. This level should support the strengths and gains the family has made in treatment and should represent a transition from the support and safety of the therapy setting to the support and safety of the family. Termination activities for groups or between therapist and child could include several interventions that aim to help children to identify their strengths and accomplishments. Dayton (1994) describes an activity she calls *"Claiming the Good."* Clients are asked to picture themselves as young children and to remember positive messages they have heard about themselves. This can be utilized effectively during termination with children by asking them to remember positive statements they have heard about themselves while in treatment. The child or therapist can list the messages on a scroll or special paper, along with the name of the person the message came from (including self). The children can then role play the message being given and explore feelings related to hearing the message.

A powerful termination activity for use with families is the creation of a safe place in the sand tray. Families are asked to work together to incorporate elements that represent safety, security, and connectedness into a cooperative sand tray. Families are then asked to tell the story of their sand tray, with a specific focus on moving forward into the future.

Family Involvement

Although the scope of this chapter does not allow the space to fully discuss the components of family and parent treatment, it is important to at least make mention of it here. It is recommended that parents/caretakers of children with sexual behavior problems become involved in an ongoing treatment or support group. Such a group offers families a safe place to voice concerns and decreases feeling of isolation through the emotional support of families in similar situations. Parent groups should also educate parents about the dynamics of child sexual behavior problems and provide support and encouragement for parents to make the necessary changes in their home environment. Several books are available to assist parents in helping their children. These include Johnson's (1998) *Helping Children with Sexual Behavior Problems* and *From Trauma to Understanding* (Pithers et al., 1993).

In addition to specific parent groups, family members, including the case child, should be involved in family therapy throughout the treatment process. Family therapy objectives will vary depending on family issues, needs, and concerns. For most families, the focus will primarily be on repairing and strengthening family bonds, roles, and relationships.

Conclusion

Children with sexual behavior problems pose a unique dilemma for child therapists. Although they are children and must be treated as such, their behaviors have caused harm to others. Treatment for these children must focus on decreasing the inappropriate behaviors while preventing the child from becoming entrenched in the victimizer role.

This chapter presented a drama therapy approach to treatment for children with sexual behavior problems that aims to reduce the problematic behaviors while repairing and enhancing the child's sense of self. Through the use of role play, enactment, and pretend play, children are given the opportunity to expand their role repertoire, explore alternative viewpoints, and experiment with solutions. The treatment protocol presented identifies strengths and focuses on healing and building resilience rather than concentrating on deficits and pathology. By trusting that drama therapy is reparative and that children are capable of participating in their own healing process, growth and positive change are possible.

References

Cattanach, A. (1993). *Play therapy with abused children.* London: Jessica Kingsley.

Cattanach, A. (1994). *Play therapy: Where the sky meets the underworld.* London: Jessica Kingsley.

Dayton, T. (1994). *The drama within: Psychodrama and experiential therapy.* Deerfield Beach, FL: Health Communications.

Emunah, R. (1995). From adolescent trauma to adolescent drama: Group drama therapy with emotionally disturbed youth. In S. Jennings (Ed.), *Dramatherapy with children and adolescents* (pp. 150–168). London: Routledge.

Friedrich, W. (1997). *Child sexual behavior inventory.* Lutz, FL: Psychological Assessment Resources.

Gallo-Lopez, L. (2000). A creative play therapy approach to the group treatment of young sexually abused children. In H. Kaduson & C. Schaefer (Eds.), *Short-term play therapy for children* (pp. 269–295). New York: Guilford.

Gallo-Lopez, L. (2001). TV show storyboard. In H. Kaduson & C. Schaefer (Eds.), *101 more favorite play therapy techniques* (pp. 8–10). Northvale, NJ: Jason Aronson.

Gil, E. (1994). *Play in family therapy.* New York: Guilford.

Gil, E., & Johnson, T. C. (1993). *Sexualized children: Assessment and treatment of sexualized children and children who molest.* Rockville, MD: Launch Press.

Haen, C., & Brannon, K.H. (2002). Superheroes, monsters and babies: Roles of strength, destruction and vulnerability for emotionally disturbed boys. *The Arts in Psychotherapy, 29*(1), 31–40.

Irwin, E. (2000). The use of a puppet interview to understand children. In K. Gitlin-Weiner, A. Sandgrund, & C. Schaefer (Eds.), *Play diagnosis and assessment* (2nd ed., pp. 682–703). New York: Wiley.

Irwin, E., & Malloy, E. (1975). Family puppet interviews. *Family Process, 14,* 179–191.

Jennings, S. (1993). *Playtherapy with children: A practitioner's guide.* Oxford, England: Blackwell.

Johnson, T. C. (1998). *Helping children with sexual behavior problems: A guidebook for parents and substitute caregivers.* South Pasadena, CA: Author.

Landy, R. J. (1994). *Drama therapy: Concepts, theories and practices* (2nd ed.). Springfield, IL: Charles C. Thomas.

Landy, R. (1996). *Essays in drama therapy: The double life.* London: Jessica Kingsley.

Landy, R. (2001). *New essays in drama therapy: Unfinished business.* Springfield, IL: Charles C Thomas.

Longo, R. E. (2002). A holistic approach to treating young people who sexually abuse. In M. Calder (Ed.), *Young people who sexually abuse* (pp. 218–230). Lyme Regis, Dorset: Russell House Publishing.

Longo, R. E., & Longo, D. P. (2003). *New hope for youth: Experiential exercises for children and adolescents.* Holyoke, MA: NEARI Press.

Pithers, W. D., & Gray, A. (1998). The other half of the story: Children with sexual behavior problems. *Psychology, Public Policy, and Law,* 4(1–2), 200–217.

Pithers, W. D., Gray, A., Cunningham, C., & Lane, S. (1993). *From trauma to understanding: A guide for parents of children with sexual behavior problems.* Brandon, VT: The Safer Society Press.

Rasmussen, L., Burton, J. E., & Christopherson, B. (1992). Precursors to offending and the trauma outcome process in sexually reactive children. *Journal of Child Sexual Abuse,* 1(1), 33–48.

Sternberg, P., & Garcia, A. (2000). *Sociodrama: Who's in your shoes?* (2nd ed.). Westport, CT: Praeger.

Tanaka, M., Kakuyama, T., & Urhausen, M. T. (2003). Drawing and storytelling as psychotherapy with children. In C. Malchiodi (Ed.), *Handbook of art therapy* (pp.125–138). New York: Guilford.

Van Fleet, R. (2001). Dynamic dinosaurs. In H. Kaduson & C. Schaefer (Eds.), *101 more play therapy techniques* (pp. 359–361). Northvale, NJ: Jason Aronson.

CHAPTER 9

Spectacle and Ensemble in Group Drama Therapy Treatment for Children with ADHD and Related Neurological Syndromes

LEE R. CHASEN

Introduction

Presently, and perhaps ironically, spectacle and ensemble are being used as dramatic vehicles in the genre of reality television programming. In a fascinating and often blurry interface between fictionalized entertainment and real life, groups of people are left on islands, placed in houses, or sent on journeys with the tasks of winning races, choosing life partners, reaching destinations, or surviving. I can only assume that the purpose of this relatively new genre, aside from the usual commercial considerations, reflects our instinctual and cultural propensity to create drama as a strategy for deepening our understanding of, and connection with, our human condition.

So far, though, it seems as if the various attempts at creating reality television have, rather than shedding light on the complexity of human relationship and emotion in any meaningful way, succumbed to the same contrived superficiality that often defines popular culture. The contrivances and banality of media-driven popular culture, in the service of commercial success, seem to use elements of spectacle and ensemble to manipulate our attention span and hold our interest. Spectacles of lavish, multimillion-dollar mansions or primitive, foreboding jungle settings are presented while ensembles of clashing personalities with potentially disruptive dynamics are knowingly put together in order to stimulate connection to our senses and sensibilities, keeping us, perhaps, from pursuing a more meaningful experience.

I would argue, though, that these shows also hold our attention and remain commercially viable because of the flashes of authentic emotional vulnerability and intensity that periodically emerge in the players. These are the moments that we, the audience, seem to latch onto in our efforts to more deeply see and understand ourselves, our emotions, and our connections with others. I would also argue that these flashes and moments of authenticity and vulnerability, such as the tearful anxiety of facing a fear brought about by the setting or the righteous rage that explodes when confronting relationship issues, are generally evoked by the same elements of spectacle and ensemble used by these shows to manipulate popular complacency. This seemingly contradictory dynamic reflects the simple make up, function, and range of drama; to serve as a mirror, constructed with various combinations of fictional elements, that enhances and reflects some aspect of our reality, from our most materialistic and superficial musings to our deepest, most mysterious connections to self and other.

This chapter will explore why and how dramatic elements of spectacle and ensemble may be applied in group drama therapy sessions, specifically for children diagnosed with Attention-Deficit/Hyperactivity Disorder (ADHD) and related neurological syndromes; to capture attention and evoke authentic emotional responses and reflection from the participants, ideally facilitating deeper understanding and higher functioning in their "real" life experiences.

The Diagnostic and Statistical Manual of Mental Disorders, Fourth Edition, Text Revision (American Psychiatric Association, 2000) identifies a "persistent pattern of inattention" and "interference with developmentally appropriate social . . . functioning" as essential features of Attention-Deficit/ Hyperactivity Disorder (p. 85). Inattention and impairment of social interaction are also listed as symptoms of Asperger's Disorder and Pervasive Developmental Disorder Not Otherwise Specified (PDD-NOS). Children with these diagnoses find it difficult to remain focused and naturally attend to tasks. They may stay fixated for long periods of time on something that stimulates the senses or is of interest to them, but attending to concepts that do not originate in their own thought patterns can be very challenging. This often sets them up for failure in traditional classroom and therapy settings that rely solely on verbal interaction.

Social interaction is also greatly impacted for these children because of their tendency toward impulsivity in thought and emotional expression. Often, they detach from attempting to function in groups in a healthy and appropriate manner, choosing instead to subsist in their own, frequently misguided perceptions and impulsively driven and fantastically based thought patterns. Even with such unpleasant results as consequences from authority figures and social rejection, detachment seems easier to these children when faced with the strain of organizing and applying their thought processes toward managing the situation at hand.

It is important to note that children who demonstrate impulsivity and oppositional defiance resulting from immaturity, poor parenting, or lack of emotional intelligence skills, rather than neurological makeup, are frequently labeled and misdiagnosed as having ADHD. Children with neurologically driven attention deficits and impulsivity, though, often develop similar oppositional and defiant behaviors. For children with ADHD, the combination of neurological factors and environmentally learned behaviors often generates frustration and power struggles between the child and those who assign and reflect the various tasks and expectations of daily life.

Behavioral expectations need to be adjusted when treating these different conditions that originate in either environmental or neurological factors. A child whose behavior is learned and promoted by his or her environment may be expected to adjust more quickly once a behavioral plan or change in family dynamic is put in place. While the treatment approach for a neurologically impaired child may be similar, substantial results and changes in behavior may not occur as readily. To significantly alter the course of the neurological impulse, a consistent and methodical approach over a longer period of time is usually needed.

Kid Esteem Inc., a nonprofit organization dedicated to the emotional health and empowerment of children, families, schools, and communities, provides treatment for children diagnosed with these behavioral and neurological disorders. Drama therapy is used in individual and group contexts to facilitate emotional intelligence as a foundation for addressing emotional and social dysfunction and issues concerning family life.

Children are referred to Kid Esteem from a range of sources, including pediatricians, neurologists, school psychologists, social workers, and guidance counselors. Criteria for group participation include the ability to follow basic group protocol and transitions, and the ability to respond verbally. These criteria reflect developmental, rather than behavioral, ability. Many of the children who attend Kid Esteem, while developmentally able to function and respond in group, have difficulty doing so because of emotional or environmentally based behavioral issues. Groups are named with child-centered titles such as "*Kid Power Hour*" and "*If You're Angry and You Know It . . .*" These names help children understand that the purpose of participating in our groups is to empower who they are, rather than conform to a pre-determined, authority-based objective. Groups usually run for either 6 or 10 weeks, meeting weekly for one hour.

There is a separate program for children with neurological challenges, but these children also need to be developmentally able to follow basic group protocol, such as demonstrating awareness of the presence of others, transitioning between activities, and responding verbally to their experience, in order to participate. There is crossover between the two programs and populations based on the severity of diagnoses and the subsequent level of group functioning. Programs are available for children between the ages of 3 and 13. Groups are comprised of no more than 15 children with at least two group leaders. In certain groups, a simultaneous parenting group is facilitated that focuses the parents on weekly topics, including specific strategies for transforming family dynamics and managing family issues, such as positive discipline, behavior management, empathic communication, and emotionally intelligent expression. For groups that do not have a parenting group component, weekly assignments (or "homework") are given to the parents, reflecting topics that they are then expected to process with their families.

Group treatment, and specifically drama therapy group treatment, empowers neurologically disabled children to face the difficulties of managing the impulses and miscues that social interaction provokes. Spectacle and ensemble in drama therapy provide a means for capturing and holding attention so that the children can focus on their significant life experiences and learn the skills of emotional intelligence in an affirming social context.

Emotional Intelligence

The skills of emotional intelligence are facilitated in the groups as a basis for helping the children to self-monitor, organize thoughts, manage impulses, and connect with others in a positive, self-aware manner. Emotional intelligence is defined as "the ability to perceive emotions, to access and generate emotions so as to assist thought, to understand emotions and emotional knowledge, and to reflectively regulate emotions so as to promote emotional and intellectual growth" (Salovey & Sluyter, 1997, p. 5). Social components of emotional intelligence include "the ability to discern emotions in others, to feel empathy, to delay gratification, to control one's own emotions, to exhibit social competence, and to be emotionally well adjusted" (Epstein, 1998, p. 19). In his popular text *Emotional Intelligence: Why It Can Matter More than IQ*, social psychologist Daniel Goleman (1995) emphasizes the importance of the ability to deal with frustrations and control impulsive behavior.

Besides helping the children to control impulses by providing a language that organizes and manages those feelings, the ability to identify and verbalize emotional experience also can serve as an antidote, or immunization of sorts, against the development of depression, anxiety, and oppositional behavior disorders that result from unmanageable or uncontrolled feelings of sadness, fear, and anger (Epstein, 1998). This furthers the goal of providing tools for impulse control, as the self-aware and self-contained language of emotional intelligence supports the children toward being less likely to act out those emotions in a dysfunctional manner against themselves, others, and their environments. Otherwise, such emotional dysfunction provides another source of fuel that provokes the desire to impulsively act out.

By addressing this dynamic in the context of a social setting, the children are able to receive positive feedback and support from peers in response to their more appropriate and contained emotional expression. The skills of emotional intelligence support neurologically challenged children in addressing issues of impulse control and social dysfunction, as well as facilitating a protocol for emotional well-being that furthers the process of empowerment and self-control.

Drama Therapy

Historically, theater and drama have functioned as collective, ritualistic events that explore the mysteries and vulnerabilities of the human condition through emotional reflection, expression and language. Drama therapy's potential to serve as a conduit for emotional intelligence is highlighted by Robert Landy's (1994) assertion that drama therapy aims "to increase the dimensions of the role so that . . . the client . . . can express a range of emotions, think a range of thoughts, [and] perform a range of actions" (p. 47).

Landy's (1994) concept of "distancing" in drama therapy facilitates the client's movement between real and fictional, and cognitive and affective experience, integrating subjective emotional feelings with objective understanding, ultimately resulting in healthier functioning. By using projective techniques, including toys, dolls, puppets, masks, storytelling, theater, sociodrama, and world technique to symbolically represent emotion and associated emotional experience, the client becomes able to navigate an effective balance between feeling and thought, initiating greater clarity, understanding, and management of personal experience.

The dramatic elements of *spectacle* and *ensemble* seem to support the facilitation of emotional intelligence skills in the drama therapy treatment of children whose neurological conditions foster inattention and social dysfunction. By incorporating elements of spectacle and ensemble into a drama therapy approach, clients are able to focus on, attend to, and process individual emotional experience in an affirming, collective context.

Spectacle

Aristotle's (1996/1895) description of spectacle in his analysis of tragedy refers to all that is visual on the stage. Tragedy, an imitation of a serious action in dramatic form that arouses emotion and empathy to a state of awareness, employs spectacle as one of the components that maintains the drama as a whole. Dramatic spectacle is similar to Landy's (1994) projective techniques in that each is comprised of visual objects or experiences that symbolize shared meaning and meaningful interaction within the dramatic enactment. Spectacle differs from projective techniques in that spectacle is used to bring attention to and support the drama, rather than symbolizing or representing the subject of the clinical encounter. In this sense, it follows Aristotle's notion that spectacle is less important than the other elements of tragedy, which include plot, characters, diction, thought, and melody.

Aristotle (1996/1895) stresses, though, that spectacle is an attraction, suggesting that it could function as a key element in clinical work with children who are inattentive and neurologically impaired. Dramatic spectacle attracts and holds attention. Colors, objects, costumes, masks, and props, when used as components to support participation in a whole dramatic encounter, can capture and guide a child's focus toward interaction, with the clinically based concept woven into the drama.

In a 6-week group called *Making Friends*, Jonathan, a 5-year-old boy, spent much of the first and second sessions apart from the group. While the other children participated in a sociometric warm-up, moving around the room, connecting to specific written sentiments tacked to the wall that measured individual emotion in response to social criteria, Jonathan stayed on the far side of the room, intermittently calling out provocative words and fragmented phrases. His responses, such as "I hate!" and "Stupid!" were not directed at anybody in particular, but toward the group as a whole. Gentle, non-judgmental attempts to coach him into connectedness and participation with phrases such as "Jonathan, is the activity making you mad or scared?" and "Come play with us!" were met with physical and verbal aggression. He would swing his arms threateningly if anybody got too close. On the intake form filled out by the parents, Jonathan's mother identified him as having a language delay and being aggressive and "tuned out" when participating in group activities.

Later in the session, puppet shows were developed by the children to provide opportunities to identify with and respond to challenging social encounters that were suggested during the sociometry. When the puppet stage was taken out and the lights were switched from the usual fluorescent to color, Jonathan's affect became hushed. He came over to where the puppet shows were about to take place and sat with the other children, looking up at the stage lit by the colors. Even though the setting consisted of a simple, brightly colored, 4-foot puppet stage and a basic track lighting system fitted with colored bulbs, the spectacle of the drama became, in a sense, larger to Jonathan than his fragmented and resistant world, helping him to organize and focus his thoughts on something outside of himself.

As the puppet shows were presented, the children were prompted to respond to and identify with the social contexts that were being enacted. Jonathan, who had shown no connection to, or understanding of, any of the previous concepts or activities, referred to a puppet representing a "mad friend" and said, "That's me! I'm a bad friend." As a group, we processed Jonathan's response and its accompanying dynamics. While Jonathan was able to only marginally participate in the ensuing discussion, he successfully focused on and related to the activity. After the session was over, his mother was surprised to hear that he participated. When she added, somewhat fatalistically, "But he didn't understand anything . . ." we described Jonathan's insightful encounter with the puppets, to which she expressed an even greater surprise.

If we had merely discussed the social contexts with the children in a more traditional setting, it is unlikely that Jonathan would have connected to the concepts. If we had merely used the puppets, perhaps sitting in a circle, Jonathan would have probably stayed on his side of the room, in his own world, relating to the group in a disconnected and pathological manner. The simple spectacle of the puppet stage and the lights created a "whole" setting that captured his attention and focused his thoughts in a manner that more conventional techniques probably would not have been able to do.

Ensemble

According to the *Oxford English Dictionary* (Simpson, 1989), the word *ensemble*, referring to "a complete whole" and "each part in relation to the whole," first surfaced as a theatrical term in 1915. Since then, ensemble has been used to describe the manner in which this particular type of theater is produced, as well as an attribute of effective performance.

Leonard (2003) acknowledges the growing movement of ensemble theater in America. He makes the following statement regarding theatrical ensemble:

(The) group is empowered to shape artistic direction through a structure of function . . . that is inclusive of all members of the group. . . . (Individuals) have a significant degree of impact on the definition of the ensemble's mission. . . (and resulting theatrical events are) strongly affected by the individual contributions. (What is Ensemble Theater? Section, para. 1–2)

Directing the drama therapy group as an ensemble, in which members are empowered to contribute as individuals in order to strengthen the function of the group, is an important aspect of effective treatment.

ADHD children show interest in group participation and social connection, but because of their inattentiveness, impulsivity, and resulting social difficulties, often disconnect from and disrupt group process due to a combination of over-stimulation and perceived or actual rejection from peers and authority figures. They often cross spatial and social boundaries with inappropriate physical contact or comments. After numerous rejections, these children may become oppositional and seek to disengage from social encounters as an act of self-preservation.

Children with Asperger's Syndrome and PDD-NOS, on the other hand, usually seem disinterested in social interaction, unless connection to another can very concretely reflect the experiences and perceptions that are in their thoughts at that moment. These thoughts, particularly for the Asperger's child, often fixate on electronic, technical, and mechanical objects and processes. If children with these conditions do connect socially, they often find it extremely difficult to negotiate the give-and-take of perceiving and responding to another's perspective unless it mirrors their own thoughts. Their presentation is similar to that of the narcissist, with the world functioning as a mirror whose sole purpose is to affirm preconceived notions about their own fragmented sense of being. The need for such mirroring, though, is fueled by an impaired neurology and resulting cognitive, rather than emotional, imbalances.

To create a sense of ensemble, the activities of the drama therapy groups focus participating individuals on their unique experiences and their potential contributions to what the group is presenting as a whole. We empower the group to shape the direction of the dramas based on their connections to the sum of the individual experiences, in a manner that has a supportive impact on the mission of the group and is inclusive of all members. The ensemble dynamic creates an environment in which the experiences of neurologically challenged children, who because of their impulsive and inappropriate behavior often are the recipients of negative discipline from authorities and social rejection from peers, can be accepted, honored, and respected.

Children diagnosed with ADHD, chronic opposition, and socially disruptive behavior such as spitting at authority figures and throwing chairs have functioned in Kid Esteem groups as cooperative and productive members because of the ensemble nature and stated mission of the groups. The ensemble informs the children that being present with a full range of who they are is not only acceptable, but also necessary and important with regard to the functioning and direction of the group. Their individual stories and experiences have significant impact on the group as a whole, providing the children with an appropriate sense of control and empowerment.

Max was a ten-year-old boy with ADHD who entered an emotional intelligence group determined to sabotage his experience and the experience of the group. The tips of his hair were fashionably dyed and his clothes reflected the latest trends, giving him the appearance of a teenager. Max's mother indicated during his intake that he "has no self-esteem, is very angry and is unable to express himself." She went on to say that Max lies, breaks things, and is extremely disrespectful to adults and peers, causing him to "get in trouble" in group settings.

Max challenged every activity of the first two sessions by rolling his eyes, smiling condescendingly, and calling the activities "stupid." He set himself apart from the group, sitting in the one chair on the other side of the room, attempting to undermine the leader's direction and lure converts over to his side of the figurative and literal space. Rather than enter into a power struggle with him, I let Max be. I focused on establishing the foundation for the ensemble experience, which would hopefully provide group members with a more interesting and valuable choice than Max's rebellion. I respected and understood his need to rebel, while coaching him to refrain from crossing specific boundaries with aggressive language or actions.

I developed the sense of ensemble through empowering mission statements and warming up a full range of emotional self-awareness and acceptance in the children. By the third session, Max began to participate and respond from across the room. By the fourth, he physically joined the group and became a productive member. The ensemble offered Max an opportunity to feel unique and empowered in a manner that did not rely on his usual resistance and opposition. Children in the group who might have joined Max in the first few sessions and fed his oppositional stance responded instead to their own sense of empowerment, envisioned by joining the ensemble.

Group Protocol

All groups at Kid Esteem begin by identifying the mission of the ensemble, which is founded in the empowerment of children. The concept of empowering the experience of each individual is introduced to the children in very concrete terms. Parents are held accountable for facilitating progress and growth, either by attending a simultaneously occurring parenting group or completing a weekly "homework" assignment that focuses on positive discipline, empathic communication, and problem solving techniques, as previously discussed. The children and parents are specifically told at the initial orientation that the parent groups and homework assignments are intended "to help the parents behave better."

Parents of children with ADHD and neurological challenges frequently have their own corresponding neurological conditions that make it difficult for them to process and stay on task with regard to effective parenting skills. They sometimes blame their children and hold them responsible for their own sense of inadequacy. The children, along with having to deal with their own impulsive and dysfunctional behavior, are put in the difficult "no-win" position of having some sort of control and power over their parents' negative behavior. The primary purpose of the parenting groups and homework assignments is to support the parents in reversing this dynamic.

The children feel inclined and are encouraged to informally report on their parents' progress at the beginning of each session. As the children exchange information about whether or not their parents are successfully completing or even attempting the homework, they build a sense of community, purpose, and direction among themselves. If children report that their parents are not doing the homework, the leader, as well as the other group members, support the notion that their parents need to take responsibility for this part of the program. Children will also ask the group leader to intervene and speak with the parents about the importance of the weekly assignments. Along with variations of sociometric and other group encounter and improvisational exercises (Fox, 1987; Moreno, 1978), these discussions warm the children up to creating and portraying their dramas and responding to the dramas of the other group members.

Differently themed groups that may focus on social skills, emotional intelligence, or self-esteem, for example, follow different protocols. However, the concept of empowerment is redefined and woven into each of the group themes at the outset of the sessions. Theatrical, psychodramatic, and projective techniques support the children in gaining access to a healthy source of power rather than attempting to exercise power over someone or at somebody's expense. By participating in the dramatic enactments, framed by elements of spectacle and ensemble, they build a pragmatic vocabulary of intelligent emotional expression with which they can successfully address and manage challenging social and family life situations presented in the dramas.

During *Puppet Interviews*, used for ages 4 to 8, for example, the children are shown various puppets characterized with different emotional facial expressions. We ask the children to verbalize what they think the puppets might be saying based on the puppets' facial expressions. We then use the puppets to model the distinction between emotionally intelligent language and emotionally aggressive language, deemed "super power" and "sour power," for the purposes of access and understanding.

An excerpt from the parent homework for that week reads as follows:

When we express anger or frustration with "Super Power," *strong and angry words*, usually beginning with "I am . . ." or "I feel like . . ." are expressed in a respectful manner to get other people to listen and help us. We also demonstrate "Super Power" when our own positive opinion of ourselves stays stronger than a negative opinion from someone else. Expressing anger with "Super Power" *does not* mean being nice, polite or apologetic. It encourages expression of a *strong statement in which the individual can accurately describe his or her anger.*

When we show "Sour Power," angry words and actions, usually starting with "You . . ." are about insulting or hurting other people or ourselves, may get others angry at us or scared, might get us into trouble and probably won't get us what we need. This is the type of anger most of us experience, usually aggressive toward others, causing us to think that expressing anger is "bad" or "wrong." We want to get across that expressing anger is "good" and "right."

The children are then directed to the puppet area and asked to choose a puppet they think "has something mad to say." Once they obtain a puppet, they walk around the room as a group for approximately 20 seconds speaking the mad words that they constructed in the role of the puppet. They may choose to enact either super power or sour power mad words with their puppets. We warm up to the language of *sad, scared, frustrated,* and *happy* emotions in the same manner.

Next, the children are asked to choose a puppet with which they would like to present a show. I ask the children to think about the name of their puppet, how old the puppet is, if the puppet is a boy or girl, where the puppet lives, if the puppet is mad, sad, scared, frustrated or happy, any story the puppet may want to tell, and whether their puppet uses super power or sour power. The children come to the puppet stage one at a time, focused, as stated earlier, by the spectacle of the puppet stage and lighting and embraced by an ensemble eager to hear and share their stories. After each presentation, the audience identifies whether the puppet used super or sour power and asks questions of the puppets, such as "What else gets you mad?" and "How does your scared come out?"

When presenting their puppets, the children enact stories that concretely represent their own life experiences, as well as creating more distanced, symbolic representations of those experiences. During this session, the primary focus is on developing a more objective understanding and context for application of emotionally intelligent language. After everyone has a turn, the children sit together and identify the puppet that reminds them of their own, real-life situations. They might speak about being teased or dealing with an aggressive sibling, teacher, or parent. Another way to facilitate closure is to have the children bring their puppets to the circle to say goodbye and express any final thoughts to the group. As the children leave the session, they take a homework sheet, which, for that particular week, instructs the parents to consider and share with the family how they might be showing sour power in their parenting and family management.

Objects of spectacle and activities that build ensemble are used throughout the first part of the program to enhance emotional self-awareness, group cohesion, and a sense of empowerment through intelligent emotional expression. A simple Karaoke microphone that amplifies the children's voice, for example, is used in the *Super Power Challenge* session to direct their emotional expression toward an individual of their choosing from real life, represented by an empty chair (Landy, 1994; Perls, 1969), while the rest of the ensemble supports the player by doubling (Moreno, 1978) potential responses from the sidelines.

The first half of the program incorporates aspects of spectacle and ensemble using more fantastical and distanced techniques as described in *Puppet Interviews. Super Power Challenge,* facilitated in the middle of the program, transitions the children toward creating and enacting dramas around real-life experiences. The final sessions of the program employ the skills developed during the first part to support the children toward exploring and managing issues from their real lives.

The *Director's Chair,* an adaptation of Fox's Playback Theatre (1987), comprises the final part of the program. While Playback uses a trained company of actors to portray an "everyday or imaginary experience" (Landy, 1994, p. 33), Director's Chair focuses on real-life experiences prompted by challenging family and social dynamics. The children volunteer to sit, one at a time, in the director's chair, and are provided with a director's megaphone and a television remote control. These props help to capture and focus the children's attention on the activity.

Sitting in the director's chair, the children are asked to tell their story regarding a certain emotional experience, where it took place, who else was present, and what occurred during the encounter. The rest of the group is prompted to listen closely since the child in the director's chair will be casting the "show" from the children in the group. The director casts someone to play him or herself, and then the remaining roles needed to enact the story.

After the children are chosen to play the roles, they are assembled in the playing area and quickly coached by the director and group leader in terms of simple blocking and lines. The director then yells "Action!" into the megaphone or says "Play!" while pushing the button on the remote control to start the scene. If the actors stray too much from the parts they are assigned, the director may yell "Cut!" or "Pause!" using the props, and clarify any blocking or lines for the actors. When the scene is played to the director's satisfaction, he or she yells "Cut!" or "Stop!" The rest of the group is then asked to use emotionally intelligent language to describe what they think it would be like to be in the director's situation that was just portrayed. A supportive and empathic dialogue ensues until the director feels doubled. Then, the next director is chosen.

Group Process

While the drama therapy groups at Kid Esteem are comprised of specifically established curricula and protocols, they are constructed to facilitate individual therapeutic process. The three cases that follow will give examples of how individual clients' goals are facilitated within the group.

Joe

Joe, a 10-year-old boy with ADHD, would jump up and down and flap his hands whenever he was excited, which he often was. His positive attitude and pleasant affect were interspersed with intense anxiety about social situations, causing him to perseverate on questions and answers about events and procedures surrounding the social encounter. Joe was mainly eager and naive when dealing with his peers, which, according to his mother, often caused him to be taken advantage of. Joe's mother also reported that his anxiety would often lead to meltdowns at home, resulting in frequent periods of excessive and confused crying and bouts of physical aggression against family members.

During *Super Power Challenge*, Joe used the spectacle of the lights, the empty chair draped with colored scarves, and the microphone to address a boy in his neighborhood who was convincing the other children not to play with Joe. Joe placed a picture he had drawn of the boy in the chair. He picked up the microphone, which projected and empowered his voice, and began expressing his anger toward the boy. Provided with prompts written on a cue card that read, "*I am* . . . ; *I feel* . . . ; *I know* . . . ; *I don't* . . ." and "*I will* . . . ," Joe was able to make empowered statements that were grounded in self-awareness.

Rather than getting caught up in the less certain experience of attempting to control the other, with phrases such as "*You* better cut it out," or "*You're* not being fair," Joe was able to assume more control through language that best represented where he stood and possible courses of action he could take. Pointing his finger at the picture of the boy, Joe authentically and forcefully proclaimed, using the prompts on the cue card, "I am sick of being left out! I don't deserve to be treated this way! I feel really mad about it! I know I can play good! I will tell your mother if you keep doing it!"

After his turn at the exercise, Joe continued to spontaneously construct and express emotionally intelligent language related to his situation as he empathized with situations that the other children addressed. Each child, as he takes his turn at the microphone, is supported and coached as needed by the leader and the rest of the ensemble watching from the "sidelines." If a child feels uncomfortable or stuck after describing their situation and the picture they have placed in the chair, the group suggests possible phrases that begin with the aforementioned cue card prompts.

It is often difficult and awkward for children (and adults!) to construct and apply empowered language and phrases that can appropriately manage conflicts with others. A lack of emotional intelligence skills in our culture often causes us to focus on attacking the other, rather than clarifying our own experience. Learning how to use emotionally intelligent language provides children with ownership of a more solid, secure platform from which they can effectively express ideas and feelings. The *Super Power Challenge,* with its elements of spectacle and ensemble, supports the children toward acquisition of these skills, while alleviating, to some extent, the anxiety and helplessness experienced in social conflicts.

During his turn in the *Director's Chair,* Joe chose to tell the recurring story of feeling anxious about being late when he gets picked up for school and his bus gets stuck in traffic. After telling his story and casting the parts, he used the megaphone to call "Action!" and the scene began. Joe watched as the bus picked him up and then went to the next house, where the boy was always a few minutes late. Joe laughed and flapped his hands as the boy he cast as himself started speaking the lines Joe had provided him. The boy playing Joe repeatedly asked the bus driver if they were going to be late. The child in role as the bus driver answered that, just like every other morning, they would be on time. The other children on the bus responded according to Joe's direction, becoming increasingly annoyed at his perseverative anxiety.

The group responded to Joe's predicament, choosing words like "frustrated" and "scared" to describe what he might be feeling. As the audience and players searched for more empowered language that Joe could possibly apply to the situation, he spontaneously jumped out of the director's chair and entered the scene. He went up to the boy he cast as himself and, in a forceful yet nurturing tone, said, "Its okay. You're not going to be late. This happens every morning." I directed the boys to reverse roles. Upon hearing the words that he had just spoken from the other boy, Joe seemed a little lost. I attempted to double him by saying, "But maybe we will be late." He flapped and jumped up and down and said, "Yeah! Maybe we will be late!" In an aside, I asked Joe if the bus was ever late and what would happen if the bus were late again. He thought for a moment and responded that the bus had been late once, but nothing had really happened as a result. I asked him if he could reassure the boy who was playing him in the scene. Joe gently explained that, even if the bus were late, nothing bad or unpleasant would occur and he would be all right. The boys reversed roles and Joe received the information and support he had just provided for himself.

Joe and his mother reported during later weeks that Joe was able to go back to the dialogue from the scene and cope more efficiently when the late boy and traffic would raise his anxiety on the bus. The dramas provided Joe with interventions that empowered cognitive and affective self-monitoring, and a better understanding of, and access to, a source of pragmatic language that facilitated higher functioning in his attempts to cope with a difficult situation.

Robert

Robert was a 6-year-old boy with ADHD who became very invested in the possibility that his parents might learn how to behave better. While his mother noted on Robert's intake form that he was "constantly in trouble at school…doesn't listen to the teacher" and was "very distracted," we found him to be extremely compliant, focused, and responsive. During the first session, upon establishing the ensemble's mission and hearing about the weekly homework assignments, Robert shared that his mother and father mostly used hitting and spanking as their main discipline strategies. Although our philosophy strongly disagrees with this approach to parenting, such behavior toward children is acceptable according to state law (New York). Robert did not show any visible signs of physical abuse. Moreover, his parents were attending the parenting component of the program. I assured Robert that we would do everything we could to help his parents stop hitting.

All of Robert's dramatizations reflected his frustration, anger, fear, and sadness about this problem. Early in the sessions, during *Puppet Interviews*, he portrayed a sad, 6-year-old puppy that gets "wild," and then is hit. During *Super Power Challenge*, Robert addressed his mother, represented in the empty chair, and said, "I get mad when you hit me. I feel sad. I know I will listen. I don't want to get hit. I will try to listen." Meanwhile, in the parenting sessions, Robert's mother was taking responsibility and working on developing alternative discipline and communication strategies to curb her physical response to Robert's behavior. Robert was eager to report on his mother's progress each week.

During his turn in the director's chair, Robert told the story of getting mad at his sister and then getting hit by his mother while they were in a park together. Robert watched intently as the child cast as his mother "stage slapped" the child playing him. He listened closely while the rest of the children expressed their feelings about his situation, and he seemed to absorb and process the possibility of empowering his position. This was reinforced as the group doubled Robert with emotionally intelligent language, such as "I don't want to get hit!" and "It hurts when you hit me!" The ensemble affirmed and supported Robert's experience and provided possible pragmatic approaches to the challenges that he and his family face.

Frank

Frank, a 9-year-old boy, fit the criteria for a diagnosis of Asperger's Syndrome. His social interaction and participation in the group was mostly conducted in a "highly eccentric, one-sided, verbose, and insensitive manner" (APA, 2000, p. 83). His interest in enactment seemed to evolve from the opportunity to use the various objects of spectacle, such as the lights, microphone and megaphone. Frank's dramas portrayed patterns of interest generally restricted to characters, objects, and parts of objects pertaining to video and board games. Initially, I allowed Frank to participate and relate to the group on his terms. For much of the process, he avoided interpersonal connection. I felt compelled to direct him a bit further, though, as the program shifted into its final phase.

When we began *Director's Chair*, Frank was enthusiastic about having his turn and using the megaphone and remote. He approached the exercise, as he had to some extent approached the others, as an opportunity to manage and control the different mechanical parts of the objects of his preoccupations. During an exploration of family relationships and the different emotions that weave through them, for example, Frank expressed an interest in portraying a time when he played Yahtzee with his father. As he cast and directed the different roles in his drama, though, it became apparent that he was only interested in seeing the interaction between the different components of his computerized Yahtzee game. Social/emotional exchange between Frank and his father were non-existent in his drama, and were merely tacked on in a perfunctory manner to satisfy my coaching. This reflected, according to Frank's parents, his general approach to managing interpersonal relationships.

During an exploration of social relationships in a future session, I told Frank that his show had to be about real people from real life, rather than characters from a video game. When it was his turn to sit in the director's chair, Frank assured me that he would do a story about participation in his little league game. As he began to tell his story, he quickly cast the roles and hurried the actors into position. I soon realized that he was re-creating a baseball video game, hoping to get it on its feet and "rolling" before I noticed. I decided to stop him and hold him to the parameters of the exercise. This caused Frank to become agitated with me and insist that I allow him to create his scene. I gently coached him to try a scene with real people and focus, perhaps, on *who was playing* the video game. He was extremely resistant, saying that he couldn't do it that way and that he had to do the video game. I told him it would be fine to direct a scene about a video game as soon as we were able to see a story from his real life.

Frank told the group, reluctantly at first, about a time when a teammate intentionally hurt him in a little league game. When the incident occurred, Frank kept it to himself, apparently feeling overwhelmed by the situation and disconnecting from it. As he told, cast, and directed the story, his mood gradually shifted from frustration to a more relaxed and thoughtful introspection. When the children in the group responded to Frank's situation and suggested various courses of action that could potentially empower him, he became genuinely interested. He asked the children questions such as, "Would *you* have told the mom?" in response to their comments.

After Frank and the group processed Frank's story, I allowed him to cast and create his baseball video game. He only spent a minute or two on this task, as his interest and focus had shifted and been satisfied, for the moment, by a deeper exploration of the social/emotional dynamics from his real-life situation. Through his initial interest in the objects of spectacle, Frank was able to connect to the process of enactment and ultimately find purpose and meaning in receiving feedback from the ensemble.

Given the degree to which children, especially those with neurological challenges like Frank, can dissociate or cut off from the reality of the sometimes overwhelming task of processing and managing social and emotional experience, it is important to know when to allow for a more symbolic representation through the drama and when to be directive and apply positive pressure toward addressing real-life issues. The leader needs to determine, to the best of his or her ability, if the participant is using the exercise to avoid the task at hand, which may ultimately reinforce the tendency for dysfunction. If the child is not willing to be prompted toward a healthier response using the drama he or she has created, then it is reasonable to redirect the child with positive encouragement fueled by a vision of his or her success. Such redirection, though, will only be successful if the foundation of the ensemble has been developed enough to process and manage the resistance.

At the end of the session, I was explaining to Frank's mother what had occurred. I told her, "It was hard for Frank to participate in sharing and directing a situation from his real life…" She said, "Oh no, he can't do that." I told her that he can, and did, with support from the group and direction from me. Frank's mother was surprised and encouraged, as she thought that his condition prohibited him from relating and processing in that manner. We used the experience to sort through, from a parenting perspective, where Frank's neurological deficiency ends and where his behavioral manipulation begins. This information, which highlights one of the quandaries of treating children with a combination of neurological and emotionally based behavioral problems, supported Frank's mother toward the delicate process of how to further address and empower Frank's social and emotional development.

Summary

While reality television may use dramatic elements of spectacle and ensemble in a way that blurs reflection of "real life," drama therapy can use these devices to capture the attention and focus of children with ADHD and related neurological disorders, guiding them toward reflection and higher functioning in their real lives. By including elements of spectacle and ensemble in group drama therapy sessions, a sense of wholeness and cohesion may be created that facilitates empowered development of the individual in a reaffirming social context. Visual elements such as the lights and props, and a focus on individual contributions to the collective process, help children with ADHD and related neurological conditions to connect to, focus on and address social challenges and family life issues in a manner that can facilitate their individual therapeutic processes. By using a drama therapy approach, neurologically impaired participants are able to gain experience and competence in self-awareness, self-monitoring, self-control and emotionally intelligent self-expression, resulting in greater impulse control and improved social functioning.

References

American Psychiatric Association. (2000). *Diagnostic and statistical manual of mental disorders* (4th ed., text rev.). Washington, DC: Author.

Aristotle (1996). *Poetics* (M. Heath, Trans.). New York: Penguin Classics. (Original work published 1895)

Epstein, S. (1998). *Constructive thinking: The key to emotional intelligence.* Westport, CT: Praeger.

Fox, J. (Ed.). (1987). *The essential Moreno.* New York: Springer.

Goleman, D. (1995). *Emotional intelligence: Why it can matter more than IQ.* New York: Bantam Books.

Landy, R. J. (1994). *Drama therapy concepts, theories and practices* (2nd ed.). Springfield, IL: Charles C. Thomas.

Leonard, B. (2003, November 5). *Network of ensemble theatre holds first festival, conference.* Retrieved from http://www.communityarts.net/readingroom/archive/01ensembleconf.php

Moreno, J. L. (1978). *Who shall survive?* Beacon, NY: Beacon House.

Perls, F. S. (1969). *Gestalt therapy verbatim.* Moab, UT: Real People Press.

Simpson, J. A. (Ed.). (1989). *Oxford English dictionary* (2nd ed., vol. 5). Oxford, England: Clarendon Press.

Salovey, P., & Sluyter, D. J. (Eds.). (1997). *Emotional development and emotional intelligence: Educational implications.* New York: Basic Books.

CHAPTER 10

Taming the Beast

The Use of Drama Therapy in the Treatment of Children with Obsessive-Compulsive Disorder

TED I. RUBENSTEIN

Introduction

The world is full of rules: rules that are imposed from without and those that are established from within. For most children, rules are anchors in a chaotic world. From the moment the child can walk, he or she begins to challenge those rules. As the maxim goes, the adults set the rules, the children break them, and the adults re-assert them. This process becomes a dialogue of sorts. Before long, the adult demonstrates some flexibility within the rules and the child begins to integrate them with an understanding that rules and rituals are necessary guidelines that function best in context. For children with obsessive-compulsive disorder (OCD), it would appear that rule making and rule adherence are the central organizing features of their personality. In fact, for these children, the strictures of daily life imposed from within are crushing, oppressive, fruitless measures to ward off an overwhelming anxiety stemming from intrusive, horrifying thoughts. These unrelenting thoughts, often quite frightening, can only be stopped by creating a set of intractable rituals and rules. In short order, the rules themselves become an organic force with a mind of their own. For the child with OCD, disobedience or defiance of the rules will bring on certain destruction to his or her loved ones or the entire universe.

Despite the potentially paralyzing effect that this disorder can have on a child's academic, family, and social life, pharmacological and psychotherapeutic treatments have made significant gains over the past 20 years. The following chapter will look at some of these treatments. In particular, it will examine the way in which drama therapy and action-oriented techniques, from a cognitive-behavioral theoretical approach, have been used to treat children with OCD. Case examples will be reviewed to explain specific treatment approaches.

A Description of OCD

According to the *Diagnostic and Statistical Manual of Mental Disorders, Fourth Edition, Text Revision* (APA, 2000), obsessive-compulsive disorder involves recurrent obsessions or compulsions that are severe enough to be time-consuming and cause distress or significant impairment. The DSM-IV-TR (APA, 2000) defines obsessions as persistent ideas, thoughts, impulses, or images that are experienced as intrusive and inappropriate and that cause marked anxiety or distress. Compulsions are defined as repetitive behaviors or mental acts aimed at preventing or reducing anxiety (APA, 2000). These obsessions are frequently accompanied by feelings such as fear, disgust, or uncertainty (March & Mulle, 1998). Developmentally, most children exhibit some degree of obsessive-compulsive behaviors in which rituals and rules become an important part of their daily lives. What distinguishes the symptoms of OCD from normative, age-dependent behaviors are the timing, content, severity, and appraisal of the intrusive thoughts (Barrett & Healy-Farrell, 2003; March & Mulle, 1998).

Recent research shows that OCD among children and adolescents is much more prevalent than was once believed (Grados & Riddle, 2001; March & Mulle, 1998). Between 1% to 3% of the child population, or 1 in every 200 children, develop obsessive-compulsive disorder (APA, 2000; March & Mulle, 1998). It is also not uncommon for children with OCD to present with tic disorders, disruptive behavior, and learning disorders (Riddle et al., 1990).

Treatment Approaches

In conceptualizing OCD, there are three prevailing theoretical models. The first is behavioral, suggesting that the fears and subsequent attempts to mitigate these fears are part of a stimulus-response contingency. While compelling in its parsimony, this theory alone fails to account for the critical role that thought processes seem to play in the manifestation of this disorder (Riggs & Foa, 1993). The cognitive models suggest that automatic thoughts function as stimuli, which are then compounded by core beliefs that one is unduly responsible for negative outcomes (Barrett & Healy-Farrell, 2003; Riggs & Foa, 1993). Several neuropsychological studies have demonstrated abnormalities in the basal ganglia and frontal cortex (March & Mulle, 1998; Swedo et al., 1989). The literature suggests that pharmacotherapy alone shows some amelioration of symptoms but does not, in isolation, consistently effect a long-lasting change (March & Mulle, 1998; Riggs & Foa, 1993).

That said, it is generally believed that most children benefit from a combined approach of pharmacotherapy and cognitive-behavioral therapy (CBT); therefore, warranting the collaboration of psychiatric consultation (Gadow, 1991; March & Mulle, 1998; McLean et al., 2001; Piacentini, Gitow, Jaffer, & Azrin, 1994). Taken together, behavioral, cognitive, and neuropsychological models provide a unified theory about OCD that flows directly toward efficacious treatments (Kendall et al., 1997; March & Mulle, 1998).

The prognosis and outcome of OCD have improved dramatically since the inception of cognitive-behavioral models (Riggs & Foa, 1993). March and Mulle (1998) suggest a combined approach of pharmacological, psychosocial, and systems approaches. Likening the disorder to diabetes, they outline a treatment strategy that includes cognitive-behavioral interventions, psycho-education, and the use of externalization. The latter technique is consistent with a medical metaphor. It also fits with a drama therapy approach, in particular the use of distancing as a way of achieving insight (Landy, 1996).

Cognitive-behavioral therapy approaches for the treatment of OCD are punctuated by techniques such as exposure/response prevention, reframing, stress inoculation, and psycho-education (Mahoney, 1991; March & Mulle, 1998; Pina et al., 2003). Where such approaches may be powerful for adults, children are less capable of engaging in the mental tasks that are required by cognitive-behavioral therapy (CBT) approaches (March & Mulle, 1998; Meyer, 1966; Riggs & Foa, 1993). For example, to benefit from cognitive reframing one must be capable of meta-cognition; however, such abstract thinking does not develop until one is at least 12 years old, and in some cases not at all (Rosen, 1985). Even the simplest approaches to CBT can be problematic when the child has a co-morbid learning disability or behavioral disorder, which, as mentioned above, is frequently the case.

On the other hand, children are able to externalize and are most certainly capable of pretend play as early as 4 years of age. As the child grows, socio-dramatic play and symbols are increasingly used to solve problems. Frequently, children will use play and skits to demonstrate knowledge in school, while during recess the social pecking order is defined by interactions within play. This proclivity to use symbol and pretense underpins the justification for using drama therapy as a treatment strategy (Grados & Riddle, 2001). In drama therapy, child and therapist are able to collaborate on a task that is familiar and accessible. Children are easily engaged in play, specifically play that starts with the phrase "let's pretend" (Santrock, 1995). Recognizing the limitations of using CBT with children, March & Mulle, in their book *OCD in Children and Adolescents: A Cognitive-Behavioral Treatment Manual* (1998), designed a treatment protocol that incorporates many of the approaches found in cognitive-behavioral therapy adapted to match the developmental abilities of children. Underlying this treatment approach is the use of metaphors for talking about anxiety, family involvement, and exposure/response training. This approach has been adapted and redesigned, applying techniques of drama therapy, to create the protocol described herein. For the purposes of discussion, it is entitled, "Taming the Beast." This title is merely a shorthand term, although it is frequently used with children to help them understand the treatment process.

Description of the Taming the Beast Protocol

Overview

The treatment protocol described in the following pages is based on work conducted with 27 clients at a clinic in an urban setting. Twenty of these clients were males and 7 were females. The median age of the entire sample was 11 years old; the mode and mean were 9 years old. Four clients were Asian-American, two were African-American, and the rest were Caucasian. These clients were referred to the clinic by two separate psychiatrists who specialize in the treatment of children with anxiety disorders. During the course of treatment, all clients remained under the medical supervision of psychiatrists, with varied medical regimes for each. The treating therapists were creative arts therapists, social workers, and psychologists. The use of drama therapy is applied to many of the concepts and guidelines described in March and Mulle's (1998) manual. Many of the adjustments to the protocol are based on insights gained from clinical experiences with these 27 clients.

The treatment protocol described by March and Mulle (1998) involves eight successive stages. These stages include psychoeducation, cognitive training, mapping, exposure/response, relapse prevention, and family involvement. Based on this progression, the "Taming the Beast" protocol is as shown in Table 10.1.

Assessment

Prior to entering into drama therapy, the child should be given a thorough evaluation. This evaluation can be conducted by an appropriately trained drama therapist but is frequently done in conjunction with a licensed psychologist. The evaluation includes an in-depth client and family interview,

Table 10.1 "Taming the Beast" Treatment Protocol

Stage	Goals	Techniques
I: Assessment	Identify the size, scope and dynamics of the child's anxiety, obsessions and compulsions	Formal and informal instruments, observations, interview
II: Naming the Beast	Create working vocabulary for further treatment Psycho-education about disorder	Role play, puppetry, mask work, empty chair techniques
III: "Building the toolkit"or "Planning the strategy"	Identify strategies for coping with anxiety	Cognitive mapping, role play
IV. Taming The Beast	Testing the strategy or testing the tools	Exposure/response prevention
V. Practice	Practice	Group therapy Mutual storytelling

a review of medical/treatment records, a psychological assessment battery, and a psychiatric evaluation (Goodman & Price, 1992).

During this assessment process, the clinician should begin to identify the role that the family system plays in the process of the obsessions and compulsions. In many cases, clinicians will find that certain family members have gone to great lengths to accommodate various compulsions. Often, families live in anticipation of the next crisis. While this level of preparedness can be psychologically draining to the family, it can be reframed as a strength to be harnessed later. This reframing should take the form of identifying for the family the level of emotional investment and commitment that is shared by the various members. Later in the treatment, that same investment will be shifted from crisis management to strategy development and coaching, as will be described later.

An important part of the assessment process includes identifying the child's specific fears, phobias, and compulsions. This can be done through direct questioning, checklists of fears, and collateral information drawn from the family. It should be noted that, at this early stage in the therapeutic relationship, many of the fears will not be readily shared. From the child's perspective, the thoughts that underlie these fears are so dark, so threatening, that merely uttering them is beyond one's ability to cope. This fear of even speaking about the fears leads directly into one of the first targets of the treatment: naming.

Naming

In many ways, the assessment process is also a part of treatment. The interview strengthens rapport and allows the child to begin revealing his or her secrets. These are the closely held secrets of their fears and worries. By telling these secrets to an empathic third party, the process of naming has begun.

Naming is a process of knowing and of agency. Once we put a name to something, we can begin to understand it and exert some agency, if not control, over it. Adam of the Old Testament named the animals of the earth in order to gain mastery over them. Similarly, once we begin to name things, we have some power to affect them. It is like a light thrown into a darkened room that makes visible what was merely a shadow. It may be quite uncomfortable, even unpleasant, to see what is in the darkened room; but what is known is more within our grasp than what is unknown. The naming process begins with identifying and sharing fears and intrusive thoughts. Once these fears have started to be catalogued, the therapist introduces the fear thermometer (March & Mulle, 1998). This fear thermometer is, in fact, a metaphor for any kind of subjective rating of the experience of fear. The child is asked to identify their internal experience of anxiety by attaching a temperature to their feelings. For example, Jonathan, a 9-year-old, Caucasian male identified several fears, including one of trucks and large automobiles. He believed that trucks would lose control and crash into him and his family. He was then asked to identify, using a thermometer scale, how he felt when he was near a truck. The therapist questioned Jonathan:

T: Now I want you to think of hot and cold. Think about a really cold day, like when it is winter. The thermometer would say what?

J: 30 below.

T: Great. Now I want you to think about a really hot day, in the middle of summer. What would the temperature read?

J: About 1000 degrees.

T: Okay. Now, let's think about the 1000 degrees as when you are really, really scared and nervous. Let's also think about 30 below as totally cool. You are totally cool and nothing bothers you.

At this point, the child is asked to physically demonstrate hot and cold, as well as cool and really scared. Once the child begins to do this, the therapist immediately mirrors these physical reactions. The therapist then asks, "Now, can you show me how hot or cold it is for you when you see a truck?"

Jonathan indicates that seeing a truck is moderately warm. The therapist then asks him to give it a temperature reading. Jonathan replies with "about 50." This indicates to the therapist that seeing a truck, while anxiety provoking, is not as highly distressing as some of his other fears. The therapist would review the entire checklist of fears and phobias with the child, asking him or her to assign a temperature to each of the fears that have been revealed at this point in the treatment.

After this initial assessment, the child is asked to create his or her thermometer. Making the thermometer becomes an elaborate and engaging art project. The child is encouraged to make the thermometer two-dimensional. Later in the treatment process, this thermometer will be referred to frequently in order to help client and therapist gauge progress and talk about the client's experience of anxiety. In one case, the child was quite invested in making a sculpture of his thermometer. This desire on the child's part was related to his compulsive behaviors. In about half of the cases in which the protocol was used, the children chose to make other kinds of measurement gauges, such as a rocket fuel gauge.

Once the thermometer is created, it is photocopied and will be used throughout the treatment. The parents are also given a copy. They are asked to identify their understanding of their child's anxiety as related to specific fears, and to place the degree of anxiety on the thermometer. In separate meetings in which the child is not included, the parent's rendering is compared with that of the child and discrepancies are noted. The clinician attempts to understand the meaning behind such discrepancies by testing several hypotheses during subsequent family sessions. These hypotheses are: Is someone in the system catastrophizing or minimizing? Are there significant breaks in communication such that parents are unaware of the depth of the child's pain? Is the child "faking bad" as yet another dimension to the OCD presentation (White, 1986)? In at least two cases, the children were underplaying their experience of fear in order to "fake good." In another instance, the family was over-estimating certain fears or narrowly focusing on one or two fears when there were others that were far more salient for the child. In this example, the child's fears really centered on doing harm to the parents.

The second step in naming is asking the child to tell stories about how their obsessions have affected their lives. Some children will tell elaborate stories while others will use only sparse detail. The level of depth seems to depend on the comfort level with the therapist, the severity of the anxiety and, in some cases, the cognitive styles of the children.

In a separate session, the parents are also asked to tell stories about how the anxiety has affected the family's life and their child's life. The stories are then shared with the entire family. In most cases, this stage is a positive one in which the family begins to validate certain experiences. The parents are often surprised to learn how certain behaviors relate to specific fears. For example Billy, a handsome 12-year-old, Caucasian boy, walked stiffly with his hands held away from his body and a robotic-like bend in his torso. As one can only imagine, this had devastating effects on his social interaction because the picture did not fit. Here was an otherwise "normal" looking child who walked like "Frankenstein," a moniker given to him by his peers. His parents knew that this had something to do with his OCD but thought it was related to his self-perception of his weight. The family highly valued physical fitness and naturally assumed that Billy was trying to appear more "athletic." When the family, including Billy, began to talk about this particular behavior, he or Billy haltingly revealed that his gait and posture were, in fact, his attempts to prevent contamination. He believed that if he touched any object that might have been touched by another child, he would certainly become contaminated. After this revelation, the family gained a deeper appreciation of Billy's internal struggle and daily battle with anxiety.

After the stories have been shared with the family, the therapist and client are ready to begin the next subphase of naming, which is externalizing. In this context, externalizing is a cognitive process whereby the disorder is separated from the individual (White, 1986). March and Mulle (1998) describe this as making OCD the problem. In this process, the child is asked to give the OCD a nickname. It is explained to the child that the OCD is "an unpleasant and oppressive neurobehavioral illness over which both the child and family already have some influence—an influence we and they desire to increase. In this way, therapist, child and family become members of the same team . . ." (March & Mulle, 1998, p. 37). This name can be anything but needs to accurately describe, almost allegorically, the child's experience of the OCD. Curiously, many of the names chosen by the children are somewhat counter-intuitive. Rather than the nearly pejorative terms one might expect, such as "sicko," "monster," or worse, some children chose benign names like "Daisy," "Roscoe," or "Sunshine." Given that this disorder is so paralyzing and painful, it was curious that some children were almost affectionate toward their externalized character. One conclusion that can be drawn is that, while OCD has exerted unwanted, unhealthy control over them, it has also served a purpose. Indeed, as far as the children can tell, the OCD has warded off disaster for some 8 to 13 years. It occurred to the author that while this section of the treatment was groundwork, in fact, this might be the beginning of the introduction of drama therapy. The child needed to directly interact with this force that was soon to be externalized.

The children are encouraged to create a picture of their OCD with the assigned name. Once the picture is drawn, the child is invited to create a puppet or life size doll using a chair and a variety of costumes that represents the OCD (Irwin, 2000; Landy, 1996; Marner, 1995). The OCD's name is emblazoned on a piece of clothing, across the forehead or on a sign that is prominently displayed on or near the doll. The therapist and child sit opposite the puppet and begin to talk about the OCD as if he is not there. The therapist begins to ask the child what it would be like if the OCD actually came to talk with him or her.

In two cases, the abstraction of pondering what the OCD might say was too complicated for the children. To solve this problem, another therapist was introduced into the treatment approach so that he might be able to "enact" this externalized character. Occasionally, albeit rarely, the therapeutic alliance with the child is strong enough that the therapist can play the part of the OCD. However, such a move should be carefully considered. It is important for the clinician to remember that the therapist and child wish to join forces against the OCD. If the therapist plays the OCD, there is the possibility of a strong transferential reaction that might undermine the therapeutic alliance. If, however, the therapist works alone with the child and does not have the luxury of a therapeutic team on site, as is often the case, either the child or therapist can verbalize the words for the doll, much the way a ventriloquist might. In all of these cases, the end goal is that the child has a conversation with his or her OCD, the content of which is driven by the child.

At some point during this process, the child is encouraged to confront the character of his or her OCD. He or she is asked to "boss it back" (March & Mulle, 1998). This language is used to imply that the child will be gaining control over the OCD. In future sessions, this will be an important strategy. Both the family and the therapist will refer to this concept of "bossing back" when the child is particularly challenged by the OCD. The child is asked to envision what "bossing back" looks like, including the physical posture. If necessary and helpful, the auxiliary player who is embodying the OCD can create that body position or the physical response of being bossed back as described by the child.

Dialogue between the OCD and the child may last two to three sessions. After the child has had ample chance to talk with his or her OCD, the treatment is ready to move to the next stage.

Building the Toolkit

The focus of the next stage is on strategy building. During the naming section, some strategies were laid down, but in this stage there is a primary focus on specific strategies. "Boss it back" is practiced frequently. Second, there is a continued referral to the thermometer. In this phase, exposure/

response prevention is initiated, during which the child is asked to begin "bossing back" the disorder in situations that are anxiety-provoking. The child is asked to role play, with the therapist, being in that situation. Starting with the least distressing situation or fear, and moving up the hierarchy of anxiety, the therapist and child begin to identify a set of verbal strategies, thought processes, and behaviors that all relate to "bossing back" the OCD and thereby taking control. The therapist and the child begin to strategize together about how they might talk with the OCD and what sorts of things they might say to "boss it back."

Using improvisational role play, set design, or even puppetry, the child and therapist will enter into a scene in which the external stimulus that triggers fear is present (Irwin, 2000). For example, in the case of Jonathon, one of his middle range fears was any kind of thunderstorm, big or small. He was certain that the storm would escalate into a raging tornado. This fear almost completely paralyzed him at times. Using a stepwise progression, the therapist and client engaged in scenes that depicted being in a storm. In the first scene, the storm was distant and the detail of the storm was entirely drawn from imagination. Each scene added an element of heightened drama and reality, including lights and sound. At the final stage, the sound and effect of a huge storm were created. Using the storm as a metaphor, the therapist asked the client to create a story about the storm but find a way in which the character is completely able to boss back their fear. Jonathan's story involved Joe DiMaggio who is batting for the New York Yankees in the final game of the World Series. Mr. DiMaggio is fearful of the storm such that he is unable to concentrate on his hitting. Just as the windstorm ensues, he hits the ball. The wind carries it away, making it a home run, and the Yankees win the World Series. Each of the child's fears is played out in this way. At the conclusion of each story, the child is asked to identify his internal experience of anxiety on the anxiety thermometer.

The work of exposure/response prevention is not isolated to the drama therapy session. The clients are then asked to cognitively talk about the ways in which they are taking control of their anxiety. Concrete, reality-based, self-soothing statements are used, such as "Tornadoes are relatively rare." A series of self-talk statements are generated during the "conversations" with the OCD. For example, in Jonathon's case, with the help of the therapist, he talked with "Smarmy the II" about the control that he was exerting when inclement weather was present.

T: What should we say to Smarmy about storms?
J: I don't know.
T: What can we say to him about storms that will keep him under better control?

J: My dad says that tornadoes never happen in the city.
T: Well, I don't know about never, but there hasn't been one for about a
hundred years. That's pretty good.

Other similar self-soothing statements were developed. It is important
to note that while things went relatively smoothly in this particular example,
the more intense the anxiety, the more difficult it is for the child to generate
self-soothing statements.

With the strategies firmly intact, the child is ready to move to the next
step. It is important to note that progression to the next phase of the treatment may occur before the child has reached the top of his anxiety hierarchy. The clinical experience thus far seems to show that children require a
sufficient scaffolding of success before they are able to begin conquering
the most intensely anxiety-provoking fears. This history of success is most
sweet when shared with others in a group context. Groups, however, can
also be among the single most anxiety-ridden experiences for these children.
The dichotomy of needing to connect and also being fearful of embarrassment in a group necessitate safe, contained group work.

Taming the Beast and Practice

Having successfully learned many coping techniques, the child is encouraged
to join one of several groups of other children also working to overcome
the symptoms of OCD. At first glance, it would seem that a homogenous
group, with varying degrees of anxiety, might create a chaotic situation.
The individual members of the group might begin to play off each other's
anxiety, and soon the group itself becomes chaotic. The members might
become fearful that the group is out of control, creating more anxiety. As
Masterpasqua (1997) points out, "Chaos, disorder and the person experiencing them must be embraced. To do otherwise is to deny 'the motion of life'
and to serve as a source of alienation" (p. 36). The chance for these children
to be understood and validated far outweighs the risks of an elevated anxiety.

Within the group, the children are encouraged to share personal triumphs
and struggles, and to swap "war stories" from their battle with OCD. They
are also encouraged to collaborate on stories that will eventually become
pieces of theatre. In collaboration, the children are encouraged to practice
coping strategies and make friends in the context of their newfound or
emerging freedom from anxiety.

In the group, each child is encouraged to create a story of some kind. The
rest of the group adds, amends, or revises the story based on their creative
response. The original author is then encouraged to find a compromise
between what they had originally intended and what was offered by the
group. Frequently, the therapist intervenes at this point and helps members

maintain a sense of control over their own actions and experiences, while at the same time contributing to a larger group activity.

The group then negotiates how this story is enacted, including the use of props and costumes. For some members, the use of props and costumes becomes its own testing of the exposure/response strategies, for they become anxious about the spread of germs when touching "community" items. Certain members of the group have very distinct ideas about how the story should be enacted with specific ideas for parts that should be played. For some children, the anxiety of planning becomes overwhelming and they either withdraw entirely or become narrowly focused on one minor aspect of the story, thereby ignoring or rejecting any further collaboration. Again, the therapist intervenes, assisting each member in maintaining a balance of active collaboration. Side coaching, in which the therapist subtly pulls a group member aside and reminds him about "bossing back" the OCD, may also be necessary.

In one group, five boys, ranging in age from 9 to 11, all of whom were diagnosed with OCD and had undergone the first part of the protocol mentioned above, met for three times prior to creating their first story. The first three sessions focused on introductions and theatre games. These first sessions had two foci: to help the group begin to become comfortable with each other and to assess the dynamics within the group. By playing a series of theatre games, some that involved rough and tumble play, some that involved guessing, and others that simply involved full creative investment, the therapist was able to identify strengths and challenges faced by these children in a social context. By session three, the group was ready to tell a story.

Alex, a 9-year-old, Caucasian boy, created a story about a space shuttle that had gone off course, leaving the crew in trouble. "Jean-Luc Picard" from TV's *Star Trek: The Next Generation* was summoned to save the day. Alex intended to play the captain. The therapist asked Alex how Picard was going to execute this difficult mission. Alex responded by saying that Picard had a special space capsule that not only could travel at lightning speed, but also was immune to whatever had imperiled the space shuttle. At this point, Alex had created a story that contained no other characters and, thus, involved no other group members. This was typical of his play in other settings. He usually had to be the winner of every game and seemed to cast others in peripheral roles. This play style had been the source of significant social problems at school. Even on pre-arranged play dates, neighborhood children stopped accepting invitations to play because they no longer wanted bit parts in Alex's sociodramatic play.

David, a 10-year-old member of the group, latched onto the idea of Jean-Luc Picard and immediately began a conflict with Alex about who would actually play this role. While the group began assigning parts, Steven, age 9, became overwhelmed by the social challenge and retreated into commenting on obscure details about the space shuttle, such as the circumstances under which it would get off course. Having some knowledge about flight, he was insistent that the space shuttle would not be able to go off course without drifting into space and, therefore, becoming irretrievable. When the notion of another space ship was introduced, a craft that was able to rescue the shuttle, Steven scoffed, saying no such space ship existed. William, a 10-year-old Asian American, was not at all interested in a story of this kind but seemed willing to play along if it was an interesting story. Tony, an 11-year-old, Caucasian male, was far more interested in adhering to the group rules, such as not talking out of turn and remaining seated while the group planned the story. Finally, Robert, an 11-year-old who had brought some trading cards with him, put his head down to look at his cards, interacting with no one.

Each of these reactions was entirely consistent with the play styles of the children and tapped into their individual issues of control. David and Alex needed to control the other members of the group and, if unable to accomplish that, wanted to overpower the activity and thereby eliminate the uncertainty that comes from a relationship. Steven, feeling overwhelmed by the task, focused on the part of the story he could understand—the aerodynamics of flight. Robert simply withdrew.

The therapist conducted "writers'" meetings in which the three boys were encouraged to function like scriptwriters who must work together to create a coherent story. The boundaries were set: (1) Jean Luc cannot do it alone; and (2) whatever technology was needed could be invented so long as it did not completely defy scientific knowledge. For this last point, the therapist observed that in much of science fiction the technology represented had not been invented but did have a root in existing knowledge. At this point in time, one of the *Star Wars* films had just been released and the group used that film as a point of inspiration. The therapist pointed out that light sabers didn't yet exist but lasers existed in the most common items such as CD players. The therapist posited, if we can accept light sabers, then why not ships that can probe deep space and return?

The group struggled with this story design and, for half of a session, remained at something of a stalemate. The therapist then broke the stalemate by suggesting plot lines with two options and asking the group to agree to one of two options. So, the therapist (in this case, the author) said, "Jean-Luc has a crew. Now each of you are on the crew. So, who are the different members and what are their jobs?" By narrowing the choices, the therapist attempted to contain some of the anxiety of the group members. This moved the group off center and Alex was among the first to start asking group members to play certain parts. Once the parts had been decided, the therapist asked the group to identify what obstacles they might encounter to obtaining their objective, which was to save the foundering space shuttle. The group, almost in unison, suggested a violent meteor storm, a character from the *Star Wars* movies (Darth Mal), and an electromagnetic disturbance (Steven's suggestion).

As a participating member of the "writing" team, the therapist also added obstacles that were germane to each child's specific fears. Therefore, there was an infestation of intergalactic bugs, a loss of oxygen pressure in the rescue craft caused by a malfunction, and other specific things that some of the kids had identified earlier as sources of anxiety. The goal here was to allow the other group members to help each child overcome his specific fear while in the cocoon of an imaginative play space.

The group enacted the story using improvisational storytelling. They were told that anything could happen during the story, with the ground rules that: (1) the entire rescue crew had to participate in the rescue and return safely; and (2) it was deep outer space, unexplored territory, and anything was possible. This last directive was aimed specifically at Steven. This rule was not enough to prevent him from stopping the action entirely and stating why something was impossible or implausible. In a private session, the therapist worked with Steven on the classic improvisational rule about never saying "no" while on stage. This rule simply states that in improvisational theatre, whenever an actor creates an object or situation, the partner cannot deny what was created. This became a powerful therapeutic vocabulary for Steven. His need to control his internal chaos would only allow him to accept that which fit with his understanding or expectation of the world. This style closed him off from friends, family, and academic progress. Steven was told that anytime he heard something in the story that he did not agree with, he could say, "Yes, and . . ." or "Yes, but. . . ." This concrete strategy, developed in the strategy building sessions, was employed in other areas of his life.

Eventually, the children enacted the story, the space shuttle was rescued, and the crew returned safely. In this first story, none of this would have been possible without significant therapist intervention. The goal for each of the subsequent stories was for the therapist to intervene less and the group to collaborate more. After 6 months, the group disbanded because two members had achieved all of their stated goals and were able to manage their OCD sufficiently. This is not to say they were without anxiety, but by using the strategies, they were able to ameliorate many of the symptoms. The remaining three members stayed in the group, but two new people joined, thus creating an entirely different group dynamic.

In the ideal setting, children end their treatment after they have achieved the goal of effectively using the strategies to mitigate symptoms of anxiety and to begin to control their OCD. The benchmark of recovery is consistent with that found in the literature, with a suggested decrease of at least six points in the Yale-Brown Obsessive-Compulsive Scale from pretreatment to post treatment, and a final score of less than 12 (Goodman et al., 1989; Goodman & Price, 1992). From the inception of this treatment, 10 children have achieved this benchmark, 4 children withdrew prematurely, and the remaining 13 are continuing their treatment as of this writing.

The two boys who left the particular group mentioned above had follow-up sessions every 3 months. During these sessions, they reviewed with the therapist moments or times when the strategies did not work. They also reviewed successes. Many times, these sessions were spent reviewing successful school reports and new friendships, and sharing the children's private reverie about being able to walk right into their fears and "boss it back."

Conclusion and Summary

Childhood OCD is a complicated disorder that, until recently, was underrepresented in the epidemiological literature. It has both neuropsychological and behavioral components. While no studies have been completed that show one treatment approach as more effective than another, there is evidence to suggest that a combination of pharmacological, cognitive, and behavioral approaches are best suited to help these children.

Drama therapy can make the CBT approach concrete while remaining consistent with a child's desire to achieve mastery through play. The introduction of group therapy techniques in conjunction with drama therapy provides the child an in vivo experience of practicing the strategies learned through CBT. The use of drama therapy in conjunction with CBT for this population was piloted with 27 clients, as described above. There is a great amount of research to be done in order to identify exactly which element of the protocol is the change agent. The size of the sample is limited and needs to be expanded with more quantifiable outcome measures. The introduction of other drama therapy techniques and a comparison to a control group are needed. On the other hand, the results at this level of inquiry are promising. By combining the practical with the pretend, the child and therapist are able to access strength in order to overcome obstacle. In many cases, this struggle can be conducted in a cocoon of fun and spontaneous enjoyment.

The giggles that erupt when the child is asked to name his or her beast, and the exasperated gestures that come when the child is asked to do battle with the beast are both indicators that the child is beginning to gain control; to step aside, for a moment, and see the absurdity in the cruelty of this disorder. Once that absurdity is harnessed, the fear seems a less dark, less foreboding entity. It is not unlike laughing at what is fearful. The times when the children become engrossed in their pretense contain the signs of hope that lead them to believe what the adults around them say: "Someday, you will beat this." Perhaps pretending will make it so.

References

American Psychiatric Association. (2000). *Diagnostic and statistical manual of mental disorders* (4th ed., text revision). Washington, DC: Author.

Barrett, P., & Healy-Farrell, L. (2003). Perceived responsibility in juvenile obsessive-compulsive disorder: An experimental manipulation. *Journal of Clinical Child and Adolescent Psychology, 32* (3), 430-441.

Gadow, K. D. (1991). Clinical issues in child and adolescent psychopharmacology. *Journal of Consulting and Clinical Psychology, 59*(6), 842–852.

Goodman, W. K., & Price, L. H. (1992). Assessment of severity and change in obsessive compulsive disorder. *Psychiatric Clinics of North America, 15*(4), 861–869.

Goodman, W. K., Price, L. H., Rasmussen, S. A., Mazure, C., Delgado, P., Heninger, G. R., & Charney, D. S. (1989). The Yale Brown Obsessive Compulsive Scale: I. Development, use and reliability. *Archives of General Psychiatry, 46*(11), 1006–1011.

Grados, M. A., & Riddle, M. A. (2001). Pharmacological treatment of childhood obsessive-compulsive disorder: From theory to practice. *Journal of Community Psychology, 30*(1), 67–79.

Irwin, E. (2000). The use of a puppet interview to understand children. In K. Gitlin-Weiner, A. Sandgrund & C. Schaefer (Eds.), *Play diagnosis and assessment* (2nd ed., pp. 617–636). New York: Wiley.

Kendall, P. C., Flannery-Schroeder, E., Panichelli-Mindel, S. M., Southam-Gerow, M., Henin, A., & Warman, M. (1997). Therapy for youths with anxiety disorders: A second randomized clinical trial. *Journal of Consulting and Clinical Psychology, 65*(3), 366–380.

Landy, R. (1994). *Drama therapy: Concepts, theories and practices* (2nd ed.). Springfield, IL: Charles C. Thomas.

Landy, R. (1996). *Essays in drama therapy: The double life.* London: Jessica Kingsley.

Mahoney, M. J. (1991). *Human change processes: The scientific foundations of psychotherapy.* New York: Basic Books.

March, J., & Mulle, K. (1998). *OCD in children and adolescents: A cognitive-behavioral treatment manual.* New York: Guilford.

Marner, T. (1995). The role a role play may play: Dramatherapy and the externalization of the problem. In S. Jennings (Ed.), *Dramatherapy with children and adolescents* (pp. 63–74). New York: Routledge.

Masterpasqua, F. (1997). Toward a dynamical developmental understanding of disorder. In F. Masterpasqua & P. A. Perna (Eds.), *The psychological meaning of chaos: Translating theory into practice* (pp. 23–40). Washington, DC: American Psychological Association.

McLean, P.D., Whittal, M. L., Thordarson, D. S., Taylor, S., Söchting, I., Koch, W. J., Paterson, R., & Anderson, K. W. (2001). Cognitive versus behavior therapy in the group treatment of obsessive–compulsive disorder. *Journal of Consulting and Clinical Psychology, 69*(2), 205–214.

Meyer, V. (1966). Modification of expectations in cases with obsessional rituals. *Behaviour Research and Therapy, 4,* 273–280.

Piacentini, J., Gitow, A., Jaffer, M., & Azrin, N. H. (1994). Outpatient behavioral treatment of child and adolescent obsessive compulsive disorder. *Journal of Anxiety Disorders, 8*(3), 277–289.

Pina, A. A., Silverman, W. K., Weems, C. F., Kurtines, W. M., & Goldman, M. L. A. (2003). A comparison of completers and noncompleters of exposure based cognitive and behavioral treatment for phobic and anxiety disorders in youth. *Journal of Consulting and Clinical Psychology, 71*(4), 701–705.

Riddle, M. A., Scahill, L., King, R., Hardin, M. T., Towbin, K. E., Ort, S. I., Leckman, J. F., & Cohen, D. J. (1990). Obsessive compulsive disorder in children and adolescents: Phenomenology and family history. *Journal of the American Academy of Child and Adolescent Psychiatry,* *29*(5), 766–772.

Riggs, D. S., & Foa, E. B. (1993). Obsessive compulsive disorder. In D. H. Barlow (Ed.), *Clinical handbook of psychological disorders: A step-by-step treatment manual* (pp. 189–239). New York: Guilford.

Rosen, H. (1985). *Piagetian dimensions of clinical relevance.* New York: Columbia University Press.

Santrock, J. W. (1995). *Life-span development.* Madison, WI: Brown and Benchmark Publishers.

Swedo, S. E., Schapiro, M. B., Grady, C. L., Cheslow, D. L., Leonard, H. L., Kumar, A., Friedland, R., Rapoport, S. I., & Rapoport, J. L. (1989). Cerebral glucose metabolism in childhood-onset obsessive-compulsive disorder. *Archives of General Psychiatry, 46*(6), 518–523.

White, M. (1986). Negative explanation, restraint and double description: A template for family therapy. *Family Process, 25*(2), 169–184.

CHAPTER 11

Group Drama Therapy in a Children's Inpatient Psychiatric Setting

CRAIG HAEN

Beyond food, clothing, and shelter, the single greatest
need in a child's life is for emotional security, or what I call
connectedness. Connectedness creates the magic.
—Edward M. Hallowell

Children's group therapy has had a long history within the inpatient, psychiatric setting (Lomonaco, Scheidlinger, & Aronson, 2000) where groups are an inherent part of the milieu treatment environment. Despite this history, there are relatively few clinical writings on inpatient group work with children. Within the field of drama therapy, several authors have addressed the use of groups with an acute, adult population (Emunah, 1983; Forrester & Johnson, 1996; Mitchell, 1987; Reif, 1981; Sheppard, Olson, Croke, Lafave, & Gerber, 1990; Winn, 1996), but there is scant literature that specifically examines the use of drama therapy as a group treatment modality in child inpatient psychiatry (see Carlson-Sabelli, 1998; Trafford & Perks, 1987).

Children are hospitalized in a psychiatric setting when they are deemed to be a danger to themselves or others, and cannot maintain safety outside the hospital. Often, aggressive, destructive, or self-injurious behaviors are the precursors to admission. The children can have one or more of a variety of pathologies and often have a history of maltreatment from adults. As such, they bring to the inpatient unit patterns of interaction that are fueled by "impulsiveness, intense competitiveness, acting out, large-scale regression, and the mechanisms of denial, splitting and projective identification" (Tsiantis, 1996, p. 140).

The Setting

Inpatient psychiatric programs for children are most often located on locked units within a hospital environment. The treatment team is usually multi-disciplinary and a behavioral system is frequently utilized for milieu management. The goals of hospitalization include psychological stabilization, the provision of a safe holding environment, diagnosis and assessment, intensive therapy (individual, group, and family), medication management, and co-ordination of ongoing services that will continue to assist the child and family after discharge (McGarvey & Haen, in press). As lengths of stay have dramatically decreased in recent years, there is a greater emphasis on focused, goal-directed treatment (Stearns, 1991). Studies have shown that, despite shorter admissions, hospitalization can still be an effective intervention for the mentally ill child (Soth, 1997).

The physical environment of an inpatient unit is qualitatively similar to what Foucault (1977) described as disciplinary space, with characteristics of enclosure, partitioning, the establishment of functional areas, and a defined rank among the members. The symbols of this rank, which include keys and identification badges, can be quite powerful. Likewise, a hierarchy often exists among the staff based on each member's title and discipline of practice (Mitchell, 1987). The issues evoked by the treatment environment are important for children to explore during the therapy process.

By its very nature, the inpatient unit is one predicated on groups. Therapists working in this setting must remain mindful of the fact that each group therapy session functions as a group within a larger system (Williams, 1999). Bronfenbrenner (1992) conceived of child development as occurring within a series of systems. He theorized that, in order to understand the child, one must understand the child's reciprocal interaction with each level of the ecological system. Likewise, a therapy group on an inpatient unit is framed by the milieu itself, the larger hospital structure, and the child's world outside the hospital. Characteristics and changes in any of these environments can affect the micro-system of the group.

On acute units, groups are constantly impacted by the rotating client base, which leads to an ever-evolving group structure and culture. The therapist has little control over group composition. Though children can be separated by age (with a range of 2 to 3 years being preferable), there are often patients with varying diagnoses, issues, and functional levels in the same group. Given the frequent termination and addition of group members, Yalom (1983) advocated for viewing each inpatient group session as separate and complete unto itself. Sarra (1998) has argued against the single-session notion. He advocates instead for the "evolving cultural matrix" of the group, pointing out how one set of patients may continue to work on issues that another group had begun, and how the creation of a milieu that communicates support for group therapy can bolster therapeutic progress.

In concordance with Sarra (1998), it is this author's experience that each group session contains a fair number of patients who are "veterans" in the group. Likewise, many patients are admitted to the unit multiple times and are thus familiar with group therapy. In addition, an active group therapy program is one in which patients may meet for several days in a row and can do ongoing work during that time period. Though changes in membership may occur, the main thrust of the group can continue over several sessions.

Unlike in outpatient settings, the group therapist on an inpatient unit often takes on multiple roles (Bellinson, 1992). For example, in addition to coordinating the group therapy program, this author also sees children individually for trauma-specific play therapy, assists with milieu management, meets with families, takes the children outside and on field trips, and may play out the roles of disciplinarian, coach, supporter, surrogate family member, advocate, guide, and clinician at different points in any given day. These varying roles allow for different patterns of interaction between the therapist and clients. As the roles become more fluid, the therapist must maintain an internal sense of consistency. The shifts allow him to experience the clients more fully, but also leaves him more vulnerable to countertransference reactions.

There are significant challenges to working on an inpatient unit. As the children project their family roles onto their interactions with peers and staff, there develops a constant level of chaos and violence that can be frightening and stressful. Likewise, it is often in the confines of the hospital where the children expose the true core of their desperation and primal rage. Many of their cries are akin to those of dying animals, and their level of damage and need is often overwhelming. In addition, the use of seclusion and restraint as management tools can evoke strong affect in both patients and staff.

In this environment, rescue fantasies are a common feature of the transference-countertransference dynamic, as are the anger and disappointment that develop when the children realize that the staff cannot meet their pervasive needs for love and nurturing. It is not uncommon for a client to simultaneously evoke anger in one staff member and the desire to protect in another. These opposing relationships are often indicative of splits within the child's family-of-origin or reflective of their extremely polarized patterns of interaction with others.

Despite the challenges, this author has found the inpatient setting to also hold certain clinical advantages. By working within the context of a treatment team, one is afforded multiple viewpoints and glimpses into the child's psyche. A team that functions together can serve as a support network for its members, helping them to navigate the frustrations inherent in providing therapy to severely disturbed children (McGarvey & Haen, in press). Likewise, inpatient treatment allows the therapist the opportunity to work intensively each day with the child. By having staff available around the clock, the clinician knows that there is someone to monitor the child's well-being if he has had a particularly difficult session. By virtue of her multiple roles, the inpatient group therapist brings to the group a more proficient understanding of each of the clients (Bellinson, 1992).

Having frequently grown up in environments of chaos and threat, the patients typically present as rigidly defended and disengaged. Despite the strong, protective outer cores that they have developed, it is this writer's experience that, after one gets past the armor, the inpatient children are much less defended than their more stable peers. Because their needs are great, they seek connection and have the capacity to provide for one another symbolically within the context of the group. Having acquired knowledge from the communal setting, the children often prove markedly perceptive in their observations of staff members and peers, and can offer effective reality testing. They are able to take emotional risks that a less acute population might not allow themselves, precisely because they have little left to lose. Clients who enter sessions with their hands over their ears, screaming, "Leave me alone!" come to take care of the more vulnerable members of the group. Children who are initially withdrawn and silent share with the group their past histories of abuse when it feels safe enough. It soon becomes evident that many of the group members' "maladaptive" behaviors are survival skills that have developed to protect them from harm.

Because of the many challenges endemic to the inpatient environment, the group therapist must be sharp, flexible, and creative. He must be able to provide containment and structure while remaining open to the needs of the group. She must be a strong advocate for the sanctity of the therapeutic space and guard it against intrusion. The therapist remains compassionate and empathic, able to look beyond the child's pathology to see his strengths and the parts of him that are healthy. She is charged with recognizing and meeting the group where they are developmentally, but also with encouraging them to rise to their own best level of functioning. Finally, the therapist must have a strong tolerance for clients who have been so damaged that they will not readily get better and will frequently return to the hospital. As will be illustrated, drama therapy can prove an effective treatment method for navigating the difficulties of treating a severely disturbed child population in a contained setting.

Inpatient Considerations and Drama Therapy's Contribution

As emotionally disturbed children often lack essential inner controls, regulation must be provided externally by the therapist (Sugar, 1991). Limit-setting, boundaries, structure, and containment become key elements in the inpatient group therapy process, and those methods that work best are those in which the group leader is an active presence (Bellinson, 1992; Haen & Brannon, 2002; Rosenberg & Cherbuliez, 1979; Scheidlinger, 1960). Likewise, successful interventions are those that take into consideration the developmental level of the group (Mosholder, Burke, & Carter, 1988), and that serve to organize psyches that are fragmented by intrusive thoughts, delusions, and paranoia. Methods in which the therapist remains non-directive or simply follows the group's fantasy play without providing safety and structure are contra-indicated for this population.

Given the short-term nature of hospitalization, it belies the group therapist to build cohesion within the group quickly and to move into a working phase in a manner that is both safe and direct. Often, particularly with younger and regressed clients, the clinical focus should be on affect recognition, identification, and tolerance. This can occur within the here-and-now of the group environment by building empathy and creating connections between members. Likewise, group therapy should be used as a venue for instilling hope (Forrester & Johnson, 1996), processing the experience of hospitalization (Kibel, 1993), and empowering clients to gradually let go of the role of patient and reconnect with healthier, more stable roles that are syntonic with family and community (Langley & Langley, 1983). Finally, if viewed in the context of a continuum of care, inpatient work can be seen as a process of planting seeds that will be cultivated as the children continue their work on an outpatient basis.

Drama therapy has much to contribute to addressing the challenges of inpatient group therapy with children. There is support in the mental health literature for the efficacy of role play as a tool for therapeutic change in group work (Bellinson, 1992; Frank, 1976; Mosholder et al., 1988; Stearns, 1991). Enactment provides the child with an avenue of expression that is in harmony with her ability to play, opening up doors that purely verbal therapy does not (Barratt & Segal, 1996). Scheidlinger (1960) wrote, "It is well known that in all children, acting is the natural form of communication. . . . Expressing problems through action rather than words is especially true of personalities with early fixation levels" (p. 360).

Upon entering a group, severely emotionally disturbed children often have difficulty because they do not know how to be an appropriate group member. They lack the essential skills of empathy, emotional communication, and listening. They struggle to perceive and understand affect, to read social cues, to navigate interpersonal boundaries, and to problem solve. The therapist's active facilitation of the children's capacities in these areas is at the heart of the drama therapy group process. Emunah (1999) wrote, "The drama therapist is not a bystander, but an active player who serves as a role model and catalyst for clients' engagement in the action-oriented treatment process" (p. 118).

The drama therapist models spontaneity and a sense of humor, as well as excitement and respect for the group members, and the group itself. This sense of respect includes setting limits in a manner that emphasizes the child's own ability to gain control of his behavior ("I notice that you're having a hard time focusing right now. Can you join the group, or do you think you need a time out?") and the therapist's use of self to foster understanding about how the child's actions make others feel ("You keep interrupting me when I try to talk, and it's starting to make me feel frustrated."). In doing so, he attempts to make the group process visible and comprehensible to the members. The therapist might also model and teach appropriate expression of affect by speaking about themes that are present in the group but remain unspoken. ("It seems like many people in the group are saying that they feel happy today. I wonder if anyone feels differently?") Thereafter, the therapist encourages the group to take collective responsibility for its members, who are engaged in providing validation, empathy, support, and affective feedback to one another.

A sense of esprit de corps must be fostered in the initial stages of the group in order for it to develop. On an inpatient unit, these initial stages are measured in minutes rather than weeks. Emunah (1996) emphasized how the use of drama therapy techniques can accelerate the coalescence of a group in the beginning by helping clients to overcome resistance, fear, and anxiety. Ritualistic ways of beginning group sessions are often grounding, specifically those that either orient the children or help them connect to one another. Warm-ups should respond to the here-and-now of the group's presentation and target increased cohesion and interaction. For example, if many of the group members enter the room unfocused and silly, the warm-up should seek to engage them and direct their attention to the task at hand. Likewise, if they are withdrawn, the warm-up should target increased energy and expression. Groups with widely disparate energy benefit from activities such as Group Mood (Emunah, 1994) and collective movement exercises that help bring the members into similar affective space.

In one session that followed a particularly stressful fight on the milieu, the group members came to the center of the circle and grabbed imaginary cans of disinfectant. They ran around the room pretending to de-contaminate the space. In another session, the group struggled to focus due to the very loud banging coming from an angry patient in an adjacent Quiet Room. The author encouraged the children to get down on the floor and join the steady, rhythmic banging. Gradually, each member was asked to transform the banging into another rhythm or sound. As they did so, their anxiety dissipated and they began to come together as a group. In both instances, the active, attuned nature of the warm-up process engaged the children, and the metaphor made the space safe for therapy to occur.

It is this author's belief that children who might not otherwise be able to interact in a group setting can be successful when endowed with a role in which the task is clear. These roles can be functional (helping to arrange the space by moving chairs in a circle; setting up the stage) or related to group interaction (tapping members to find out how they feel inside; checking in with a silent peer). Within the working phase of the session, the roles can extend from the dramatic framework and include those that develop the observing ego (audience member, camera-person) or the ability to be assertive and remain focused (director, actor). Likewise, the expression of roles within the enactment can serve to address many of the issues characteristic of children with mental illness.

In a group of 5- to 8-year-olds, the members used small toys and blocks to build an imaginary town. During the construction, this writer remained on the outside as a witness, reflecting to the group the dynamics that he saw—children who worked in pairs and sub-groups, those who played on the periphery, conflicts that arose in the group, and so on. He then enroled as a reporter, interviewing each child through a toy he or she chose. He asked each how long he had been in the town, how safe she felt, and his or her wishes for the future of the town. Derrick, who had spent time in the care of his homeless, substance-abusing mother, enroled as a vagrant drunk who wandered the town until he was welcomed into the home of Ruby, a female group member whose character offered to be his new mommy. Reggie, a psychotic 6-year-old who had great difficulty connecting to peers, built an elaborate fortress in the middle of the room, responding to questions from the leader by shouting, "Nobody home!" Veronica, who had accidentally set herself on fire prior to hospitalization, suffering third-degree burns, called out for help, saying that her house was on fire. The group banded together to rescue her family characters from their imaginary home. Lilly, an 8-year-old witness of domestic violence, talked about how she did not feel safe in the town because of all the robbers who wandered the streets at night. A closure process helped them to disengage from the intimate expression of these characters and to return to a grounded sense of self.

Affect, Cognition, and Self-Control

There exists a misconception, particularly from those charged with management of the milieu environment, that the arts have the potential to activate clients in an unhealthy and destabilizing way. In actuality, drama therapy can serve to organize an otherwise fragmented client. As Irwin (1983) wrote, "The very nature of the arts process necessitates organization and control. The creative experience demands limits, with a new order emerging out of the old, clarity and control supplanting chaos and confusion" (p. 45). In playing a role, the client takes on and demonstrates the function and qualities specific to that role, finding within themselves those same characteristics. The role provides distance, safety, and a framework that allows for the expression of feelings (Landy, 1993). Clients who are the most fragmented often speak with lucidity and insight while in the guise of character.

In an interview, neurologist Oliver Sacks stated:

Sometimes literally with patients you see a temporary wholing or healing. . . . Sometimes very disorganized people with retardation or dementia or autism, may be able to take on a role and act, and in so doing can take on the coherence and the unity of an active identity, if only for a little while. Acting, like music, can sometimes . . . bring a very damaged person into a brief unity which could not otherwise be imagined of them (Delgado & Heritage, 1996, p. 325).

As most actors will attest, the process of creating a character is one that demands empathy, and being a good actor is equivalent to being in partnership with another, requiring listening, focus, control, and trust. For children, playing the role of a teacher, parent, staff member, sibling, or friend allows them to gain perspective. Role reversal, mirroring, and engagement of the group in creating alternate endings are effective interventions that stimulate patients' empathic capacity. Witnessing a peer's enactment of a scene, creation of a picture, or projection onto an object allows for empathic connection as well. Even when the group process is primarily verbal, the psychodramatic technique of doubling (Kellerman, 1992) can be profound in establishing bonds between members. A client who is stuck, unable to find words, can be asked to choose a group member who they think can speak for them—to say what they are thinking or feeling under the surface. By experiencing empathy in the drama therapy group setting, the child feels seen, heard, and validated, often for the first time in her life.

In a session with older children, the group engaged Matthew, a resistant and angry member, by creating a sculpture (with his permission) in which each member embodied a part of him. Intrigued, Matthew tapped each child on the shoulder and listened as they said, "I understand the part of Matthew that feels angry . . . quiet . . . silly . . . scared . . ." and so on. After taking each of his peers into account, Matthew remarked with delight and surprise, "You guys *really* get me!" Matthew grew to gradually trust the group and often sought to engage newer group members through the creation of sculptures that represented aspects of their personalities.

Drama therapy can contribute to clients' sense of empowerment, allowing them mastery at a time in their lives when much is out of their control. In the safety of the group environment, the children often use their metaphors and characters not only to express what is, but also to test out fantasies of how things could be. In so doing, their viewpoint is expanded, as they try on alternate roles for themselves and activate latent aspects of the self (Haen & Brannon, 2002). Lederer (1964) wrote of the act of creation as an act of defiance—of rejecting what exists and creating a new possibility. Through scene work, the children often re-story their lives, choosing roles that reflect strength and power (Haen, 2002). One obese 8-year-old, who was often a bully on the unit, chose to enrole as a superhero whose job it was to "protect all the fat kids." With sudden affect, the child quietly added, "I know what it's like for those kids."

In another session, an 11-year-old girl, who was extremely disorganized with poor insight and boundaries, was able to step into the role of a therapist meeting for the first time with a frightened client. She was encouraged to stay in touch with the client's fears and to empathize with the character by reversing roles with the child playing the client. As the therapist, she was more eloquent and organized than she had ever been during her hospitalization. Afterwards, she was able to reflect on how the choices she made in the scene—her posture, tone of voice, stillness—allowed the other character to feel safe in her presence. She said that when she played the role she felt respected.

Drama therapy is a powerful medium in which to explore problem solving. The dramatic space allows for a dilemma to be examined from multiple angles, to be frozen and rewound. Clients can rehearse varied strategies and outcomes for a given situation. Role play can be used to assist children with cause-and-effect as they begin to learn how their actions impact others (Frank, 1976). Problem solving is effective in the dramatic space because the child's whole self—body and mind—is engaged in the process. Thompson (1999) elucidated the connection between drama therapy and Cognitive Behavioral Therapy, discussing how drama can be used with offenders to re-work behavior patterns and to rehearse alternate responses, appropriate reactions, and reflective abilities.

Often, this author will utilize group as a laboratory to examine conflictual relationships between group members. The children frequently enjoy creating courtroom scenes in which they are the jury or participating in activities during which they provide feedback and suggestions to peers on how to handle difficult situations. For younger children, this author has found that an adaptation of Boal's (2002) forum theater that uses puppets instead of actors can be successful. In this method, the therapist presents a scene of conflict (e.g., being teased by a bully, trying to get a parent's attention) and has the group members step in for the protagonist to practice different approaches to the situation. Through the role, the therapist challenges the clients' approaches and deepens their processing of the issue at hand. By engaging in the scene, the children rehearse how they might handle this problem the next time it arises in real life. Differences of opinion among group members are encouraged, and the children are invited to think about the consequences that might follow each choice made by the protagonist.

Group drama therapy provides a space for the children to process their experience of hospitalization. It is often during group sessions that patients talk about their anger at the staff for enforcing limits, and the therapy space can be used to de-escalate rising tensions on the milieu. Hospitalized children frequently become excited about the prospect of creating an idealized hospital, exploring how they would like to see children cared for. In doing so, they are symbolically caring for themselves. However, at some point, the therapist must bring to the group's awareness that it is often easier to talk about their temporary frustrations with the staff than it is to process the ongoing pain, anger, and confusion that is connected to their lives outside the hospital.

When the group feels safe enough, the children explore their family experiences, enacting imaginary phone conversations with relatives, creating family sculptures and scenes, and using empty chairs to address parents who disappoint, fail, or hurt. It is a challenge for the therapist to sit with the intense affect that can emerge and to balance the tension in the group so that it does not overwhelm the members, whose egos are often not fully intact. Nevertheless, while in the transitional space of the unit, the children have the opportunity to grieve the failed attachments that arise from a staggering history in multiple foster families or institutions (McGarvey & Haen, in press). If the children *do* have an internalized sense of family, their roots are often dirty, weak, or broken. By processing these experiences within the safety of the group, the clients experience the security of a *symbolic* family. They discover that in the group, just as in a family, the members must learn to listen, to support, to compromise, and to say goodbye.

Transitions and Closure

Therapists on an inpatient unit soon realize how difficult transition times can be for mentally ill children. It is often around change of shift, transport from one setting to another, the end of an activity, or bedtime that acting out occurs. For this reason, group members benefit from a short period of downtime after sessions, before returning to school or moving to the next activity. Likewise, special attention should be paid to both the opening and closure of the group, as well as shifts in the staffing and unit population.

Termination is a frequent topic in group sessions, as children are often preparing to leave the unit and move on to another level of care. While discharges are common events, the importance of recognizing and processing them cannot be overlooked. For emotionally disturbed and chronically traumatized children, the opportunity to say goodbye in a healthy way can be corrective and can open the door for processing other experiences of loss. Often, however, the topic is fraught with the potential to flood clients and needs to be addressed safely through dramatic metaphor and action. Termination can be processed experientially and metaphorically through the giving of symbolic gifts or the packing of pretend suitcases within the group.

In one session, the children used an imaginary crystal ball as a vehicle for saying goodbye to a core group member. Each child gazed into the crystal ball and shared one picture he or she saw of their departing peer in the future. One boy said that he saw his peer being successful and having a wife and children, while another stated that he saw them reunited as a famous rap duo. One girl offered her wishes that the group of children would meet again someday to form their own hospital to care for "children with problems." In many ways, the pictures that the group members imagined reflected the dreams they had for themselves. When the boy who was leaving shared a wish that he had for each of the remaining group members, his words reflected an accurate knowledge of what each peer needed to do to stabilize and leave the hospital.

As mentally ill children often lack the ability to self-regulate (Levy & Orlans, 1998), the group leader must facilitate an active closure process. Closure is a time to de-role, to become grounded and centered, and to prepare to transition from the group. It can mean moving from a state of activity to one of stillness. It can be a time to reconnect to the group by making eye contact with members and breathing. It can also be a time to concretize the symbolic—by asking the members to name one way they are like their character or one thing from the enactment they would like to retain—or to set future goals. Often, this author uses the magic box (Johnson, 1986) as a closing ritual, asking the members to discard a feeling, life circumstance, or behavior, and to take out something they need, a gift for another member, or a quality they are proud to possess.

An essential component to working within a system is the transfer of information from the group setting to the other members of the treatment team. It belies the group therapist to maintain reciprocal communication with the other clinicians and staff who interact with the child. For the drama therapist, this means translating the aesthetic work done within the session into clinical terms that are comprehensible to those from other disciplines. It also means understanding the work that is being done with each client in the other treatment modalities. Without a proper understanding of context, the drama therapist will find himself operating within a vacuum.

Clinical Vignette

David was a 10-year-old, Caucasian male whose parents had recently divorced. He was hospitalized for increased suicidal ideation following their separation and his father's subsequent relocation to a town several hours away. In addition to depression, David's clinical picture included gender variant behaviors, which he had been unable to explore in outpatient treatment and unwilling to discuss during his hospitalization. Kathy was an 11-year-old, African-American female with a history of aggressive acting out in her current foster home, which was her third foster placement in a year. She was intelligent and engaging, and the source of her sudden rage attacks (which often escalated to damaging property and threatening the safety of those around her) was unclear. Lucas was a 9-year-old Hispanic male whose mother had recently welcomed a new boyfriend into the home. Lucas was the eldest of three children and previously had functioned as "Man of the House" in the absence of a father whom he had never met. He had been unable to verbally process the reasons for his resentment of his mother's boyfriend.

All three attended a drama therapy group session that began with a warm-up in which each client was handed an imaginary magic wand and took a turn transforming the group members into a character of his or her choosing. Together, they tried on the roles of athlete, student, monster, infant, and unit staff, as chosen by each "magician." When David was handed the magic wand, he paused, made a motion to speak, and then hesitated. When the group leader asked about his hesitation, David expressed uncertainty about naming his role. He was encouraged to consult with the group, who validated his choice. David excitedly transformed the group into supermodels. Each took turns demonstrating their model walk. David was the last to go. He moved reluctantly, and then with increasing confidence, as his peers communicated acceptance of seeing him enact a feminine posture.

The group rejoined their circle of chairs. They were asked to each identify a favorite and least favorite role from the many they had enacted. Lucas stated that the baby was his favorite, Kathy chose the student, and David chose the model. The group was asked to think about a context in which all three of their role choices could interact. They quickly suggested a family, casting Kathy as the eldest daughter and Lucas as the 2-year-old son. They changed David's supermodel character into a mother.

The group leader asked where the scene would take place and they mutually decided that it should happen over dinner in the family kitchen. He suggested to the group that the scene should involve the mother delivering some important news to the family. The two boys excitedly suggested that the news be that the father had gone to jail. Kathy added that maybe the mother was worried about the children, and that her daughter character no longer wanted to live in the home.

The group leader asked each to find a place in the house that their character was located prior to gathering for dinner, and to take a frozen position in that space. Each was tapped on the shoulder and asked to talk about how they felt about being in the family. Kathy's character spoke about liking school and wanting to leave the home because she did not feel cared for. David talked about his worry that the children would hate their mother and blame her for the dissolution of the family. Lucas said he wanted to "poop on Daddy's head" and giggled mischievously.

In the course of the scene, David became gradually at ease in portraying a female, wearing a necklace he found in the room, and presenting the mother as an unstable alcoholic on the verge of tears and given to hysterics. Kathy began to tell the family of her desire to leave and live with her aunt, stating that she no longer felt noticed at home. Lucas enjoyed the regressive, id-driven nature of his character and spent the majority of the scene expressing anger at the father for being imprisoned, talking about the many primal revenge fantasies he had—of beating up the father, of puking on him, and the like.

The group was assisted in processing how they would like the scene to end. They agreed that they needed the mother to be strong and to attempt to unite the family by promising to spend more time with them. In the course of enacting this, the family begged Kathy to stay with them and give them another chance, promising to allow her the space she needed to be comfortable. Lucas's character remained angry, but he expressed pleasure at the idea of his sister remaining with the family. The group members de-roled through breathing out their character, putting away the costume pieces and chairs used in the scene, and returning to the circle. They talked briefly about their experience in the enactment, though on this particular day the metaphor had the effect of holding much of what needed to be said.

For these three clients, the safety and distance provided by the role play allowed them the containment they needed to explore what had previously been impasses in their treatment. After this session, Kathy began to gradually talk more with her individual therapist about her anger at being placed in foster care and her unfulfilled needs for attention in her foster family. For Lucas, this session constituted the first time that he expressed rage at his mother's new boyfriend. This was the only time during his admission that David explored his gender variance. It gave the treatment team a better understanding of the instability that David perceived in his mother and his subsequent fears that she would not be able to take care of the family, as well as his strong identification with her.

Conclusion

It can be extremely difficult working within an inpatient setting, knowing that, as one colleague has so aptly stated, "We are merely a blip on the radar screen for these kids," merely one stop in their long journey through a mental health system full of many therapists and caregivers. While success stories *do* exist, the triumphs are more often measured in inches than miles—a violent boy who progresses from being able to tolerate group for 5 minutes to staying for the duration of the session; a girl with a lengthy past history of sexual victimization who feels safe enough to talk about it for the first time; an autistic boy who learns his first word while on the unit; a child who makes her first friend. The successful therapist is one who can appreciate these small steps forward while reconciling the steps backward that the children take on their road to healing. At the same time, one cannot underestimate the value of each therapeutic interaction the child has. This writer has often found solace in the words of de Becker (1997), who wrote:

No ceremony attaches to the moment that a child sees his own worth reflected in the eyes of an encouraging adult. Though nothing apparent marks the occasion, inside that child a new view of self might take hold. He is not just a person deserving of neglect or violence, not just a person who is a burden to the sad adults in his life, not just a child who fails to solve his family's problems, who fails to rescue them from pain or madness or addiction or poverty or unhappiness. No, this child might be someone else, someone whose appearance before this one adult revealed specialness or lovability, or value. (p. 227)

References

Barratt, G., & Segal, B. (1996). Rivalry, competition and transference in a children's group. *Group Analysis, 29*, 23–25.

Bellinson, J. (1992). Group psychotherapy with children in psychiatric hospitals. In J. D. O'Brien, O. W. Lewis, & D. J. Pilowsky (Eds.), *Psychotherapies with children and adolescents: Adapting the psychodynamic process* (pp. 313–335). Washington, DC: American Psychiatric Press.

Boal, A. (2002). *Games for actors and non-actors* (2nd ed.) (A. Jackson, Trans.). New York: Routledge.

Bronfenbrenner, U. (1992). Ecological systems theory. In R. Vasta (Ed.), *Six theories of child development: Revised formulations and current issues* (pp. 187–249). London: Jessica Kingsley.

Carlson-Sabelli, L. (1998). Children's therapeutic puppet theatre—Action, interaction, and cocreation. *International Journal of Action Methods, 51*(3), 91–112.

de Becker, G. (1997). *The gift of fear: Survival signs that protect us from violence.* Boston: Little, Brown & Co.

Delgado, M. M., & Heritage, P. (1996). *In contact with the gods: Directors talk theatre.* Manchester: Manchester University Press.

Emunah, R. (1983). Drama therapy with adult psychiatric patients. *The Arts in Psychotherapy, 12*(2), 71–79.

Emunah, R. (1994). *Acting for real: Drama therapy process, technique, and performance.* New York: Brunner/Mazel.

Emunah, R. (1996). Five progressive phases in dramatherapy and their implications for brief dramatherapy. In A. Gersie (Ed.), *Dramatic approaches to brief therapy* (pp. 29–44). London: Routledge.

Emunah, R. (1999). Drama therapy in action. In D. J. Wiener (Ed.), *Beyond talk therapy: Using movement and expressive techniques in clinical practice* (pp. 99–123). Washington, DC: American Psychological Association.

Forrester, A. M., & Johnson, D. R. (1996). The role of dramatherapy in an extremely short-term in-patient psychiatric unit. In A. Gersie (Ed.), *Dramatic approaches to brief therapy* (pp. 125–138). London: Routledge.

Foucault, M. (1977). *Discipline and punish: The birth of the prison* (A. Sheridan, Trans.). New York: Pantheon Books. (Original work published 1975)

Frank, M. G. (1976). Modified activity group therapy: Responses to ego impoverished children. *Clinical Social Work Journal, 4*(2), 102–109.

Haen, C. (2002). The dramatherapeutic use of the superhero role with male clients. *Dramatherapy, 24*(1), 16–22.

Haen, C., & Brannon, K. H. (2002). Superheroes, monsters and babies: Roles of strength, destruction and vulnerability for emotionally disturbed boys. *The Arts in Psychotherapy, 29*(1), 31–40.

Irwin, E. (1983). The role of the arts in mental health. *Design for the Arts in Education, 86*(1), 43–47.

Johnson, D. R. (1986). The developmental method in drama therapy: Group treatment with the elderly. *The Arts in Psychotherapy, 13*(1), 17–33.

Kellerman, P. F. (1992). *Focus on psychodrama: The therapeutic aspects of psychodrama.* London: Jessica Kingsley.

Kibel, H. (1993). Inpatient group psychotherapy. In A. Alonso & H. I. Swiller (Eds.), *Group therapy in clinical practice* (pp. 93–111). Washington, DC: American Psychiatric Press.

Landy, R. J. (1993). *Persona and performance: The meaning of role in drama, therapy, and everyday life.* New York: Guilford.

Langley, D. M., & Langley, G. E. (1983). *Dramatherapy and psychiatry.* London: Croom Helm.

Lederer, W. (1964). Dragons, delinquents, and destiny: An essay on positive superego functions. *Psychological Issues, 4*(3).

Levy, T. M., & Orlans, M. (1998). *Attachment, trauma, and healing: Understanding and treating attachment disorder in children and families.* Washington, DC: Child Welfare League of America.

Lomonaco, S., Scheidlinger, S., & Aronson, S. (2000). Five decades of children's group treatment—An overview. *Journal of Child and Adolescent Group Therapy, 10*(2), 77–96.

McGarvey, T., & Haen, C. (in press). Intervention strategies for treating traumatized siblings on a pediatric inpatient unit. *American Journal of Orthopsychiatry.*

Mitchell, R. (1987). Dramatherapy in in-patient psychiatric settings. In S. Jennings (Ed.), *Dramatherapy: Theory and practice for teachers and clinicians* (pp. 257–276). Cambridge, MA: Brookline Books.

Mosholder, A., Burke, W., & Carter, W. (1988). Insight-oriented group psychotherapy of latency-age children in an acute care setting. *Group, 12*(4), 226–232.

Reif, R. (1981). Drama therapy with short-term psychiatric patients in a hospital setting:

Observations of a student. In G. Schattner & R. Courtney (Eds.), *Drama in therapy: Vol. 2. Adults* (pp. 67–82). New York: Drama Book Specialists.

Rosenberg, J., & Cherbuliez, T. (1979). Inpatient group therapy for older children and preadolescents. *International Journal of Group Psychotherapy, 28*, 393–406.

Sarra, N. (1998). Connection and disconnection in the art therapy group: Working with forensic patients in acute states on a locked ward. In S. Skaife & V. Huet (Eds.), *Art psychotherapy groups: Between pictures and words* (pp. 69–86). London: Routledge.

Scheidlinger, S. (1960). Experiential group treatment of severely deprived latency-aged children. *American Journal of Orthopsychiatry, 30*, 356–368.

Sheppard, J., Olson, A., Croke, J., Lafave, H. G., & Gerber, G. J. (1990). Improvisational drama groups in an inpatient setting. *Hospital and Community Psychiatry, 41*(9), 1019–1021.

Soth, N. B. (1997). *Informed treatment: Milieu management in psychiatric hospitals and residential treatment centers.* Lanham, MD: Medical Library Association.

Stearns, F. (1991). Inpatient group treatment of children and adolescents. In R. L. Hendren & I. N. Berlin (Eds.), *Psychiatric inpatient care of children and adolescents: A multicultural approach* (pp. 176–193). New York: Wiley.

Sugar, M. (1991). Planning group therapy for children. *Journal of Child and Adolescent Group Therapy, 1*(1), 5–14.

Thompson, J. (1999). *Drama workshops for anger management and offending behavior.* London: Jessica Kingsley.

Trafford, G., & Perks, A. (1987). Drama therapy in a child and family psychiatry unit. *British Journal of Occupational Therapy, 50*(3), 94–96.

Tsiantis, J. (1996). Transference and countertransference issues in the in-patient psychotherapy of traumatized children and adolescents. In J. Tsiantis (Ed.), *Countertransference in psychoanalytic psychotherapy with children and adolescents* (pp. 137–153). Madison, CT: International Universities Press.

Williams, J. C. (1999). Inpatient settings. In C. E. Schaefer (Ed.), *Short-term psychotherapy groups for children* (pp. 439–482). Northvale, NJ: Aronson.

Winn, R. (1996). Dramatherapy in forensic psychiatry. In J. Pearson (Ed.), *Discovering the self through drama and movement* (pp. 167–171). London: Jessica Kingsley.

Yalom, I. D. (1983). *Inpatient group psychotherapy.* New York: Basic Books.

Families and the Larger System

CHAPTER 12

Aikido and Drama Therapy with Families and Children

CHRISTOPHER DOYLE

I was working on a locked adolescent psychiatric unit in Belmont, California. A young woman had just been admitted to the unit. She was extremely agitated, banging her fist on the counter at the nurse's station. She was screaming about how staff at the hospital were in a secret coalition designed to kill her. There was a very long hallway between the nurse's station and the exit door of the unit. I was by the exit door, making my way out to go to another part of the hospital. I approached the door and took the keys out of my pocket. This young woman, who was a good 40 pounds heavier than me and full of terror and rage, saw the keys. She saw the door. She saw me with the keys. She let out a howl and made a direct, full-speed charge for me. It was very clear at that moment that this woman had no other intention than to break out of the hospital. I was the object in her way. She was charging me like a mother bear charges anything that gets between her and her cubs.

Turning to face the young woman directly, I gently let the keys slide back into my pocket. I took a soft, long breath in and let it out slowly. I found my palms opening toward her, hands soft, raised slightly, extending right into the center of her being. I smiled and relaxed. I relaxed some more. I continued to breathe and extend my breath to her. All this happened in a few seconds, without any thought or effort on my part.

Without any thought or effort on her part, the screaming, running woman responded. What had begun as a full-speed charge transformed into a trot. She continued to slow down. Soon she was walking. She completely stopped 2 feet in front of me and peacefully stared into my eyes, mouth slightly

207

open, as if she were about to say something but had forgotten what to say. Without a word, I gently put my arm around her shoulder and turned her around. We walked back down the long hall. As we walked, I said, "Hi, I'm Christopher. What's your name?" She told me her name and we chatted a bit as I escorted her pleasantly to her room.

At this time, I had been practicing the nonviolent martial art of Aikido for a few years. The hours of training I had done had proven themselves to be there, alive and well, in my body. I did not have time to plan any kind of response to this attack. The woman had full intent to destroy me.

Aikido was created in the first part of the twentieth century by a great Japanese warrior named Morehei Ueshiba. Ueshiba had mastered many of the classic forms of Japanese martial arts. He is considered by many to be the greatest martial artist in Japanese history. Ueshiba had several spiritual awakenings that led him to create a new martial art. He realized that all beings are connected as one family, and that to injure someone else is to injure yourself. He dedicated the second half of his life to taking the techniques he had mastered from other martial arts and transforming them into new techniques, techniques that do not injure but seek instead to end conflict and restore balance to the universe. When someone attacks someone else, that person is out of balance and harmony with the perfect love of the universe. The purpose of Aikido is to restore balance and harmony to the universe—without inflicting injury upon the attacker. The word "Aikido" may be translated as "The Way of Peace" or "The Way of Love."

In that hallway on the psychiatric unit with the woman, I was surprised to discover: (1) how I no-mindedly had already absorbed Aikido principles in my body; (2) how completely effective Aikido was for me in that potentially violent situation; (3) how, ultimately, the highest aim in Aikido is to have no actual physical confrontation at all. If I had taken on a fighting stance or hurriedly tried to run away—had I done just about anything other than what I ended up doing—that woman would have confronted me physically. The results could have been devastating for at least one of us, most likely me.

This chapter is about how I incorporate Aikido into my drama therapy practice with families and children. I will first discuss essential concepts of the martial art of Aikido and how these concepts apply to clinical practice. I will then present examples of techniques that I have used combining Aikido and Drama Therapy principles. Finally, I will provide a case example from my private practice.

Aikido and Drama Therapy

The central aim of Aikido is to bring peace to the world. This is accomplished through meeting violence with nonviolence. When someone attacks, they are out of balance and harmony with themselves and with the universe. Applied Aikido blends with the attack by moving to safety and allowing the attack to complete itself. It ultimately restores the person or situation to universal harmony. I will discuss five principles of Aikido that apply directly to clinical work. These principles are: blending, ki, centering, nonresistance, and redirection. People explore these principles for their entire lives and never cease to deepen their understanding of them. My goal here is to briefly introduce the fundamental concepts.

The operative principle in Aikido is blending. The Aikidoist follows the energy of the attack and helps it go where it wants to go, thereby neutralizing the "attack" and helping the "attacker" to be restored to harmony. Through blending with an "attack," the attack ceases to be an attack. It becomes a guide. The Aikido practitioner has no intention to harm the other person. On the contrary, an Aikidoist trains with a commitment to protect all life and to not inflict injury upon anyone.

There is an energetic force at work here. This energy is called ki, the universal energy flowing through everything. Some people would call this love. Other words for it could be God, Peace, Flow, breath. An Aikidoist seeks to harmonize with this energy and allow it to run through his body. When someone attacks, the Aikido practitioner draws the attacker into his sphere of energy and allows the energy to take care of the attack.

When I am practicing Aikido on the mat, the times when I really experience Aikido "working" (or, in other words, the times when I am in harmony with ki) are when I get "myself" out of the way and allow the ki to complete its full expression. It is about being open to things exactly as they are. It is more than being open to it. It is welcoming life as it is, on life's terms. When a big, mean-looking attacker comes at me full speed, I have trained myself to smile inside and say, "Welcome! Let's explore this together and see what we discover!"

There is one very important thing I do when I am physically attacked. I practice centering. Being centered means being grounded in the body, in the earth, in the ki energy enveloping everything. It means being totally present to myself and whatever is around me. We use breath a lot to center, to relax, to drop into the Earth and the universal energetic field. Relaxation is an important part of centering. In Aikido, we train in a state of relaxation. The stronger someone comes at us, the more we relax, get present, and get soft.

Nonresistance is related to centering. Nonresistance allows things to be exactly as they are. It means having no intent to resist, fight with, or overpower the attacker. There is no struggle. The Aikidoist allows the attack to come through, as it wants to, joining with the energy of the attack and drawing the attacker into his circle of influence, and then finally to resolution.

Finally, when attacked, once an Aikidoist blends with the attack, opens to ki, is centered and nonresistant, she re-directs the attack. Re-direction is a very important yet subtle concept. If someone were to strike me with a fist to my face, I could step off the line, not resisting the strike, letting the strike meet the open space created when I moved. But the event does not stop there. Following the energy and movement of the strike, I re-direct the strike to a safe and harmonious conclusion. I was struck with the intent to be harmed. I not only re-direct the physical strike so that no one gets hurt, but through my influence, I change the intent of the strike from one of harm to one of peace. I join with the attack and the attacker and, together, we find something new.

We could take everything I have said about Aikido and apply it to therapy. In fact, you can re-read the last few paragraphs, take out the words "Aikidoist" and "Aikido practitioner" and put in the word "Therapist." The principles of blending, ki, centering, nonresistance, and re-direction create a central theoretical model of how I work as a drama therapist. A new term is born: Aiki-Drama Therapy.

When a client is before me, above all, I seek to be present and centered in myself, in ki, or universal energy. I trust this energy with all my being, allowing it to guide me. I blend with my clients, accepting them as they are without needing them to change or be different—even if they are "attacking" me with words or some other non-verbal exchange. Finally, I seek appropriate opportunities for redirection. I ask questions that change perspectives. I change the scene. I do something with the energy and intent coming from the client. I blend with the client and, together, we walk down a path that both of us discover along the way, a path that neither of us would have been able to take alone. This is Aiki-Drama Therapy.

It is necessary at this point to say a few words about resistance. We all know what resistance means. It means to oppose, to fight against, and to not give in. Resistance usually occurs because the person doing the resisting or fighting feels some kind of threat or attack. There is a sense of a need to protect. It is often a life-or-death feeling. Everyone coming into therapy has resistance, whether it is conscious or unconscious. Clients can feel threatened and their resistance can be activated simply by the fact of therapy.

In Aiki-Drama Therapy, there is no such thing as "resistance." What many clinicians think of as resistance, I think of as a Holy Guide showing both the client and me the direction in which to travel. I have come to view resistance as the client's way of communicating to me which door or window to open or to not open. It is the client's way of letting me know where they need help and how I can begin to help them. Resistance can be the heartbeat of therapy. It gives life to the work; it shows me what to do. When I am with clients, I seek to discover the resistance, open up to it completely, welcome it, blend with it, and see where the ki or universal energy wants to go with it. It is helpful to remember that resistance from clients has nothing to do with me personally. It is an indication of where the client is out of balance with the universe.

This does not mean that I do not think. On the mat, not thinking is highly appropriate—even completely necessary—for Aikido to be effective. In a clinical setting, not thinking can be deadly. I have to rely on my years of training, education, experience, and study. I would say that I take my thinking, clinical mind and blend it with the universal energy. In this way, I become a decision maker. I join with resistance, see where the energy wants to go and then, very importantly, I make a decision. This decision of what to do next is based in psychological theory and my years of experience as a therapist.

Finally, Aiki-Drama Therapy is also about my blending with myself. It is crucial that I be alive and awake to my internal world while in the presence of my clients and their resistance. How do I feel? What are my thoughts and fantasies? What does my body want to do? I seek to not fight against my internal responses, but to join with them and allow them to teach me about what is going on with my client.

I once worked with a woman who was creating a scene from her childhood about when her mother was deathly ill and confined to a bed upstairs in the house. As this woman was talking about the scene and setting it up, I started hearing someone whistling in my imagination. As I listened to this whistling, I experienced an image of a child being very afraid and whistling in the dark as a way to soothe herself. I became aware of a growing and very strong impulse to whistle. I thought about this impulse to whistle. I considered the ramifications. I weighed it against the psychological theories I use, as well as my relationship with my client and others in the room. I made a decision that it would cause no harm, and that it might lead somewhere useful. (These are the two criteria I often use when making a decision in therapy. I have enough experience with this process of *thinking* that it happens in a few seconds.) I followed my impulse and began to whistle. The woman continued to set up her scene. And then she stopped short. She remembered something—the whistling. When the woman's mother wanted her to come upstairs to the bedside for a visit, she would whistle. The woman had forgotten about her mother's whistling until she heard me whistling. My whistling opened up entire new pathways, insights, and levels of learning for this woman.

If you combine the fact of my whistling to the image I had—of a scared little girl in the dark soothing herself—you can get a glimpse of how effective and powerful it can be to blend, trust and be in tune with ki, be centered, be nonresistant to clients, be nonresistant to internal experiences and impulses, and allow for the possibility of redirection.

Techniques

In Aikido training, there is an unlimited number of specific, physical techniques. We practice these techniques over and over, thousands of times. But ultimately, there are no techniques. When I am faced with an "attacker," there really is no "attacker." What exists, and what is relevant, is the energy field created by our relationship with one another. In a sense, the "attacker" and I become one. The rest of what happens in the energy field is always a surprise, always a mystery, always resolved through bodily wisdom and universal energy—never through reliance on techniques or thinking with the mind.

I am sure that you can read this chapter, perhaps do a little more reading about Aikido, perhaps even try Aikido on the mat, and you will bring to life countless drama therapy techniques of your own that fit who you are and how you think and work. I don't try to invent or think of techniques. What I ultimately seek to do as a therapist is simply be present with myself and my client. If there is anything I am *trying* to do, that is it. *Techniques* come to me from the universe. Then I decide if it seems like a good idea or not.

What I am about to present here are not really techniques or any kind of formula. I am not a formula follower. I think we all have to discover techniques for ourselves. The way to discover a technique is to be present, open, and welcoming to whatever fact is before us. From this openness and acceptance of the present moment—within us and outside us—we can be awake to the wisdom of the universe to be our source of guidance. What I can do here, in this section called "Techniques," is name and describe some techniques that have come to me, techniques that I have used in working with children and families. Each "technique" has infinite manifestations that depend on you, your client, and billions of other factors. With each technique described, I will provide examples of how that technique manifested at least once for me.

In Aiki-Drama Therapy, there are two fields of techniques: Blending and Redirection. It is the art of the therapist to blend with the client and then to redirect the energy to its harmonious completion.

Blending

Blending means going with, not fighting against. It is something I seek to do all the time when I am with clients. I blend with the direction they want to go, I blend with their ideas and perceptions, I blend with who they are.

Blending means accepting the client and the situation. It is an inner attitude as much as it is something I do. It is, above all, being present to myself and the client with an attitude of nonresistance. The result of being blended with leads the client to feeling accepted, valued, taken seriously, and honored. In self-psychology terms (Doyle, 1998), blending can provide a selfobject experience of proper mirroring for a client. Blending, in and of itself, can build self structure. Terms for more specific ways of blending are: Acceptance, Encouragement, Reflection, and Manifestation.

Acceptance   When a therapist is blending, she has a stance of acceptance toward the client. Acceptance is at the heart of Aiki-Drama Therapy and is the core of blending. Acceptance means allowing someone to be exactly who they are without criticizing or shaming them. Acceptance does not mean "like" or "approve of." If someone describes something about himself that I find despicable, I do not have to get into my personal judgments about it. But I can stay open to myself and be accepting toward my client. I can understand that he has good reasons for being exactly who he is in that moment. I can help him explore and understand these reasons. Along with having an inner attitude of acceptance, it is paramount that the therapist communicates this acceptance back to the client.

I once had a teenager tell me that he wanted to rape a woman. In fact, he enacted a spontaneous, solo scene in which he raped and beat a woman. The content was beyond grotesque to me. I did not get involved with my specific personal reactions necessarily. I stayed in touch with how I was feeling—grossed out, repulsed, angry. Instead of doing or saying anything that might shame or criticize the boy, I blended with acceptance. I empathically placed myself inside my client's world to the extent that I could. After the boy enacted the rape, I held it with him. My stance was open and curious. There was room for this boy in my office and in my heart—all of him. I let him know this by my open physical stance, my tone of voice, and my non-judgmental/noncritical energy toward him. He was encouraged to explore his scene further.

I had him play the woman who had just been raped to see if he was capable of other feelings about this; specifically, to see if he could have empathy. He was not capable of empathy toward the woman. But as the woman, we discovered that she had a little boy. I had my client play this little boy. My client realized in the role play that he was playing himself as a little boy. He had witnessed these things happening to his mother and had no way of telling me about this experience or how he felt about it. But, because of my blending through acceptance, my allowing him to be exactly who he was without shaming him, he was able to begin to heal.

Encouragement   Another way to blend is to encourage people to be exactly who they are, or to do exactly what they are already doing. Encouragement takes acceptance to the next step. You not only accept clients, but you positively support them in being fully who they are, to think what they think, do what they do, and so on. Whatever the clients are thinking, doing, or feeling, you help them to do as fully and completely as possible. Encouragement can happen verbally, non-verbally, through physical action, or in countless other ways. In working dramatically with clients, I have encouraged them by initiating scenes in which what they are doing is the perfect role needed for the scene.

Phil was 13 years old and did not want to do therapy with me. He came into my office and laid on the couch, face down, motionless. He looked like he was asleep. Maybe he was. He was not responsive to any verbal exchange. Instead of demanding that Phil sit up and do "therapy" with me, I blended with Phil. I walked out an imaginary door and returned as his mother, trying to wake him up. "Come on, honey, it's time for school." Phil laid there, grinning. As his mother, I got on the phone and called the doctor. I exited and returned as the doctor. This doctor could not wake up Phil, so the doctor called in a world-renowned specialist in teenage sleeping disorders. I returned as the specialist. I had Phil cracking up as I dragged him all over the room, hooked up his brain to monitors that tape recorded his thoughts and videotaped his dreams, which I played back on a monitor and consulted about with imaginary colleagues.

Phil ended up having a marvelous time doing exactly what he wanted to do—lie there and "not participate." I simply blended with him and supported him in doing exactly what he was doing. Most importantly, Phil got to experience being accepted exactly as he was. In fact, who he was and who he wanted to be in that moment was valuable and even extremely necessary. Phil never got to experience being needed like this in his real life.

Reflection   An important way of blending is to reflect back to a client whatever he is presenting. In reflection, the therapist seeks to mirror the client's inner world, in concrete terms or through physical action of some kind. Reflection is a very important part of blending in that it communicates back to the client that you see him, that you understand him. Perhaps reflection is the other half of acceptance.

A simple way to do a reflection is literally showing back exactly what I see or hear. The most basic way to do this kind of reflection is to verbally summarize and restate back to the client his position, feelings, or ideas: "So what I hear you saying is that when your dad comes into your room and shouts at you to clean up your room, you really don't like it. And it makes you not want to clean up your room. Is this right?" With reflections, it is important to keep in mind that we are blending. We are not adding our insights, criticisms or judgments. We are merely reflecting back something true for the client.

I often have family members do this simple kind of verbal reflection with each other. A child will talk to her mom, and I will have the mom repeat back to the child what she heard her say. It is astonishing to me how difficult this exercise can be for so many people! But if therapists can train families to be good reflectors for each other, through their blending, the members feel more accepted and valued.

Reflections can be done physically. The most obvious physical simple reflections are mirror and sculpting work (Emunah, 1994). It is my experience that if a family can be trained to be good mirrors for each other, if they can learn to do a "leaderless" mirror game, they feel blended with, accepted, and seen. Sometimes, after someone talks about a problem, I'll have someone else in the family sculpt *another* family member in response to what they heard the first family member say.

A more complex reflection takes the client's world to a deeper level. Once I have blended by providing a literal reflection of what the client is saying, doing, or feeling, I might add a guess or insight about what is going on beneath the surface to deepen the client's experience or understanding. For example, after saying the above example and seeing how it was accepted, I might add: "You know, I'll bet it also makes you very sad that your dad yells at you . . ." In this way, I am doing more than just reflecting back what the client said. I am also reflecting back something that perhaps was just below the surface.

I often use doubling (Moreno, 1946) to do reflections, or have family members double for themselves. I recently had a set of parents and their two teenage children in my office. I went around and had each person talk about what it is like to be in this family. Then, we went around again. One person would sit in a chair, and the other three would stand behind him or her. I invited these three family members to reflect back what they heard the seated member say. Next, we dropped it to a deeper layer. I invited the three doubles to take a shot at what might be there just beneath the surface such as, ". . . and I feel mad about how you treated me the other day," or ". . . and I'm sad about all this." The seated person could repeat anything he or she wanted, and also had the right to tell someone, "No, that's not it, you're wrong."

Finally, I employ the use of video. I film families interacting verbally or playing a game. We play back the video and watch it together. This is a very powerful way to reflect back to the family their transactions, feedback loops, triangulations, and so on; and I don't have to say a word.

Manifestation   Manifestation is about making the inside outside. It is about taking something real that is inside the client and concretizing it in the physical world. Like any of these other techniques, there are countless ways to manifest something in the therapy office. Here are a few ways I have done it:

> If two people are having a hard time communicating with each other, I put an imaginary wall between them. I also have had the clients build a physical wall with objects and furniture in my office. We then continue the session with the wall there. Another way I have done this is to have clients turn their backs to each other and continue the session.
>
> Sometimes the way I deal with power struggles is to get the two people involved to stop talking. I set them up to arm wrestle with each other. I had a family in which the 13-year-old boy had the most power in the family. I had the family build a "mountain" in the office. The boy sat on top of the mountain while the rest of the family members crawled around on the floor beneath the mountain, asking the boy for permission to come up.
>
> With families that fight a lot, especially when sibling rivalry is present, I have taught fake WWF wrestling techniques and had the family members slow-motion wrestle with each other. If one or both of the parents are under-involved and need to be more involved with the kids, I have the parents be the referees. If one or more of the parents are overly involved, I ask the kids to choreograph a fight in private at home and bring the fight in next week to demonstrate for their parents.

When Blending "Does Not Work"   A final note about blending. When blending does not work, as in the case of an extremely resistant client, I do not fight against the not working. I blend with it.

Jack was an extremely resistant 14-year-old boy I was seeing with his parents and older sister. Jack simply refused to say a word, literally, session after session. Jack did not respond to my initiating scenes, using his silence, or any physical ways of blending I had tried. One day, Jack sat in the waiting room and refused to come into my office with his family. Instead of fighting against Jack's decision to not join us, I commended Jack on how he was seeking to help his family. "I imagine what you are doing here is seeing the need for me to meet alone with your parents and your sister," I said. "I've been thinking that this might be a good idea" (and I really had), "and so today will be a perfect opportunity to do that. See you next week—and thanks!" Jack waited patiently in the waiting room the entire session and returned with his family week after week—as a participant. In fact, the next session, Jack spoke for the first time. He told his parents how he felt that they valued his sister more than him. This naturally led me to have the next session with just Jack and his parents, which Jack attended and in which he participated.

Redirection

If blending is the joining with the client, redirection is the working through of the client's issues, pathology, problems, and conflicts. Redirection is the part of the therapy where the therapist leads. In redirection, the therapist challenges the client to see things differently, to alter his or her behavior, to explore their understanding, to clear out emotional energy, to create a new story. It is important that the client has first been blended with before the therapist begins to redirect. Redirection also means for me to be willing to change directions inside myself if the client does not go where I think we might be going or need to go. Ultimately, redirection can refer to any intervention that is initiated by the therapist, as long as the purpose of the intervention is to work through the client's issues.

Redirection can be fairly subtle. A dad named Mark was talking to his family about how he is a caretaker at the expense of his own integrity. As he talked about giving to others, I noticed he crossed his arms and legs. His voice was getting more and more constricted. I could energetically feel him going away and shutting down. Instead of continuing along the path of exploring his caretaking, I redirected. Blending with his body language and my inner impulse that he did not want to continue, I simply asked Mark how he was feeling right now. Mark began to cry, moving deeply into his despair. He talked about how he has been living his whole life giving to others and how hard this is to look at. My re-direction opened up a new door for Mark that he *was* ready and wanting to walk through—the door of his resistance to looking at this issue. Instead of working on his caretaking, which was too overwhelming, we explored his resistance to the work, his fears of what he might discover. This led to a number of sessions in which Mark taught his children about how he was wounded in his childhood and how these wounds had impacted his ability to be a parent.

Sometimes redirection does not look like an organic growth out of the blending, but is more like a bolt of lightning. Diane and her 17-year-old, substance-abusing daughter were in my office. The daughter, Karen, was crying and going on and on about how unfair people were to her and how her mother didn't understand her. If I tried to say something, Karen would angrily cut me off by saying, "NO! Let me finish!" Then, she would go back to lengthy monologues of how the world has been unfair to her and how her mother should trust her and give her more freedom. I paid attention to the energy in my body. I was angry. I wanted this young woman to shut up. She was stuck and completely dominating Diane and me, blocking any attempts to change. I could have used an infinite number of techniques or interventions. Here are just a few redirection possibilities that could have been very effective. (Please keep in mind that some of these examples require a sense of humor):

Have them reverse roles
Have Karen complain even more
Tape Karen's mouth shut (with pretend tape) and let Diane talk
Role reverse with either Karen or Diane
Place Karen in a "sound proof room," let her continue talking into a pretend tape recorder, and interview Diane separately
Have Karen write down all her complaints while I talk to Diane
Have Diane write down all her complaints while I talk to Karen
Have the two of them tell a story together

We could go on and on. None of these techniques are any more right or wrong than others. So what did I actually do? First, I was soft. Then, I became a thunderbolt. I let Karen go on and on, watching to see if Diane would do anything. After about 10 minutes, I could see that this is just what they did. Diane has no voice, no power, no boundaries with her daughter. Karen walked all over her mom. I offered several opportunities for Karen to try something different, to see the mom's perspective, to work toward movement. She blocked everything and continued talking. Here is where the thunder came in: I shouted, "STOP TALKING! HOLD IT! STOP! STOP!!!"

I finally was big enough to shock Karen into closing her mouth, and it was silent for the first time. I knew I had to deal with Karen first. I calmly asked her if I had frightened her or if anyone had ever done that to her before. She said no. We engaged in a quiet conversation about what I had just done. I joked about it, "It's not too often I have to do something like that to get a word in. Man! You can talk! On and on!! You've got a lot to say!" Karen was laughing. We were finally walking on the same path. I assured her that everything she wanted to say would get said. But, perhaps, just not all at once.

Then I turned to Diane and said, "Don't you ever want to do that? Stand up and shout SHUT UP?" Karen and Diane cracked up. Diane said no, that she never wants to tell Karen to shut up. This response lit Karen's fire "Oh Mom! That's not true! You'd love to tell me to shut up! Admit it!" (Thank God, Karen was feisty.)

With some more persuading, Diane told the truth. "Yes," she said. In fact, it came out that Diane had long wanted to tell Karen to shut up but was afraid it would hurt their relationship. Karen was delighted. I contracted with Karen that she and I were now going to teach her mom to tell her to shut up. Everyone was laughing as we continued on with this very serious work.

On the surface, it might seem that my shouting at Karen to stop talking was an act of violence. In order for something to be violent there needs to be a disregard for the other person. My intervention was done with love, for loving reasons. Nothing else that I knew of (or that came to me) in that moment was going to help these people become more conscious. The most compassionate thing I could do was strike hard.

A Final Word about Techniques

As I indicated earlier, any technique can be a redirection if the intent of the technique is to work through the client's process. Likewise, any technique can be blending if the intent of the technique is to blend. As is obvious by now, all techniques are part of each other. If you do one thing, you are probably doing everything.

It is important to note that not every technique is going to be accepted by the client. I may offer for the parent to do a role reversal in order to deepen their understanding of their child. The client may refuse. This does not mean therapy is failing. It simply means to keep blending and try another redirection.

My favorite quote from Ueshiba (1992) is, "Failure is the key to success. Each mistake teaches us something" (p. 87). I apply this stance to all my work as a therapist. It is my job to try things and fail, learn from it, and try again. This is how therapy works. On the mat in Aikido, I don't always get it "right." My blend will not blend, the technique I apply may not be the right technique for that moment. The art of Aikido is to be able to instantly readjust. This ability is a central feature that distinguishes the black belt from the brown belt.

Case Example

This is an example of one of the most "resistant" boys I have ever worked with. I am not including this particular example because it is pretty. I want to show you something with which I really struggled.

Tim was an 11-year-old with Axis I diagnoses of Asperger's Syndrome, Depression, Obsessive Compulsive Disorder, and Trichotillomania. His mother (dad was not in his life) brought him in to see me because Tim had suicidal ideation, severe social problems, no friends, and great difficulty getting along with his older sister. He would not "listen" to adults or participate in family events, and was obsessed with computers and computer games.

I did a thorough, two-session assessment with just the mom and reviewed past psychological test results, IEP's, and Occupational Therapy reports. The day came when I finally met Tim with his mom, Mary. When I asked Tim to tell me a little about himself, he would only say, "I like eggs." I asked him to tell me about the kinds of eggs he likes. His only reply was, "I like eggs." I even offered Tim some pretend eggs to eat. To this, Tim made a fart noise and his mom told him to be polite.

I asked Tim about his interest in computers and he would not talk to me about it. I asked him if he had any idea why his mom wanted him to see me, and Tim looked away. I asked him if he knew what counseling was all about and he said, "The whale on the float. Fart. Eat my shorts." About fifteen minutes into the session, I had his mom leave the room so I could assess Tim on his own. He instantly began making continuous noises of sorts and yawned in an exaggerated fashion when I would say anything.

I pulled out all the stuff I pull out when nothing works. I joined with his resistance. When he would babble, I would babble back. I initiated improvisational scenes with him based on his body language, words, or anything he was doing. I invited him to play board games, make videos, create a sandtray picture. . . . I matched his silence with being silent and just sitting there with him. I tried making jokes and I tried not making jokes. All the while, I felt a great sense of hostility directed toward me, and I was feeling hostility toward him. So, I used this hostility and began to playfully wrestle with him. He would not engage. Even when I would go flying across the room at his slightest movement—a technique that has never failed—Tim would not connect. The disconnection I felt was the most severe disconnect I have ever felt in the presence of another person.

I sat across from him and said, "You know, I really would like to get to know you. I'd like to make some kind of connection with you. But it seems like everything I'm trying isn't working. It feels to me like you don't like me and don't want to be here. Is that true?"

"Pajamas and peanut butter," he said, not looking at me, of course.

"I don't know what to do or say!" I said. I had had enough experience with Tim to know that if I tried to make something out of his "pajamas and peanut butter," it would be cut down. I found myself feeling so distanced from this boy. I had tried all the stuff that is irresistible to the most resistant clients. Nothing was working. The session ended and he walked out without returning my "goodbye" or "see you next week."

The next day, Mary called me and said that Tim didn't want to come back by himself. He was requesting that I get another boy in there, or at least someone else in the room. I invited Mary to be the "someone else" for the next session. She agreed. I felt so at a loss about how to connect with

Tim. I was hoping that I might be able to engage with him with his mom there.

The next session with Tim and Mary, he presented as resistant as always: not engaging with me, no eye contact, interrupting conversation between Mary and me with body function noises. I asked Tim a few questions. To each, he responded, "I don't know." I took this as a sign of progress. His response to me was at least on the same planet as my question.

I told Mary that she and I were going to play the I Don't Know Game. I was going to ask her questions, and the only thing she could say in the whole game was, "I don't know." I instructed Tim to watch carefully and not say anything.

"So, Mary, what did you have for breakfast today?" I said.

Mary hesitated. And then, "I . . . don't know."

"Come on, you don't know what you had for breakfast? Surely you know that!"

"I don't know."

Tim cracked up, but tried to hide it.

"Who lives in your house?"

"I don't know."

"What is your name, anyway?"

"I don't know."

"Now come on, Mary!" I said, "You know your name!"

"I don't know!"

I continued with this, asking Mary questions and having her say, "I don't know." Tim was visibly having a good time watching his mom "misbehave/ not participate/be stupid." I eventually included Tim in the game and he readily played. He and his mom began whispering to each other, planning other things that they could say to me.

I had Tim hooked. I spent the rest of the session engaging both of them with each other doing guessing games, theater games, card tricks, and hiding games. I ended the session having the two of them engage in mirror work with each other. Finally, I entered into the mirror with them so the three of us were mirroring each other, taking turns leading.

I had two more sessions with Tim and Mary. Tim returned to being extremely difficult to engage. The dynamic that kept repeating with Tim was that he would offer a little something, like a word, babble, or gesture. When I would respond to the offer, Tim would cut it off, interrupting any flow that could have been established. I would end up feeling so smashed down. I knew he was probably communicating to me how he felt in his life— smashed down, cut off, discouraged, disengaged, devalued. I tried working with this countertransference, playing out being smashed down, cut off, dismissed, destroyed. I tried wondering with him if he ever felt these feelings. Nothing would go anywhere. It was constant cut off, and cut off, and cut off . . .

The next session, Mary came in with Tim and announced that she wasn't feeling well that day. She said she needed to wait in the waiting room and had a doctor's appointment after the session. I readily agreed to her request to remain in the waiting room. As she left the room, she said to Tim, "Now you behave. Don't give him too hard a time."

"Oh, we'll be just fine, Mary," I said.

Tim started talking to me in gibberish. I spoke back to him in gibberish. He discounted me with his body language and would not respond to my gibberish communication with him. Tim had a CD walkman and head-phones in his lap that he was fumbling with. I asked him what CD he had . . . no visible or felt sense of connection. I tried engaging him about his interests in music . . . nothing.

I pulled out the CD player in my office. "How about if we listen to your CD on this? I'd like to hear it," I offered.

"How about not," he said.

I was feeling so frustrated. I had never had such a difficult time engaging a client. Even with the most resistant clients I had had up to that point, I could at least go over and sit on them or something and I would get a smile of playfulness. I was not getting even that much from Tim.

"There's a hospital down the street," he said.

"That's right. And good for me because I think I'm going to check myself in."

"I like eggs," he said.

I had tried everything I could think of in working with his egg line: serving him eggs, asking him what it is he likes about eggs, asking him what else he likes, using the metaphor of the new life in an egg, the potential of new birth, throwing eggs at things . . . and so on. Nothing would connect with him. He would block anything I did or said with his body language—yawning, telling me this was boring, sighing deeply. The only thing he did not do was leave the room. I took this as a huge indication that *something* was working.

However, during this session, I began to have thoughts of calling Mary in and telling her that I thought this was no use, that I didn't want them to waste their time and money. The thought of terminating brought me some relief. Then I wondered—who would I refer this child to? It was the old thing of saying, "Boy, we need to send this guy to a therapist," and then remembering that I am the therapist! The only person I could think of qualified to work with this boy was . . . me. I had tons of experience working with children and teens with Asperger's. I had volumes of notes from successful, engaging sessions filled with connection, expression, intimacy, eye contact, fun, and growth.

I connected with my despair and fantasy and shared it with Tim. "I just don't know what to do with you," I said. "No matter what I try, you just shoot it down. I'm really, seriously, at a loss." A silence passed. I considered that maybe Tim was thinking about what I had just said. I also considered that maybe he did not understand a word of anything I've ever said.

Tim put his headphones on and turned on his CD. This pissed me off. I told him that he couldn't do that. I stood up. I felt myself wanting to rip the headphones off his body and shake him. Forget about blending, ki, being centered, nonviolence! I felt so hopeless with this child. I wanted to call in Mary and terminate with them both. What I really wanted to do was say, "Fuck you. Go ahead and stay miserable! I'll work with someone who *wants* to get better!" Fortunately, I did not say this.

I knew that I could physically take the headphones away from Tim. I also knew that my overpowering him would do nothing to further our relationship. I sat back in my chair and did nothing. I heard so many voices in my head telling me, "You can't let a child listen to headphones in therapy! Show him you care! Show him who's in charge! Show him you won't give up on him! Take them away!"

I sat and recovered. I remembered to breathe. Then I did something that I had not really done yet. I became *present* with Tim. I sat with him and accepted him, myself, the entire situation, just as it was. *I did nothing.* Tim listened to his headphones. *I relaxed.* I told myself that no matter what happens, *I will be okay.* A number of minutes went by.

Something significant happened inside me. Up to this point, I had been trying to *get* a response from Tim. I had forgotten to blend with his non-responsiveness, with his disconnect. Unconsciously, I had been trying to forge Tim into someone who can connect. As I sat there watching Tim listen to his music, I let go. I gave up on trying to change him or have him be anyone other than who he was. This was not a giving up; it was a letting go. I let Tim be Tim. I let me be me. I sat back in my chair and actually enjoyed myself. I enjoyed Tim, too, sitting there listening to his headphones. I let it all be okay.

Finally, Tim turned the volume down and said, "You can't stop me."

"That's so true," I said quietly. "I cannot stop you. You have a tremendous amount of power."

Tim continued to listen to the music. He made another comment, something about technology and the CD. I wasn't sure what he said. I asked him to repeat his comment, but he was silent. I asked him if he had burned that CD himself; he was still and quiet. I sat back and remained present to him. I once let a teenage client with Asperger's sleep for 30 minutes on my couch.

This experience with Tim was kind of like that, except I felt much more engaged with the teenage client who was sleeping. I deeply felt my despair about working with Tim. I kept returning to how hopeless I felt about him, about my ability to work with him, about our relationship. I got a strong sense that we needed a third person in the room to help us. Then, without any thought or effort on my part, that third person arrived.

"And so, the therapist just sat there while the Young Man listened to his music on his headphones," I found myself saying. "Yes, the therapist was at a complete loss about what to do, so he just stupidly sat there. The Young Man totally ignored anything the therapist did or said. The Therapist considered checking himself into the hospital down the street. 'I need a vacation,' he thought to himself. 'Maybe I'm just a totally lousy therapist and should give it up!'"

I went on like this. Tim did not make any indication that he was interested or even listening for quite a while. Finally, he said, "This is stupid."

"And the Young Man said, 'This is stupid,'" I said. "'Of course this is stupid,' thought the therapist, but what else could he do? The therapist leaned back in his chair and considered the options. The Young Man turned away slightly, and the Therapist began breathing out of the side of his mouth . . ."

After a few more minutes of this, Tim had taken off his headphones and was staring in front of him. He smiled slightly. He would make comments from time to time, and I would just include the comments in the commentary.

"Stop this stupid story!" he would say.

"'Stop this stupid story!' said the Young Man, getting more and more upset that the Therapist was going on and on like an idiot for no reason. The Young Man made a face and the therapist wondered, 'What does this all mean?' He, of course, had great difficulty figuring it all out, but he had a huge head full of brains and he was working on it . . ."

"I like eggs," Tim said.

"The Young Man said, 'I like eggs.' The Young Man had said that many, many times to the therapist. The Therapist was not sure what to do with this."

"I like eggs," Tim said.

"He said it again. And he kept saying it."

"I like eggs, I like eggs," Tim went on.

"The therapist would be sitting there looking, thinking, not having the slightest clue about what was going on or what to do, and the Young Man would say . . ."

"I like eggs!"

We continued like this for a while. The commentary would go on and then prompt Tim for his line, "I like eggs." Tim would say his line and, together, the two of us were writing a script. Then, Tim changed the story. "Let's play checkers!" he said, looking at my checkers game in the corner.

"The Young Man said, 'Let's play checkers!' The therapist considered this. Was the Young Man just saying this to set the therapist up? To get the therapist to get up and get the checkers out, only to reject the game and the therapist, only to perhaps knock the game over when it is set up?"

"Let's play checkers!" Tim said again.

"The Young Man said it again—'Let's play checkers!' Was the Young Man serious? Did he really want to play?"

I made Tim work hard for it, but I finally got the checkers game out and put it by Tim's feet. Tim came down to the checkers game and set the game up with me. We played the game and I stopped the third-person commentary. From time to time, during the game, Tim would say things to me about the game, like, "Did you notice that I had a jump here but took this one instead?" We engaged with the game, and Tim played extremely well. He really gave me a hard time. I ended up winning the game, but just barely.

"Man, you are really good!" I said.

Tim smiled a little bit. "You can do anything if you set your mind to it," he said.

"Is that the kind of guy you are?" I said. "The kind of guy who can do anything once he sets his mind to it?"

"Yes," he said.

I was so amazed. We were having a conversation. We had connected. I was genuinely, deeply moved.

"Tell me, Tim," I said, "What is it that you are the most interested in, in the whole world?"

There was a pause as he thought about it.

"Eggs," he said.

I cracked up. Tim cracked up. We sat there laughing together. I told him that I liked his sense of humor. I also told him I liked him.

I said goodbye. Tim said goodbye. I said see you next week. Tim said okay.

"And Tim," I said, "have a great week."

"You too," he said.

Conclusion

Every human being wants to be accepted, valued, seen, understood . . . loved. This is my bottom-line creed. When I work with a family or a client, I keep this creed in my heart and in my mind. I remember that the people before me are doing the best they can to connect with me, themselves, and with each other, even if it looks and feels like they are doing the opposite. I also remember that the doorway to connection and growth is often through what seems like resistance, or even violence.

There is a calligraphy by Ueshiba himself in my Aikido dojo that translates, "Practice the Aikido that cannot be seen by the human eye." When I am doing Aiki-Drama Therapy with clients, no one knows that I am blending, flowing with ki, being centered, practicing nonresistance, and redirecting. It does not matter that no one can see what I am doing. The main thing that does matter is my authentic presence: being present to myself and my clients. Above all, I trust presence and let go to it. It is in this mystical place of presence where worlds meet and souls heal.

References

Doyle, C. (1998). A self psychology theory of role in drama therapy. *The Arts in Psychotherapy,* *25*(4), 223–235.

Emunah, R. (1994). *Acting for real: Drama therapy process, technique, and performance.* New York: Brunner/Mazel.

Moreno, J. (1946). *Psychodrama: First volume.* Ambler, PA: Beacon House.

Ueshiba, M. (1992). *The art of peace: Teachings of the founder of Aikido* (J. Stevens, Trans.). Boston: Shambhala Publications.

Suggested Readings on Aikido

Dobson, T. (1978). *It's a lot like dancing: An Aikido journal.* Berkeley, CA: North Atlantic Books.

Saotome, M. (1993). *Aikido and the harmony of nature.* Boston: Shambhala Publications

Stevens, J. (1987). *Abundant peace: The biography of Morihei Ueshiba, founder of Aikido.* Boston: Shambhala Publications.

Stevens, J. (1995). *The secrets of Aikido.* Boston: Shambhala Publications.

Stevens, J., & Rinjiro, S. (1984). *Aikido: The way of harmony.* Boston: Shambhala Publications.

Ueshiba, K., & Ueshiba, M. (1985). *Aikido.* Tokyo: Hozansha Publications.

Ueshiba, M. (1992). *The art of peace: Teachings of the founder of Aikido* (J. Stevens, Trans.). Boston: Shambhala Publications.

CHAPTER **13**

Co-Working with Adoptive Parents to Support Family Attachments

ANN CATTANACH

Hansel and Gretel

Close to a large forest there lived a woodcutter with his wife and his two children. The boy was called Hansel and the girl Gretel. The family was very poor, and now there was famine in the land and they could find nothing to eat.

The woodcutter was distraught and said to his wife, "What is to become of us? How are we to feed our poor children when we have nothing for ourselves?"

"I'll tell you what, husband," said the wife. "Tomorrow morning, we will take the children out into the thickest part of the forest. We will light a fire and give each of them a piece of bread; then we will go out to work, and leave them alone. They won't be able to find their way back, so we shall be rid of them."

The woodcutter said he could never find it in his heart to leave the children in the forest, but his wife gave him no peace until he consented.

"But I grieve over the poor children all the same," said the woodcutter.

Coming into Care

In the United Kingdom, a child comes into care to be "looked after" by the state when family life breaks down and the child is no longer safe at home. There are many reasons for the breakdown of the family, both within the

227

family structure and through external circumstances, as in the story of Hansel and Gretel. Once in the care system, a child can be looked after in residential accommodation or in foster care, which is the preferred option, especially for the younger child. After a thorough assessment of the child's needs, if appropriate, the local authority can make an application to free the child for adoption. Parental rights are then transferred from the birth family to the local authority or adoption agency. If, by this time, prospective adopters have been found, then they can make an application to adopt.

Some children waiting to be adopted can be in foster care for quite some time before a family is found and the legal processes are completed. In Scotland, 2002/2003 figures show that more than one in three children in care have been looked after for 2 years or more (Scottish Executive National Statistics, 2003). Many children move from foster placement to foster placement, so that continuity of care is lacking and changes of school become frequent. Education suffers and the child feels a loss of family security. A study of 234 children (Hill & Tisdall, 1997) found that one third had experienced five or more moves since coming into care. In many cases, these moves included a change of school.

The various moves are often expressed in play as children tell "moving house" stories. Jane, age nine, told this story:

The Brown family was moving house because their old house had been burnt down.

Luckily, they had just come back from holiday and had all their things with them so nothing got burnt.

They didn't mind about the old house because they were going to move house anyway.

Everybody is going to the new house.

At last, they get there.

They like the new house.

It is small but they still like it.

This lorry came up with all their furniture, and the baby started to cry because of the loud noise the lorry made.

The family set up the furniture in the new house.

The baby is trying to sleep and the rest of the family is trying to sort out the furniture.

They bring the suitcases in and begin to unpack.

Everybody gets fed up and they have a little rest.

The baby stops crying and goes to sleep.

Once an adoptive family is found and the placement is approved, the child can move to live with the prospective adopters, and the legal process for adoption can proceed. By this time, the child may have moved from birth family to a variety of foster homes and, in the course of that journey, may see many professionals. It can be very hard for the child to discriminate the roles of all these adults who have intervened in his or her life. This can create difficulties for the child and adoptive parents in attaching to each other and forming a family unit.

Attachment Theory

The two major attachment theorists, Bowlby (1969–1980) and Ainsworth (1978), argued that secure attachments in the early years are central to the development of social competence, while insecure attachments create difficulties in relationships and problems in later development. With secure attachments, the infant uses the caregiver as a secure base from which to explore the environment. With insecure attachments, the infant either avoids the caregiver or demonstrates resistance or ambivalence in the relationship. The theory claims that throughout life the person monitors the physical attachment figure.

Ainsworth and colleagues (1978) described three principal patterns of attachment:

1. *Secure Attachment* occurs when the person is confident that her parent or parent figure will be available, responsive, and helpful when he or she encounters difficult or frightening situations. With this assurance, he or she can explore the world. The parent, especially the mother, promotes this confidence by being readily available—sensitive to her child's signals and lovingly responsive when he or she seeks comfort.

2. *Insecure Anxious Resistant Attachment* develops when the child is uncertain whether the parent will be available, responsive, or helpful when called upon. Because of the uncertainty, the person is always prone to separation anxiety, tends to cling, and is anxious about exploring the world. The parent promotes the pattern by being unpredictable to some extent: sometimes available and helpful, but not at other times. The pattern is shown by persons who have been separated from the parent, and also by parents who threaten abandonment as a means of control.

3. *Insecure Anxious Avoidant Attachment* occurs when the child has no confidence that he or she will be comforted when seeking care; on the contrary, they expect a rebuff. When such a person tries to live life without the love and support of others, he or she tries to become emotionally self-sufficient and may become self-absorbed in ways that damage social relationships.

These three categories of attachment were further extended by the work of Main (1991) to include a fourth category:

4. *Insecure Disorganized Disorientated Attachment* occurs when the person has an unusually high level of fear and might be disorientated. This can result from experiences of abuse by adults or the death of parents or caregivers.

Many children who come into care have experienced insecure attachments and develop a view of themselves as unlovable, not worthy of love and affection. James, age seven, felt that he was disgusting and that nobody could possibly want to take care of him. He created an imaginary boy in play and narrated his life, using small dolls and slime to tell that story:

There was once a boy called Mad Boy and his head was full of slime.
It was leaking out of his brain, his eyes and his mouth.
People said, "This is disgusting," and nobody would play with him.
He managed to get rid of his slime by squeezing his head and it shot out of his brain, mouth, and eyes.
When he was clean, his biggest wish was to have clothes and shoes.
He lived on his own, but he wanted a nice family.
He got a family and he was happy about his family, but he misses his birth family, especially his mum.
Even though he was adopted, he saw his birth mum.
He wasn't cross with her, even though he didn't live with her.

Some children find the loss of the birth parents very difficult to manage and often create an unrealistic picture of that primary attachment figure. As they no longer meet their parents on a day-to-day basis, they imagine an ideal parent to help cope with their loss. It is very important to understand how painful parental loss is for a child—no matter how inappropriate the parenting.

James described this feeling in his story. His hero is a green pen called Harry who lived in a bag with a lot of rats:

He had a mum and dad but was fostered.
He missed his mum 100 times very much.
He remembered his dad but didn't miss him, as mum is mum.
The rats touched him and made him stink.
And he didn't like it.
His mum and dad couldn't keep him clean and tidy.
Then he went out with his new foster mum and he got new, clean clothes.

One day, he heard that he was coming home to his mum and dad.
And he had a very nice time and he lived happily ever after.
When he went home this time, his mum kept him clean.

James has minimized his home circumstances because his attachment
and loyalty to his birth mother is so strong. But, he also wants the love,
affection, and family life in his foster family, and feels torn between the two.

Working with the Adoptive Family

If a child in an adoptive placement is referred for therapy, I discuss the needs
of the child with the parents and the child together. The key issue is usually
about the struggle for attachment and the child's confusion about finding a
way into the life of the family. If you have had to learn the rules of five
families before meeting the new mum and dad, it is difficult to process yet
another family structure or understand how parents can care for you.

In these circumstances, we usually negotiate a way of working that offers
creative time with the child, then time with the parents and child together
to help to cement the family relationship. This can mean a pivotal role for
the therapist in explaining the parents to the child and the child to the parents. For example, if the child shows impulsive behavior, then it helps the
parents understand if we talk about such children's needs to be first. If at
school, these children might put up their hand to answer a question even if
they don't know the answer. They just want to be first, I explain.

The adoptive parents might have struggles with their own history of attachment, and this difficulty can influence the way they perceive family life.
Adult narratives of childhood have been codified. Steele (2002) described
four patterns of attachment defined in the Adult Attachment Interview:

Dismissing. You were parentally rejected or neglected during childhood,
but this is only mentioned indirectly. You work hard to protect your
unrealistically positive or normalized image of your parents and your
childhood. You tend to dismiss or devalue the significance of childhood attachment relationships.

Autonomous. You were well loved and supported by your parents during
childhood and/or experienced adversity and perhaps severe pain. You
understand the past and its influence on the present. Yours is a coherent, credible narrative that conveys a strong valuing of attachment.

Preoccupied. You had many caregiving duties toward your parents during childhood, such that roles were frequently reversed, with your attachment needs being compromised. You are angry and confused
about these experiences but you value attachments. The task of narrating your experiences is rather painful.

Unresolved. You have suffered loss and trauma in childhood or adulthood and you are still grieving. You feel responsible in some way for the loss or trauma and you don't see that as unreasonable on your part. The loss or trauma does not yet belong to your past.

Part of the process of creating a new family with child and adopters can be to reflect with the parents about their own experiences of attachment and how these influence their roles as parents. When I provide treatment for a child in such a family, I usually work in the family home. In the private time I spend with the child, we play together and I utilize imaginative play with toys and small objects, dramatic play, and story work. I use a narrative approach to explore themes and dominant stories that the child wants to express.

The Function of Narratives and Stories in Play and Drama Therapy

If the drama therapist uses a narrative approach, then the following functions can underpin and support the intervention:

1. Telling stories and playing stories can be a way of controlling our world and what happens to us in that world. For a child who lacks power, it can be an enriching experience. For once, the child can say, "I'm the king of the castle, and you're the dirty rascal," and not experience the consequences of their reality world.
2. The use of narratives and stories in Play and Drama Therapy can help children make sense of their own lives and also learn empathy through imagining how other characters in their stories might feel.
3. Working with stories and narrative play means that there is collaboration between child and therapist, where what happens in the sessions is co-constructed between the two.
4. This model is based on social construction theory and narrative therapy, which describe the development of identity as based on the stories we tell about ourselves and the stories others in our environment tell about us.
5. Some dominant stories we have about ourselves are not helpful and can lead to victimization. In Play and Drama Therapy, we can explore ways to shift and expand aspects of identity through exploring roles and ways of being in play, knowing that we do not have to take all these experiments into our lived lives.
6. This approach also recognizes the fact that the developing child is part of an ecological system, not an isolated individual. We live in a time and culture, and this influences our way of seeing.

7. In this kind of collaboration, the child can play with small toys and objects, create a dramatic event, draw a picture, or just make marks on clay or slime. But as they do so, they tell a story about what they are doing. My role as therapist is to listen, perhaps ask questions about the story if required, and record the story by writing it down if the child requests it. If the play becomes a drama, then I might take a role if the child wishes. I might also share a story that might be congruent with the play of the child or as a way to deepen the relationship through the shared experience of telling and listening.

Social Construction Theory

If we are to use narratives in a collaborative approach between child and therapist, we need to understand aspects of social construction theory, which defines narratives as the way we construct our identity. This theory (Burr, 1995) states that all ways of understanding are historically and culturally relative, specific to particular cultures and periods of history. Products of that culture and history are dependent on particular social and economic arrangements prevailing in that culture at that time. Knowledge is sustained by social processes, and shared versions of knowledge are constructed in the course of our daily lives together. We make use of words in conversations to perform actions in a moral universe. What we define as truth is a product not of objective observation of the world, but of the social processes and interactions in which people are constantly engaged with each other.

So, child and therapist construct a space and a relationship together where the child can develop a personal and social identity through finding stories to tell about the self and the lived world of that self. The partnership agreement between child and therapist gives meaning to the play as it happens. The stories children tell in therapy are imaginative expressions of what it feels like to live in their real and imagined worlds. The worlds of the stories can be mediated by the therapist, who can assist in sorting out cognitive confusions present in the play. Sometimes, there is a process of re-storying in which the child can try out new aspects of self by taking on a role and exploring a world from the perspective of that role. A major aspect of this kind of play is the constant affirmation between child and therapist that it is "only a story" that does not necessarily have to be lived in the reality world.

Narrative Therapy

These processes of storying experiences are also explored in narrative therapy. Le Vay (2002) described the expression of narrative identity as one of the fundamental processes in play therapy because this process enables the child and therapist to explore relationships via the symbolic and meta-phoric imagery that is co-created during the course of the play. Humans have a natural inclination to story personal experience, and the richness of symbolism and metaphor in this process becomes embedded in the relation-ship between child and therapist. Thus, narrative frameworks are constructed that allow children to begin to sequence, order, predict, and make sense of complex feelings that can exist as a result of trauma and abuse. Le Vay (1998) believes that we realize ourselves through the stories that we tell both others and ourselves. The words we say, the sentences we construct, and the events that we choose to include or omit all contribute to the generation of narrative identity through which we aim to make sense and order out of experience.

Lax (1992) stated that the interaction itself is where the text exists and where the new narrative of one's life emerges. This unfolding text occurs between people. In treatment, the therapist is always co-author of the un-folding story, in partnership with the client. The resulting text is neither the client's nor the therapist's story, but a co-construction of the two.

Lax (1999) defined a narrative therapist as someone who assists persons to resolve problems by enabling them to deconstruct the meaning of the reality of their lives and relationships, and who shows the difference between that reality and the internalized stories of self. The narrative therapist encour-ages clients to re-author their lives according to alternative and preferred stories of self-identity.

Narrative therapy has links with those therapies that have a common respect for the client and an acknowledgment of the importance of context, interaction, bonding, and the social construction of meaning. Narrative therapy parallels drama therapy in that both modalities explore roles, identity, and story life events in order to make sense of experience. In both processes, the narratives can be about lived life or imaginary worlds.

The Child as Part of an Ecological System

Children need adults to care for them if they are to survive in the world. When working with a child in adoptive placements, it is important to con-sider the ecological system within which the child lives if the intervention is to make any sense or help keep the child safe. Sometimes, the desire to res-cue overcomes the therapist, who does not consider the consequences of an intervention for the child in their environment, and then the child feels betrayed. The therapist becomes just another person in the adult world who has let the child down. If children are learning to attach to a new family, it is important that the therapist does not distort that attachment. Therefore, supporting the children within their family is crucial.

Bateson (1972) described the person and the symbolic world of culture within a system of interdependent relations. We live within a specific culture at a particular moment of time and develop our identity through our interaction within that culture. Bateson defined the unit of survival as a flexible organism-in-its-environment. He viewed the individual as part of a larger aggregate of interactional elements. These interactions involve information exchanges. It is the totality of these exchanges that makes up the mental process of the system, of which the individual is only one part.

Bronfenbrenner (1979) defined the ecology of human development as progressive mutual accommodation between the growing human being and the changing properties of the immediate settings in which he or she lives. This development is affected by relations between these settings and by the larger contexts in which the settings are embedded. He defined three systems: the micro- (small) systems, the meso- (middle) systems, and the exo- (large) systems. All these systems are contained in a Macro- (large) system.

The Micro-system is the developing child's life in the family, with the daily routines, roles, and interpersonal relations within the immediate settings of home and school. The Meso-system is the interrelations among two or more settings in which the developing child actively participates; for example, the relations among home, school, and the local peer group. A "looked after" child may have a constantly changing system as he or she moves from foster home to foster home, also potentially resulting in changes of school and peer group.

The Exo-system refers to one or more systems that do not involve the developing person as an active participant. However, events that occur in these systems influence what happens in the setting containing the developing person. So, what happens in the parent's workplace, for example, could profoundly affect the environment of the child. The Macro-system is the culture and the society into which the individual is born. This system contains the cultural beliefs of the society; for example, what it is like to be a child and how children should be reared.

Bronfenbrenner (1979) defines human development as a process through which the developing person acquires a more extended, differentiated and valid conception of the ecological environment. They, in turn, become motivated and able to engage in activities that can reveal the properties of, sustain, or restructure the environment at levels of similar or greater complexity in form and content. The child in an adoptive placement has had many encounters with social systems in his culture and often wants to make sense of aspects of his environment while in the therapeutic setting. The child needs to place some issues into a social context in order to understand how he came to leave his family and what it might mean to be adopted.

Although it is stated in the legislation that the views of the child are paramount, for the child moved from placement to placement, it is hard to believe that he or she has any say in the process. Many children express this lack of autonomy or control over what happens to them in their play.

Alan's Story

Alan is 7 years old and has lived in his adoptive family for 2 years. He has not yet been adopted, but the legal process is nearing completion. Alan came into the care system at an early age because his mother was 15 years old when he was born, had been in care herself, and found it impossible to care for him, although she had tried very hard for 2 years. She asked social services to find adoptive parents for him and he was subsequently fostered from the age of 2. From 2 to 5 years, Alan was cared for in seven different foster homes before being placed with his adoptive family.

Alan found it a struggle to feel secure in the family and was convinced that he would be rejected. Sometimes, he found family life so difficult that he wanted to run away. He was confused about the rules and could be destructive of his own possessions and family objects. When I met Alan and his new parents, there were tensions about helping him feel comfortable in the family, and Alan himself felt anxious and worried. He found the building safer than the people, feeling secure within the physical structure of the house, especially the garden. He enjoyed the quiet of his bedroom and other secret places where he could play. He found sleeping at night difficult and had nightmares about monsters who chased after him. Alan was confused about all the families who had cared for him and found it difficult to differentiate one caregiver from another. He had seen many professionals and had had numerous social workers. He wasn't quite sure what parents were for.

In my play with Alan, he liked to tell stories as he played. He also liked me to share stories with him. He enjoyed folk tales and looking at picture books with me if the story was sympathetic. One of the first folk tales we shared was the story of the Scottish Broonie. I told Alan that, in some ways, he reminded me of the Scottish Broonie:

> The Broonie is described as a wild and shaggy creature, usually a small man about 25" in height. He is wrinkled and brown and wears tattered brown clothes. The Broonies in the Highlands have no fingers or toes. Most humans are afraid of them because they look so fierce. The Broonie hides in the dark corners of old houses, which he haunts. He watches the coming and goings in the house and, at night, he cleans the home and does all the tasks that he thinks members of the household might find useful. He is devoted to the family who live in his house, and his only purpose is to please them. He doesn't do this for

reward but because he is attached to them. Some Broonies are attached to the house more than the people who live there, but they still work in the house to keep it clean and tidy.

Broonies are very touchy creatures and sometimes, if family members give him a reward, he will take umbrage and leave. He is especially offended by the offer of food other than a bowl of milk or cream or cake covered with honey. Any other offer of food sends him into paroxysms of rage and hurt. You mustn't pay him. You can thank him, but that is all. Otherwise, he will say farewell and leave . . . never to be seen again.

We laughed together at this folklore. We always met at Alan's house. We sat together on the floor in the sitting room in front of the log fire with a drink and biscuits. It was easy to imagine magical creatures in his house. Alan liked me to tell him the story of the Broonie of Blednock:

This Broonie had a name, although many have no name. He was called Aitken Drum. He lived on a farm and worked hard at night doing all the farm work required. But he always disappeared before sunrise, after drinking his bowl of cream left out for him by the farmer's wife.

This Broonie had no nose and his mouth was just a gash; but he was very hard working, and the farmer was short of workers and needed his services. The neighbors were shocked at the sight of the Broonie, but the farmer's wife was wise and realized they had a good bargain; for, Aitken Drum could do the work of 10 men.

He worked by starlight and by moonlight whenever there was work to be done, but he always disappeared before sunrise and nobody saw him drink the cream that was left for him by the farmer's wife.

Aitken Drum stayed at the farm for many years and, eventually, the children lost their fear of him. They loved to listen to his strange, unearthly songs and play the Broonie games he taught them when he came to work at twilight.

For many years, all went well; until one day a foolish young woman thought it was time that Aitken Drum dressed like other folk in the village, and left a pair of dirty breeches for him next to the cream left by the farmer's wife. And, from that evening, he was never seen again. Only a shepherd passing near a farm one night heard the voice of Aitken Drum crying and grieving because he had been given his fee and could work no more.

And, on dark nights, when the river is in spate, the villagers tremble when they think of the first time they saw Aitken Drum. Children lying in bed at night listening to the wind in the trees think they hear the voice of Aitken Drum singing them to sleep with his mystical song.

I often told this story to Alan when he requested it during our time to-gether. He liked sad stories and had great empathy for heroes who struggled to find their place in the world. He was especially fond of two picture books, *That Pesky Rat* (Child, 2002) and *Ginger Finds a Home* (Voake, 2003). *That Pesky Rat* is the story of a rat who wants to belong to someone. His friends tell him about their homes and their owners, and the rat puts an advertisement in the pet shop to find a home for himself. Old Mr. Fortesque reads the ad, but his eyesight isn't good and he thinks he has a cat as a pet. So the pesky rat ends up with Mr. Fortesque, pretending he is a cat. He finally has a name, Tiddles, and even though he has to wear a jumper, he is content. Alan laughed at the story and at how the rat had to compromise to get what he wanted. We thought about fitting people together with each other, not perfect but good enough.

Alan loved *Ginger finds a Home* because it describes a kitten surviving at the bottom of a garden and the little girl who brings food for him. Gradu-ally, she befriends Ginger and persuades him to come into her house. But, when she tries to shut the door, Ginger runs away because he is frightened. In the end, he returns to the house and eventually lives with the little girl in her house. He is happy and only goes to the bottom of the garden to sun-bathe.

Alan had great sympathy for Ginger and identified with his life at the bottom of the garden. He liked the progress of the story and the fear Ginger felt when he entered the girl's house for the first time. We both liked the happy ending. Alan's own stories were usually about cars. Initially, the cars were driverless, controlled by external forces, and the environment was full of danger. *Traffic* is an example of these stories:

This traffic is in the village called Legoland.
There is lots of traffic in the village waiting for the traffic lights.
The cars are remote control.
But, suddenly, one car slipped when turning and made a big hole in the road.
The cars were never sad or angry, only happy, even in the traffic jams.
In the traffic jam, they just whistle.
One day, a car drives up the ramp of its house
When it got to its house, it stopped.
Then another car came, its neighbor, and parked behind.
The green car reversed onto the road.
The orange car reversed onto the road.
The cars drove away.
The cars came back and parked at the side of the house in the park-ing bit.

They didn't notice a hole in the road, but didn't fall in it.
And all the cars got parked.

There was a sense of aimlessness about the movements of the cars in Alan's stories—as though they did what they did because they had been told to do it. The environment was also full of unexpected dangers, some of which were avoided by the cars. But, there seemed to be no rhyme or reason for the dangers and no strategies employed by the cars to keep safe. The characters were mechanical in their responses. We were able to share this sense of powerlessness, which Alan felt about himself and his circumstances, with his parents. They were able to acknowledge how difficult it must be to be moved from place to place without any control over what was happening.

Then, Alan began to include more characters in his stories, although the environment was still dangerous:

Look Out
This story takes place in Russia.
It is very, very, very, very, very, very hot.
There are lots of little cars which are magic.
Nobody drives the cars because they are magic.
A dog lives there, too. He lives in the cage.
He lives on his own because he is old enough to look after himself.
If he gets into trouble, he'll fix it.
A car comes and doesn't turn and goes into the cage.
The dog wasn't in the cage.
When the dog was coming home, he saw the car and nearly jumped higher than the cage.
He put his nose in the cage and got buried in the sand.
He was knocked off the cage.
Then, the car got blown away.
And the dog went to America.

We talked about the story together—how home was a cage for the dog, the cage was not safe, and the dog left to go to America, which was the furthest place he could go. Alan was settling in with his new family but still feeling unsafe. When he felt this way, he wanted to run or find a place on his own, away from everybody, where he could play and relax. Alan wanted me to read his story to his parents, and we talked together with them about wanting to run away when you don't feel safe. They helped him find a warm, comfy place in a corner of the house where he could play undisturbed when he felt anxious.

Alan began to feel safer with his family, but school was a great problem. He found concentration difficult and didn't have the social skills to make friends. His teacher was very sympathetic but it was still a daily struggle. This was expressed in the story of Birdsigh:

> Once, there was a little robin called Birdsigh.
>
> Birdsigh was very upset one morning because all the other children thought he was a stinky poo-poo, but he wasn't.
>
> He went into his home for two days because he was very unhappy.
>
> He was on his own.
>
> He looked after himself.
>
> One day, a train came along and Birdsigh flew away, and he went to the big city where the train never goes.
>
> Birdsigh was a very frightened little bird.
>
> He was a very naughty bird.
>
> He said sorry to everyone in the class who had been hurt by him.
>
> Then, he got the train, who was number three train, and he went to the next city in the train.
>
> He just gently flew around until he was exhausted.
>
> He was so tired he wanted to run back home.
>
> It was too far to run.
>
> He got the train again and went home.
>
> And in the house was his mum and dad.
>
> "Where have you been, you daft little bird?"

Alan's parents were well aware of his school problems. They often felt helpless as they tried to support him while also fighting the wider system to get the help in school that they thought Alan needed. Resources are scarce, and there are no easy answers.

Reflections

The meetings with Alan and his parents continue. There are finite resources for these meetings, so we do what we can with the time allotted. There are relaxed times when the family enjoys their life together, and other moments when events at school, or home, or with friends create anxiety and fear for the family. Sometimes the task of creating a loving family seems overwhelming for parents and child, but strong determination and the desire to understand each other creates hope for all.

Alan's play and stories help the parents to understand how it feels to be him and helps them to make sense of some of his behavior. Alan likes and needs to play as a soothing activity, and as a way to gain self-esteem through being heard by an adult who admires his playing skills. He also indicates which stories he wants his parents to hear and what he thinks they should know about how he is feeling. Some parts of our discussions are confidential, and he is very clear about what he wants his parents to hear about our meetings.

Alan's latest story shows how his self-confidence is growing. There are people in this story who communicate with each other and a sense that they have some autonomy over events:

The Car Race in the Desert Sand

There are four cars in the race.

The race starts and one car is ahead.

Then another joins the fast car.

The two other cars watch as the black car storms ahead.

But the black car went much too sharply round the bend.

The other car stayed behind and stopped in the sand.

"Why have you stopped?"

"This is a race and we are trying to win," said Michael.

Sandy said, "I have to change my wheel because my tire is broken down."

"Oh no, I am in the water," says Michael who is driving the black car.

Sandy helps push Michael's car out of the water.

Michael goes storming ahead.

The other two cars are racing away as fast as they could.

But the other cars stop or get stuck in the sand.

So Michael wins the race.

The End.

End Piece

This is a story from the island of South Uist in Scotland. I live in a culture where storytelling is still a way to communicate with your neighbors and ease some of the fears of living in a harsh, natural environment. In the cold and snow of winter, when darkness comes early, a story helps to keep the community together.

Why Everyone Should be Able to Tell a Story

There was once an Uist man traveling home to Uist by the Isle of Skye. He had been working the harvest on the mainland. He was walking through Skye and, at nightfall, he called at a house and asked to stay until morning as he had a long way to go.

He went in the house and was made welcome by the owner who asked him if he had any tales or stories to tell. He said he had none.

"It's very strange that you have no stories to tell," said his host

"I can't remember any," replied the man.

His host was telling stories all night until it was time to go to bed. The Uist man was given the small room between the parlor and the kitchen to sleep in. Hanging in the room was the carcass of a sheep.

The Uist man hadn't been in bed long when two men came and took the sheep. The Uist man followed the thieves. He had gone some way after them when one thief noticed him and said to the other, "Look at that man following us. He will betray us. Let's go back and do away with him."

The two men went after him. The Uist man ran as fast as he could back to the house, but the two thieves got between him and the house. The Uist man kept going until he heard the sound of a big river. He made for the river but, in his panic, he fell into the river, and the stream took him away.

But he got hold of a branch of a tree on the riverbank and clung to it. He was too frightened to move. He heard the two thieves walking up and down the riverbank throwing stones whenever they saw shadows in the water. He stayed there until dawn.

It was a frosty night and, when he tried to get out of the river, he couldn't do it. At last, he managed to make one shout and made a leap, and he woke up and found himself on the floor beside the bed holding the bedclothes in his hands. His host had been casting spells on him in the night.

In the morning, at breakfast, his host said, "Well, I'm sure that wherever you are tonight, you'll have a story to tell, though you hadn't one last night."

That's what happens to a man who couldn't tell a story.

Everyone should be able to tell a story to help pass the night.

References

Ainsworth, M. D. S., Blehar, M. C., Waters, E., & Wall, S. (1978). *Patterns of attachment: A psychological study of the strange situation.* Hillsdale, NJ: Erlbaum.

Bateson, G. (1972). *Steps to an ecology of mind: Collected essays in anthropology, psychiatry, evolution and epistemology.* Northvale, NJ: Jason Aronson.

Bowlby, J. (1969–1980). *Attachment and loss* (Vols. 1–3). New York: Basic Books.

Bronfenbrenner, U. (1979). *Ecology of human development: Experiments by nature and design.* Cambridge, MA: Harvard University Press.

Burr, V. (1995). *An introduction to social constructionism.* London: Routledge.

Child, L. (2002). *That pesky rat.* London: Orchard Books.

Hill, M., & Tisdall, E. K. M. (1997). *Children and society.* London: Longman.

Lax, W. (1992). Post-modern thinking in a clinical practice. In K. Gergen & S. McNamee (Eds.), *Therapy as social construction* (pp. 69–85). Thousand Oaks, CA: Sage.

Lax, W. (1999, July). *Definitions of narrative therapy.* Paper presented at the Dulwich Centre Conference on Narrative Therapy, Adelaide, Australia.

Le Vay, D. (1998). *The self is a telling.* Unpublished master's thesis, University of Surrey, Roehampton Institute, London, England.

Co-Working with Adoptive Parents • **243**

Le Vay, D. (2002). The self is a telling: A child's tale of alien abduction. In A. Cattanach (Ed.), *The story so far: Play therapy narratives* (pp. 35–58). London: Jessica Kingsley.
Main, M. (1991). Metacognitive knowledge, metacognitive monitoring, and singular (coherent) vs. multiple (incoherent) model of attachment: Findings and directions for future research. In C. M. Parkes, J. Stevenson-Hinde, & P. Marris (Eds.), *Attachment across the life cycle* (pp. 127–159). London: Routledge.
Scottish Executive National Statistics. (2003). *Children's social work statistics 2002–2003.* Retrieved December 1, 2003, from http://www.scotland.gov.uk/stats/bulletins/00287-00.asp
Steele, H. (2002). State of the art: Attachment theory. *The Psychologist, 15*(10), 518–522.
Voake, C. (2003). *Ginger finds a home.* London: Walker Books.

CHAPTER 14

Stories from the Islands

Drama Therapy with Bullies
and Their Victims

STEVE HARVEY

During a pick-up basketball game among sixth graders, Reggie, a large 12-year-old boy, turns and runs after a much smaller classmate who had accidentally stepped on his foot. Reggie hits the boy in the face when he catches up with him on the other side of the room, where no teacher can see what is going on. Earlier in the year, Reggie had continually touched two girls of the same age on their buttocks. Next to his home, he sought out a younger boy whose mother had recently been killed in a car accident and teased him relentlessly about her death. In his earlier years, Reggie had been extensively physically abused and was threatened with being killed by a family relative. His mother was never clear who his birth father was, due to her early "crazy" drug years. Reggie is a continual behavioral problem at home, where he often threatens to harm himself or becomes assaultive toward his younger sisters.

On another day in the same middle school, Jennifer, a 12-year-old girl, yelled at and hit another girl who had developed a rumor that Jennifer had been performing oral sex on several male classmates. The girl had also told others that Jennifer was more interested in sexual activities with other girls and was, therefore, "gay." Neither of these statements was true, as Jennifer had not yet become sexually active. She had, however, experienced ongoing sexual assault in preschool. Her grandmother, who had raised her and been her protector throughout the abuse, had recently passed away. Jennifer had also experienced ongoing physical abuse from her birth father, whom she had rarely seen in recent years.

Such episodes occur regularly in the school lives of children, particularly at the end of elementary school, and with increasing frequency in middle school. It is often difficult for adults who are in charge of discipline to sort out who is the perpetrator and who are the victims. Often, children who are identified as being the "bullies" state that they, too, are targets of ongoing verbal and physical attacks from other groups of peers. These children tend to be among the most severe cases referred for mental health. It is sometimes hard to define where the ongoing, peer-related violence stops and the disrupted family relationships begin.

In a recent survey about violence, youth reported that their biggest concern was the emotional cost of episodes such as those presented above. According to children, they primarily experience bullying interactions as being cruel and leading to emotional alienation (Gatinsky & Salmond, 2002). While actual violence does matter, the intent behind behaviors such as teasing, excluding others from activities, put-downs, and sexually oriented harassment can itself make social life emotionally painful. Intentional, emotionally hurtful behaviors are so much a part of children's peer experience that many children believe that things will not change (Khosropour & Walsh, 2001).

While these statements refer to emotionally abusive peer relationships, clearly adult interactions contribute to the "sting" of the hurt as well. Many adults simply do not believe the extent and scope of the bullying behavior or its emotional cost on their children and students. Nor do they understand how such events trigger very painful memories from a conflicted family past or current, ongoing family problems. Teachers, school administrators, and even parents simply do not talk about bullying, leading students to feel that adult intervention is infrequent and ineffectual. Students report that telling adults only brings more unwanted harassment and further social isolation (Charach, Papler, & Ziegler, 1995). Peer witnesses also tend to add to the intensity and frequency of these episodes, as many of the onlookers want to be seen as popular and, therefore, offer verbal and physical encouragement to the "bullies" (Espelage & Holt, 2001). In general, these interactions contribute to an overall social climate of "meanness," distrust, and lacking of real emotional connection, particularly for those students who already have experienced significant interpersonal violence.

Bullying behaviors continue in earnest during the middle school years as children are developing more complex relationships with their peers. A majority of adults remember the ages of 11 through 13 as the primary period of their most severe bullying experiences (Estea & Rouse, 2001). Children of this age report a strong pressure to "fit in" and be like everyone else, with little tolerance for personal difference. Such lack of acceptance for individuality is only one of the prime causes of negative peer relationships. Many students also engage in bullying because it is modeled by others or simply because it is a good defense in the chaotic social atmosphere in which they find themselves. Families in which physical punishment is used and where domestic violence occurs also contribute to the development of negative peer socialization.

Weinhold (2000) suggests that children who have experienced psychological trauma, loss, and poor attachment might be particularly vulnerable to becoming a bully or victim as they enter middle childhood, due to their past history of poor interpersonal, intimate relationships, and learned distrust of others. Such factors contribute to the problematic situations presented earlier. Traumatized and maltreated youth are particularly vulnerable to increased psychological challenges as they attempt to find peer groups and friends.

This chapter will present a working model in which dramatically oriented, interactive play therapy can be used with late elementary to early high-school-aged children who are both bullying others and being bullied in their schools and communities. While school prevention programs are invaluable in helping to improve peer socialization and create more positive school culture (Olweus, 1993a, 1993b), individual, family, and group dramatic interactions have an important role in addressing bullying. This is particularly important for those children whose basic attachments to others have been compromised. For these children, the negative peer harassment, encouragement of onlookers, and adult indifference they experience at school can become a very painful extension of their family lives, in which emotional exchanges with others have been characteristically negative, hurtful, and disorganizing. The interventions presented here address those children who are bullies or victims and have a history of poor intimate family relationships, insecure attachment, and psychological trauma.

Dynamic Play Therapy

Dynamic Play Therapy (Harvey, 1990, 1993, 1994a, 1994b, 1994c, 1995, 1997, 2000; Harvey & Kelly, 1993) is an interactive intervention in which creative arts therapy modalities are used in an integrated way to address basic interpersonal, emotional conflict with the goal of developing corrective experiences within relationships. Case studies (Harvey, 1993a, 1995, 1997) present relationally oriented interventions that address children's psychological and attachment traumas arising from adoption, physical and sexual abuse, and loss of an attachment figure through death or family breakup. These interventions involve assisting parental figures and children to engage in expressive play together using drama, art, movement, and video to actively develop metaphorical interactions with a sense of playfulness and sponta-neity. The interventions make use of extensive therapist "coaching" to guide families or individual children to play in a productive and attuned manner.

Central to this intervention style is the belief that the experience of shared, spontaneous, or "naturally creative" play produces intimacy, trust, and mutual reciprocal positive feelings that are necessary for the formation of basic, secure attachment, the intimacy of friendships, and the development of a hopefulness that future relationships can be emotionally fulfilling. In addition, the play episodes that result from such interaction have value in terms of helping children develop an understanding of their basic emotional distress and conflicts. Russ (1998) noted that emotional expressiveness in play is related to creativity and positive overall adjustment. In Dynamic Play Therapy, children are helped to expand their emotional expressiveness, leading to increased creativity and improvement in important socialization with significant others. Guided use of the metaphors generated in a child's interactive play can also help him to develop more adaptive self regulation skills in social situations.

Researchers and clinicians working with young children (Harvey, 1994a; Stern, 1985; Tortera, 1994) have emphasized how the episodes of shared, interactive play between a parent and her or his child are fundamental to the process of creating joint emotional realities. However, children who have experienced significant psychological trauma, separation, and loss are not able to generate such beneficial, joint play flow. From an early age, their play is often characterized by significant breaks, stops, and interruptions. Rather than creating mutual, positive feelings, such play often produces fur-ther alienation among the players. This alienation reflects the generalized, negative emotional atmosphere a problematic family typically experiences. As these children become older, they have great difficulty engaging with their peers in playful and enjoyable ways. They develop expectations that their peers will mistreat them, and often attack others for actions they mis-interpret as being negative.

The main goal of Dynamic Play intervention is to utilize creative arts therapy modalities in helping child and adult players begin to identify how their play breaks down, to understand the negative emotional atmosphere such play creates among them, and to create more improvisational flow in their interactions. Throughout this process, the therapist discusses how the play has meaning as it relates to the child's emotional history. This discussion can help develop more resonant emotional meaning in resulting play epi-sodes through shared metaphor making. These discussions also assist chil-dren in beginning to understand how to generate more socially responsive interactions in their everyday life.

To accomplish these goals, the therapist guides the participants through a series of stages: evaluation, use of initial games, coaching toward more spontaneous play, and the development of ritual and more planned play episodes to achieve resolution of core emotional issues. The therapist often structures interactive play as games that organize initial interactions, so that a family's or child's more spontaneous play can develop once they become more willing and able to use basic expressive art modalities.

As players become increasingly able to generate their own play improvisations, the therapist helps them to transition their play, so that metaphors develop that can express their unique emotional struggles, especially in relational situations. Finally, rituals are planned and completed to resolve past core issues (see Harvey, 1994b, 1997, 2000 for more complete descriptions of this process).

Adaptations for Middle-School Bullies and Victims

As mentioned earlier, many middle-school students who are engaged in negative peer interactions are both bullies and victims. This is particularly true for the kind of children being discussed in this chapter, who have had family histories of loss, separation, and violence. As social pressure increases for children to form peer groups in fifth though ninth grade, children with trauma/attachment difficulties have many problems forming trusting relationships and friendships. As their social "scene" gains more importance, peer interactions become the new playground. Children with traumatic pasts can easily lose their sense of connection and empathic give-and-take with their age mates. The result is a diminished hope that things will work out right for them.

Some adaptations of Dynamic Play are necessary to better engage late-elementary/middle-school children, as the imaginative play, art, or drama that younger children regularly produce is no longer expressed so freely. Most children this age who have been involved in bullying are usually quite angry toward, and alienated from, adults and peers. Many are in trouble with school administrators for their social behavior and they have a high degree of conflict with their parent(s). In order to accommodate these social/family situations, parents participate less than they normally would in interventions with younger children. The older children spend far more time with the therapist as the initial, responsive play partner in one-to-one sessions. Once these youths can engage with an adult therapist, the clinician helps to plan sessions with parents or other important adults. Initial games are used with greater frequency to structure and organize interactive play and expression in the beginning of treatment.

Evaluation with older children does not include family play, and resolution scenes are more likely to be addressed individually. Family corrections (when they can occur) are usually conducted verbally and are planned to occur as home activities outside of the therapy session. Parents are included to assist with behavioral management ideas, as well as to communicate with the teachers and school administrators with whom their children are involved. The majority of expressive activity occurs between the child and therapist. The therapist also needs to get a realistic report of the peer harassment the youth receives, and engages in, from a reliable outside source such as a teacher or counselor. Often, the bullying behavior the youth engages in, or is subjected to, is denied or distorted greatly in self-reports.

Evaluation includes: parent and child interviews to gain an understanding of current problematic behavior; a history that includes past experiences with psychological trauma and attachment-related problems; and a review of current peer relationships. It is important to get information about the child's thoughts of death or self-harm, as well as their experience with bullying/being bullied. Such information usually must be asked for directly, as children may not provide it without direction. Therapy goals are then developed with parents, children, and therapist to include plans that address peer relationships. Some descriptions of interactive play activities are given to the family. The child is also given an idea of the kinds of play interactions and the expectation of parent involvement in later sessions. Interactive play then occurs with the therapist. These sessions are more structured in the beginning to help organize activity and generate interest.

Initial Play Activities

It is important for youths to enjoy their initial play sessions with the therapist, as most of their interactions with others have been unsuccessful. To help accomplish this, initial, simple, interactive games are used to provide a sense of freedom, as well as structure and rules. In general, activities that involve some kind of safe, physically aggressive competition between adult therapist and child seem to work best to achieve such engagement. Some good examples of these first games include: tug of war, "scarf wars" (the therapist and child throw large scarves at each other while avoiding the other's scarves), and "scribble wars" (the therapist and child each try to produce more scribbles on a large paper using markers or crayons). These activities can involve high-intensity physical activity in a safe manner. When throwing scarves made of light material, for example, the youth can use his whole body in a very intense way without causing harm to someone else.

The therapist then continues to attune to the play of the child and uses the resulting episodes to coach the development of longer play scenarios using the emotional themes and the theme shifts of the resulting dramas.

The therapist also uses verbal coaching to assist the child in giving the activity emotionally relevant meaning (e.g., "Why not throw a scarf at the kid who teased you yesterday? . . . Here, this stuffed animal will be that boy.") This verbal coaching mostly occurs while the interactive play is happening, rather than before or after the action. It seems that metaphorical expressions are easily built while youth are in the act of play. Most children this age tend to be highly resistant to discussing emotion when directly asked. However, such resistance is not as high during the action phase of expression.

Using similar verbal coaching, the therapist can help guide these initial activities into longer and more elaborate versions of the original, and develop brief dramatic enactments of scenes from the child's current life. For example, tug-of-war can become a struggle to get away from a harassing peer, a scarf can become anger thrown at a peer or teacher, or a scribble war can turn into an imagined argument with an adult authority figure. The goals of these initial interactions are to help the youth participate in an engaged and motivated way in a playful interaction in which they contribute ideas, use "expressive momentum" (Harvey, 2000), and develop play that can represent a feeling from their social experience. This process is successful if the child can play without prompts, challenges, and/or limit setting from the adult therapist. It is during this phase that the therapist is most likely to use information provided by the teacher's or parent's school reports to create scenes of actual, recent peer interaction.

Transition to Scene Work

The goal of the next stage of treatment is to help the child develop his or her own independent play that contains meaningful content related to social interactions. Such play episodes mostly take on the structure of a dramatic or narrative scene. The therapist introduces activity structures that can be further developed or transitioned into more personal narrative. Ideas to facilitate such a transition include the following: (1) making a home base; (2) attempting to pull the youth away from the "home"/capture games; (3) constructing an obstacle course; and (4) creating a drama such as an underwater scene, an imagined dream, or a TV wrestling match.

Home Base

A home base is created when the child is able to use props (such as large pillows) to construct a place in which he is "safe" in any game action. Often, the home base flows easily out of the action of throwing scarves, and the child spontaneously, or through direction, makes a structure behind which the scarves can't hit him. Any number of games can then develop in which the child uses his "home" as a point of return while the therapist tries to catch, tag, or use props to contact him while he is outside of the house.

As improvisation of these games develops, more personally relevant drama emerges. One boy, who had a long history of physical abuse and current bullying behavior toward peers, developed a series of dramatic episodes in which he would attempt to make a stronger "base" using several sets of pillows, while he asked the therapist to "bomb" the house with large stuffed animals. While the animals easily knocked down his initial building, he was finally able to design a home that was resistant to attack. The therapist and boy then developed a scene whereby the thrown stuffed animals came to represent the insults and verbal attacks he had experienced throughout his life. His new, strongly constructed pillow home became a place in which he could experience self-containment, the feeling of a positive, more relaxed self. During this drama, the therapist was able to talk to the boy about developing and using self-restraint strategies with his peers. The learned behavior proved to be effective for him during his daily interactions.

Capture

This activity is a version of home base. It involves the youth making a base and the therapist throwing a large elastic band to catch him or her. If the child is captured, the therapist then attempts to pull him or her out of/off of the base. This usually initiates some kind of struggle. At times, the capture can turn into being "rescued" as the therapist pulls him or her out. During this interaction, the therapist can ask questions such as "Who or what is pulling at you?" or "What are you trying to escape?" As the youth answers these questions during the action, a scene can be developed that has metaphoric significance.

One older, elementary-school-aged boy who was quite involved in bullying developed a game in which he would actively dive into a large pile of pillows to get away from the therapist. As the episodes developed through improvisation, he changed the scene to become about being stuck in a "collapsed cave" (the pillows) and needing rescue from the therapist, who pulled him out with the elastic band. When the therapist asked him about the emotional aspects of the play, the boy identified the cave as being like the feeling of being "caught up" in an aggressive episode with peers. The rescue led to a discussion about the boy's need for adult help with his aggressive behavior.

Obstacle Course

In this activity, the therapist asks the child to use all the props in the room to make an obstacle course that requires some kind of physical exertion to negotiate. This course can also be "mapped" with the use of art activities, as well. Usually, the development of a good course takes some experimentation with both the physical aspects as well as the art media. Examples include using the pillows to make a wall to be jumped, using a parachute to crawl through with eyes closed, or having the therapist use the elastic band to pull the child across a portion of the room with various props as resistance.

Once the child has developed enough obstacles (usually three or four), the therapist asks the child to identify a real-life problem to associate with each obstacle. The child then completes the "problem course" with discussion as to how these problems and potential solutions are occurring in "real" life. This activity is one that has proven very useful in sessions involving parents because of the highly prescribed, supportive action involved between parent and youth. Before completing the course, the parent and child are asked to discuss and prepare mutual activity to enable the child to solve his problems through the course. Various obstacles can be identified as involving specific, peer-related problem situations. These episodes can be effective in helping parent and child problem solve about family or social dilemmas.

Imagined Scenes

Often, a child has a difficult time developing metaphorical value in his or her play and requires therapist assistance in allowing his or her activity to express inner states. One dramatic activity that helps to encourage such expression involves having the youth assume a restful position with his or her eyes closed. While he or she are not looking, the therapist uses the scarves, pillows, parachutes, and stuffed animals to design a scene (an imagined dream or an underwater scene) around him or her. The youth then opens his or her eyes and describes what he or she sees, next engaging in improvised action. It is helpful to use video during these scenes and review the resulting movies with the youth in order to plan further developments and script his or her own ideas

The goal of using these initial activities is for the youth to develop his or her own dramatic scenes, in which the therapist maintains a witnessing role or takes on minor roles in support of the main drama. As such youth-directed drama unfolds, the therapist helps to identify important emotional themes, coach more effective improvisation, and suggest positive outcomes. For example, the therapist could help the youth develop companionship for those characters who find themselves constantly abandoned. If parent–child relationships are sufficiently positive, the parents are invited in to help complete these more corrective scenes.

Real-life scenes involving peer-related conflict can be introduced at this point. However, some attempt to use imagination to transform reality (e.g., by casting a cruel peer or rejecting parent as a stuffed animal involved in physical interaction) offers emotional distance and assists the youth in maintaining a more creative and metaphor-making state. Often at this point, the verbal suggestions made during the action are intended to encourage the metaphor making and are imaginative in nature rather than equating actions to real people or events. Once the youth is able to make an expressive episode that has some meaning, the therapeutic goals shift to assisting the youth in developing more imaginative and personal narratives, rather than verbally acknowledging how the play relates directly to real life.

Case Example

Jim was an 11-year-old boy in the fifth grade who constantly pushed smaller, more popular boys down on the playground. He was referred for Dynamic Play Therapy after the school refused to let him return without medication. During the initial interview, Jim's mother reported that her son was attacked and almost killed by a very large dog when he was much younger. Prior to this, he had also witnessed his father physically assault his mother on several occasions. His parents divorced and Jim now resided with his mother. He reported that he greatly missed seeing his father. Before the referral, Jim had also witnessed his dog, which he had received as a way to help him resolve his past attack, being killed by a larger dog while on a walk. Shortly after this event, the school reported that he had become significantly aggressive toward other children and simply didn't seem to have the social understanding to develop friendships. After the school administrator asked that he not return to class without medication, Jim had started thinking about harming himself. These comments compelled his mother to seek out services.

During the evaluation, Jim verified that he had indeed been thinking about killing himself. He contracted to not harm himself in any way and to tell his mother and/or the therapist about his thoughts of self-harm. The therapist and mother told him that they would periodically ask about the topic, as well. Once the therapy sessions started, Jim reported that his thoughts of self-harm stopped.

The therapist also asked Jim directly about any bullying behaviors he had experienced or engaged in. His mother provided school reports of discipline incidents in which her son had physically hurt or intimidated his peers. The reports from Jim and his mother indicated that he had physically bullied other classmates and had also been the victim of many cruel comments and rumors, peer-initiated conflicts, and social exclusion in his class. He said that these patterns of interaction contributed to his not being able to pay attention in class and feeling that peers and teachers did not want him in the school nor respect him. He feared that other students might bring a weapon to school and he would subsequently become a victim of some kind of school violence.

Jim reported that he still clearly remembered the dog attack in which he almost died and the several days he spent in the hospital recovering. He was very frightened by these thoughts, experiencing them as intrusive, even though the attack occurred several years prior. Both he and his mother said they had never really talked to each other about this event because of the strong fear and helplessness the memory evoked. They both emphasized how emotionally upsetting the recent attack and killing of the boy's dog had been.

After a few sessions of discussion, Jim and his mother agreed that these events would need to be addressed in some way, but felt that they could not discuss their feelings together, at least not initially. The mother also reported that she was having problems establishing discipline with her son. They both said they could consider how the dog attacks might be related to the current difficulties in school once the strong, fearful feelings of the past were somewhat resolved.

Further evaluations were not consistent with ADHD and medication was not recommended. The school did agree to allow Jim to return with the provision that the family complete some kind of counseling. The therapist, mother, and son agreed that individual, dramatically oriented play would initially occur between Jim and the therapist, as the mother was currently having difficulty listening to her son's feelings. The mother would be asked to join when Jim felt he could talk about his feelings with her. She agreed to this plan. The therapist described the playroom to the boy, and he was eager to try something "that was fun" after having talked about so many events that were upsetting to him.

During the first dynamic play session, the therapist suggested that Jim and he have a "war" with the scarves. After a brief description of playroom rules in which he agreed to slow down should the activity become dangerous and to help with the cleanup of the room at the end of the session, the therapist and Jim divided the scarves. They began throwing them at each other using large, strong movements. The object was for each player to try to "hit" the other by throwing the scarves, while avoiding the other's attempts to hit him. The two used the entire playroom space, moving rapidly to find ways to either get away from the other or approach for a good "attack."

After several exchanges in which the boy was highly engaged in the activity, the therapist suggested that each player use the pillows to build a "fort" to make a place to rest from the thrown scarves. Jim made a fort that was completely sealed off, such that the scarves couldn't get in and he couldn't get out to stage "attacks." The session ended at this point, as time ran out. Jim said he wanted to return and continue the game. The therapist suggested that the two of them could begin to make a story, as well.

During the next week, Jim's teacher and mother reported that he had been oppositional in the class and had engaged in some arguments with his peers that included insults and pushing. In the next session, the therapist told Jim that the teacher and his mother had told him of the arguments with peers and problems in class. The therapist suggested that the two could again have a scarf war and play out various parts of the incidents. During the following scene, the therapist asked Jim to make some school-related comments while throwing the scarves, to express the emotions that were triggered. The therapist occasionally took on the roles of a peer or teacher, while also maintaining supportive coaching to encourage different ways of using the scarves to attack and the pillows to make a "base." The boy again made a tightly enclosed fort as the session ended.

Jim was engaged and able to generate his own "expressive momentum" with a balance of form (rules, reciprocity, and awareness of the therapist) and energy (internal motivation and curiosity to generate ongoing, independent play). Thus, the therapist decided to introduce a transition activity to help him begin to use the physical expression to generate more independent metaphor and story making. During the next session, the two began again with a "scarf war" and the building of a "home" without any mention of peers, school, or family. As before, Jim made a fort in which he could hide from the scarves. As the drama could not actually continue without Jim playing outside the fort, this action was taken as suggesting a change in theme. The therapist used this cue to introduce a new dramatic improvisation. He asked Jim to begin to create a narrative of being in his room asleep and then coming out into a dream. The therapist then arranged the large stuffed animals and other props around the room.

Jim was asked to come out and enact the "dream" he found. When he did leave the pillow "home," he described a dream of having crashed a plane on a threatening, foreign island where he was surrounded by several characters that wanted to harm him. One was going to throw Jim in jail, another was going to attack him, causing him to fight for his life, and only one or two smaller creatures would offer him help in any way.

From this point through the next seven sessions, Jim created independent, dramatic scenes around the theme of arriving on a dangerous island and having to overcome several struggles before he could find some way to escape to a safe homeland. The therapist adapted to this change by joining the drama, playing several of the minor roles (e.g., the attacking animals, the jail keeper, and even those who helped the "hero" find his way to safety or win a conflict). The therapist also provided narration to connect the action, highlighting the emotional themes of threat, struggle, and abandonment, and the hero's ultimate resourcefulness during his escapes. In this way, the therapist was able to help reframe Jim's expressions of helplessness at being on a hostile island to focus instead on his resourcefulness at overcoming a much larger enemy.

The therapeutic coaching used during these sessions departed from a more reality-based orientation of actual peer or school behavior, instead helping to elaborate the metaphorical and imagined dramatic action. In this way, the therapist as narrator could give voice to strong emotional expressions—such as fear of attack or serious physical injury, abandonment, hopefulness, and relief at having survived intense struggles—as they occurred in the story line. The therapist also facilitated Jim's improvisational play and story telling when he did not have any new ideas, much like an improvisational drama teacher might. When Jim could not find a way to get out of "jail" in his story, for example, the therapist pointed out where a small crack existed in the arrangement of pillows to see if it might suggest a further story line. Jim then invented several escape plans incorporating a small animal "ally." Importantly, he shifted into a more creative playfulness with these suggestions. The creative shifts and problem solving were helpful in pointing out the boy's "natural creativity" during moments of stress, if even in metaphor.

Over the next several sessions, Jim continued to independently enact stories in which he, as an "explorer," had found his way to some very dangerous places (usually a far-off island). The hero had many narrow escapes from danger until he could finally develop an escape plan to return to his "home base." During one of the final struggles, he generated dramatic action in which he was being eaten by a large animal that jumped on top of him. The therapist coached Jim to remember his resourcefulness in his role as the "hero," and reminded him of how he had escaped in the past.

It was not until the next session that the therapist pointed out to Jim how much his improvised dramatic activity was like the dog attack his mother and he had briefly described many weeks before. It was important that the therapist waited to make this connection between the dramatic action and the real traumatic event until Jim developed sufficient ego strength. The timing allowed for important emotional and cognitive distance from the affect associated with the event. The risk of making this connection during the enactment was that Jim would have experienced a re-traumatization in his play. In discussion some time after the enactment, the therapist could help Jim see how his metaphors contained both the fearful elements of the attack as well as the creative struggle for escape and remaining alive (both actually alive, as well as in his imagination). After these talks, Jim agreed he was ready to talk about the attack with his mother. The mother was contacted and a conjoint session was set up.

During the next meeting, Jim and his mother were assisted in retelling the specifics of the attack as they remembered it. The therapist coached them to recall how the experience felt, including the mother's terror at discovering her son was missing and realizing what had occurred when she heard the ambulance coming to assist him. Jim was able to recall how he had approached the large dog in anticipation of playing with it when it suddenly attacked him. He was supported in remembering how he was able to keep the dog from actually killing him by his physical strength and struggle. This conversation was the first time these two had ever talked about the event, as well as some of their important experiences. It proved quite cathartic for them.

In a following session, Jim was able to describe and show his mother the general theme of his "Stories from the Islands." At this time, the therapist was able to assist both the mother and son in making the connection between the boy's general experiences of threat (be it from a peer's or teacher's behavior, or from his memory of the attack) and his strong need for physical struggle. Jim was able to use his story to understand how, on an emotional level, the two very different experiences of peer harassment and the dog attack could be related. Importantly, he was able to use his stories to see how he was able to survive on the island using his creativity, and how he was able to actually survive the real attack using his physical struggles and resourcefulness. From this, the therapist could begin to talk about how Jim could change his social behavior with his peers. Instead of being victimized by their negative comments, isolating himself, or becoming too aggressive without cause, he could generate pro-social solutions by accessing his creativity and resourcefulness. By the end of the year, it was noteworthy that Jim had made a best friend in a younger and much smaller girl who herself was very anxious.

Summary

As children enter middle childhood and early adolescence, they experience more social demands to be like their peers in order to have relationships. Often, this means that social, physical, verbal, and social aggression toward others who are seen as different becomes an accepted way to create social identity. Adults can be perceived as unhelpful by youth who become involved in bullying or who are victimized. This social dilemma is particularly challenging for those children who have already experienced histories of attachment disruption and trauma within their families. Without intervention that addresses their primary relational deficits, difficulties with trust, and basic inability to "play" with others with a sense of reciprocity and experiential give-and-take, these children can become emotionally isolated, sometimes seeming beyond help. They continue to experience social failure with adults, peers, and parents.

Relationally oriented play therapy can be very useful in introducing such youths to an experience in which they can begin to respond with creativity, spontaneity, and organization by using expressive modalities with a responsive adult. Dynamic Play Therapy (Harvey, 2000) is an intervention style in which youth can be "coached" to develop relationships using drama, art, movement, and video with a therapist who functions initially as a "master player." Play episodes are eventually used to enhance the parent–child relationship and to improve peer interaction.

In this intervention style, the therapist needs to address concrete, current peer problems as reported by school and community sources, as well as by the child. The therapist initially guides the client to participate in interactive improvisations using expressive media. He then uses verbal coaching to help transition the play into dramatic scenes that represent emotionally relevant interactions with peers and teachers. During an initial phase of treatment, the therapist helps the client develop organized and enjoyable improvisation ability. Children are then assisted in using improvisation to generate independent play narratives, such as the "Stories from the Islands." Finally, the therapist can begin to use these narratives to help children reflect on their emotional and social experience. It is this reflection, in combination with the creative experience of play with an empathic, attuned therapist, that contributes to lasting change and growth.

References

Charach, A., Papler, D., & Ziegler, S. (1995). Bullying at school—A Canadian perspective: A survey of problems and suggestions for interventions. *Education Canada, 35*(1), 12–18.

Espelage, D. L., & Holt, M. K. (2001). *Bullying victimization during early adolescence: Peer influences and psychological correlates.* Bingham, NY: Haworth Press.

Estea, M., & Rouse, J. (2001). At what age are children most likely to be bullied at school? *Aggressive Behavior, 27*(6), 419–429.

Gatinsky, E., & Salmond, K. (2002). *Ask the children: Youth and violence.* New York: Families and Work Institute.

Harvey, S. A. (1990). Dynamic play therapy: An integrated expressive arts approach to the family therapy of young children. *The Arts in Psychotherapy, 17*(3), 239–246.

Harvey, S. A. (1993). Ann: Dynamic play therapy with ritual abuse. In T. Kottman & C. Schaefer (Eds.), *Play therapy in action: A case book for practitioners* (pp. 371–416). Northvale, NJ: Jason Aronson.

Harvey, S. A. (1994a). Dynamic play therapy: Expressive play intervention with families. In K. O'Connor & C. Schaefer (Eds.), *Handbook of play therapy: Volume two. Advances and innovations* (pp. 85–110). New York: Wiley.

Harvey, S. A. (1994b). Dynamic play therapy: Creating attachments. In B. James, *Handbook for treatment of attachment-trauma problems in children* (pp. 222–233). New York: Lexington Books.

Harvey, S. A. (1994c). Dynamic play therapy: An integrated expressive arts approach to family treatment of infants and toddlers. *Zero to Three, 15*, 11–17.

Harvey, S. A. (1995). Sandra: The case of an adopted, sexually abused child. In F. Levy (Ed.), *Dance and other expressive arts therapies: When words are not enough* (pp. 167–180). New York: Routledge.

Harvey, S. A. (1997). Dynamic play therapy: A creative arts approach. In K. O'Connor & L. Braverman (Eds.), *Play therapy theory and practice: A comparative presentation* (pp. 341–367). New York: Wiley.

Harvey, S. A. (2000). Family dynamic play. In P. Lewis & D. Johnson (Eds.), *Current approaches in drama therapy* (pp. 19–43). Springfield, IL: Charles C. Thomas.

Harvey, S. A., & Kelly, E. C. (1993). The influence of the quality of early interactions on a three year old's play narratives. *The Arts in Psychotherapy, 17*(4), 387–395.

Khosropour, S. & Walsh, J. (2001, April). *That's not teasing—that's bullying: A study of fifth graders' conceptualization of bullying and teasing.* Paper presented at the meeting of the American Educational Research Association, Seattle, WA.

Olweus, D. (1993a). Bully/victim problems and school children: Long-term consequences and an effective intervention program. In S. Hodgins, *Mental disorders and crime* (pp. 317–349). Thousand Oaks, CA: Sage.

Olweus, D. (1993b). *Bullying at school: What we know and what we can do.* Cambridge, MA: Blackwell Publishers.

Russ, S. W. (1998). *Affect, creative experience, and psychological adjustment.* Philadelphia, PA: Brunner/Mazel Publishers.

Stern, D. (1985). *The interpersonal world of the infant: A view from psychoanalysis and developmental psychology.* New York: Basic Books.

Tortera, S. (1994). Join my dance: The unique movement style of each infant and toddler can invite communication, expression, and intervention. *Zero to Three, 15,* 1–10.

Weinhold, B. (2000). Uncovering the hidden causes of bullying and school violence. *Counseling and Human Development, 32*(6), 1–18.

CHAPTER 15

Through the Eyes
of the Therapists and Children
*Drama Therapy during and
after September 11th*

KRISTIN LONG and ANNA MARIE WEBER

For therapists who work with traumatized clients, the concept of creating a safe space infuses the therapeutic process, regardless of one's orientation. However, when we, as therapists, are also experiencing the trauma with which our clients are struggling, and the treatment takes place in a city shrouded in danger, the ability to feel truly safe is tested. While therapists working in war-torn countries have long understood and grappled with this treatment dilemma—the challenge of finding safety when surrounded by danger—it hit home for American mental health professionals following the terrorist attacks on New York City and Washington, D.C. on September 11, 2001. This article will examine our shared process, that of two drama therapists struggling to make sense of the attacks on the World Trade Center while called upon to help heal young clients in the New York City area.

As we explored writing about 9/11 and our reactions to the traumatic events, we discovered that we had so much to talk about, yet so little seemed to become concrete on paper. Our memories were scattered and disconnected. We started to look at how our relationship, that of the authors, began. At first, our connection was through the people we knew in common who were trying to draw us together. During those days, we heard, over the telephone and through messages, each other's comforting words of support in the wake of terrifying loss. Our trust in each other grew through the pain and loss we witnessed. Our common fear was that we wouldn't be "good enough" to meet the needs of so many caught in the web of terror and grief. One therapist was so close, only blocks away, and the other trapped, unable to travel the deserted roads off Long Island. Though miles apart, we employed the same style. We stayed in tune with the needs of clients, staff, interns, and loved ones.

Here are the moments from our individual stories, our clients' stories, and those who touched and continue to touch our lives. While struggling with our own emotional, spiritual, and physical reactions to the traumatic events, we constantly questioned how to provide a safe enough holding environment in which our child clients could address deep pain and grieve. The intensity of multiple emotions varied for us, the authors, as well as for the children and staff we worked with, depending on the specific experiences and relationships. Each, however, had his or her own personal degree of impact and needed to discover a way to begin the healing process.

Through our work, drama therapy provided a container for both child and therapist. As Dale (1997) wrote, ". . . the aim is not to avoid stress but to *recognize when it is present*, to be able to manage and contain it, and to be able to understand what it is telling us about what is happening inside the child, inside ourselves, and in the interaction between the child and therapist" (p. 57). The therapist, clients, modality, and the play space itself allowed true affect to emerge without the pressure of verbalization, while coping skills and a sense of safety were reinforced. For the traumatized client and therapist, the drama therapy process empowered both to begin healing. Drewes (2002) spoke in her training of the need for the therapists to stay with the scary terrorist play, while being the mediators, reminding the children that "not everyone in the world is bad." To carry out this role, we access supervision, personal therapy, interpersonal support, and spiritual connections.

The individual client and professional narratives that follow cycle through the stages of trauma response and healing. Figley (1985) identified the phases of trauma recovery: catastrophe, relief and confusion, avoidance, reconsideration, and adjustment. Trauma triggers often cycle a person back and forth through the phases. Therapists, child clients, their caregivers, and community members all had, and continue to have, times when trauma triggers take hold. A traumatic wound was suffered that, for many, also triggered past trauma. We begin in Lower Manhattan.

Kristin writes:

I was dog-sitting on the morning of September 11, 2001. The penthouse apartment in which I was staying, only a block away from my own, had an amazing balcony that faced south toward downtown Manhattan with a breathtaking view of the Twin Towers. I had my coffee on the balcony that morning, as my dog and the two I was watching slept in the morning sun. I allowed myself to fantasize for a moment about what it would be like to have this view every morning—to be able to afford an apartment that allowed such a luxury.

I went back inside, gathered my things for the day, and walked out the door. I never imagined I wouldn't return until after midnight. As I walked to my worksite, I looked up at the sky and thought how it looked like a *Simpsons* cartoon sky—bright blue, a few passing clouds—overall, a beautiful Tuesday morning.

As I walked to my job, I thought about the interns with whom I worked—one just starting, the other soon to terminate her work. A new colleague also had started the day before. I arrived at 8:45. The phone started ringing minutes later and, as I picked it up, I heard my friend's voice. Simultaneously, the hospital's internal speaker system started to make an announcement about a "Code 3." As my friend informed me over the phone that a plane had hit one of the buildings of the World Trade Center, I glanced at my ID card to remind myself what Code 3 meant. "Disaster Plan" was written in small, black type. I paused, questioning if this was yet another drill to prepare us for an upcoming audit. "What kind of plane? What do you mean?" I asked, imagining that a small airplane that takes tourists on flights to view the skyline had hit the tower. Then I wondered, "How could that be possible?" My friend didn't have any more information and, at that point, the chaos I heard on the unit reminded me that my presence was needed in the hallway.

The nurses and supervisors were running out the locked front door of the inpatient child and adolescent unit, racing toward the elevators. I asked what I could do to help and was told to stay with the kids in the day room. The TV was turned on and the news was playing in the room where all the kids were gathered. Within seconds, I could tell from the newscaster's face that something tragic had happened. I wasn't sure what it was; there was mumbling among the staff but nothing I heard made much sense. I guided the children into the dining room and they sat down while breakfast was served. Not all the children seemed aware that something had happened outside the hospital, but they were beginning to internalize the anxiety they felt from the staff rushing in and out. A few of the older children asked me what was happening. Such an innocent question; I found myself wishing I had an answer. I felt a pit inside my stomach unlike anything I had experienced before. I was unsure of the answers myself, but slowly began to realize from staff conversations that the airplane that had hit the tower was a commercial flight with many passengers. I answered the children who were still asking, honestly stating that a plane had hit one of the World Trade Center buildings. I told them I did not know any of the details yet, and gingerly encouraged them to finish eating. Staff continued to rush in and out of the front door. I wondered what they knew that I did not.

My memory seems to blur at this point, as if someone or something else was responsible for my thoughts and actions throughout the day. Even as I write this now, I question the accuracy of my recollections. Yet, this is how my mind has recorded the events. All of the children were somehow brought back into the day room—the youngest being about 5 years old, the oldest 15. The TV was still on; no one seemed to consider turning it off for a while, or that maybe the images weren't meant for the children to see over and over. By this time of the morning, the towers were on fire. Watching my beautiful view of downtown ablaze, I wretchedly realized both towers had been hit. One child recalled that he had a perfect view of downtown from his bedroom window. He stood up and started to rush down the hallway to get a live view of the action the TV was broadcasting. I flashed back to my morning coffee, not sure I wanted him, or me, to see this event live; but I hurried down the hall after him.

I have thought repeatedly of my decision to not try to stop him from seeing. I have spent much time trying to determine if it was "right" or "okay." Still without an answer, I have finally been able, through this writing, to focus on the process of all that happened that day. Sometimes that nagging question returns, though: "Would he be better off today if I had prevented him from seeing those images through his hospital room window?" At times, I am tormented by this unanswered question.

By the time I rushed down the hall and into the child's bedroom, a few other children were congregated around the window. We stood in the child's bedroom, a huddle of us, staring together at the burning towers. We could actually see the yellow, orange, and red flames consuming the buildings. It reminded me of some violent video game, something I was watching though a TV screen, not a window. I wanted to stop looking but, like the children, I was drawn to the view.

The children were making a few comments, asking who knew someone there, noting the smoke, wondering how far away we were. I found myself reassuring them that we were blocks away; the fire from the towers could not reach us. At this point, the TV had broadcast that the planes had been highjacked and that the attacks were intentional. I was scared, but with such an intense energy that the fear was never fully transmitted throughout my body.

New kids came into the room as others left, or wandered into a new room down the hall to see a slightly different version. I reflected about the unit rules, specifically the one that states that no child is allowed in another's room. Usually these rules were so well enforced; the structure of the unit had to be maintained for everyone's safety. No one seemed to be enforcing much of anything at this point. I also thought about the day room—who was monitoring the TV and what were the children watching? As I started to comprehend the immensity of what had happened, still not convinced that it was an attack and not a horrible mistake, staff members were starting to identify people they knew who worked in or near the World Trade Center, "down there." *There* seemed like such a strange word, symbolizing a far-off, make-believe place. I was horrified, scared, and suddenly protective—of the children, the staff, myself, and the city.

At one point in the morning, the telephone became such a lifeline. Children wanted to connect with foster parents, siblings, and friends. I heard something on the news about a plane in Pennsylvania and thought immediately of my brother living in Philadelphia. What was happening to my friends in Washington, D.C.? I had no idea what was going on in the outside world, but in our community the loudspeaker kept blurting out commands; cots were being dragged up the emergency stairwell, sirens were loud and constant outside, and large bottles of water were being transported on and off the unit.

Staff members came into the office I shared with this new employee, requesting to use the telephone. I offered the new intern the opportunity to leave, but she was committed to staying for the day. I wasn't sure how I felt about this. Should I, as her supervisor, tell her she *had* to go? I couldn't imagine experiencing all of this so early in my training. I followed my instinct and I chose not to force her to leave. She spent the day with the children, playing games and talking, running back to the office to try to help others reach out to people via telephone—a telephone that suddenly wasn't a very reliable form of communication.

While I was in my office assisting children in making phone calls, the towers collapsed. My office window didn't face downtown, so I wasn't aware until I went back out into the hallway. One of the mental health workers simply said, "They fell. Did you know?" I had to repeat what he said; it didn't seem possible. It wasn't until I went to the TV and saw the instant replay that I believed him. My memory immediately flashed back to how the skyline looked when coming out of the Holland Tunnel—a view I had seen hundreds of times. It was a perfect view of the skyline of my massive city. I instinctively went to the window where I was huddled with children earlier and looked. There was smoke, lots of smoke, but it was as if they never stood. I couldn't even remember exactly where they had been. I spent a while trying to reconstruct the image. As I walk down Fifth Avenue, I still find myself trying to remember where they stood.

Finally, I reached my parents by telephone. My mother was worried I had chosen that day to take a trip to the top of the towers. I was able to check my messages and was shocked to hear so many voices—my friends from overseas calling. Someone asked if I could please just send an e-mail, surely that would allow me to get through to everyone if I couldn't call. I felt very far away from everything, but mostly far away from "down there." For others, though, I was their closest link to the attacks. The sadness of the trauma had hit, but I tucked it away. I started to make mental notes of all the people I knew who worked there, but there was no idea at this time how many people had escaped. My job was to continue to sit with the kids, to be there with them. There were so many unanswerable questions to which these children were demanding responses. The ongoing run of news showed the Towers falling over and over. I missed it live, but watched the retelling throughout the day.

It was lunchtime and, as the kids went into the dining room, I took a break. I remember walking past one of the doctor's offices and seeing her sitting at a desk reading the newspaper, chair leaning back, legs propped up. I was so angry. Didn't she realize the kids needed her? It seemed like too casual of a pose given the day. I later realized how many people struggled to find some sense of normalcy amid all the chaos.

12:00 p.m. It was the first time I had been outside since the attacks on the World Trade Center and had offered to go for a drink and snack run for the children and staff. The hospital was hectic. I took the elevator to the seventh floor gymnasium and saw that it had been transformed into an emergency triage station; cots were lined up along the basketball court, waiting to be filled with injured bodies that never arrived. Bottled water had been brought upstairs, and oxygen tanks and medical machinery lined the periphery of the gym. I took the stairs down and headed outside.

On my way to the corner store, I found myself immobilized as I reached Sixth Avenue. Leaning against the fire hydrant, which I still walk by a couple times a week, I looked down the street as I had done hundreds of times before. I saw an image I can only describe as a scene out of *Night of the Living Dead.* Men in business suits, covered with ashes, were trying desperately to get a signal on their cell phones. Conversation after conversation was filled with the same plea: "Have you heard/seen/talked to . . . ?" There was a stream of faces, men and women, with such blank stares of horror, disbelief, and shock. The dirt is what I remember, the soot. Everyone was so filthy. And there was a bizarre silence. It wasn't quiet, but the absence of the cars, buses, and horns in this city usually filled with traffic was jarring. It was the most unnatural image I have ever seen, and it is forever pasted in my memory. As I leaned against that fire hydrant, I looked up and saw the downtown skyline missing its two massive towers. I tore myself away, feeling like a secret observer who had no right to be watching this somber parade, and went into the deli for some snacks.

The rest of the day passed somehow. The usual 4:15 p.m. change of staff never happened, as too many people were unable to get into the city and many were unable to leave. I remember hearing that Manhattan was "closed." How can that be? There were people I wanted to see, needed to connect to, who were locked outside. The newest announcement inside the hospital was that no staff person was allowed to leave until further notice. At 5:00, however, the staff decided that the intern should leave. I was grateful for the time she spent with the kids and was aware of how valuable her time was to them. I was also extremely concerned about her, given the traumatic events of the day.

I had never been at the hospital past 6:00 p.m., at least not on the unit where I worked. I joined the children for dinner and then sat down with some of the younger ones to read bedtime stories. *Chicka Chicka Boom Boom* (Martin & Archambault, 2000) had been a favorite in drama therapy groups earlier that week, so out it came again for bedtime. I helped tuck them in and I sat myself on the edge of the bed. My mind flashed to a class lecture I had at some point in my career as a student. The topic was on boundaries and working with children. I wondered what guidelines applied in this situation.

Finally, a few minutes after midnight, we were advised that we could leave. Everyone was to return the next morning, as there were quite a few staff who were unable to get into Manhattan. I left the hospital alone and turned onto Sixth Avenue again. I started crying for the first time that day as I walked back to the apartment where I was dog-sitting. I resented not being able to just go home. I again leaned against the same fire hydrant, just being still for a few moments. There were no vehicles, but many people were still outside. I have never experienced so many people making eye contact in New York City. Everyone who passed was either staring downward or looking deep into another's eyes, hoping to find answers to unspoken questions.

I walked to Fourteenth Street to go home and continued crying until I arrived at the apartment. I spent a few moments just holding and hugging my dog. I was so aware that to him the day was like any other, except I was a bit late for the evening walk. I found such comfort in his unconditional love. I realized I needed to be somewhere familiar for a few minutes. Logging onto the Internet, I sent out a mass e-mail and spent some time reading messages from far-off friends. I felt so disturbed and wasn't sure I could sleep. I hesitated to go onto the balcony, but something pulled me outside. I started crying again, sobbing this time.

When I stepped back inside, I turned on the news and stared at the images for a few minutes, then wanted an escape. After making a few more phone calls, I just wanted to watch some old *Seinfeld* repeat. I started flipping though the cable channels, getting more and more agitated that all that was on was either the news or the loud snow that comes from not having a signal. As I was cursing at the TV, it hit me—I literally felt such a blow— that the antenna that had served as New York City's cable connection had been on top of the towers. I had a crushing sense of guilt for being irritated about not getting cable. People had died horrible deaths and I was upset over television. I don't know when I finally drifted off, but I fell asleep feeling very alone.

The next few days blur together. People I worked with were still waiting to hear from loved ones who were missing. I met with the intern who was getting ready to terminate, suddenly feeling inadequate as a supervisor. All the things we discussed her doing the last week there seemed trivial. She wasn't sure she wanted to leave now and volunteered extra time translating for families searching for people who were missing.

I remember taking a lunch break on September 12 and seeing the long lines at the hospital: lines of people wishing to volunteer, wanting to donate blood, needing to get in to see if the person they were looking for was inside. Every time I walked outside, I was bombarded with questions and requests to get people in.

I went to the seventh floor where the emergency triage room was created, and became filled with anguish when I saw that all the cots were empty. I knew it meant that there weren't people to fill them—not enough people had gotten out alive. As the days went on, this gym area transformed into a place for survivors, workers, and family members to gather and tell stories, get information—what little there was—and simply sit together.

As the week continued, my walk to the hospital became more of a journey. First, I had to identify myself as a hospital employee to go below Fourteenth Street. This act filled me with a sense of pride and, at the same time, I felt like I just wasn't worthy. After all, I wasn't going down to the disaster site to do work, just to the hospital; and not to do medical work that was "really needed," just children's psychiatry. I kept asking myself what *I* was doing there. I felt at times like an imposter, showing up where I had no right to be.

I had such contrasting feelings. Sometimes, I was filled with a concrete desire to do something, like so many of the people waiting to offer their services. Other times, such a large part of me felt my trauma responses were for another time. I needed to force the feelings I had down somewhere inside of me so that I could go to work and sit and play with the kids.

About a week after the attack, I had a day off from work. I felt like I was returning to the community being behind in the grieving process. It seemed as if people were a week into their processing and I was just getting ready to start. Many people had reached the point where they had heard enough; they didn't want to hear stories anymore. They had become overwhelmed. I still wanted to share and to listen, not just to the children at this point, but also to my peers.

As these feelings emerged, I kept trying to reach out to the New York University Drama Therapy Program for some supervision, especially around how to supervise the two students who were interning at the hospital. I kept hearing the same message from everyone: "Talk to Anna Marie." I resisted. I didn't really know Anna Marie. I knew other staff—people who I couldn't reach by phone. Those who I could connect with were telling me to reach out to her. I knew they were right. When we spoke, I told her the story of my experience on 9/11. I told her about the lines of people, about the phone calls, about my anger, my intense sadness, and my feelings of just not being good enough to do this. I felt such relief as we finally connected.

Over the next few days, we talked and talked. We talked about how to use drama therapy to ground ourselves and the children; to provide comfort and to reinforce coping skills and a sense of safety through the use of familiar stories, activities, and rituals. I had such vivid pictures in my head. I needed to share and release them so that I could hear more from others; for, as the medical side of the hospital started to realize that no one else was coming, that there were no survivors, the psychiatric side of the hospital started to overfill. Children who had never before required this level of care were now coming into the locked unit, and they needed someone to be able to listen to their stories.

As the week passed, the lines of people outside the hospital started to diminish. No donated blood was needed; there was really nothing for the volunteers to do. I felt so sad as I saw people being turned away, people who had such a need to just *do something*. There were no more people waiting by the ER. But what had replaced them were pictures, walls and walls of pictures of people who were missing. It was truly indescribable. I stood and watched a young woman hang a photocopied picture of a man on the wall near the entrance I used. She used such care to make sure her picture would be seen and stay on the wall, but not cover anyone else's picture. During the few days following the attacks, more and more pictures emerged; not just on the walls of the hospitals, but around the parks and streets as well. Restaurant doors had pictures. There were photos inside flower shops. I remember seeing the photo of one man in several locations. His name was Dave and he had a little girl and a young wife. I started to recognize his face and could pick him out of the wall of pictures. I wondered often about his family, their story, and their sadness. As staff members started to return to their jobs, still hopeful for a call or message from someone who was missing, I wondered if they knew, prior to returning to work, that the pictures were there. I often think of how hard it must have been for people to just walk in through those doors again after 9/11.

The first rainfall after the attacks left the pictures, the candle wax, and the artwork a patchwork collage. I felt devastated as I walked to work one day and saw people cleaning up the park. It seemed to signify a push to move on, to clean up the images and get on with life. I didn't feel ready. I wasn't sure how.

Anna Marie writes:

The worry, the fear, the unanswered calls, news videos . . . and the questions: "Who's alive? Who's trying to find their way home? Who's missing?" Each person had his or her own needs. How do we stay attuned at so many levels—moment to moment, person to person, each one unique, following their lead, yet being present and offering choices?

When I headed for the train, an agency volunteer stepped off the elevator. I said, "I am on my way to catch the train to the city" (as I always did on Wednesdays). He turned to me with a face of terror—frozen as he held on to the doorknob, saying, "I haven't been able to go back." I felt so horrible as I realized that my weekly trip to New York University had triggered such terror for this man who had had airplane parts fall at his feet only a few days before. He was so close to the World Trade Center.

As I walked outside, I had images running through my head from another volunteer's story about escaping from her office covered in ashes, searching for her way home. She, too, was afraid to go back to the city. I had to push aside my fear and race to catch my train into the city. So many thoughts and memories came back to me as I rode in. We were so worried about our friends' children and, for hours, we wondered if they had escaped. Some did not, while others were greeted with grasping hugs and tears. I came to realize that my living and working in New York caused great pain for my nephew as he watched the news and called home from his first few weeks at college. "Has anyone heard from Anna Marie?" They had not. It would take hours to connect by phone. That was the trigger for my feelings of guilt, which would emerge months later in staff debriefing sessions.

Back to the task at hand. I was going to travel through the tunnel—taking the train and a subway to the Village downtown. I had heard of many being trapped in the tunnels. I was heading toward the war zone—to meet students and colleagues caught in the center of it all. What horrors would I hear on this day, only a week after the tragedy; this September 19th, which was also the anniversary of my own brother's death? He had fallen while mountain climbing. Images of him falling have haunted me for years, and now thousands of people were also haunted by images of people falling. As one child, whose story was told on the radio, said to her father, "I saw birds falling on fire." Later that evening, she stated to her dad before falling asleep, "I know they weren't birds." An eerie silence came over the train as we went through the tunnel, entering New York City.

I walked into the NYU office that day so sensitive to deep grief, in touch with the greatest loss of my life—so aware of others' grief around me. Guiding myself to stay in the moment and be open to other's pain, staying present to the fear and loss in those touched by personal tragedy, I witnessed the deepest soul-wrenching grief and loss that evening. My students had been through so much, each harboring their own personal sense of loss and trauma. My own tears would wait for the train ride home.

Kristin writes:

The weeks following 9/11, the child psychiatric unit received many children with diagnoses of Major Depressive Disorder and Posttraumatic Stress Disorder. The unit shifted in some ways, usually serving children with conduct disorder or psychosis. While there was still aggression on the unit, the sadness had really taken over. Again, I was left with such doubt about my abilities. Teddy bears, books, and hugs goodbye replaced my usual drama therapy interventions. These concrete things seemed to provide some of the safety for which the children were looking. I still wondered what else I could offer them. What could I say? Landy (2002), recounting his speech to New York University staff following the attacks, posed the same question: "Reflecting on the early days following September 11, I wondered why such a strong sense of inadequacy struck again, some 35 years into my career as a drama therapist?" He continued, "The answer seemed very clear. Like so many others, I was deeply affected by the massive terrorist attack and the great sense of threat that hung over New York and the United States" (p. 136).

I clearly remember one child who was admitted to the hospital in the month that followed the attacks. Tyrone was an eight-year-old boy diagnosed with conduct disorder and currently living in foster care. He had been admitted to the children's psychiatric unit previously for a brief stay because of increased violent behavior. Following 9/11, he was again hospitalized after becoming aggressive at home and school. He'd had a positive relationship with his uncle, who had just died in the World Trade Center attack. Tyrone had a difficult time readjusting to the unit rules and the highly structured environment. He was constantly being redirected for "acting out" behavior, which receives an automatic time-out. During the first drama therapy session with five other children, Tyrone was provided, for the first time, with a space to explore his feelings about the World Trade Center disaster and the death of his uncle in a non-verbal way.

The group began with an invitation for each member to offer a movement. The other members of the group then joined. I will never forget Tyrone's movement. His limbs seemed to slowly melt as he fell to the ground. His knees bent, hips buckled, shoulders slouched; he hung his head low as he collapsed onto the floor. This movement didn't seem calculated; rather, he appeared to be in slow motion. When I invited him to get up and repeat the movement with the rest of the group, he refused. My first thought was that he was being oppositional, something seen so often on the unit. After several unsuccessful attempts to have him rise, mostly by trying to set limits or reinforce the rules, I finally began to listen and watch him on the floor. As my frustration level increased, I noted he was repeating, "I'm dead. Try to get me to be alive."

The group gradually began to respond to his request for help. One by one, and then collectively, we all tried to verbally persuade him to stand up. After a few moments, Tyrone put his hands over his ears, stating, "I can't hear you, I am deaf. Try something else." The children knew that I am conversational in American Sign Language, so they suggested I try to communicate with him through signs. I taught the children how to say, "We miss you" and "Please get up." Once again, through our rudimentary signs, we all encouraged him to stand. Tyrone looked up at us from his position on the floor and, with sad eyes, said, "I am blind. I can't see you." I felt myself wanting to shed tears for this child, unable to see, hear, or understand all that had happened in the last month.

The group came together again for a brainstorming session. The children looked to me for help, and I felt at a loss. There was a part of me that wanted to suddenly set a firm limit, to tell Tyrone he had to get up or he would have a time-out. This felt much easier than continuing. I realized, though, that he needed to work through this, to play though this, not be cut off in the middle of his process. I was also aware of the frustration and anxiety that I was struggling with, my own fears of not being seen or listened to by the children with whom I was working. I was feeling overwhelmed, not sure if I had enough of whatever it took to get him up at all.

I recalled a past client who was diagnosed with Usher Syndrome (the diagnosis given to Helen Keller). I gently took Tyrone's hand from the floor and began to sign into his palm. As I did, I explained to the other children that when someone can't see or hear, they still have a strong need to communicate and connect with people. They use their hands, placed in each other's hands, to talk. I signed and spoke, "We miss you Tyrone, please get up." The other children began to form their own signs and joined me in asking Tyrone to stand up again. They used their hands on his legs, feet, and arms to make this request. As we all chanted our new mantra, Tyrone opened his eyes and slowly got to his feet without a word. The group came back into a standing circle, and I wondered how to move on from there. I struggled with words to express or validate what had happened, but Tyrone took care of that for me. He looked at each member in his or her eyes, and offered a half smile, both with his mouth and his eyes.

It wasn't until later in supervision that I fully comprehended how, in falling down, he was impersonating the falling buildings. The images that had been replayed over and over on the TV now surfaced in the somewhat chubby body of an 8-year-old boy struggling to make sense of something no one can understand. In some ways, it seemed as if he was decompensating along with the buildings. In this state, he no longer was able to connect to any of his senses. However, his ability to ask for help though his body and play, his desire to come alive, demonstrated the strong, healthy child somewhere inside Tyrone.

In a later session, Tyrone chose to play on a rug that I often used during sessions with the children. This rug has images of roads, buildings, and a city on it. Using toy cars, bendable people, and other objects, the children created their own play world. While Tyrone was playing during one group session, he began to bury the police and firefighters under a pile of cars, trucks, construction vehicles, and other people. Another staff member who witnessed his process kept telling him not to play "so violently," and to "be nice with the toys." At one point, he was even informed that he would receive a time out if he continued. I chose to join him on the rug and encouraged him to persist with his play, while assuring the staff that I would make sure his "violence" remained within the boundaries of the rug. Trusting the process, I witnessed his play and hoped I would be able to maintain my promise to the staff. Only after every last pliable firefighter was buried under the rubble of toy cars, planes, buses, and trucks was Tyrone able to quietly mention to me that his uncle died in the towers. He looked at me and said he wondered if his uncle jumped out the window. I sat quietly, not trusting any words that I might speak, and looked at this child whose sadness had been injected into me. Tyrone stared at me and unhurriedly put each toy back into the container that once held them. Those toys became so loaded for me; they were overflowing with Tyrone's projection. Each time I used them with other children, his face emerged in my thoughts.

The work with Tyrone in some ways seemed to mirror the mental health system. My work as a drama therapist was to create an area where expression was able to emerge. Yet, at the same time, the building blocks of this foundation—the staff, the structure of the session—were collapsing, as well. Everyone's grief was seeping through the walls of the hospital. The self-expression Tyrone needed to release through play could have become buried by the staff's request for him to "play nice." In discussing the world of play that children enter, Hoey (1997) wrote, ". . . children are not concerned about contradictions, unless some adult is trying to pin them down to explain, in logical sentences, the maelstrom of half-experienced thoughts and emotions that sometimes flood their consciousness. In play, there is no need to explain" (pp. 29–30). The arts can be a similar catalyst in the healing process; they provide a bridge to the verbal expression, allowing children to eventually name feelings that accompany the reactions and thoughts they are physically holding.

One comment I heard repeatedly following 9/11 was how inadequate professionals felt in counseling others, especially children. As adults struggled to make sense of the images that were replayed repeatedly in the media, or even in their own mind, they began to understand that children were also struggling to cope with these images. Landy (2002) wrote:

> Since the terrorist attacks, the public has been bombarded with images of crashing planes, burning towers, firefighters, policeman, and rescue workers digging through the rubble, Afghani men in turbans and women in burkas, Osama bin Laden and his cronies, bombings, and soldiers scattered throughout the world. Clients carry these images with them and while in treatment creative arts therapists can encourage them to create their own healing images through words and movement, drawings, songs and stories. (p. 139)

Anna Marie writes:

"Ground Zero" became a phrase familiar to the whole world through the news. Day after day, the dust could be seen hanging over all of downtown, as well as the odor unlike any other. Children of parents working at Ground Zero as rescue workers carried added fears: "What if the pile falls on them? Will they get sick? Will the ground collapse? Will something fall and kill them?" Not only were their parents returning home from long shifts, but some also appeared angry and stressed, while others were numb and spaced out. Some parents exhibited extraordinary kindness, while others tried to control their families. A few turned to aggression, escalating the violent behavior they had used before 9/11. Gentry (2002) wrote:

> Many kind and good-hearted emergency service professionals, caregivers, friends and family members who have witnessed the pain, grief and terror in their service to survivors will themselves end up wrestling with encroaching intrusive images, thoughts, and feelings from these interactions in the weeks, months and years ahead. (p. 55)

Some of the children went to the site, others to the fire stations where their parents worked. Ground Zero was a part of their lives. It was where they imaged their parent; the pile of devastation was like a mountain to them. If the towers fell, then in their young minds, the other buildings could fall. Their parents could be buried like the people everyone was looking for.

Unless asked, they rarely spoke of their fears as the world focused on the dead and the missing. I only found out about this by inquiring (Terr, 2003), as I do with all my clients, inviting them to speak and/or play. "What do you think about just before you go to sleep at night?"

Therapy goals shifted. Support and guidance became prominent in order that the children might discover new coping skills that would allow them to speak about and play through their fears. In time, they were able to verbally share their feelings with friends and loved ones.

The rescuers at Ground Zero had an extraordinary influence, the extent of which few knew. Many children who are exposed to domestic violence, for example, feel conflicted loyalty, often identifying with the aggressor in an attempt to hold on to their fathers. Those who have been totally separated from their fathers often long for a father figure, fluctuating between feelings of hate and sadness. The firemen and women, as well as all the other rescuers, gave the children new, strong, empathic role models.

My clients' sessions often contained World Trade Center and tower images, as did those of many of the children throughout New York (Haen, 2002, in press; Landy, 2002). Towers and crashing airplanes were repeated themes. For some, however, an extraordinary thing happened as they connected with those they saw on TV and in person. More and more rescue figures appeared in their play. When the communities held candlelight vigils, carrying signs of "Thank You," children and their mothers attended and participated. They spoke with the firefighters and police officers, many seeing them in a new light. The rescuers became the heroes of the world as they took time to greet the little children who came out to honor them. It was amazing to witness something so beautiful come out of such a tragedy, as these wounded children discovered positive male role models.

The First Anniversary

I live across the street from our local volunteer fire department. Often, I witness their strength and vulnerability. They have children climbing on their trucks as they demonstrate their tools on weekends. As they carry out their hero roles for the children, the memorial stone for their Chief has been placed on the front lawn. Adorned with flowers, it reminds us of the loss and devastation of only a year ago, or was it just this morning? We spiral through time.

Kristin writes:

September 11, 2002. I was no longer working at the hospital. I had left a month prior and was regretting my decision to resign. As the anniversary drew near, I feared I would feel lost not working there. I had an intense desire to have *something* to do on that day. The images of the volunteers and the long lines materialized in my mind, being turned away because their offers to help simply were not required.

People's responses to the anniversary fell along such a continuum. Anniversaries seem to give us the impression that we need to be at a certain stage in our healing process. I was working several jobs at this time, one of which was with an agency that provided counseling services for people following the attack. I was working individually with some people, as well as at an elementary school. While I felt the agency I was working with had arranged some poignant memorial activities, I missed the hospital and the staff. Articles were published that offered explanations on how to support children throughout the day, how to recognize signs of trauma . . . "How To" seemed to fill the pages of every informational packet I received the month prior to the anniversary. Most clinicians and educators appeared to concur that the best way to handle all the expected emotions was to allow the people who were grieving to grieve, and that it should be acceptable for those who were not at that stage in their process to not participate. But what about children?

The school where I worked on the Lower East Side decided to have a "regular" school day. After all, I was told, it is only the second week of school! I worked in the after-school program and, when I arrived, the kids had an option to have a discussion about 9/11, do some creative processing, or play outside. Most chose the latter. An art therapist and I worked with a few children who opted to do some drawing. They drew pictures of the towers, some of which were in the process of burning. Many children simply wanted to retell where they were that day and what they saw. Landy (2002) wrote about the importance of allowing children to work through their images. He affirmed, "By encouraging work with images of horror, creative arts therapists have the opportunity to help traumatized clients engage in a playful dialogue effective enough to achieve a greater sense of control and mastery of their lives" (p. 140).

One adolescent spoke of her younger brother coming into the TV room long after his bedtime. Their mother had been away on a business trip on 9/11, but usually worked in the towers. The children had been to visit her worksite a few months prior. The family had tried to shield the child from so many of the visuals reshown on television and seen in the newspaper. As this young child entered the living room, the late night news again showed the towers standing tall on a beautiful afternoon. The boy ran to his mother's lap, gave her a huge hug, and exclaimed how happy she must be: the towers were back standing and she could now return to work! I listened to this story and others, commented occasionally, and wondered yet again what the "right thing" to do was.

That evening, I allowed myself to play back my memories of the past year. I had attended two memorial services for members of my church and listened to stories of many others who had done the same. I had spent time remembering everyone I knew who had died during my lifetime, especially the death of my grandmother in November, 2001. I recalled my feelings of loneliness on the day of the attack, my sadness, my feeling unworthy yet proud. I remembered my adamant refusal to write anything down. Solidifying my memories of the events as they unfolded wasn't something I was willing to do. I felt like I should write, especially that week in 2001.

March, 2003. I was still working on the Lower East Side in an after-school program. Yolanda, a 9-year-old girl, asked me on March 12 if we were all going to die. She had heard on TV that the "deadline" (what a word!) for war with Iraq was approaching. Her large, brown eyes were filled with terror and wonder. This 9-year-old and I had spent many drama sessions together throughout the last few months. She was the only consistent group member, often described as shy by other staff at the school. Her quiet intelligence often captured me.

"Will we have another war in New York City?" she asked. I looked at her, feeling unable to find an answer in my own mind. As I was sitting with this now-familiar feeling of not knowing, I listened to her say, "Don't they get it? New York City *had* war already." I stared in her eyes, silently agreeing, as she picked up her snack tray and walked away.

I have often wondered what kept me going those days at the hospital. What draws me to continue to seek out children who have lived through trauma? As I look back, I realize how crucial my own therapy, supervision, and support from people close to me was during these last 2 years. Through ongoing therapy and supervision, I am able to understand, or at least begin to understand, my reactions to what that has unfolded in our world. Being offered a consistent space to explore my sadness, anger, impatience, and other feelings granted me insight I never would have found on my own.

Combined Reflections

Much has been written about vicarious traumatization, secondary trauma, and countertransference in relation to treating traumatized children (James, 1994; Johnson, 1998). Yet, this experience had an added dimension, for all Americans were touched by the events of 9/11 in some way. We rose to the occasion, focusing on others. Later, we knew we had to address our own feelings in order to go back to work, back to being open to the children and the therapeutic process. Cattanach (1992) wrote, "The therapist needs to understand the emotional effects of her work on herself...To keep the children safe the therapist must also be safe" (p. 147).

This co-writing process has freed us to do the clinical work asked of us in the wake of the second and third anniversaries, with all their triggers of pain, fear, grief, and loss. As we worked on the first draft deadline, the 9/11 Commission was reviewing and planning to speak to the public about the events of that day and before. During August, New Yorkers were retraumatized when an electrical blackout left the city in darkness. Clients and staff were locked in buildings behind electric doors and caught in elevators. Memories were triggered as the past and present collided. Buildings no longer felt safe in a crisis. The city was still cycling through phases of traumatic recovery, and continues to do so with every new crisis event. There are so many levels of impact, each unique, yet each somewhat the same. What continues to happen from the children's eyes? We are still searching for the answer.

We write this in order that we might be able to stay in tune with the child clients in our care as the anniversary month and other triggers emerge again. We are bringing the events of that time and its aftermath into present memory. We are exploring our emotions and the parallel process that continues to emerge so that we can carry on as children's drama therapists. As Johnson (1998) wrote:

> Whether we are teachers, health care providers, social workers or psychotherapists, service to others in need and pain provides a crucible. By finding the inner and outer resources to meet the demands of our work—demands so intrinsically challenging that we daily risk sliding backward into despair—we grow farther and more fully than would otherwise be possible. By facing and transforming the fires of our work, we may refine our very souls. (p. 253)

References

Cattanach, A. (1992). *Play therapy with abused children.* London: Jessica Kingsley.

Dale, F. (1997). *Stress in child psychotherapists.* In V. P. Varma (Ed.), *Stress in psychotherapists* (pp. 44–57). London: Routledge.

Drewes, A. (2002, October). *When disaster strikes.* Training presented for the Suffolk County Mental Health Association, Port Jefferson, NY.

Figley, C.R. (1985). From victim to survivor: Social responsibility in the wake of catastrophe. In C. R. Figley (Ed.), *Trauma and its wake: The study and treatment of Post–traumatic Stress Disorder* (Vol. I, pp. 398–415). New York: Brunner/Mazel.

Gentry, E. R. (2002). Compassion fatigue: A crucible of transformation. *Journal of Trauma Practice* (pp. 37–61). New York: Haworth Press.

Haen, C. (2002). The dramatherapeutic use of the superhero role with male clients. *Dramatherapy,* 24(1), 16–22.

Haen, C. (in press). Rebuilding security: Group therapy with children affected by September 11th. *International Journal of Group Psychotherapy.*

Hoey, B. (1997). *Who calls the tune? A psychodramatic approach to child therapy.* New York: Routledge.

James, B. (1994). *Handbook for treatment of attachment-trauma problems in children.* New York: Free Press.

Johnson, K. (1998). *Trauma in the lives of children: Crisis and stress management techniques for counselors, teachers, and other professionals.* Alameda, CA: Hunter House.

Landy, R. (2002). A creative arts therapist's reflections on the trauma of September 11, 2001. *The Arts in Psychotherapy, 29*(3), 135–141.

Martin, B., & Archambault, J. (2000). *Chicka chicka boom boom.* New York: Simon & Schuster.

Terr, L. (2003, May). *Using play therapy to mimic natural healing: What we have learned from Columbine and 9/11.* Paper presented at the meeting of the New York Association for Play Therapy, Melville, NY.

Name Index

Subject Index